SENTENCE SKILLS

A WORKBOOK FOR WRITERS
FORM B

Sentence Skills is also available in alternate editions known as Form A and Form C. The explanatory text is essentially the same in each book, but the activities, tests, and writing assignments are different. An instructor can therefore use alternate versions of the book from one semester to the next.

Learning Aids Accompanying Sentence Skills

- The *Annotated Instructor's Edition* is identical to the student book except that it includes answers to all the activities and tests.
- A set of *thirty ditto masters,* free to instructors adopting the text, provides extra activities and tests for many skills.
- A *software disk* will help students review and practice many of the skills.
- An *Instructor's Manual and Test Bank* contains a full answer key, additional tests, and a guide to the computer disk.

SENTENCE SKILLS

A Workbook for Writers

FIFTH EDITION

FORM B

JOHN LANGAN

Atlantic Community College

McGRAW-HILL, INC.

New York St. Louis San Francisco Auckland Bogotá Caracas
Lisbon London Madrid Mexico City Milan Montreal New Delhi
San Juan Singapore Sydney Tokyo Toronto

SENTENCE SKILLS
A WORKBOOK FOR WRITERS
FORM B

This book is printed on acid-free paper.

4567890   DOC DOC   909876

ISBN 0-07-036410-9

This book was set in Times Roman by Monotype Composition Company.
The editors were Alison Husting Zetterquist, Laurie Pisierra, Lesley Denton, and Susan Gamer;
the production supervisor was Annette Mayeski.
The designer was Rafael Hernandez.
R. R. Donnelley & Sons Company was printer and binder.

Library of Congress Cataloging-in-Publication Data is available: 93-28530 (Student Version)

About
the Author

John Langan has taught reading and writing at Atlantic Community College near Atlantic City, New Jersey, for over twenty years. The author of a popular series of college textbooks on both subjects, he enjoys the challenge of developing materials that teach skills in an especially clear and lively way. Before teaching, he earned advanced degrees in writing at Rutgers University and in reading at Glassboro State College. He also spent a year writing fiction that, he says, "is now at the back of a drawer waiting to be discovered and acclaimed posthumously." While in school, he supported himself by working as a truck driver, machinist, battery assembler, hospital attendant, and apple packer. He presently lives with his wife, Judith Nadell, near Philadelphia. Among his everyday pleasures are running, working on his Macintosh computer, and watching Philadelphia sports teams or *60 Minutes* on TV. He also loves to read: newspapers at breakfast, magazines at lunch, and a chapter or two of a recent book ("preferably an autobiography") at night.

Contents

PART THREE
SENTENCE VARIETY THROUGH COMBINING ACTIVITIES   389

PART FOUR
WRITING ASSIGNMENTS

APPENDIXES   **465**

To the Instructor

Sentence Skills will help students master the essential rules of grammar, mechanics, punctuation, and usage needed for clear writing. The book contains a number of features to aid instructors and their students.

- ***Coverage of basic writing skills is exceptionally thorough.*** The book pays special attention to fragments, run-ons, verbs, and other areas where students have serious problems. At the same time, a glance at the table of contents shows that the book treats skills (such as dictionary use and spelling improvement) not found in other texts. In addition, entire sections of the book are devoted to editing, proofreading, and sentence variety.

- ***The book has a clear and flexible format.*** Part One presents and gives practice in all the essential basic writing skills. Part Two then reinforces those skills through mastery, editing, and proofreading tests. Part Three uses sentence-combining exercises to help students achieve variety in their writing. Part Four presents writing assignments that enable students to transfer the skills they have learned to realistic writing situations. Since parts, sections, and chapters are self-contained, instructors can move easily from, for instance, a rule in Part One to a mastery test in Part Two to a combining activity in Part Three or a writing assignment in Part Four.

- **Practice materials are numerous.** Most skills are reinforced by activities, review tests, and mastery tests, as well as ditto masters and tests in the *Instructor's Manual.* For most of the skills in the book, there are over one hundred practice exercises.

- **Practice materials are varied and lively.** In many basic writing texts, exercises are monotonous and dry, causing students to lose interest in the skills presented. In *Sentence Skills,* exercises involve students in various ways. An inductive opening project allows students to see what they already know about a given skill. Within chapters, students may be asked to underline answers, add words, generate their own sentences, or edit passages. And the lively and engaging practice materials in the book both maintain interest and help students appreciate the value of vigorous details in writing.

- **Terminology is kept to a minimum.** In general, rules are explained using words students already know. A clause is a *word group;* a coordinating conjunction is a *joining word;* a nonrestrictive element is an *interrupter.* At the same time, traditional grammatical terms are mentioned briefly for students who learned them earlier and are comfortable seeing them again.

- **Self-teaching is encouraged.** Students may check their answers to the introductory projects and the practice activities in Part One by referring to the answers in Appendix B. In this way, they are given the responsibility for teaching themselves. At the same time, to ensure that the answer key is used as a learning tool only, answers are *not* given for the review tests in Part One or for any of the reinforcement tests in Part Two. These answers appear in the *Annotated Instructor's Edition* and the *Instructor's Manual;* they can be copied and handed out to students at the discretion of the instructor.

- **Diagnostic and achievement tests are provided.** These tests appear in Appendix A of the book. Each test may be given in two parts, the second of which gives teachers a particularly detailed picture of a student's skill level.

- **Valuable learning aids accompany the book.** A set of *thirty ditto masters,* ready to run, enables instructors to check students' progress on most of the skills in the book. A *software disk* will help students review and practice many of the skills in the text. The *Annotated Instructor's Edition* includes answers. The comprehensive *Instructor's Manual* includes (1) a complete set of additional mastery tests, (2) a model syllabus along with suggestions for teaching the course and using the software, and (3) an answer key. The manual is 8½ by 11 inches, so that both the answer pages and the added mastery tests can be conveniently reproduced on copying machines.

These aids are available by contacting the local McGraw-Hill representative or by writing to the College English Editor, College Division, McGraw-Hill, Inc., 1221 Avenue of the Americas, New York, New York 10020.

CHANGES IN THE FIFTH EDITION

The helpful comments of writing instructors who have used previous versions of *Sentence Skills* have prompted some important changes in this new edition.

1   The convenient *Annotated Instructor's Edition* is identical to the student book except that it includes answers to all the activities and tests.

2   A revised set of ditto masters, free to instructors adopting the book, provides more tests and activities than were available previously.

3   Additions have been made to key chapters:

- The chapter on sentence fragments provides additional hints on using the comma when correcting fragments.
- The chapter on run-ons has been expanded to show subordination as a method of correcting run-ons.
- The chapter on the apostrophe has simplified the use of the apostrophe with words ending in *s*; also, it now provides more practice in distinguishing between possessive words and simple plurals.
- The chapter on commas now offers practice from the very start with the problem of unnecessary commas.
- The chapter in Part One on paper format has been reinforced by the addition of two combined editing tests in Part Two.

4   Three chapters (''Misplaced Modifiers,'' ''Dangling Modifiers,'' and ''Faulty Parallelism'') have been resequenced; changes have been made in the format of certain tests; and practice materials have been updated, corrected where necessary, and in general freshened throughout.

5   Part Four, ''Writing Assignments,'' has been almost completely rewritten. It now provides step-by-step instructions to beginning students on how to write a variety of simple paragraphs and an essay.

ACKNOWLEDGMENTS

Reviewers who have provided assistance include Michele Benacquista, Lakeland Community College; Alice Cleveland, College of Marin; Matthew Corcoran, York College; Jean Garrett, Mt. San Antonio College; Marjorie B. Green, Caldwell Community College; Judy Harvey, Wilmington College; Martha L. Hughes, East Georgia College; Mikelyn Stacey, Ohlone Community College; and Lisa M. Wernsman-Mehlig, Rock Valley Community College. I am also grateful for Janet M. Goldstein's help as I worked on the *Instructor's Edition* of the text, and I much appreciate the exceptional design and editing skills she has brought to preparing the *Instructor's Manual* for the book.

John Langan

SENTENCE SKILLS

A WORKBOOK FOR WRITERS
FORM B

Sentence Skills

INTRODUCTION

Part One explains the basic skills needed to write clear, error-free sentences. Before you begin working with these skills, however, you will want to read the first chapter—"Learning Sentence Skills"—which explains how you will benefit personally from writing standard English. While the skills are presented within four traditional categories (grammar, mechanics, punctuation, and word use), each section is self-contained so that you can go directly to the skills you need to work on. Note, however, that you may find it helpful to cover "Subjects and Verbs" before turning to other skills. Typically, the main features of a skill are presented on the first pages of a section; secondary points are developed later. Numerous activities are provided so that you can practice skills enough to make them habits. The activities are varied and range from underlining answers to writing complete sentences involving the skill in question. One or more review tests at the end of each section offer additional practice activities.

Learning Sentence Skills

WHY LEARN SENTENCE SKILLS?

Why should someone planning a career as a nurse have to learn sentence skills? Why should an accounting major have to pass a competency test in grammar as part of a college education? Why should a potential physical therapist or graphic artist or computer programmer have to spend hours on the rules of English? Perhaps you have asked questions like these after finding yourself in a class with this book. On the other hand, perhaps you *know* you need to strengthen basic writing skills, even though you may be unclear about the specific ways the skills will be of use to you. Whatever your views, you should understand why sentence skills—all the rules that make up standard English—are so important.

Clear Communication

Standard English, or "language by the book," is needed to communicate your thoughts to others with a minimal amount of distortion and misinterpretation. Knowing the traditional rules of grammar, punctuation, and usage will help you write clear sentences when communicating with others. You may have heard of the party game in which one person whispers a message to the next person; the message is passed, in turn, along a line of several other people. By the time the last person in line is asked to give the message aloud, it is usually so garbled and inaccurate that it barely resembles the original. Written communication in some form of English other than standard English carries the same potential for disaster.

To see how important standard English is to written communication, examine the pairs of sentences on the following pages and answer the questions in each case.

1. Which sentence indicates that there might be a plot against Ted?
   a. We should leave Ted. These fumes might be poisonous.
   b. We should leave, Ted. These fumes might be poisonous.
2. Which sentence encourages self-mutilation?
   a. Leave your paper and hand in the dissecting kit.
   b. Leave your paper, and hand in the dissecting kit.
3. Which sentence indicates that the writer has a weak grasp of geography?
   a. As a child, I lived in Lake Worth, which is close to Palm Beach and Alaska.
   b. As a child, I lived in Lake Worth, which is close to Palm Beach, and Alaska.
4. In which sentence does the dog warden seem dangerous?
   a. Foaming at the mouth, the dog warden picked up the stray.
   b. Foaming at the mouth, the stray was picked up by the dog warden.
5. Which announcer was probably fired from the job?
   a. Outside the Academy Awards theater, the announcer called the guests names as they arrived.
   b. Outside the Academy Awards theater, the announcer called the guests' names as they arrived.
6. On the basis of the opening lines below of two student exam essays, which student seems likely to earn a higher grade?
   a. Defense mechanisms is the way people hides their inner feelings and deals with stress. There is several types that we use to be protecting our true feelings.
   b. Defense mechanisms are the methods people use to cope with stress. Using a defense mechanism allows a person to hide his or her real desires and goals.
7. On the basis of the following lines taken from two English papers, which student seems likely to earn a higher grade?
   a. A big problem on this campus is apathy, students don't participate in college activities. Such as clubs, student government, and plays.
   b. The most pressing problem on campus is the disgraceful state of the student lounge area. The floor is dirty, the chairs are torn, and the ceiling leaks.

8. On the basis of the following sentences taken from two employee reports, which worker is more likely to be promoted?
   a. The spring line failed by 20 percent in the meeting of projected profit expectations. Which were issued in January of this year.
   b. Profits from our spring line were disappointing. They fell 20 percent short of January's predictions.

9. On the basis of the following paragraphs taken from two job application letters, which job prospect would you favor?
   a. Let me say in closing that their are an array of personal qualities I have presented in this letter, together, these make me hopeful of being interviewed for this attraktive position.

      sincerly yours'

      Brian Davis

   b. I feel I have the qualifications needed to do an excellent job as assistant manager of the jewelry department at Horton's. I look forward to discussing the position further at a personal interview.

      Sincerely yours,

      Richard O'Keeney

In each case, the first choice (a) contains sentence-skills mistakes. These mistakes range from missing or misplaced commas to misspellings to wordy or pretentious language. As a result of these mistakes, clear communication cannot occur—and misunderstandings, lower grades, and missed job opportunities are probable results. The point, then, is that all the rules that make up standard written English should be a priority if you want your writing to be clear and effective.

Success in College

Standard English is essential if you want to succeed in college. Any report, paper, review, essay exam, or assignment you are responsible for should be written in the best standard English you can produce. If not, it won't matter how fine your ideas are or how hard you worked—most likely, you will receive a lower grade than you would otherwise deserve. In addition, because standard English requires you to express your thoughts in precise, clear sentences, training yourself to follow the rules can help you think more logically. And the basic logic you learn to practice at the sentence level will help as you work to produce well-reasoned papers in all your subjects.

Success at Work

Knowing standard English will also help you achieve success on the job. Studies have shown repeatedly that skillful communication, more than any other factor, is the key to job satisfaction and steady career progress. A solid understanding of standard English is a basic part of this vital communication ability. Moreover, most experts agree that we are now living in an "age of information"—a time when people who use language skillfully have a great advantage over those who do not. Fewer of us will be working in factories or at other types of manual labor. Many more of us will be working with information in various forms—accumulating it, processing it, analyzing it. No matter what kind of job you are preparing yourself for, technical or not, you will need to know standard English to keep pace with this new age. Otherwise, you are likely to be left behind, limited to low-paying jobs that offer few challenges or financial rewards.

Success in Everyday Life

Standard English will help you succeed not just at school and work but in everyday life as well. It will help you feel more comfortable, for example, in writing letters to friends and relatives. It will enable you to write effective notes to your children's schools. It will help command attention to a letter of complaint that you write to a company about a product. It will allow you to write letters of inquiry about bills—hospital, medical, utility, or legal—or about any kind of service. To put it simply, in our daily lives, those who can use and write standard English have more power than those who cannot.

HOW THIS BOOK IS ORGANIZED

- A good way to get a quick sense of any book is to turn to the table of contents. By referring to pages vii–x, you will see that the book is organized into four basic parts. What are they?

  _____

  _____

  _____

  _____

- Part One deals with the sentence skills themselves. How many skills areas are covered in all (count them)? _____

- Part Two reinforces the skills presented in Part One. What are the four kinds of reinforcement activities in Part Two?

  _____

  _____

  _____

  _____

- Turn to the introduction to Part Three to learn the purpose of that part of the book and write the purpose here: _____

  _____

- Turn to the introduction to Part Four to find the purpose of that part of the book and write the purpose here: _____

  _____

  _____

- Helpful charts in the book include (*fill in the missing words*) the _____ _____ on the inside front cover, the _____ charts in Appendix C, and the _____ of sentence skills on the inside back cover.

- Finally, three appendixes at the end of the book contain:

  _____

  _____

  _____

HOW TO USE THIS BOOK

The first step in getting the most out of *Sentence Skills* is to take the diagnostic test on pages 467–472. By analyzing which sections of the test gave you trouble, you will discover which skills you need to concentrate on. When you turn to an individual skill, begin by reading and thinking about the introductory project. Often, you will be pleasantly surprised to find that you know more about this area of English than you thought you did. After all, you have probably been speaking English with fluency and ease for many years; you have an instinctive knowledge of how the language works. This knowledge gives you a solid base for refining your skills.

Your next step is to work on the skill by reading the explanations and completing the practices. You can check your answers to each practice activity by turning to the answer key at the back of the book. Try to figure out *why* you got some answers wrong—you want to uncover any weak spots in your understanding.

Finally, use the review tests at the ends of chapters to evaluate your understanding of a skill in its entirety. Your instructor may also ask you to take the mastery tests or other reinforcement tests in Part Two of the book. To help ensure that you take the time needed to learn each skill thoroughly, the answers to these tests are *not* in the answer key.

While you are working through individual skills, you should also take time for the sentence-combining activities in Part Three and the writing assignments in Part Four. The writing assignments in Part Four are a brief but important part of the book. To make standard English an everyday part of your writing, you must write not just single sentences but paragraphs and essays. The writing assignments will prove to you that clear, logical writing hinges on error-free sentences. You will see how the sentence skills you are practicing ''fit in'' and contribute to the construction of a sustained piece of writing. In the world of sports, athletes spend many days refining the small moves—serves, backhands, pitches, lay-ups—so that they can reach their larger objective of winning the game. In the same way, you must work intently on writing clear sentences in order to produce effective papers.

The emphasis in this book is, nevertheless, on writing clear, error-free sentences, not on composition. And the heart of the book is the practice material that helps reinforce the sentence skills you learn. A great deal of effort has been taken to make the practices lively and engaging and to avoid the dull, repetitive skills work that has given grammar books such a bad reputation. This text will help you stay interested as you work on the rules you need to learn. The rest is a matter of your personal determination and hard work. If you decide—and only you can decide—that effective writing is important to your school and career goals and that you want to learn the basic skills needed to write clearly and effectively, this book will help you reach those goals.

Section 1: Grammar

Subjects and Verbs

INTRODUCTORY PROJECT

Understanding subjects and verbs is a big step toward mastering many sentence skills. As a speaker of English, you already have an instinctive feel for these basic building blocks of English sentences. See if you can insert an appropriate word into each space below. The answer will be a subject.

1. The _____ will soon be over.

2. _____ cannot be trusted.

3. A strange _____ appeared in my backyard.

4. _____ is one of my favorite activities.

Now insert an appropriate word into the following spaces. Each answer will be a verb.

5. The prisoner _____ at the judge.

6. My sister _____ much harder than I do.

7. The players _____ in the locker room.

8. Rob and Marilyn _____ with the teacher.

Finally, insert appropriate words into the following spaces. Your answers will be a subject and verb, respectively.

9. The _____ almost _____ out of the tree.

10. Many _____ today _____ sex and violence.

11. The _____ carefully _____ the patient.

12. A _____ quickly _____ the ball.

The basic building blocks of English sentences are subjects and verbs. Understanding them is an important first step toward mastering a number of sentence skills.

Every sentence has a subject and a verb. Who or what the sentence speaks about is called the *subject;* what the sentence says about the subject is called the *verb.* In the following sentences, the subject is underlined once and the verb twice:

> People gossip.
> The truck belched fumes.
> He waved at me.
> Alaska contains the largest wilderness area in the United States.
> That woman is a millionaire.
> The pants feel itchy.

A SIMPLE WAY TO FIND A SUBJECT

To find a subject, ask *who* or *what* the sentence is about. As shown below, your answer is the subject.

> *Who* is the first sentence about? People
> *What* is the second sentence about? The truck
> *Who* is the third sentence about? He
> *What* is the fourth sentence about? Alaska
> *Who* is the fifth sentence about? That woman
> *What* is the sixth sentence about? The pants

It helps to remember that the subject of a sentence is always a *noun* (any person, place, or thing) or a pronoun. A *pronoun* is simply a word like *he, she, it, you,* or *they* used in place of a noun. In the preceding sentences, the subjects are persons (*People, He, woman*), a place (*Alaska*), and things (*truck, pants*). And note that one pronoun (*He*) is used as a subject.

A SIMPLE WAY TO FIND A VERB

To find a verb, ask what the sentence *says about* the subject. As shown below, your answer is the verb.

> What does the first sentence *say about* people? They gossip.
> What does the second sentence *say about* the truck? It belched (fumes).

What does the third sentence *say about* him? He waved (at me).

What does the fourth sentence *say about* Alaska? It contains (the largest wilderness area in the United States).

What does the fifth sentence *say about* that woman? She is (a millionaire).

What does the sixth sentence *say about* the pants? They feel (itchy).

A second way to find the verb is to put *I, you, he, she, it,* or *they* in front of the word you think is a verb. If the result makes sense, you have a verb. For example, you could put *they* in front of *gossip* in the first sentence above, with the result, *they gossip,* making sense. Therefore, you know that *gossip* is a verb. You could use the same test with the other verbs as well.

Finally, it helps to remember that most verbs show action. In ''People gossip,'' the action is gossiping. In ''The truck belched fumes,'' the action is belching. In ''He waved at me,'' the action is waving. In ''Alaska contains the largest wilderness area in the United States,'' the action is containing.

Certain other verbs, known as *linking verbs,* do not show action. They do, however, give information about the subject of the sentence. In ''That woman is a millionaire,'' the linking verb *is* tells us that the woman is a millionaire. In ''The pants feel itchy,'' the linking verb *feel* gives us the information that the pants are itchy.

Practice I

In each of the following sentences, draw one line under the subject and two lines under the verb.

Ask *who* or *what* the sentence is about to find the subject. Then ask what the sentence *says about* the subject to find the verb.

1. Fran froze six pounds of hamburger patties.
2. The company offered a ten-dollar rebate on every toaster oven.
3. The sports announcer talked nonstop during the game.
4. Jill peeled the bandage off her cut finger.
5. The warm sunshine felt good on my bare legs.
6. Our backyard is knee-deep in weeds.
7. Alicia snagged her stocking with her broken fingernail.
8. The steel comb scratched my scalp.
9. The pen leaked all over my finger.
10. That outlet store carries only damaged or outdated goods.

Practice 2

Follow the directions given for Practice 1. Note that all the verbs here are linking verbs.

1. The best shows on television this week were the ads.
2. In some countries, an after-dinner burp is a compliment to the cook.
3. Mirror sunglasses always look eerie, like a robot's eyes.
4. My voice sounds terrible in the morning.
5. Tina became engaged to Roy after just three dates.
6. Harold's new after-shave lotion smells like cleaning fluid.
7. Visitors often appear fearful at my German shepherd's bark of greeting.
8. To a female fly, a male's wing vibrations are a love song.
9. My head cold feels like a combination of fatal headache and torture by sneezing.
10. In some ways, the change from tadpole to frog seems as much of a miracle as the change from frog to prince.

Practice 3

Follow the directions given for Practice 1.

1. One lonely neon light glowed in the distance.
2. The kite soared into the sky at the end of a taut, vibrating string.
3. Manuel caught a foul ball at the game.
4. The skaters shadowed each other's movements perfectly.
5. Fluorescent lights emphasized the tired lines in the man's face.
6. Tracy reads to her bedridden grandmother every night.
7. Marsha's oversized glasses slipped down her nose twenty times a day.
8. Carelessly, Jane allowed the children to light the kerosene heater.
9. The squirrel jumped from one tree branch to another.
10. Carpenters constructed a wooden wheelchair ramp next to the stone steps of the church.

MORE ABOUT
SUBJECTS AND VERBS

Distinguishing Subjects
from Prepositional Phrases

The subject of a sentence never appears within a prepositional phrase. A *prepositional phrase* is simply a group of words beginning with a preposition and ending with the answer to the question *what*, *when*, or *where*. Here is a list of common prepositions.

Common Prepositions

about	before	by	inside	over
above	behind	during	into	through
across	below	except	of	to
among	beneath	for	off	toward
around	beside	from	on	under
at	between	in	onto	with

Cross out prepositional phrases when looking for the subject of a sentence.

In the middle of the night, we heard footsteps on the roof.
The magazines on the table belong in the garage.
Before the opening kickoff, a brass band marched onto the field.
The hardware store across the street went out of business.
In spite of our advice, Sally quit her job at Burger King.

Practice

Cross out prepositional phrases. Then draw a single line under subjects and a double line under verbs.

1. Stripes of sunlight glowed on the kitchen floor.
2. The black panther draped its powerful body along the thick tree branch.
3. A line of impatient people snaked from the box office to the street.

4. At noon, every siren in town wails for fifteen minutes.

5. The tops of my Bic pens always disappear after a day or two.

6. Joanne removed the lint from her black socks with Scotch tape.

7. The mirrored walls of the skyscraper reflected the passing clouds.

8. Debris from the accident littered the intersection.

9. Above the heads of the crowd, a woman swayed on a narrow ledge.

10. The squashed grapes in the bottom of the vegetable bin oozed sticky purple juice.

Verbs of More Than One Word

Many verbs consist of more than one word. Here, for example, are some of the many forms of the verb *help:*

Some Forms of the Verb **Help**

helps	should have been helping	will have helped
helping	can help	would have been helped
is helping	would have been helping	has been helped
was helping	will be helping	had been helped
may help	had been helping	must have helped
should help	helped	having helped
will help	have helped	should have been helped
does help	has helped	had helped

Below are sentences that contain verbs of more than one word:

Diane is working overtime this week.

Another book has been written about the Kennedy family.

We should have stopped for gas at the last station.

The game has just been canceled.

Notes

1   Words like *not, just, never, only,* and *always* are not part of the verb although they may appear within the verb.

Diane is not working overtime next week.
The boys should just not have stayed out so late.
The game has always been played regardless of the weather.

2   No verb preceded by *to* is ever the verb of a sentence.

Sue wants to go with us.
The newly married couple decided to rent a house for a year.
The store needs extra people to help out at Christmas.

3   No *-ing* word by itself is ever the verb of a sentence. (It may be part of the verb, but it must have a helping verb in front of it.)

We planning the trip for months. (This is not a sentence, because the verb is not complete.)
We were planning the trip for months. (This is a complete sentence.)

Practice

Draw a single line under subjects and a double line under verbs. Be sure to include all parts of the verb.

1. Only Einstein could have passed that math test.
2. She could have been killed by that falling rock.
3. The children did not recognize their father in his Halloween costume.
4. The hunger strikers have been fasting for four days.
5. I could not see the tiny letters on the last row of the eye doctor's chart.
6. People may be wearing paper clothing by the year 2000.
7. He should have studied longer for the final.
8. Rosa has been soaking in the bathtub for an hour.
9. Long lines of southbound geese were flying overhead.
10. My little brother can ask the same stupid question five times in a row.

Compound Subjects and Verbs

A sentence may have more than one verb:

The dancer stumbled and fell.
Lola washed her hair, blew it dry, and parted it in the middle.

A sentence may have more than one subject:

Cats and dogs are sometimes the best of friends.
The striking workers and their bosses could not come to an agreement.

A sentence may have several subjects and several verbs:

Holly and I read the book and reported on it to the class.
Pete, Nick, and Fran caught the fish in the morning, cleaned them in the afternoon, and ate them that night.

Practice

Draw a single line under subjects and a double line under verbs. Be sure to mark *all* the subjects and verbs.

1. The trees creaked and shuddered in the powerful wind.
2. The little girl fell off the jungle gym and landed in the dirt.
3. On Sunday, I will vacuum the upstairs rooms and change the linens.
4. The late afternoon sun shone on the leaves and turned them to gold.
5. Sam and Billy greased their chapped lips with Vaseline.
6. The tall, masked man and his Indian friend rode off into the sunset.
7. My sister and I always race each other to the bathroom in the morning.
8. Amy breathed deeply and then began her karate exercises.
9. At the party, Phil draped a tablecloth over his head and pretended to be Lawrence of Arabia.
10. The professional wrestler and his opponent strutted around the ring and pounded on their chests.

Review Test 1

Draw one line under the subjects and two lines under the verbs. As necessary, cross out prepositional phrases to help find subjects. Underline all the parts of a verb. Remember that you may find more than one subject and verb in a sentence.

1. The endings of most movies are happy.
2. I should have filled the car with gas before work.
3. The female of many animals is larger than the male.
4. Three buildings on our block are for sale.
5. Dozens of ants gathered around a scoop of pink ice cream on the sidewalk.
6. Many shoppers saw the pennies on the floor but would not pick them up.
7. Squirrels can collect thousands of nuts in one season.
8. Fruits and vegetables with dangerous sprays should be banned from this country.
9. An extra key was placed under the big empty planter by the front door.
10. Harry dieted for a year, lost a hundred pounds, and cured his high blood pressure.

Review Test 2

Follow the directions given for Review Test 1.

1. A pair of Ohio twins were born forty-eight days apart.
2. Everything in that linen store is on sale at 40 percent off.
3. My son is looking for dinosaur bones in the backyard.
4. According to surveys, most people talk to their dogs.
5. Jay and Elise were married two years ago and are divorced already.
6. At dinnertime, my cat meows and rubs against my leg.
7. The huge tree outside our kitchen window throws lovely shadows on the kitchen wall in the afternoon.
8. My parents and the Greens played bridge for hours and argued constantly.
9. Deanna took a chocolate from the box, took one bite, and put the piece back.
10. Mona removed Ed's arm from her shoulders and ran from the theater with tears in her eyes.

Sentence Fragments

INTRODUCTORY PROJECT

Every sentence must have a subject and a verb and must express a complete thought. A word group that lacks a subject or a verb and that does not express a complete thought is a *fragment*.

Listed below are a number of fragments and sentences. See if you can complete the statement that explains each fragment.

1. Children. *Fragment*
   Children cry. *Sentence*

   ''Children'' is a fragment because, while it has a subject (*Children*), it lacks a ~~predicate~~ verb (*cry*) and so does not express a complete thought.

2. Dances. *Fragment*
   Lola dances. *Sentence*

   ''Dances'' is a fragment because, while it has a verb (*Dances*), it lacks a _____ (*Lola*) and so does not express a complete thought.

3. Staring through the window. *Fragment*
   Bigfoot was staring through the window. *Sentence*

   ''Staring through the window'' is a fragment because it lacks a _____ (*Bigfoot*) and also part of the _____ (*was*) and because it does not express a complete thought.

4. When the dentist began drilling. *Fragment*
   When the dentist began drilling, I closed my eyes. *Sentence*

   ''When the dentist began drilling'' is a fragment because we want to know *what happened when* the dentist began drilling. The word group does not follow through and _____.

Answers are on page 480.

WHAT SENTENCE FRAGMENTS ARE

Every sentence must have a subject and a verb and must express a complete thought. A word group that lacks a subject or a verb and that does not express a complete thought is a *fragment*. Following are the most common types of fragments that people write:

1   Dependent-word fragments
2   *-ing* and *to* fragments
3   Added-detail fragments
4   Missing-subject fragments

Once you understand the specific kind or kinds of fragments that you might write, you should be able to eliminate them from your writing. The following pages explain all four types of fragments.

1   DEPENDENT-WORD FRAGMENTS

Some word groups that begin with a dependent word are fragments. Here is a list of common dependent words:

Adverbs

Common Dependent Words	
after	unless
although, though	until
as	what, whatever
because	when, whenever
before	where, wherever
even though	whether
how	which, whichever
if, even if	while
in order that	who
since	whose
that, so that	

Whenever you start a sentence with one of these dependent words, you must be careful that a dependent-word fragment does not result. The word group beginning with the dependent word *After* in the selection below is a fragment.

After I stopped drinking coffee, I began sleeping better at night.

A *dependent statement*—one starting with a dependent word like *After*—cannot stand alone. It depends on another statement to complete the thought. ''After I stopped drinking coffee'' is a dependent statement. It leaves us hanging. We expect in the same sentence to find out *what happened after* the writer stopped drinking coffee. When a writer does not follow through and complete a thought, a fragment results.

To correct the fragment, simply follow through and complete the thought:

After I stopped drinking coffee, I began sleeping better at night.

Remember, then, that *dependent statements by themselves* are fragments. They must be attached to a statement that makes sense standing alone.*

Here are two other examples of dependent-word fragments:

Brian sat nervously in the dental clinic. While waiting to have his wisdom tooth pulled.
Maria decided to throw away the boxes. That had accumulated for years in the basement.

''While waiting to have his wisdom tooth pulled'' is a fragment; it does not make sense standing by itself. We want to know in the same statement *what Brian did* while waiting to have his tooth pulled. The writer must complete the thought. Likewise, ''That had accumulated for years in the basement'' is not in itself a complete thought. We want to know in the same statement what *that* refers to.

---

* Some instructors refer to a dependent-word fragment as a *dependent clause*. A *clause* is simply a group of words having a subject and a verb. A clause may be *independent* (expressing a complete thought and able to stand alone) or *dependent* (not expressing a complete thought and not able to stand alone). A dependent clause by itself is a fragment. It can be corrected simply by adding an independent clause.

How to Correct
Dependent-Word Fragments

In most cases, you can correct a dependent-word fragment by attaching it to the sentence that comes after it or to the sentence that comes before it:

> After I stopped drinking coffee, I began sleeping better at night.
> (The fragment has been attached to the sentence that comes after it.)
>
> Brian sat nervously in the dental clinic while waiting to have his wisdom tooth pulled.
> (The fragment has been attached to the sentence that comes before it.)
>
> Maria decided to throw away the boxes that had accumulated for years in the basement.
> (The fragment has been attached to the sentence that comes before it.)

Another way of correcting a dependent-word fragment is to eliminate the dependent word and make a new sentence:

> I stopped drinking coffee.
> He was waiting to have his wisdom tooth pulled.
> They had accumulated for years in the basement.

Do not use this second method of correction too frequently, however, for it may cut down on interest and variety in your writing style.

Notes

1 Use a comma if a dependent-word group comes at the *beginning* of a sentence (see also page 189):

> After I stopped drinking coffee, I began sleeping better at night.

However, do not generally use a comma if the dependent-word group comes at the end of a sentence:

> Brian sat nervously in the dental clinic while waiting to have his wisdom tooth pulled.
> Maria decided to throw away the boxes that had accumulated for years in the basement.

2   Sometimes the dependent words *who, that, which,* or *where* appear not at the very start but *near* the start of a word group. A fragment often results.

Today I visited Hilda Cooper. A friend who is in the hospital.

''A friend who is in the hospital'' is not in itself a complete thought. We want to know in the same statement *who* the friend is. The fragment can be corrected by attaching it to the sentence that comes before it:

Today I visited Hilda Cooper, a friend who is in the hospital.
(Here a comma is used to set off ''a friend who is in the hospital,'' which is extra material placed at the end of the sentence.)

Practice 1

Make each dependent-word group a sentence by adding a complete thought. Put a comma after the dependent-word group if it starts the sentence.

Examples   After I got out of high school
               After I got out of high school, I spent a year traveling.

               The watch which I got fixed
               The watch which I got fixed has just stopped working again.

1. After I got home from the party

    _____

    _____

2. Because I finished all my assignments

    _____

    _____

3. When my grandfather died

    _____

    _____

4. The discount store that just opened

    _____

    _____

5. Although my daughter is only five years old

    _____

    _____

Practice 2

Underline the dependent-word fragment (or fragments) in each selection. Then correct each fragment by attaching it to the sentence that comes before or the sentence that comes after it—whichever sounds more natural. Put a comma after the dependent-word group if it starts the sentence.

1. Since she was afraid of muggers, Barbara carried a small can of Mace on her key ring. A hat pin was hidden under her coat lapel.

    _____

    _____

    _____

2. When I began watching the TV mystery movie, I remembered that I had seen it before. I already knew who had murdered the millionaire.

    _____

    _____

    _____

3. Tulips had begun to bloom, Until a freakish spring snowstorm blanketed the garden. The flowers perished in the unseasonable cold.

    _____

    _____

    _____

4. Whenever I'm in the basement and the phone rings, I don't run up to answer it. If the message is important, The person will call back.

    _____

    _____

    _____

5. Since she is a new student, Carla feels shy and insecure. She thinks she is the only person, Who doesn't know anyone else.

    _____

    _____

    _____

2 -ING AND TO FRAGMENTS

When a word ending in -ing or the word to appears at or near the start of a word group, a fragment may result. Such fragments often lack a subject and part of the verb.

Underline the word groups in the examples below that contain -ing words. Each is an -ing fragment.

Example 1

I spent all day in the employment office. Trying to find a job that suited me. The prospects looked bleak.

Example 2

Lola surprised Tony on the nature hike. Picking blobs of resin off pine trees. Then she chewed them like bubble gum.

Example 3

Mel took an aisle seat on the bus. His reason being that he had more legroom.

People sometimes write -ing fragments because they think the subject in one sentence will work for the next word group as well. In the first selection above, they might think the subject I in the opening sentence will also serve as the subject for "Trying to find a job that suited me." But the subject must actually be in the sentence.

How to Correct -ing Fragments

1   Attach the fragment to the sentence that comes before or the sentence that comes after it, whichever makes sense. Example 1 above could read, "I spent all day in the employment office, trying to find a job that suited me." (Note that here a comma is used to set off "trying to find a job that suited me," which is extra material placed at the end of the sentence.)

2   Add a subject and change the -ing verb part to the correct form of the verb. Example 2 could read, "She picked blobs of resin off pine trees."

3   Change being to the correct form of the verb be (am, are, is, was, were). Example 3 could read, "His reason was that he had more legroom."

How to Correct *to* Fragments

As noted above, when *to* appears at or near the start of a word group, a fragment sometimes results.

> To remind people of their selfishness. Otis leaves handwritten notes on cars that take up two parking spaces.

The first word group in the example above is a *to* fragment. It can be corrected by adding it to the sentence that comes after it:

> To remind people of their selfishness, Otis leaves handwritten notes on cars that take up two parking spaces.

(Note that here a comma is used to set off ''To remind people of their selfishness,'' which is introductory material in the sentence.)

Practice 1

Underline the *-ing* fragment in each of the three items below. Then make the fragment a sentence by rewriting it, using the method described in parentheses.

Example   The dog eyed me with suspicion. <u>Not knowing whether its master was at home.</u> I hesitated to open the gate.
(Add the fragment to the sentence that comes after it.)

Not knowing whether its master was at home, I hesitated to open the gate.

1. Julie spent an hour at her desk, Staring at a blank piece of paper. She didn't know how to start her report.
   (Add the fragment to the preceding sentence.)

   _____

   _____

2. Rummaging around in the kitchen drawer, Bob found the key he had misplaced a year ago.
   (Add the fragment to the sentence that comes after it.)

   _____

   _____

3. I went back to get a carton of Fresca, ~~As a result,~~ losing my place in the checkout line.
   (Add the subject *I* and change *losing* to the correct form of the verb, *lost.*)

   _____

   _____

Practice 2

Underline the *-ing* or *to* fragment in each of the five items below. Then rewrite each item correctly, using one of the methods of correction described on pages 24–25.

1. Last night, my bedroom was so hot I couldn't sleep. Tossing and turning for hours, I felt like a blanket being tumbled dry.

   _____

   _____

   _____

2. A sparrow landed on the icy windowsill. Fluffing its feathers to keep itself warm.

   _____

   _____

   _____

3. Alma left the party early. The reason being that she had to work the next day.

   _____

   _____

   _____

4. Grasping the balance beam with her powdered hands, The gymnast executed a handstand, Then she dismounted.

   _____

   _____

   _____

5. To cover his bald spot, Walt combed long strands of hair over the top of his head, Unfortunately, no one was fooled by this technique.

   _____

   _____

   _____

3 ADDED-DETAIL FRAGMENTS

Added-detail fragments lack a subject and a verb. They often begin with one of the following words.

also	except	including
especially	for example	such as

See if you can underline the one added-detail fragment in each of these examples:

Example 1

Tony has trouble accepting criticism. Except from Lola. She has a knack for tact.

Example 2

My apartment has its drawbacks. For example, no hot water in the morning.

Example 3

I've worked at many jobs while in school. Among them, busboy, painter, and security guard.

People often write added-detail fragments for much the same reason they write *-ing* fragments. They think the subject and verb in one sentence will serve for the next word group as well. But the subject and verb must be in *each* word group.

How to Correct
Added-Detail Fragments

1   Attach the fragment to the complete thought that precedes it. Example 1 could read: "Tony has trouble accepting criticism, except from Lola." (Note that here a comma is used to set off "except from Lola," which is extra material placed at the end of the sentence.)

2   Add a subject and a verb to the fragment to make it a complete sentence. Example 2 could read: "My apartment has its drawbacks. For example, there is no hot water in the morning."

3   Change words as necessary to make the fragment part of the preceding sentence. Example 3 could read: "Among the many jobs I've worked at while in school have been busboy, painter, and security guard."

Practice 1

Underline the fragment in each of the three items below. Then make it a sentence by rewriting it, using the method described in parentheses.

Example   My husband and I share the household chores. <u>Including meals.</u>
I do the cooking and he does the eating.
(Add the fragment to the preceding sentence.)
My husband and I share the household chores, including meals.

1. My father has some nervous habits, For instance, folding a strip of paper into the shape of an accordion.
    (Correct the fragment by adding the subject *he* and changing *folding* to the proper form of the verb, *folds*.)

    _____

    _____

2. Marco stuffed the large green peppers, With hamburger meat, cooked rice, and chopped parsley. Next, using toothpicks, he reattached the stemmed pepper tops.
    (Add the fragment to the preceding sentence.)

    _____

    _____

3. My little brother is addicted to junk foods, For example, Bugles and Doritos. If something is good for him, he won't eat it.
    (Correct the fragment by adding the subject and verb *He craves.*)

    _____

    _____

Practice 2

Underline the added-detail fragment in each of the five items below. Then rewrite as needed to correct the fragment. Use one of the three methods of correction described on page 27.

1. My husband keeps all his old clothes, For instance, his faded sweatshirt from high school. He says it's the most comfortable thing he owns.

    _____

    _____

2. My sister has some very bad habits. For example, borrowing my sweaters. She also returns them without washing them.

    _____

    _____

3. To improve her singing, Donna practiced some odd exercises. Such as flapping her tongue and fluttering her lips.

    _____

    _____

    _____

4. When she spotted her ex-husband, Leona left the party. She did not want him to see how much she had changed. For example, put on forty pounds.

    _____

    _____

    _____

5. Stanley wanted a big birthday cake. With candles spelling out STAN. He wanted to see his name in lights.

    _____

    _____

    _____

4   MISSING-SUBJECT FRAGMENTS

In each example below, underline the word group in which the subject is missing.

Example 1

One example of my father's generosity is that he visits sick friends in the hospital. And takes along get-well cards with a few dollars folded in them.

Example 2

The weight lifter grunted as he heaved the barbells into the air. Then, with a loud groan, dropped them.

People write missing-subject fragments because they think the subject in one sentence will apply to the next word group as well. But the subject, as well as the verb, must be in *each* word group to make it a sentence.

How to Correct
Missing-Subject Fragments

1   Attach the fragment to the preceding sentence. Example 1 could read: "One example of my father's generosity is that he visits sick friends in the hospital and takes along get-well cards with a few dollars folded in them."
2   Add a subject (which can often be a pronoun standing for the subject in the preceding sentence). Example 2 could read: "Then, with a loud groan, he dropped them."

Practice

Underline the missing-subject fragment in each item below. Then rewrite as needed to correct the fragment. Use one of the two methods of correction described above.

1.   Embarrassed, Sandra looked around the laundromat, Then quickly folded her raggedy towels and faded sheets.

   _____

   _____

2.   Wally took his wool sweaters out of storage, And found them full of moth holes.

   _____

   _____

3.   My sister is taking a word processing course, Also, is learning two computer languages. Machines don't frighten her.

   _____

   _____

4.   When someone comes to the door, my dog races upstairs, Then hides under the bed. Strangers really terrify him.

   _____

   _____

5.   A tiny bug crawled across my paper, And sat down in the middle of a sentence. There was suddenly one comma too many.

   _____

   _____

A REVIEW: HOW TO CHECK FOR SENTENCE FRAGMENTS

1   Read your paper aloud from the *last* sentence to the *first*. You will be better able to see and hear whether each word group you read is a complete thought.

2   Ask yourself of any word group you think is a fragment: Does this contain a subject and a verb and express a complete thought?

3   More specifically, be on the lookout for the most common fragments:

   ● Dependent-word fragments (starting with words like *after, because, since, when,* and *before*)

   ● *-ing* and *to* fragments (*-ing* or *to* at or near the start of a word group)

   ● Added-detail fragments (starting with words like *for example, such as, also,* and *especially*)

   ● Missing-subject fragments (a verb is present but not the subject)

 ## Review Test I

Turn each of the following word groups into a complete sentence. Use the space provided.

Examples   Feeling very confident
Feeling very confident, I began my speech.

Until the rain started
We played softball until the rain started.

1. Before you leave work today

2. When the game show came on

3. Since I have to gain some weight

4. While I was looking in the store window

5. Will be in town next week

_____

6. Stanley, who has a terrible temper

_____

7. Down in the basement

_____

8. Flopping down on the couch

_____

9. Who fixed my car

_____

10. To wake up early

_____

Review Test 2

Underline the fragment in each item below. Then correct the fragment in the space provided.

Example   Sam received all kinds of junk mail. <u>Then complained to the post office.</u> Eventually, some of the mail stopped coming.
Then he complained to the post office.
_____

1. Since she was afraid of mussing her hair, Terry refused to go swimming.

_____

_____

2. The first time I took a college course, I was afraid to say anything in class. I didn't open my mouth, Not even to yawn.

_____

_____

3. Looking like a large dish of vanilla fudge ice cream, Our black-and-white cat went to sleep on the table.

_____

_____

4. Fran read that a sure sign of age is forgetting things. She wanted to show the article to her doctor, But couldn't remember where it was.

_____

_____

5. Dave insisted on wearing a silly hat, Which his girlfriend hated. It had two horns like a Viking helmet.

_____

_____

6. A box of frozen vegetables slipped out of Mark's grocery bag, And split open on the sidewalk. Little green peas rolled in every direction, while hard white onions bounced down the street.

_____

_____

_____

7. Even though Laurie isn't disabled, She used to park in ''handicapped only'' parking spaces. After receiving several tickets, however, she gave up this selfish habit.

_____

_____

_____

8. Thinking that the Halloween get-together was a costume party, Vince came dressed as a boxer. Unfortunately, the other guests were dressed normally.

_____

_____

_____

9. My doctor is using disposable equipment, Such as paper examining gowns and plastic thermometers. He says these are more hygienic.

_____

_____

_____

10. Stanley painted his house lemon-yellow, With orange shutters and a lime-green roof. People say his house looks like a fruit salad.

_____

_____

Review Test 3

In the space provided, write *C* if a word group is a complete sentence; write *frag* if it is a fragment. The first two are done for you.

frag	1. As I was driving my car to work last Monday morning.
C	2. I saw an animal die.
C	3. It was a beautiful, breezy fall day.
C	4. With colorful leaves swirling across the road.
f	5. Suddenly, a squirrel darted out from the bushes.
f	6. And began zigzagging in the path of approaching cars.
C	7. Soundlessly, the car in front of me hit the animal.
f	8. Sending its tiny gray-brown body flying off the road in a flurry of leaves.
C	9. After the incident, I thought about how fragile life is.
f	10. And how easily and quickly it can be taken away.

Now correct the fragments you have found. Attach each fragment to the sentence that comes before or after it, or make whatever other change is needed to turn the fragment into a sentence. Use the space provided. The first one is corrected for you.

1. *As I was driving my car to work last Monday morning, I saw an animal die.*
   _____

2. _____
   _____

3. _____
   _____

4. _____
   _____

5. _____
   _____

 **Review Test 4**

Write quickly for five minutes about the house or apartment where you live. Don't worry about spelling, punctuation, finding exact words, or organizing your thoughts. Just focus on writing as many words as you can without stopping.

After you have finished, go back and make whatever changes are needed to correct any fragments in your writing.

Run-Ons

INTRODUCTORY PROJECT

A run-on occurs when two sentences are run together with no adequate sign given to mark the break between them. Shown below are four run-on sentences and four correctly marked sentences. See if you can complete the statement that explains how each run-on is corrected.

1. A man coughed in the movie theater the result was a chain reaction of copycat coughing. *Run-on*

    A man coughed in the movie theater. The result was a chain reaction of copycat coughing. *Correct*

    The run-on has been corrected by using a _____ and a capital letter to separate the two complete thoughts.

2. I heard laughter inside the house, no one answered the bell. *Run-on*

    I heard laughter inside the house, but no one answered the bell. *Correct*

    The run-on has been corrected by using a joining word, _____, to connect the two complete thoughts.

3. A car sped around the corner, it sprayed slush all over the pedestrians. *Run-on*

    A car sped around the corner; it sprayed slush all over the pedestrians. *Correct*

    The run-on has been corrected by using a _____ to connect the two closely related thoughts.

4. I had a campus map, I still could not find my classroom building. *Run-on*

    Although I had a campus map, I still could not find my classroom building. *Correct*

    The run-on has been corrected by using the subordinating word _____ to connect the two closely related thoughts.

Answers are on page 481.

WHAT ARE RUN-ONS?

A *run-on* is two complete thoughts that are run together with no adequate sign given to mark the break between them.* As a result of the run-on, the reader is confused, unsure of where one thought ends and the next one begins. Two types of run-ons are fused sentences and comma splices.

Some run-ons have no punctuation at all to mark the break between the thoughts. Such run-ons are known as *fused sentences*: they are fused or joined together as if they were only one thought.

Fused Sentence

Rita decided to stop smoking she didn't want to die of lung cancer.

Fused Sentence

The exam was postponed the class was canceled as well.

In other run-ons, known as *comma splices,* a comma is used to connect or ''splice'' together the two complete thoughts. However, a comma alone is *not enough* to connect two complete thoughts. Some connection stronger than a comma alone is needed.

Comma Splice

Rita decided to stop smoking, she didn't want to die of lung cancer.

Comma Splice

The exam was postponed, the class was canceled as well.

Comma splices are the most common kind of run-on. Students sense that some kind of connection is needed between thoughts, and so they put a comma at the dividing point. But the comma alone is *not sufficient.* A stronger, clearer mark is needed between the two thoughts.

---

* Some instructors refer to each complete thought in a run-on sentence as an *independent clause.* A *clause* is simply a group of words having a subject and a verb. A clause may be *independent* (expressing a complete thought and able to stand alone) or *dependent* (not expressing a complete thought and not able to stand alone). A run-on sentence is two independent clauses that are run together with no adequate sign given to mark the break between them.

A Warning:
Words That Can Lead to Run-Ons

People often write run-ons when the second complete thought begins with one of the following words; be on the alert for run-ons whenever you use them:

I	we	there	now
you	they	this	then
he, she, it		that	next

CORRECTING RUN-ONS

Here are four common methods of correcting a run-on:

1 Use a period and a capital letter to separate the two complete thoughts. (In other words, make two separate sentences of the two complete thoughts.)

Rita decided to stop smoking. She didn't want to die of lung cancer.
The exam was postponed. The class was canceled as well.

2 Use a comma plus a joining word (*and, but, for, or, nor, so, yet*) to connect the two complete thoughts.

Rita decided to stop smoking, for she didn't want to die of lung cancer.
The exam was postponed, and the class was canceled as well.

3 Use a semicolon to connect the two complete thoughts.

Rita decided to stop smoking; she didn't want to die of lung cancer.
The exam was postponed; the class was canceled as well.

4 Use subordination.

Because Rita didn't want to die of lung cancer, she decided to stop smoking.
When the exam was postponed, the class was canceled as well.

The following pages will give you practice in all four methods of correcting run-ons. The use of subordination will be explained further on page 394, in a section of the book that deals with sentence variety.

METHOD 1:
PERIOD AND A CAPITAL LETTER

One way of correcting a run-on is to use a period and a capital letter at the break between the two complete thoughts. Use this method especially if the thoughts are not closely related or if another method would make the sentence too long.

Practice 1

Locate the split in each of the following run-ons. Each is a *fused sentence*—that is, each consists of two sentences that are fused or joined together with no punctuation at all between them. Reading each sentence aloud will help you ''hear'' where a major break or split in the thought occurs. At such a point, your voice will probably drop and pause.

Correct the run-on by putting a period at the end of the first thought and a capital letter at the start of the second thought.

Example   Gary was not a success at his job. his mouth moved faster than his hands.

1. Michael gulped two cups of strong coffee his heart then started to flutter.

2. Ellen defrosted the freezer in her usual impatient way. she hacked at the thick ice with a screwdriver.

3. The engine was sputtering and coughing, a strong smell of gas came from under the hood.

4. A bright-yellow Volkswagen ''bug'' pulled up beside me it looked like a deviled egg on wheels.

5. The phone in the next apartment rings all the time the new tenants keep complaining about the sound.

6. Numbered Ping-Pong balls bounced in the machine, we clutched our raffle tickets tightly.

7. The store clerk watched the girls closely they must have looked like shoplifters to her.

8. It's hard to discuss things with Lauren she interprets almost everything as criticism.

9. Kate's books look like accident victims they have cracked spines and torn covers.

10. I got to the sale too late the last ceiling fan had been sold just five minutes before.

Practice 2

Locate the split in each of the following run-ons. Some of the run-ons are fused sentences, and some of them are *comma splices*—run-ons spliced or joined together only with a comma. Correct each run-on by putting a period at the end of the first thought and a capital letter at the start of the next thought.

1. Human teenagers must be descended from cockroaches, both like to stay out late and eat junk food.

2. Only the female mosquito drinks blood the male lives on plant juices.

3. Jane has the experience to be an excellent marriage counselor she's already been married four times.

4. My uncle's final words probably express everyone's feeling about death he said, ''Wait a minute.''

5. I remember every rainbow I've ever seen one actually circled the sun.

6. The beach was once beautiful now it is covered with soda cans, plastic six-pack rings, and cigarette butts.

7. In eighteenth-century Russia, smoking carried a death penalty the same is true of chain-smoking today.

8. The business school near our home just closed down it ran out of money.

9. The frankfurter or hot dog did not begin in Germany, in fact, it first appeared in China.

10. The man about to be shot by a firing squad had a last request he wanted to be given a bulletproof vest.

Practice 3

Write a second sentence to go with each sentence below. Start the second sentence with the word given at the left.

Example *He* My dog's ears snapped up. *He had heard a wolf howling on television.*

They 1. The M&Ms spilled all over the floor. _____

_____

Then 2. I closed every window in the house. _____

_____

She 3. Elena saves everything. _____

_____

It 4. The car needed to be vacuumed. _____

_____

There 5. The street was flooded. _____

_____

METHOD 2:
COMMA AND A JOINING WORD

Another way of correcting a run-on is to use a comma plus a joining word to connect the two complete thoughts. Joining words (also called *coordinating conjunctions*) include *and, but, for, or, nor, so,* and *yet.* Here is what the four most common joining words mean:

and in addition, along with

> Lola was watching Monday night football, and she was doing her homework as well.

(*And* means *in addition:* Lola was watching Monday night football; *in addition,* she was doing her homework as well.)

but   however, except, on the other hand, just the opposite

I voted for the president two years ago, but I would not vote for him today.

(*But* means *however:* I voted for the president two years ago; *however,* I would not vote for him today.)

for   because, the reason why, the cause for something

Saturday is the worst day to shop, for people jam the stores.

(*For* means *because:* Saturday is the worst day to shop *because* people jam the stores.) If you are not comfortable using *for,* you may want to use *because* instead of *for* in the activities that follow. If you do use *because,* omit the comma before it.

so   as a result, therefore

Our son misbehaved again, so he was sent upstairs without dessert.

(*So* means *as a result:* Our son misbehaved again; *as a result,* he was sent upstairs without dessert.)

Practice I

Insert the comma and the joining word (*and, but, for, so*) that logically connect the two thoughts in each sentence. You will notice that all these run-ons are *fused sentences* (there is no punctuation between the two complete thoughts).

Example   I hate to see animals in cages, ^so^ a trip to the zoo always depresses me.

1. We knew the old desk had a secret drawer, *but* no one could find it.

2. I had to retype my term paper, *for* my little boy had scrawled on it with a purple crayon.

3. Last year my nephew needed physical therapy, *and* the whole family pitched in to work with him.

4. My new car is a pleasure to drive, *for* there isn't the slightest squeak or rattle.

5. A cat food commercial came on, *and* Marie started to sing along with the jingle.

6. It rained a lot this summer, *so* we have not had to water our lawn.

7. I heard the grinding of the garbage truck [so] I ran downstairs and grabbed the trash bags.

8. Ella wanted to take a break [but] the boss wanted the inventory list right away.

9. I couldn't read the map [for] an ink stain had blotted out an entire country.

10. The two little boys had a giggling fit [so] their father hustled them out of the church.

Practice 2

Add a complete and closely related thought to go with each of the following statements. Use a comma plus the italicized joining word when you write the second thought.

> **Example**   *but*   I was sick with the flu, *but I still had to study for the test.*

so   1. I couldn't resist the banana cream pie _____

_____

but   2. We tried to follow the directions _____

_____

and   3. Bob took three coffee breaks before lunch _____

_____

for   4. The car seat was drenched _____

_____

but   5. I don't usually pick up hitchhikers _____

_____

METHOD 3: SEMICOLON

A third method of correcting a run-on is to use a semicolon to mark the break between two thoughts. A *semicolon* (;) is made up of a period above a comma and is sometimes called a *strong comma.* The semicolon signals more of a pause than a comma alone but not quite the full pause of a period.

Occasional use of a semicolon can add variety to sentences. For some people, however, the semicolon is a confusing mark of punctuation. Keep in mind that if you are not comfortable using it, you can and should use one of the first two methods of correcting a run-on sentence.

Semicolon Alone

Here are some earlier sentences that were connected with a comma plus a joining word. Notice that a semicolon, unlike a comma, can be used alone to connect the two complete thoughts in each sentence:

Lola was watching Monday night football; she was doing her homework as well.

I voted for the president two years ago; I would not vote for him today.

Saturday is the worst day to shop; people jam the stores.

Practice

Insert a semicolon where the break occurs between the two complete thoughts in each of the following sentences.

Example   She had a wig on; it looked more like a hat than a wig.

1. Alan had to go up the ramp backwards; his wheelchair's strongest gear is reverse.
2. A cockroach is almost indestructible; it can live for weeks with its head cut off.
3. Pat read the funny birthday cards; she laughed aloud in the quiet store.
4. My brother captured the fluttering moth; it bumped around inside his hands.
5. Alex couldn't finish the book; it was giving him nightmares.

Semicolon with a Transition

A semicolon is sometimes used with a transitional word and a comma to join two complete thoughts:

I figured that the ball game would cost me about ten dollars; however, I didn't consider the high price of food and drinks.

Fred and Martha have a low-interest mortgage on their house; otherwise, they would move to another neighborhood.

Sharon didn't understand the teacher's point; therefore, she asked him to repeat it.

Note: Sometimes transitional words do not join complete thoughts but are merely interrupters in a sentence (see page 190):

My parents, moreover, plan to go on the trip.
I believe, however, that they'll change their minds.

Transitional Words

Here is a list of common transitional words (also known as *adverbial conjunctions*).

Common Transitional Words		
however	moreover	therefore
on the other hand	in addition	as a result
nevertheless	also	consequently
instead	furthermore	otherwise

Practice 1

Choose a logical transitional word from the box above and write it in the space provided. In addition, put a semicolon *before* the transition and a comma *after* it.

Example   It was raining harder than ever _____; however,_____ Bobby was determined to go to the amusement park.

1. Most people can do without food for a month_; nevertheless_ they need two quarts of water a day to survive.

2. Jean's son was sick_; therefore_ she delivered his newspapers for him.

3. Linda felt safe living near a fire hydrant _; on the other hand_ she wished that the neighborhood dogs didn't like it so much.

4. The bride's father apologized to the waiting guests_; also_ he promised to return all the wedding gifts.

5. Mindy thinks gift wrapping paper is a waste of money_; as a result_ she wraps presents in shelf paper.

Practice 2

Punctuate each sentence by using a semicolon and a comma.

Example A band rehearses in the garage next door;as a result,I'm thinking of moving.

1. The hostess told us there would be a twenty-minute wait however she then seated the couple who came in after us.
2. Ricki knows nothing about computers as a result she decided to sign up for a word processing course.
3. All too many children are emotionally abused moreover many are physically abused as well.
4. I insisted that my wife stop smoking otherwise I would have suffered the effects of the secondhand smoke from her cigarettes.
5. We packed the groceries carefully nevertheless the bread was squashed and two eggs were broken.

METHOD 4: SUBORDINATION

A fourth method of joining related thoughts together is to use subordination. *Subordination* is a way of showing that one thought in a sentence is not as important as another thought. Here are three sentences where one idea is subordinated to (made less emphatic than) the other idea:

Because Rita didn't want to die of lung cancer, she decided to stop smoking.

The wedding reception began to get out of hand when the guests started to throw food at each other.

Although Suzie wanted to watch a *Star Trek* rerun, the rest of the family insisted on turning to the network news.

Dependent Words

Notice that when we subordinate, we use dependent words like *because, when,* and *although.* On the opposite page is a brief list of common dependent words (see also the list on page 19). Subordination is explained in full on page 399.

Common Dependent Words		
after	before	unless
although	even though	until
as	if	when
because	since	while

Practice 1

Choose a logical dependent word from the box above and write it in the space provided.

Example _____Although_____ going up a ladder is easy, looking down can be difficult.

1. _____ an emotional reunion between a mother and son, the talk-show host paused for a commercial about chewing gum.

2. You should have looked at the label _____ you washed that wool sweater.

3. _____ the instructor announced there were only ten minutes left in the test, students began writing even more quickly to finish their essay answers.

4. _____ you open the windows, the paint fumes will disappear more quickly.

5. The directions say to continue on the main highway _____ a large red barn and a small road appear on the right.

Practice 2

Rewrite the five sentences below so that one idea is subordinate to the other. Use one of the dependent words in the box above. As in the example below, use a comma if a dependent statement starts a sentence. (All the sentences are taken from this chapter.)

Example   I hate to see animals in cages; a trip to the zoo always depresses me.

Because I hate to see animals in cages, a trip to the zoo always

depresses me.

1. I had a campus map; I still could not find my classroom building.

   _____

   _____

2. A cat food commercial came on; Marie started to sing along with the jingle.

   _____

   _____

3. The phone in the next apartment rings all the time; I'm beginning to get used to the sound.

   _____

   _____

4. Michael gulped two cups of strong coffee; his heart began to flutter.

   _____

   _____

5. A car sped around the corner; it sprayed slush all over the pedestrians.

   _____

   _____

A REVIEW: HOW TO CHECK FOR RUN-ONS

1 To see if a sentence is a run-on, read it aloud and listen for a break marking two complete thoughts. Your voice will probably drop and pause at the break.

2 To check an entire paper, read it aloud from the *last* sentence to the *first*. Doing so will help you hear and see each complete thought.

3 Be on the lookout for words that can lead to run-on sentences:

I	he, she, it	they	this	then
you	we	there	that	next

4 Correct run-on sentences by using one of the following methods:
   - Period and a capital letter
   - Comma and a joining word (*and, but, for, or, nor, so, yet*)
   - Semicolon
   - Subordination (as explained above and on page 399)

● **Review Test I**

Some of the run-ons that follow are *fused sentences,* having no punctuation between the two complete thoughts; others are *comma splices,* having only a comma between the two complete thoughts.

Correct the run-ons by using one of the following three methods:

● Period and a capital letter
● Comma and a joining word (*and, but, for,* or *so*)
● Semicolon

Use whichever method seems most appropriate in each case.

Example Fred pulled the cellophane off the cake,the icing came along with it.
  and

1. The runner was called safe even he couldn't believe it.

2. I looked all over for my new shirt all I could find was the empty bag.

3. Libby tried to fold the road map neatly she gave up and stuffed it into the glove compartment.

4. First we can't wait to go on vacation then we can't wait to come home again.

5. One step was sagging Mary hired a carpenter to fix the porch.

6. I ran toward the supermarket the manager had just locked the doors.

7. Ted tried to assemble the barbecue the instructions were impossible to understand.

8. I reached into the pretzel bag all that was left was salt.

9. Tina was starving she bought a limp sandwich from the vending machine.

10. Bev was bored she drew rocket ships in the margins of her notebook.

Review Test 2

Correct the run-on in each sentence below by using subordination. Choose from among the following dependent words:

after	before	unless
although	even though	until
as	if	when
because	since	while

Example   Tony hated going to a new barber, he was afraid of butchered hair.

Because Tony was afraid of butchered hair, he hated going to a

new barber.

1. The fan started throwing beer cans onto the field security guards hustled him away.

_____

_____

2. I had three cups of coffee my eyes looked like huge globes.

_____

_____

3. The boy didn't want to talk to his mother he pretended to be asleep.

_____

_____

4. The check arrived in the mail we didn't really believe that we had won the contest.

_____

_____

5. We forgot to put film in the camera the only pictures we have of our vacation are the ones in our memory.

_____

_____

6. I left school this afternoon hailstones as big as marbles were falling from the sky.

_____

_____

7. The plumber comes quickly our kitchen will look like a swamp.

_____

_____

8. The man circled the crowded parking lot in their car his wife ran into the store to return a sweater.

_____

_____

9. The boy was wearing headphones nearly everyone on the bus could hear the beat of the song on his radio.

_____

_____

10. The computer went dead a message appeared on the screen saying, "System error."

_____

_____

Review Test 3

On separate paper, write six sentences, each of which has two complete thoughts. In two of the sentences, use a period and a capital letter between the thoughts. In another two sentences, use a comma and a joining word (*and, but, or, nor, for, so, yet*) to join the thoughts. In the final two sentences, use a semicolon to join the thoughts.

Next, choose two of your six sentences and rewrite them so that each uses a dependent word and contains a subordinated thought.

Review Test 4

Write quickly for five minutes about something that makes you angry. Don't worry about spelling, punctuation, finding exact words, or organizing your thoughts. Just focus on writing as many words as you can without stopping.

After you have finished, go back and make whatever changes are needed to correct any run-on sentences in your writing.

Standard English Verbs

> ### INTRODUCTORY PROJECT
>
> Underline what you think is the correct form of the verb in each pair of sentences below.
>
> That radio station once (play, played) top-forty hits.
> It now (play, plays) classical music.
>
> When Jean was a little girl, she (hope, hoped) to become a movie star.
> Now she (hope, hopes) to be accepted at law school.
>
> At first, my father (juggle, juggled) with balls of yarn.
> Now that he is an expert, he (juggle, juggles) raw eggs.
>
> On the basis of the above examples, see if you can complete the following statements.
>
> 1. The first sentence in each pair refers to an action in the (past time, present time), and the regular verb has an _____ ending.
> 2. The second sentence in each pair refers to an action in the (past time, present time), and the regular verb has an _____ ending.
>
> Answers are on page 482.

Many people have grown up in communities where nonstandard verb forms are used in everyday life. Such nonstandard forms include *they be, it done, we has, you was, she don't,* and *it ain't.* Community dialects have richness and power but are a drawback in college and the world at large, where standard English verb forms must be used. Standard English helps ensure clear communication among English-speaking people everywhere, and it is especially important in the world of work.

This chapter compares the community dialect and the standard English forms of a regular verb and three common irregular verbs.

REGULAR VERBS: DIALECT AND STANDARD FORMS

The chart below compares community dialect (nonstandard) and standard English forms of the regular verb *talk.*

TALK

Community Dialect (Do not use in your writing)		*Standard English* (Use for clear communication)	
Present Tense			
I talks	we talks	I talk	we talk
you talks	you talks	you talk	you talk
he, she, it talk	they talks	he, she, it talks	they talk
Past Tense			
I talk	we talk	I talked	we talked
you talk	you talk	you talked	you talked
he, she, it talk	they talk	he, she, it talked	they talked

One of the most common nonstandard forms results from dropping the endings of regular verbs. For example, people might say "Rose work until ten o'clock tonight" instead of "Rose work*s* until ten o'clock tonight." Or they'll say "I work overtime yesterday" instead of "I work*ed* overtime yesterday." To avoid such nonstandard usage, memorize the forms shown above for the regular verb *talk.* Then use the activities that follow to help make the inclusion of verb endings a writing habit.

Present Tense Endings

The verb ending -*s* or -*es* is needed with a regular verb in the present tense when the subject is *he, she, it,* or any one person or thing.

He	He lifts weights.
She	She runs.
It	It amazes me.
One person	Their son Ted swims.
One person	Their daughter Terry dances.
One thing	Their house jumps at night with all the exercise.

Practice 1

All but one of the ten sentences that follow need -*s* or -*es* endings. Cross out the nonstandard verb forms and write the standard forms in the spaces provided. Mark the one sentence that needs no change with a *C.*

ends   **Example**   The sale ~~end~~ tomorrow.

_____   1. Lucille wear a wig to cover up her thinning gray hair.

_____   2. My horoscope say that today is a good day for romance.

_____   3. Eric subscribe to the *Beer Can Collectors' Newsletter* to keep up with current prices.

_____   4. Stanley ride a bicycle to work to save money on gas.

_____   5. A dog see only tones of gray, black, and white.

_____   6. At Thanksgiving, our church distribute turkeys to the needy.

_____   7. Margo breaks her cigarettes in half before smoking them.

_____   8. Chris feed chopped-up flies and mosquitoes to his tropical fish.

_____   9. That diner overcook all its food.

_____   10. He polish his shoes using a melted wax crayon and an old towel.

Practice 2

Rewrite the short selection on the opposite page, adding present tense -*s* verb endings wherever needed.

Lou work for a company that deliver singing telegrams. Sometimes he put on a sequined tuxedo or wear a Cupid costume. He compose his own songs for birthdays, anniversaries, bachelor parties, and other occasions. Then he show up at a certain place and surprise the victim. He sing a song that include personal details, which he get in advance, about the recipient of the telegram. Lou love the astonished looks on other people's faces; he also enjoy earning money by making people happy on special days.

_____

_____

_____

_____

_____

_____

_____

_____

_____

_____

Past Tense Endings

The verb ending *-d* or *-ed* is needed with a regular verb in the past tense.

Yesterday we finished painting the house.
I completed the paper an hour before class.
Fred's car stalled on his way to work this morning.

Practice 1

All but one of the ten sentences on the next page need *-d* or *-ed* endings. Cross out the nonstandard verb forms and write the standard forms in the spaces provided. Mark the one sentence that needs no change with a *C*.

jumped **Example** The cat j̶u̶m̶p̶ onto my lap when I sat down.

_____ 1. The first time I baked a pound cake, it turn out to be a ton cake.

_____ 2. The line drive slammed into the fence and bounce into the stands for a ground-rule double.

_____ 3. Ben page through the book, looking for the money he had hidden there.

_____ 4. Mario crush the sunglasses in his back pocket as he flopped on the sofa.

_____ 5. The sweating workers shoveled hot tar on the road and then smoothed it out.

_____ 6. The surgeons wash their hands before they entered the operating room.

_____ 7. The detective crack the case after finding a key witness.

_____ 8. When she was a teenager, Rita collect pictures of her favorite rock stars.

_____ 9. As they struggled, the mugger pull the gold chain from Val's neck.

_____ 10. Ken knew he lack the ability to make the varsity team, but he tried out anyway.

Practice 2

Rewrite this selection, adding past tense -*d* or -*ed* verb endings where needed.

Mrs. Bayne stroll across the street to her neighbor's yard sale. She examine the rack of used clothes, check the prices, and accidentally knock a blouse off its hanger. She poke through a box of children's toys, spilling a carton full of wooden blocks. She leaf through some old magazines, ripping a few of the brittle pages. At a table of kitchen equipment, she push down the buttons on a toaster and force them up again. Mrs. Bayne then wander off without buying anything.

_____

_____

_____

_____

_____

_____

_____

_____

_____

_____

_____

THREE COMMON IRREGULAR VERBS: DIALECT AND STANDARD FORMS

The following charts compare the community dialect (nonstandard) and standard English forms of the common irregular verbs *be, have,* and *do.* (For more on irregular verbs, see the next chapter, beginning on page 62.)

BE

Community Dialect		*Standard English*	
(Do not use in your writing)		(Use for clear communication)	

Present Tense

I be (*or* is)	we be	I am	we are
you be	you be	you are	you are
he, she, it be	they be	he, she, it is	they are

Past Tense

I were	we was	I was	we were
you was	you was	you were	you were
he, she, it were	they was	he, she, it was	they were

HAVE

Community Dialect		*Standard English*	
(Do not use in your writing)		(Use for clear communication)	

Present Tense

I has	we has	I have	we have
you has	you has	you have	you have
he, she, it have	they has	he, she, it has	they have

Past Tense

I has	we has	I had	we had
you has	you has	you had	you had
he, she, it have	they has	he, she, it had	they had

DO

Community Dialect
(Do not use in your writing)

Standard English
(Use for clear communication)

Present Tense

I does	we does	I do	we do
you does	you does	you do	you do
he, she, it do	they does	he, she, it does	they do

Past Tense

I done	we done	I did	we did
you done	you done	you did	you did
he, she, it done	they done	he, she, it did	they did

Note: Many people have trouble with one negative form of *do.* They will say, for example, ''She don't listen'' instead of ''She doesn't listen,'' or they will say ''This pen don't work'' instead of ''This pen doesn't work.'' Be careful to avoid the common mistake of using *don't* instead of *doesn't.*

Practice 1

Underline the standard form of the irregular verbs *be, have,* or *do.*

1. My brother Ronald (be, is) a normal, fun-loving person most of the time.
2. But he (have, has) a hobby that changes his personality.
3. He (be, is) an amateur actor with our community theater group.
4. When he (do, does) a part in a play, he turns into the character.
5. Once the company (done, did) a play about Sherlock Holmes, the detective.
6. In the show, Ronald (was, were) a frightened man stalked by a murderer.
7. The role (had, have) a strange effect on my brother.
8. At home, he (were, was) nervous and jittery.
9. I (done, did) my best to calm him.
10. However, he remained convinced that he (was, were) being followed.

Practice 2

Cross out the nonstandard verb form in each sentence. Then write the standard form of *be, have,* or *do* in the space provided.

_____ 1. That music store, Platters, be the largest in the area.

_____ 2. It have all the latest releases.

_____ 3. In addition, a special section have classic CDs at reasonable prices.

_____ 4. The salespeople is very knowledgeable about music.

_____ 5. They is willing to help a customer find any CD in the store.

_____ 6. They also does their best to order any CD available.

_____ 7. The owners of Platters does a good job promoting local recording artists, too.

_____ 8. The store have posters of local groups in the windows.

_____ 9. It do special promotions of their performances.

_____ 10. My friends and I be loyal and satisfied customers of Platters.

Practice 3

Fill in each blank with the standard form of *be, have,* or *do.*

My friend Brad _____ a real bargain hunter. If any store _____ a sale, he runs right over and buys two or three things, whether or not they _____ things he needs. Brad _____ his best, also, to get something for nothing. Last week, he _____ reading the paper and saw that the First National Bank's new downtown offices _____ offering gifts for new accounts. "Those freebies sure _____ look good," Brad said. So he went downtown, opened an account, and _____ the manager give him a Big Ben alarm clock. When he got back with the clock, he _____ smiling. "I _____ a very busy man," he told me, "and I really need the free time."

Review Test 1

Underline the standard verb form.

1. We (pay, pays) more for car insurance since the accident.
2. Two years ago, my brother and his wife (adopt, adopted) a handicapped child.
3. The baby (grasp, grasps) his mother's long hair in his tiny fist.
4. The original Frisbees (was, were) tin pie plates from a baking company.
5. Greta (don't, doesn't) approve of her brother's deer hunting.
6. My stepmother likes to work in the yard whenever the sun (be, is) shining.
7. Lorraine looks like a squirrel when she (chews, chew) a big wad of gum.
8. My little sister (has, have) an unusual ailment—an allergy to homework.
9. Louise (grease, greases) the casserole dish with melted chicken fat.
10. My brother (own, owns) a World War II flyer's leather jacket that belonged to our father.

Review Test 2

Cross out the nonstandard verb forms in the sentences that follow. Then write the standard English verb forms in the space above, as shown.

Example   For most of the morning, the children ~~play~~ *played* quietly in the sandbox.

1. Sandra dunk the chicken wings into sweet-and-sour sauce.
2. My parents locks themselves in the bathroom during an argument.
3. A suspicious-looking man ask if I wanted to buy a new microwave oven for fifty dollars.
4. My sister bite the erasers off her pencils.
5. Stanley ride a bicycle to work in order to save money on gas.
6. The school don't allow anyone to use the darkroom without an appointment.
7. For the third time in the movie, a car bounce headlong down a cliff and burst into flames.

8. The mail carrier give us a pink slip when we have a package waiting at the post office.

9. The ceilings was ringed with water marks from the leaky roof.

10. Instead of a keyhole, each hotel room door have a slot for a magnetic card.

Irregular Verbs

INTRODUCTORY PROJECT

You may already have a sense of which common English verbs are regular and which are not. To test yourself, fill in the past tense and past participle of the verbs below. Five are regular verbs and so take *-d* or *-ed* in the past tense and past participle. Five are irregular verbs and will probably not sound right when you try to add *-d* or *-ed*. Put *I* for *irregular* in front of these verbs. Also, see if you can write in their irregular verb forms.

Present	*Irregular*	*Past*	*Past Participle*
fall	I	fell	fallen
1. scream			
2. write			
3. steal			
4. ask			
5. kiss			
6. choose			
7. ride			
8. chew			
9. think			
10. dance			

Answers are on page 482.

A BRIEF REVIEW
OF REGULAR VERBS

Every verb has four principal parts: present, past, past participle, and present participle. These parts can be used to build all the verb tenses (the times shown by a verb).

The past and past participle of a regular verb are formed by adding *-d* or *-ed* to the present. The *past participle* is the form of the verb used with the helping verbs *have, has,* or *had* (or some form of *be* with passive verbs). The *present participle* is formed by adding *-ing* to the present. Here are the principal forms of some regular verbs:

Present	Past	Past Participle	Present Participle
laugh	laughed	laughed	laughing
ask	asked	asked	asking
touch	touched	touched	touching
decide	decided	decided	deciding
explode	exploded	exploded	exploding

Most verbs in English are regular.

LIST OF IRREGULAR VERBS

Irregular verbs have irregular forms in the past tense and past participle. For example, the past tense of the irregular verb *grow* is *grew;* the past participle is *grown.*

Almost everyone has some degree of trouble with irregular verbs. When you are unsure about the form of a verb, you can check the list of irregular verbs on the following pages. (The present participle is not shown on this list, because it is formed simply by adding *-ing* to the base form of the verb.) Or you can check a dictionary, which gives the principal parts of irregular verbs.

Present	Past	Past Participle
arise	arose	arisen
awake	awoke *or* awaked	awoke *or* awaked
be (am, are, is)	was (were)	been
become	became	become
begin	began	begun
bend	bent	bent
bite	bit	bitten
blow	blew	blown
break	broke	broken
bring	brought	brought
build	built	built
burst	burst	burst
buy	bought	bought
catch	caught	caught
choose	chose	chosen
come	came	come
cost	cost	cost
cut	cut	cut
do (does)	did	done
draw	drew	drawn
drink	drank	drunk
drive	drove	driven
eat	ate	eaten
fall	fell	fallen
feed	fed	fed
feel	felt	felt
fight	fought	fought
find	found	found
fly	flew	flown
freeze	froze	frozen
get	got	got *or* gotten
give	gave	given
go (goes)	went	gone
grow	grew	grown
have (has)	had	had
hear	heard	heard
hide	hid	hidden
hold	held	held
hurt	hurt	hurt
keep	kept	kept
know	knew	known

Present	*Past*	*Past Participle*
lay	laid	laid
lead	led	led
leave	left	left
lend	lent	lent
let	let	let
lie	lay	lain
light	lit	lit
lose	lost	lost
make	made	made
meet	met	met
pay	paid	paid
ride	rode	ridden
ring	rang	rung
rise	rose	risen
run	ran	run
say	said	said
see	saw	seen
sell	sold	sold
send	sent	sent
shake	shook	shaken
shrink	shrank	shrunk
shut	shut	shut
sing	sang	sung
sit	sat	sat
sleep	slept	slept
speak	spoke	spoken
spend	spent	spent
stand	stood	stood
steal	stole	stolen
stick	stuck	stuck
sting	stung	stung
swear	swore	sworn
swim	swam	swum
take	took	taken
teach	taught	taught
tear	tore	torn
tell	told	told
think	thought	thought
wake	woke *or* waked	woken *or* waked
wear	wore	worn
win	won	won
write	wrote	written

Practice 1

Cross out the incorrect verb form in the following sentences. Then write the correct form of the verb in the space provided.

began   **Example**   When the mud slide started, the whole neighborhood begun going downhill.

_____   1. The boys taked cigarettes into the darkened theater.

_____   2. The fire department has finally chose two women for its training program.

_____   3. The daredevil catched a bullet in his teeth.

_____   4. Someone has stole the tape deck from my car.

_____   5. After I seen my new haircut, I cried.

_____   6. I have went to the lost-and-found office several times, but my leather gloves haven't turned up yet.

_____   7. The stunt man has fell off hundreds of horses without injuring himself.

_____   8. Jack has swore to control his temper.

_____   9. The bacon strips in the pan had shrank into blackened stubs.

_____   10. Why haven't you spoke up about your problems?

Practice 2

For each of the italicized verbs in the following sentences, fill in the three missing forms in the order shown in the box:

> a. Present tense, which takes an *-s* ending when the subject is *he, she, it,* or any *one person* or *thing* (see page 54)
>
> b. Past tense
>
> c. Past participle—the form that goes with the helping verb *have, has,* or *had*

Example   My little nephew loves to *break* things. Every Christmas he (a) _____ *breaks* _____ his new toys the minute they're unwrapped.

Last year he (b) _____ *broke* _____ five toys in seven minutes and then went on to smash his family's new china platter. His mother says he won't be happy until he has (c) _____ *broken* _____ their hearts.

1. My husband always seems to *lose* things. He (a) _____ his eyeglasses about three times a day. Once he (b) _____ one of his running shoes while he was out jogging. He has (c) _____ so many car keys that we keep one taped inside the bumper of our Chevy.

2. Jamie is often asked to *bring* her gorgeous sister to parties. Poor Jamie (a) _____ Rita and then fades into the wallpaper. Last week she (b) _____ Rita to a pool party. Jamie felt as if she had (c) _____ a human magnet instead of a sister, since all the men clustered around Rita the entire night.

3. Small babies can be taught to *swim*. They don't (a) _____ like adults, but they do float and keep their heads above water. Babies are accustomed to a watery environment, since they (b) _____ inside their mothers' bodies in a bath of fluid. Babies who have (c) _____ in pools shortly after birth seem to become more confident swimmers as children.

4. My brother actually likes to *go* to the dentist. He (a) _____ at least every three months for a checkup. He (b) _____ last week just to have his teeth flossed. He has (c) _____ to his dentist so regularly that Dr. Ross has been able to afford a new sports car.

5. The vast crowd in the stadium waits for the rock concert to *begin*. The fans don't care if it (a) _____ late, since they are having a great time eating, drinking, and listening to cassette tapes. In fact, if the concert (b) _____ on time, they would feel cheated. Once it has (c) _____, the stadium will vibrate from the screams of the fans and the roar of the music.

6. My little boy likes to *hide* from me. I usually find him, since he (a) _____ in obvious places, like under the bed or inside the closet. Once, however, he (b) _____ in an unusual place. I searched all over until I discovered that he had (c) _____ inside an empty garbage can.

7. I like to *choose* unusual items when I order from a restaurant menu. My friends always (a) _____ something safe and familiar, but I'm more adventurous. Once I (b) _____ stuffed calves' brains, which were delicious. I have (c) _____ items like squid, sea urchins, and pickled pigs' feet just to see how they would taste.

8. Last month I had to *speak* before the PTA members at my daughter's school.
I can (a) _____ comfortably to small groups, but this was a meeting of hundreds of people in an auditorium. Before I gave my report, I (b) _____ to the principal and told him how nervous I was. He assured me that even though he had (c) _____ in public many times over the years, he still got butterflies in his stomach.

9. Sheila has to *take* her dog to the veterinarian. Whenever she (a) _____ him, though, he howls in the waiting room or lunges at the other pets. The last time Sheila (b) _____ Bruno, he had an accident on the linoleum floor. This time, however, Sheila has (c) _____ the precaution of keeping Bruno away from his water bowl for several hours.

10. Sean hates to *wake* up. When he does (a) _____ up, he is groggy and miserable. Once he (b) _____ up and yelled at his pet hamster for looking at him the wrong way. He has (c) _____ up this way so often that his family won't speak to him until noon.

TROUBLESOME IRREGULAR VERBS

Three common irregular verbs that often give people trouble are *be, have,* and *do.* See pages 57–58 for a discussion of these verbs. Three sets of other irregular verbs that can lead to difficulties are *lie-lay, sit-set,* and *rise-raise.*

Lie–Lay

The principal parts of *lie* and *lay* are as follows:

Present	Past	Past Participle
lie	lay	lain
lay	laid	laid

To lie means *to rest* or *recline. To lay* means *to put something down.*

To Lie

Tony *lies* on the couch.

This morning he *lay* in the tub.

He has *lain* in bed all week with the flu.

To Lay

I *lay* the mail on the table.

Yesterday I *laid* the mail on the counter.

I have *laid* the mail where everyone will see it.

Practice

Underline the correct verb. Use a form of *lie* if you can substitute *recline.* Use a form of *lay* if you can substitute *put.*

1. Unknowingly, I had (lain, laid) my coat down on a freshly varnished table.
2. Like a mini solar collector, the cat (lay, laid) in the warm rays of the sun.
3. He was certain he had (lain, laid) the tiles in a straight line until he stepped back to look.
4. (Lying, Laying) too long in bed in the morning can give me a headache.
5. I (lay, laid) on the doctor's examining table, staring into the bright bars of fluorescent light on the ceiling.

Sit–Set

The principal parts of *sit* and *set* are as follows:

Present	Past	Past Participle
sit	sat	sat
set	set	set

To sit means *to take a seat* or *to rest. To set* means *to put* or *to place.*

To Sit

I *sit* down during work breaks.

I *sat* in the doctor's office for three hours.

I have always *sat* in the last desk.

To Set

Tony *sets* out the knives, forks, and spoons.

His sister already *set* out the dishes.

They have just *set* out the dinnerware.

Practice

Underline the correct form of the verb. Use a form of *sit* if you can substitute *rest*. Use a form of *set* if you can substitute *place*.

1. Harriet (sat, set) the bowl of strawberries on the table, and four pairs of hands lunged for it.
2. The insurance agent (sat, set) down his briefcase and began his sales pitch.
3. You can't (sit, set) on my couch in those filthy jeans.
4. Maureen (sat, set) the heavy pumpkin on the front step.
5. I was (sitting, setting) my bag on the rack above my seat when the bus lurched away.

Rise–Raise

The principal parts of *rise* and *raise* are as follows:

Present	*Past*	*Past Participle*
rise	rose	risen
raise	raised	raised

To rise means *to get up* or *to move up*. *To raise* (which is a regular verb with simple *-ed* endings) means *to lift up* or *to increase in amount*.

To Rise	*To Raise*
The soldiers *rise* at dawn.	I'm going to *raise* the stakes in the card game.
The crowd *rose* to applaud the batter.	I *raised* the shades to let in the sun.
Dracula has *risen* from the grave.	I would have quit if the company had not *raised* my salary.

Practice

Underline the correct verb. Use a form of *rise* if you can substitute *get up* or *move up*. Use a form of *raise* if you can substitute *lift up* or *increase*.

1. When food prices (rise, raise), people living on Social Security suffer.
2. They have (risen, raised) their daughter to be a self-sufficient person.
3. As the crowd watched, the World War II veteran (rose, raised) the flag.
4. The reporters (rose, raised) as the president entered the room for the press conference.
5. The promising weather report (rose, raised) our hopes for an enjoyable camping trip.

Review Test I

Cross out the incorrect verb form. Then write the correct form of the verb in the space provided.

_____ 1. The famous recording star first sung in his hometown church choir.

_____ 2. After Lola was bit by the parrot, her finger was sore for a week.

_____ 3. Last August, Carmen taked her family to Yellowstone National Park.

_____ 4. The plane would have ran off the runway if the pilot hadn't been so skillful.

_____ 5. He heard a frightening hissing sound before the pipes busted.

_____ 6. I couldn't believe I got a B on the first paper I writed in college.

_____ 7. Steven laid in a lounge chair, staring up at the moon through his new binoculars.

_____ 8. The class clown had went too far, and the students waited to see what the teacher would do.

_____ 9. The sun had already rose by the time I got home from the party.

_____ 10. As we approached the quiet pond, a beaver slid into the water and swum toward its underwater lodge.

Review Test 2

Write short sentences that use the form requested for the following irregular verbs.

Example   The past of *ride*   *The Lone Ranger rode into the sunset.*

1. Past of *drink* _____

2. Present of *bring* _____

3. Past participle of *grow* _____

4. Present of *swim* _____

5. Past participle of *write* _____

6. Past of *give* _____

7. Present of *do* _____

8. Past participle of *begin* _____

9. Past of *go* _____

10. Present of *know* _____

Subject-Verb Agreement

INTRODUCTORY PROJECT

As you read each pair of sentences below, place a check mark beside the sentence that you think uses the underlined word correctly.

There <u>was</u> many applicants for the position. _____

There <u>were</u> many applicants for the position. _____

The pictures in that magazine <u>is</u> very controversial. _____

The pictures in that magazine <u>are</u> very controversial. _____

Everybody usually <u>watch</u> the lighted numbers in an elevator. _____

Everybody usually <u>watches</u> the lighted numbers in an elevator. _____

On the basis of the above examples, see if you can complete the following statements.

1. In the first two pairs of sentences, the subjects are _____
   and _____. Since both these subjects are plural, the verb must be plural.
2. In the last pair of sentences, the subject, *Everybody,* is a word that is always (singular, plural), and so that verb must be (singular, plural).

Answers are on page 483.

A verb must agree with its subject in number. A *singular subject* (one person or thing) takes a singular verb. A *plural subject* (more than one person or thing) takes a plural verb. Mistakes in subject-verb agreement are sometimes made in the following situations:

1   When words come between the subject and the verb
2   When a verb comes before the subject
3   With indefinite pronouns
4   With compound subjects
5   With *who, which,* and *that*

Each situation is explained on the following pages.

WORDS BETWEEN THE SUBJECT AND THE VERB

Words that come between the subject and the verb do not change subject-verb agreement. In the following sentence,

> The breakfast cereals in the pantry are made mostly of sugar.

the subject (*cereals*) is plural, and so the verb (*are*) is plural. The words *in the pantry* that come between the subject and the verb do not affect subject-verb agreement. To help find the subject of certain sentences, you should cross out prepositional phrases (explained on page 13):

> One of the crooked politicians was jailed for a month.
> The posters on my little brother's wall included rock singers, monsters, and blond television stars.

Following is a list of common prepositions.

Common Prepositions				
about	before	by	inside	over
above	behind	during	into	through
across	below	except	of	to
among	beneath	for	off	toward
around	beside	from	on	under
at	between	in	onto	with

Practice

For each item below, underline the subject and cross out any words that come between the subject and the verb. Then double-underline the verb in parentheses that you believe is correct.

Example   The price of the stereo speakers (is, are) too high for my wallet.

1. The leaders of the union (has, have) called for a strike.
2. One of Robin's pencil sketches (hangs, hang) in the art classroom.
3. Three days of anxious waiting finally (ends, end) with a phone call.
4. The members of the car pool (chips, chip) in for the driving expenses.
5. The woman with the teased, sprayed hairdo (looks, look) as if she were wearing a plastic helmet.
6. The addition of heavy shades to my sunny windows (allows, allow) me to sleep during the day.
7. Several houses in the old whaling village (has, have) been designated as historical landmarks.
8. The stack of baseball cards in my little brother's bedroom (is, are) two feet high.
9. Gooey puddles of egg white (spreads, spread) over the stove as Mike cracks the shells against the frying pan.
10. The giant-size box of Raisinets (sells, sell) for three dollars at the theater's candy counter.

VERB BEFORE THE SUBJECT

A verb agrees with its subject even when the verb comes *before* the subject. Words that may precede the subject include *there, here,* and, in questions, *who, which, what,* and *where.*

> Inside the storage shed are the garden tools.
> At the street corner were two panhandlers.
> There are times I'm ready to quit my job.
> Where are the instructions for the microwave oven?

If you are unsure about the subject, ask *who* or *what* of the verb. With the first sentence above, you might ask, "What is inside the storage shed?" The answer, garden *tools,* is the subject.

Practice

Underline the subject in each sentence. Then double-underline the correct verb in parentheses.

1. Lumbering along the road (was, were) six heavy trucks.
2. There (is, are) now wild coyotes wandering the streets of many California suburbs.
3. Lining the country lanes (is, are) rows of tall, thin poplar trees.
4. At the back of my closet (is, are) the high platform boots I bought ten years ago.
5. Helping to unload the heavy sofa from the delivery truck (was, were) a skinny young boy.
6. Nosing through the garbage bags (was, were) a furry animal with a hairless tail.
7. Here (is, are) the rug shampooer I borrowed last month.
8. Along the side of the highway (was, were) a sluggish little stream.
9. Where (is, are) the box of kitchen trash bags?
10. On the door of his bedroom (is, are) a sign reading, ''Authorized personnel only.''

INDEFINITE PRONOUNS

The following words, known as *indefinite pronouns,* always take singular verbs:

Indefinite Pronouns			
(-one words)	*(-body words)*	*(-thing words)*	
one	nobody	nothing	each
anyone	anybody	anything	either
everyone	everybody	everything	neither
someone	somebody	something	

Note: *Both* always takes a plural verb.

Practice

Write the correct form of the verb in the space provided.

is, are 1. Neither of those last two books on the list _____ required for the course.

remembers, remember 2. Nobody _____ seeing a suspicious green car cruising the street.

fits, fit 3. Both of these belts no longer _____.

has, have 4. Somebody _____ been playing my records.

wanders, wander 5. Nobody _____ in those woods during hunting season without wearing bright-colored clothing.

needs, need 6. Each of those dogs _____ to be inoculated against rabies.

keeps, keep 7. One of my friends _____ a pet iguana in her dorm room.

sneaks, sneak 8. Everyone _____ stationery and pens out of our office.

is, are 9. Either of those motels _____ clean and reasonably priced.

eats, eat 10. One of my children _____ raw onions as if they were apples.

COMPOUND SUBJECTS

Subjects joined by *and* generally take a plural verb.

> <u>Yoga</u> and <u>biking</u> <u>are</u> Lola's ways of staying in shape.
> <u>Ambition</u> and <u>good luck</u> <u>are</u> the keys to his success.

When subjects are joined by *either . . . or, neither . . . nor, not only . . . but also,* the verb agrees with the subject closer to the verb.

> Either the <u>restaurant manager</u> or his <u>assistants</u> <u>deserve</u> to be fired for the spoiled meat used in the stew.

The nearer subject, *assistants,* is plural, and so the verb is plural.

Practice

Write the correct form of the verb in the space provided.

looks, look   1. This coat and scarf _____ warm, but the wind seems to go right through them.

is, are   2. The bridge and the tunnel _____ closed for repairs.

confuses, confuse   3. The pitcher's unusual stance and strange grip _____ his opponents.

is, are   4. The footnotes and one picture in this book _____ printed upside down.

stars, star   5. Either a giant jellyfish or oversize lobsters _____ in this Japanese monster movie.

WHO, WHICH, AND THAT

When *who, which,* and *that* are used as subjects, they take singular verbs if the word they stand for is singular and plural verbs if the word they stand for is plural. For example, in the sentence

Gary is one of those people who are very private.

the verb is plural because *who* stands for *people,* which is plural. On the other hand, in the sentence

Gary is a person who is very private.

the verb is singular because *who* stands for *person,* which is singular.

Practice

Write the correct form of the verb in the space provided.

roams, roam   1. The dogs which _____ around this area are household pets abandoned by cruel owners.

begins, begin   2. A sharp pain that _____ in the lower abdomen may signal appendicitis.

thunders, thunder   3. The heavy trucks that _____ past my Honda make me feel as though I'm being blown off the road.

fears, fear   4. The canyon tour isn't for people who _____ heights.

tastes, taste   5. This drink, which _____ like pure sugar, is supposed to be 100 percent fruit juice.

⬤ Review Test 1

In the following sentences, underline the subject. Then complete each sentence using *is, are, was, were, have,* or *has.* Note that you will have to add a subject in some cases.

Example   The hot dogs in that luncheonette *are hazardous to your health.*

1. Either of those small keys _____.
2. The practical joker in our office _____.
3. The rock star and his bodyguard _____.
4. He was the kind of customer who _____.
5. Posted on the office door _____.
6. There's always someone who _____.
7. The old boiler, along with the rusty water tanks, _____

_____.

8. Hanging from her rearview mirror _____.
9. The first few times that I tried to roller-skate _____

_____.

10. The spectators outside the courtroom _____

_____.

⬤ Review Test 2

Underline the correct word in the parentheses.

1. The number of commercials between television shows (is, are) increasing.
2. Joan and Phil (works, work) all night at the motel's registration desk.
3. A report on either book (counts, count) as extra credit.
4. Both the mattress and the box spring on this bed (is, are) filled with rusty, uncoiling springs.
5. Nobody in that class ever (argues, argue) with the professor.
6. Remembering everyone's birthday and organizing family reunions (is, are) my sister's main hobbies.
7. Lying like limp little dolls on the bed (was, were) the exhausted children.

8. The woman from the telephone company who (empties, empty) the pay phones wears a photo ID tag around her neck.

9. The illegal dogfights which (occurs, occur) regularly in our town are being investigated by the SPCA.

10. Sewn into the sweater's seam (was, were) an extra button and a small hank of matching yarn for repairs.

 Review Test 3

There are eight mistakes in subject-verb agreement in the following passage. Cross out each incorrect verb and write the correct form above it. In addition, underline the subject of each of the verbs that must be changed.

What are the factors that makes a third-grade child aggressive and destructive? And, on the other hand, what experiences help a third-grader make friends easily and earn good grades in school? Years of research on a group of children from infancy through elementary school has provided an answer, or at least a new theory. A psychologist from one of our leading universities claim that success in the early grades are the direct result of a close relationship with the mother. Babies who have this relationship with a mother seems to gain the strength and self-esteem they need for future success in the classroom and in life. A strong, secure bond between a mother and child are formed when mothers respond quickly and consistently to their babies' needs. Both the speed and the attention is important in earning a baby's trust. The researcher points out that there are no evidence of a link between day-care arrangements and weaker mother-baby attachments. It is the quality of the relationship, not the actual hours spent, that causes a child to feel secure.

Consistent Verb Tense

INTRODUCTORY PROJECT

See if you can find and underline the two mistakes in verb tense in the following selection.

When Stereo Warehouse had a sale, Alex decided to buy a videocassette recorder. He thought he would plug the machine right in and start taping his favorite shows. When he arrived home, however, Alex discovers that hooking up a VCR could be complicated and confusing. The directions sounded as if they had been written for electrical engineers. After two hours of frustration, Alex gave up and calls a TV repair shop for help.

Now try to complete the following statement:

Verb tenses should be consistent. In the above selection, two verbs have to be changed because they are mistakenly in the (present, past) tense while all the other verbs in the selection are in the (present, past) tense.

Answers are on page 484.

KEEPING TENSES CONSISTENT

Do not shift tenses unnecessarily. If you begin writing a paper in the present tense, don't shift suddenly to the past. If you begin in the past, don't shift without reason to the present. Notice the inconsistent verb tenses in the following selection:

Smoke spilled from the front of the overheated car. The driver opens up the hood, then jumped back as steam billows out.

The verbs must be consistently in the present tense:

Smoke spills from the front of the overheated car. The driver opens up the hood, then jumps back as steam billows out.

Or the verbs must be consistently in the past tense:

Smoke spilled from the front of the overheated car. The driver opened up the hood, then jumped back as steam billowed out.

Practice

In each item below, one verb must be changed so that it agrees in tense with the other verbs. Cross out the incorrect verb and write the correct form in the space at the left.

looked   **Example**   I gave away my striped sweater after three people told me I ~~look~~ like a giant bee.

_____   1. Dana swabbed the inside of her cheek with a Q-tip, smears the cells on a glass slide, and then looked at them through the microscope.

_____   2. Debbie, a moody adolescent, threw the blouse down, shouted at her mother, and then starts to cry.

_____   3. On the highway, one rescuer rolled the unconscious man onto his back, pinched his nostrils shut, and then breathe into his mouth.

_____   4. In this neighborhood, the kids play stickball in the street; they sawed off broom handles for bats and borrow garbage can lids for bases.

_____   5. Unknowingly, Marvin picked a box of detergent with a hole in it. He left a thin trail of white powder as he rolls his cart around the store.

_____   6. To get a clear picture, Vernon jiggles the TV tuning knob, adjusts the horizontal control, and pointed the antenna out the window.

_____   7. While Dan searches for the pizza cutter in the kitchen drawer, Tony picks the pepperoni slices off the pie and quickly swallowed them.

——————— 8. Alfonso lunged for the child and pushes him to safety as the speeding cyclist whizzed by.

——————— 9. Because the kitchen lacks an exhaust fan, cooking fumes fill the house and thin layers of grease coated the ceilings.

——————— 10. As she unpacks the wall planking, Becky discovers large knotholes in some of the boards and noticed one piece with a long vertical crack.

Review Test 1

Change verbs where needed in the following selection so that they are consistently in the past tense. Cross out each incorrect verb and write the correct form above it, as shown in the example. You will need to make ten corrections.

Making a foul shot that won a basketball game was a special moment for me. For most of the year, I sat on the bench. The coach put me on the team after the tryouts and then ~~forgets~~ *forgot* about me. Then my chance appears near the end of the Rosemont High School game. The score was tied 65 to 65. Because of injuries and foul-outs, most of the substitutes, except me, were in the game. Then our last first-stringer, Larry Toner, got an elbow in the eye and leaves the game. The coach looked at me and said, "Get in there, Watson." The clock showed ten seconds to go. Rosemont had the ball when, suddenly, one of their players misses a pass. People scramble for the ball; then our center, Kevin, grabbed it and starts down the court. He looked around and saw me about twenty feet from the basket. I caught his pass, and before I could decide whether to shoot or pass, a Rosemont player fouls me. The referee's whistle blew, and I had two free throws with two seconds left in the game. My stomach churns as I stepped to the foul line. I almost couldn't hold the ball because my hands were so damp with sweat. I shot and missed, and the Rosemont crowd sighs with relief. My next shot would mean a win for us or overtime. I looked at the hoop, shot, and waited for what seemed like forever. The ball circles the rim and dropped in, and then the buzzer sounded. Everyone on the team slapped me on the back and the coach smacks my rear end, saying, "All right, Watson!" I'll always remember that moment.

Review Test 2

Change verbs where needed in the following selection so that they are consistently in the past tense. Cross out each incorrect verb and write the correct form in the space provided. You will need to make ten corrections in all.

According to an old Greek myth, the goddess of the harvest had one child, a beautiful daughter. One day, as the daughter was gathering flowers, the god of the underworld drove by in his chariot. He sees her and fell madly in love with her. He reaches out, grabbed the frightened girl, and pulled her into the chariot beside him. The daughter's screams were useless as the two drove below the surface of the earth. Soon they reached the land of the dead, where he forces her to become his wife. Not long afterward, the goddess realizes her daughter was missing. She searched for her all over the world. When she could not find her, she became so grief-stricken that she neglects her duties, and all over the earth, the crops weakened and died. Finally she threatened that nothing would grow until her daughter was returned to her. Zeus, king of the gods, then commanded that the daughter has to be released—but only if she had not eaten anything. The god of the underworld agreed to let her go, but he tricks her into eating six seeds before she leaves. Because the girl had eaten the food of Death, she had to live in Death's kingdom six months of the year, one for each of the seeds. In this way, the Greeks said, the seasons came into being. When the daughter was permitted to rejoin her mother, she brought spring and summer with her—and the crops begin to grow. But when fall came, she is forced to return to the land of the dead, and all growing things on earth died with her.

1. _____   6. _____

2. _____   7. _____

3. _____   8. _____

4. _____   9. _____

5. _____   10. _____

Additional Information about Verbs

The purpose of this special chapter is to provide additional information about verbs. Some people will find the grammar terms here a helpful reminder of earlier school learning about verbs. For them, the terms will increase their understanding of how verbs function in English. Other people may welcome more detailed information about terms used elsewhere in the text. In either case, remember that the most common mistakes people make when writing verbs have been treated in earlier sections of the book.

VERB TENSE

Verbs tell us the time of an action. The time that a verb shows is usually called *tense*. The most common tenses are the simple present, past, and future. In addition, there are nine other tenses that enable us to express more specific ideas about time than we could with the simple tenses alone. Shown on the next page are the twelve verb tenses and examples of each tense. Read them over to increase your sense of the many different ways of expressing time in English.

Tenses	Examples
Present	I *work.*
	Jill *works.*
Past	Howard *worked* on the lawn.
Future	You *will work* overtime this week.
Present perfect	Gail *has worked* hard on the puzzle.
	They *have worked* well together.
Past perfect	They *had worked* eight hours before their shift ended.
Future perfect	The volunteers *will have worked* many unpaid hours.
Present progressive	I *am* not *working* today.
	You *are working* the second shift.
	The clothes dryer *is* not *working* properly.
Past progressive	She *was working* outside.
	The plumbers *were working* here this morning.
Future progressive	The sound system *will be working* by tonight.
Present perfect progressive	Married life *has* not *been working* out for that couple.
Past perfect progressive	I *had been working* overtime until recently.
Future perfect progressive	My sister *will have been working* at that store for eleven straight months by the time she takes a vacation next week.

The perfect tenses are formed by adding *have, has,* or *had* to the past participle (the form of the verb that ends, usually, in *-ed*). The progressive tenses are formed by adding *am, is, are, was,* or *were* to the present participle (the form of the verb that ends in *-ing*). The perfect progressive tenses are formed by adding *have been, has been,* or *had been* to the present participle.

Certain tenses are explained in more detail on the following pages.

Present Perfect
(*have* or *has* + past participle)

The present perfect tense expresses an action that began in the past and has recently been completed or is continuing in the present.

The city has just agreed on a contract with the sanitation workers.
Tony's parents have lived in that house for twenty years.
Lola has watched *Star Trek* reruns since she was a little girl.

Past Perfect
(*had* + past participle)

The past perfect tense expresses a past action that was completed before another past action.

Lola had learned to dance by the time she was five.
The class had just started when the fire bell rang.
Bad weather had never been a problem on our vacations until last year.

Present Progressive
(*am, is,* or *are* + the *-ing* form)

The present progressive tense expresses an action still in progress.

I am taking an early train into the city every day this week.
Karl is playing softball over at the field.
The vegetables are growing rapidly.

Past Progressive
(*was* or *were* + the *-ing* form)

The past progressive expresses an action that was in progress in the past.

I was spending twenty dollars a week on cigarettes before I quit.
Last week, the store was selling many items at half price.
My friends were driving over to pick me up when the accident occurred.

Practice

For the sentences that follow, fill in the present or past perfect or the present or past progressive of the verb shown. Use the tense that seems to express the meaning of each sentence best.

Example *park* This summer, Mickey _____*is parking*_____ cars at a French restaurant.

watch 1. The police _____ the house for months before they made the arrests.

write 2. She _____ to the newspaper several times, but the editors never publish her letters.

take 3. I _____ a course in adolescent psychology; maybe it will help me understand my teenagers.

lift 4. The fog _____ well before the morning rush hour began.

improve 5. For the last two years, our community group _____ our street by cleaning up trash and planting trees.

protest 6. The waitresses _____ against the skimpy new uniforms that they are being told to wear.

dread 7. I _____ heights ever since one of my brothers pushed me off a wall when I was six.

vow 8. This semester, he _____ to stick to an organized study schedule.

peek 9. Some students _____ into their notes when the professor entered the exam room.

get 10. You _____ some gray hairs; why don't I pull them out?

VERBALS

Verbals are words formed from verbs. Verbals, like verbs, often express action. They can add variety to your sentences and vigor to your writing style. The three kinds of verbals are *infinitives, participles,* and *gerunds.*

Infinitive

An infinitive is *to* plus the base form of the verb.

> I started *to practice.*
> Don't try *to lift* that table.
> I asked Russ *to drive* me home.

Participle

A participle is a verb form used as an adjective (a descriptive word). The present participle ends in *-ing.* The past participle ends in *-ed* or has an irregular ending.

> *Favoring* his *cramped* leg, the *screaming* boy waded out of the pool.
> The *laughing* child held up her *locked* piggy bank.
> *Using* a shovel and a bucket, I scooped water out of the *flooded* basement.

Gerund

A gerund is the *-ing* form of a verb used as a noun.

> *Studying* wears me out.
> *Playing* basketball is my main pleasure during the week.
> Through *jogging,* you can get yourself in shape.

Practice

In the space beside each sentence, identify the italicized word as a participle (*P*), an infinitive (*I*), or a gerund (*G*). (Italic is slanted type that looks *like this.*)

_____ 1. In the cave, dozens of *grinning* skulls greeted the explorer.

_____ 2. *Launching* a new business can be a risky proposition.

_____ 3. Gwen likes *to rearrange* her living room furniture.

_____ 4. *Fixing* minor car problems is one of the skills taught at the women's center.

_____ 5. The children tried *to make* a tent by throwing a blanket over a clothesline.

_____ 6. The little girl wore the *gleaming* patent leather shoes home from the store.

_____ 7. *Listening* intently, the students translated Spanish sentences into English.

_____ 8. I read the *gripping* spy novel until two o'clock in the morning.

_____ 9. *Writing* reports for the judge is part of Grace's job as a probation officer.

_____ 10. *To fasten* the buttons on the back of her dress, Connie twisted her arms.

ACTIVE AND PASSIVE VERBS

When the subject of a sentence performs the action of a verb, the verb is in the *active voice*. When the subject of a sentence receives the action of a verb, the verb is in the *passive voice*.

The passive form of a verb consists of a form of the verb *be* plus the past participle of the main verb. Look at the active and passive forms of the verbs below.

Active	*Passive*
Lola *ate* the vanilla pudding. (The subject, *Lola,* is the doer of the action.)	The vanilla pudding *was eaten by* Lola. (The subject, *pudding,* does not act. Instead, something happens to it.)
The plumber *replaced* the hot water heater. (The subject, *plumber,* is the doer of the action.)	The hot water heater *was replaced by* the plumber. (The subject, *heater,* does not act. Instead, something happens to it.)

In general, active verbs are more effective than passive verbs. Active verbs give your writing a simpler and more vigorous style. The passive form of verbs is appropriate, however, when the performer of an action is unknown or is less important than the receiver of the action. For example:

My house was vandalized last night.
(The performer of the action is unknown.)

Mark was seriously injured as a result of your negligence.
(The receiver of the action, *Mark,* is being emphasized.)

Practice

Change the sentences on the next page from the passive to the active voice. Note that you may have to add a subject in some cases.

Examples   The moped bicycle was ridden by Tony.
Tony rode the moped bicycle.

The basketball team was given a standing ovation.
The crowd gave the basketball team a standing ovation.

(Here a subject had to be added.)

1. Kate's long hair was snipped off by the beautician.

   _____

2. The teachers' strike was protested by the parents.

   _____

3. The silent alarm was tripped by the alert bank teller.

   _____

4. The escaped convicts were tracked by relentless bloodhounds.

   _____

5. The new CAT scanner was donated to the hospital by a famous entertainer.

   _____

6. A gallon glass jar of pickles was dropped in the supermarket aisle by a stock clerk.

   _____

7. The deer was struck as it crossed the highway.

   _____

8. I was referred by my doctor to a specialist in hearing problems.

   _____

9. One wall of my living room is covered by family photographs.

   _____

10. The town was gripped by fear during the accident at the nuclear power plant.

    _____

Review Test

On separate paper, write three sentences apiece that use:

1. Present perfect tense
2. Past perfect tense
3. Present progressive tense
4. Past progressive tense
5. Infinitive
6. Participle
7. Gerund
8. Passive voice (when the subject is unknown or is less important than the receiver of an action—see page 90)

Pronoun Reference, Agreement, and Point of View

INTRODUCTORY PROJECT

Read each pair of sentences below. Then see if you can choose the correct letter in each of the statements that follow.

1. a. None of the nominees for ''best actress'' showed their anxiety as the names were being read.
    b. None of the nominees for ''best actress'' showed her anxiety as the names were being read.
2. a. At the mall, they are already putting up Christmas decorations.
    b. At the mall, shop owners are already putting up Christmas decorations.
3. a. I go to the steak house often because you can get inexpensive meals there.
    b. I go to the steak house often because I can get inexpensive meals there.

In the first pair, (a, b) uses the underlined pronoun correctly because the pronoun refers to *None,* which is a singular word.

In the second pair, (a, b) is correct because otherwise the pronoun reference would be unclear.

In the third pair, (a, b) is correct because the pronoun point of view should not be shifted unnecessarily.

Answers are on page 484.

Pronouns are words that take the place of nouns (persons, places, or things). In fact, the word *pronoun* means *for a noun*. Pronouns are shortcuts that keep you from unnecessarily repeating words in writing. Here are some examples of pronouns:

Martha shampooed *her* dog. (*Her* is a pronoun that takes the place of *Martha*.)
As the door swung open, *it* creaked. (*It* replaces *door*.)
When the motorcyclists arrived at McDonald's, *they* removed *their* helmets. (*They* and *their* replace *motorcyclists*.)

This section presents rules that will help you avoid three common mistakes people make with pronouns. The rules are as follows:

1   A pronoun must refer clearly to the word it replaces.
2   A pronoun must agree in number with the word or words it replaces.
3   Pronouns should not shift unnecessarily in point of view.

PRONOUN REFERENCE

A sentence may be confusing and unclear if a pronoun appears to refer to more than one word, or if the pronoun does not refer to any specific word. Look at this sentence:

We never buy fresh vegetables at that store, because they charge too much.

Who charges too much? There is no specific word that *they* refers to. Be clear:

We never buy fresh vegetables at that store, because the owners charge too much.

Here are sentences with other kinds of faulty pronoun reference. Read the explanations of why they are faulty and look carefully at the ways they are corrected.

Faulty	*Clear*
Lola told Gina that she had gained weight.	Lola told Gina, ''You've gained weight.''
(*Who* had gained weight: Lola or Gina? Be clear.)	(Quotation marks, which can sometimes be used to correct an unclear reference, are explained on page 177.)

Faulty	*Clear*
My older brother is an electrician, but I'm not interested in it.	My older brother is an electrician, but I'm not interested in becoming one.
(There is no specific word that *it* refers to. It would not make sense to say, ''I'm not interested in electrician.'')	
Our teacher did not explain the assignment, which made me angry.	I was angry that the teacher did not explain the assignment.
(Does *which* mean that the teacher's failure to explain the assignment made you angry, or that the assignment itself made you angry? Be clear.)	

Practice

Rewrite each of the following sentences to make the vague pronoun reference clear. Add, change, or omit words as necessary.

Example   Lana thanked Rita for the gift, which was very thoughtful of her.
Lana thanked Rita for the thoughtful gift.

1. At the gas station, they told us one of our tires looked soft.

   _____

   _____

2. Nora dropped the heavy ashtray on her foot and broke it.

   _____

   _____

3. Ann asked for a grade transcript at the registrar's office, and they told her it would cost three dollars.

   _____

   _____

4. Don't touch the freshly painted walls with your hands unless they're dry.

   _____

   _____

5. Maurice stays up half the night watching *Chiller Theater,* which really annoys his wife.

_____

_____

6. Robin went to the store's personnel office, where they are interviewing for sales positions.

_____

_____

7. Matt told his brother that he needed to lose some weight.

_____

_____

8. I wrote to the insurance company, but they haven't answered my letters.

_____

_____

9. Because my eyes were itchy and bloodshot, I went to the doctor to see what he could do about it.

_____

_____

10. I took the loose pillows off the chairs and sat on them.

_____

_____

PRONOUN AGREEMENT

A pronoun must agree in number with the word or words it replaces. If the word a pronoun refers to is singular, the pronoun must be singular; if the word is plural, the pronoun must be plural. (Note that the word a pronoun refers to is known as the *antecedent.*)

Lola agreed to lend me her Billy Joel albums.

The gravediggers sipped coffee during their break.

In the first example, the pronoun *her* refers to the singular word *Lola*; in the second example, the pronoun *their* refers to the plural word *gravediggers.*

Practice

Write the appropriate pronoun (*they, their, them, it*) in the blank space in each of the following sentences.

Example   My credit cards got me into debt, so I burned _____*them*_____.

1. I peeled off my sweaty bandanna and dipped _____ into the cool stream.

2. Jamie sanded the cabinets and coated _____ with clear varnish.

3. Since my parents retired, _____ have started to share the household chores.

4. Waiting in the stalled school bus, the children threw _____ books out the windows and lobbed potato chips at each other.

5. The dog pawed at the flower and pulled _____ out of the ground.

Indefinite Pronouns

The following words, known as *indefinite pronouns,* are always singular.

Indefinite Pronouns		
(-one words)	**(-body words)**	
one	nobody	each
anyone	anybody	either
everyone	everybody	neither
someone	somebody	

Either of the apartments has (its) drawbacks.

One of the girls lost (her) skateboard.

Everyone in the class must hand in (his) paper tomorrow.

In each example, the pronoun is singular because it refers to one of the indefinite pronouns. There are two important points to remember about indefinite pronouns.

Point 1:   The last example above suggests that everyone in the class is male. If the students were all female, the pronoun would be *her*. If the students were a mixed group of males and females, the pronoun form would be *his or her:*

Everyone in the class must hand in *his or her* paper tomorrow.

Some writers still follow the traditional practice of using *his* to refer to both men and women. Many now use *his or her* to avoid an implied sexual bias. Perhaps the best practice, though, is to avoid using either *his* or the somewhat awkward *his or her.* This can often be done by rewriting a sentence in the plural:

All students in the class must hand in *their* papers tomorrow.

Here are some examples of sentences that can be rewritten in the plural.

A young child is seldom willing to share her toys with others.
Young children are seldom willing to share their toys with others.

Anyone who does not wear his seat belt will be fined.
People who do not wear their seat belts will be fined.

A newly elected politician should not forget his or her campaign promises.
Newly elected politicians should not forget their campaign promises.

Point 2:   In informal spoken English, *plural* pronouns are often used with indefinite pronouns. Instead of saying

Everybody has *his or her* own idea of an ideal vacation.

we are likely to say

Everybody has *their* own idea of an ideal vacation.

Here are other examples:

Everyone in the class must pass in *their* papers.
Everybody in our club has *their* own idea about how to raise money.
No one in our family skips *their* chores.

In such cases, the indefinite pronouns are clearly plural in meaning. Also, the use of such plurals helps people avoid the awkward *his or her.* In time, the plural pronoun may be accepted in formal speech or writing. Until that happens, however, you should use the grammatically correct singular form in your writing.

Practice

Underline the correct pronoun.

Example   Neither of those houses has (<u>its</u>, their) own garage.

1. Girls! Did everyone remember to bring (her, their) insect repellent?
2. Anyone can pass our men's physical education course if (he, they) will laugh at all the instructor's jokes.
3. Each of the jockeys wore (his, their) own distinctive racing silks.
4. Neither of the Mets' relief pitchers was able to get (his, their) curve ball across.
5. If any student wants to apply for the scholarship offered by the women's college, (she, they) will need two recommendations.
6. Either type of video recording system has (its, their) drawbacks.
7. Each woman rushed to pick up (her, their) forms and secure a place in line.
8. Three boys were suspected, but nobody would confess to leaving (his, their) fingerprints all over the window.
9. All women leaving the room should pick up (her, their) lab reports.
10. During the fire, any one of those men could have lost (his, their) balance on that narrow ledge.

PRONOUN POINT OF VIEW

Pronouns should not shift their point of view unnecessarily. When writing a paper, be consistent in your use of first-, second-, or third-person pronouns.

Type of Pronoun	Singular	Plural
First-person pronouns	I (my, mine, me)	we (our, us)
Second-person pronouns	you (your)	you (your)
Third-person pronouns	he (his, him) she (her) it (its)	they (their, them)

Note: Any person, place, or thing, as well as any indefinite pronoun like *one, anyone, someone,* and so on (page 96), is a third-person word.

For instance, if you start writing in the first-person *I,* don't jump suddenly to the second-person *you.* Or if you are writing in the third-person *they,* don't shift unexpectedly to *you.* Look at the examples.

Inconsistent	*Consistent*
One reason that *I* like living in the city is that *you* always have a wide choice of sports events to attend. (The most common mistake people make is to let a *you* slip into their writing after they start with another pronoun.)	One reason that *I* like living in the city is that *I* always have a wide choice of sports events to attend.
Someone who is dieting should have the help of friends; *you* should also have plenty of willpower.	*Someone* who is dieting should have the help of friends; *he or she* should also have plenty of willpower.
Students who work while *they* are going to school face special problems. For one thing, *you* seldom have enough study time.	Students who work while *they* are going to school face special problems. For one thing, *they* seldom have enough study time.

Practice

Cross out inconsistent pronouns in the following sentences and write the corrections above the errors.

Example   I work much better when the boss doesn't hover over ~~you~~ *me* with instructions on what to do.

1. As we drove through the Pennsylvania countryside, you saw some of the horse-drawn buggies used by the Amish people.

2. One of the things I like about the corner store is that you can buy homemade sausage there.

3. In our family, we had to learn to keep our bedrooms neat before you were given an allowance.

4. No matter how hard we may be working, the minute you relax, the supervisor will be watching.

5. People shouldn't discuss cases outside of court if you serve on a jury.

6. As I read the daily papers, you get depressed by all the violent crime occurring in this country.

7. I never eat both halves of a hamburger bun, because you save calories that way.

8. If someone started a bakery or doughnut shop in this town, you could make a lot of money.

9. Fran likes to shop at the factory outlet because you can buy discount clothing there.

10. I can't wait for summer, when you can stop wearing heavy coats and itchy sweaters.

Review Test I

Underline the correct word or words in the parentheses.

1. Leon spent all morning bird-watching and didn't see a single (one, bird).

2. Of the six men on the committee, no one was prepared to give (his, their) report, so the deadline was extended.

3. If a student in that women's college wants to get a good schedule, (she, you) must enroll as soon as possible.

4. Neither of the luncheonettes near our office has a very wide choice of sandwiches on (its, their) menu.

5. My father has cut down on salt because it can give (you, him) high blood pressure.

6. Well, gentlemen, if anyone objects to the plan, (he, they) should speak up now.

7. I put my wet umbrella on the porch until (it, the umbrella) was dry.

8. I don't like that fast-food restaurant, because (they, the employees) are inefficient.

9. Doctors make large salaries, but (you, they) often face the pressure of dealing with life and death.

10. After eight hours in the cramped, stuffy car, I was glad (it, the trip) was over.

Review Test 2

Cross out the pronoun error in each sentence and write the correction in the space provided below it. Then circle the letter of the phrase that accurately describes the error.

Examples   Anyone turning in their papers late will be penalized.

_____*People*_____

Mistake in: a. pronoun reference   (b.) pronoun agreement

When Clyde takes his son Paul to the park, he enjoys himself.

_____*Paul*_____

Mistake in: (a.) pronoun reference   b. pronoun point of view

From where we stood, you could see three states.

_____*we*_____

Mistake in: a. pronoun agreement   (b.) pronoun point of view

1. In our company, you have to work for one year before getting vacation time.

   _____

   Mistake in: a. pronoun reference   b.   pronoun point of view

2. Amy signed up for a word processing course because she heard that they are in demand.

   _____

   Mistake in: a.   pronoun reference   b. pronoun agreement

3. We did not eat much of the fruit, for you could tell that it was not fresh.

   _____

   Mistake in: a. pronoun reference   b.   pronoun point of view

4. Eric visited the counseling center because they can help him straighten out his schedule.

   _____

   Mistake in: a.   pronoun reference   b. pronoun agreement

5. Every student who was in the chemistry lab has their own memories of the fire.

———————————

Mistake in: a. pronoun reference   b. pronoun agreement

Hint: You may want to rewrite item 5 in the plural, using the lines below:

———————————————————————————————

———————————————————————————————

6. After Lee put cheese slices on the hamburgers, the dog ate them.

———————————   ———————————

Mistake in: a. pronoun reference   b. pronoun point of view

7. If people feel that they are being discriminated against in jobs or housing, you should contact the appropriate federal agency.

———————————

Mistake in: a. pronoun agreement   b. pronoun point of view

8. Norma told her neighbor that her house needed a new coat of paint.

———————————

Mistake in: a. pronoun reference   b. pronoun agreement

9. One of the actors forgot their lines and tried to ad-lib.

———————————

Mistake in: a. pronoun agreement   b. pronoun point of view

10. If anyone wants a tryout, they should be at the gym at four o'clock.

———————————

Mistake in: a. pronoun reference   b. pronoun agreement

Hint: You may want to rewrite item 10 in the plural, using the lines below:

———————————————————————————————

———————————————————————————————

Pronoun Types

INTRODUCTORY PROJECT

In each pair, write a check beside the sentence that you think uses pronouns correctly.

Andy and *I* enrolled in a computer course. _____

Andy and *me* enrolled in a computer course. _____

The police officer pointed to my sister and *me*. _____

The police officer pointed to my sister and *I*. _____

Lola prefers men *whom* take pride in their bodies. _____

Lola prefers men *who* take pride in their bodies. _____

The players are confident that the league championship is *theirs'*. _____

The players are confident that the league championship is *theirs*. _____

Them concert tickets are too expensive. _____

Those concert tickets are too expensive. _____

Our parents should spend some money on *themself* for a change. _____

Our parents should spend some money on *themselves* for a change.

_____

Answers are on page 485.

This section describes some common types of pronouns: subject and object pronouns, possessive pronouns, demonstrative pronouns, and reflexive pronouns.

SUBJECT AND OBJECT PRONOUNS

Pronouns change their form depending upon the place they occupy in a sentence. Here is a list of subject and object pronouns:

Subject Pronouns	Object Pronouns
I	me
you	you (no change)
he	him
she	her
it	it (no change)
we	us
they	them

Subject Pronouns

The subject pronouns are subjects of verbs.

They are getting tired. (*They* is the subject of the verb *are getting.*)
She will decide tomorrow. (*She* is the subject of the verb *will decide.*)
We women organized the game. (*We* is the subject of the verb *organized.*)

Several rules for using subject pronouns, and mistakes people sometimes make, are explained starting below.

Rule 1: Use a subject pronoun in a sentence with a compound (more than one) subject.

Incorrect	Correct
Nate and *me* went shopping yesterday.	Nate and *I* went shopping yesterday.
Him and *me* spent lots of money.	*He* and *I* spent lots of money.

If you are not sure what pronoun to use, try each pronoun by itself in the sentence. The correct pronoun will be the one that sounds right. For example, "*Me* went shopping yesterday" does not sound right; "*I* went shopping yesterday" does.

Rule 2: Use a subject pronoun after forms of the verb *be*. Forms of *be* include *am, are, is, was, were, has been, have been,* and others.

> It was *I* who telephoned.
> It may be *they* at the door.
> It is *she*.

The sentences above may sound strange and stilted to you, since this rule is seldom actually followed in conversation. When we speak with one another, forms such as "It was me," "It may be them," and "It is her" are widely accepted. In formal writing, however, the grammatically correct forms are still preferred. You can avoid having to use a subject pronoun after *be* simply by rewording a sentence. Here is how the preceding examples could be reworded:

> *I* was the one who telephoned.
> *They* may be at the door.
> *She* is here.

Rule 3: Use subject pronouns after *than* or *as* when a verb is understood after the pronoun.

> You read faster than I (read). (The verb *read* is understood after *I.*)
> Tom is as stubborn as I (am). (The verb *am* is understood after *I.*)
> We don't go out as much as they (do). (The verb *do* is understood after *they.*)

Notes

a   Avoid mistakes by mentally adding the "missing" verb at the end of the sentence.

b   Use object pronouns after *than* or *as* when a verb is not understood after the pronoun.

> The law applies to you as well as me.
> Our boss paid Monica more than me.

Object Pronouns

The object pronouns (*me, him, her, us, them*) are objects of verbs or prepositions. (Prepositions are connecting words like *for, at, about, to, before, by, with,* and *of.* See also page 13.)

> Rita chose *me.* (*Me* is the object of the verb *chose.*)
> We met *them* at the ball park. (*Them* is the object of the verb *met.*)
> Don't mention UFOs to *us.* (*Us* is the object of the preposition *to.*)
> I live near *her.*   (*Her* is the object of the preposition *near.*)

People are sometimes uncertain about what pronoun to use when two objects follow the verb.

Incorrect	*Correct*
I spoke to George and *he.*	I spoke to George and *him.*
She pointed at Linda and *I.*	She pointed at Linda and *me.*

Hint: If you are not sure what pronoun to use, try each pronoun by itself in the sentence. The correct pronoun will be the one that sounds right. For example, ''I spoke to he'' doesn't sound right; ''I spoke to him'' does.

Practice 1

Underline the correct subject or object pronoun in each of the following sentences. Then show whether your answer is a subject or an object pronoun by circling the *S* or *O* in the margin. The first one is done for you as an example.

S	Ⓞ	1. I left the decision to (her, she).
S	O	2. At a sale, my mother and (I, me) get bargain-hunting fever.
S	O	3. As he gazed at (she, her) and the children, he knew he was happy.
S	O	4. The panhandler asked my brother and (I, me) for some change.
S	O	5. Without (she, her) and (he, him), this club would be a disaster.
S	O	6. Susie can change a tire faster than (I, me).
S	O	7. (We, Us) athletes always have to stay in shape.
S	O	8. It was (she, her) who noticed that the phone was off the hook.
S	O	9. The bad feelings between you and (I, me) have lasted too long.
S	O	10. Before the wedding, Jack and (he, him) tried, without much luck, to put on the cummerbunds that came with the tuxedos.

Practice 2

Write in a subject or object pronoun that fits in the space provided. Try to use as many different pronouns as possible. The first one is done for you as an example.

1. Lola ran after Sue and _____*me*_____ to return the suntan lotion she had borrowed.

2. That video equipment belongs to Barry and _____.

3. Sally and _____ decided to open a bookstore together.

4. Herb has worked at the welding shop longer than _____.

5. Take that box of candy from the shelf and give it to _____.

6. Why do you and _____ always get stuck with the cleaning up?

7. I really envy _____ and their ability to get along with people.

8. The police caught Francis and _____ as they were trying to break into the boarded-up store.

9. My neighbor and _____ are soap-opera addicts.

10. Neither Ron nor _____ is afraid of walking through the cemetery at night.

RELATIVE PRONOUNS

Relative pronouns do two things at once. First, they refer to someone or something already mentioned in the sentence. Second, they start a short word group which gives additional information about this someone or something. Here is a list of relative pronouns, followed by some example sentences:

Relative Pronouns	
who	which
whose	that
whom	

The only friend *who* really understands me is moving away.
The child *whom* Ben and Arlene adopted is from Korea.
Chocolate, *which* is my favorite food, upsets my stomach.
I guessed at half the questions *that* were on the test.

In the example sentences, *who* refers to *friend, whom* refers to *child, which* refers to *chocolate,* and *that* refers to *questions.* In addition, each of these relative pronouns begins a group of words that describes the person or thing being referred to. For example, the words *whom Ben and Arlene adopted* tell which child the sentence is about, and the words *which is my favorite food* give added information about chocolate.

Points to Remember about Relative Pronouns

Point 1:   *Whose* means *belonging to whom.* Be careful not to confuse *whose* with *who's,* which means *who is.*

Point 2:   *Who, whose,* and *whom* all refer to people. *Which* refers to things. *That* can refer to either people or things.

> I don't know *whose* book this is.
> Don't sit on the chair *which* is broken.
> Let's elect a captain *that* cares about winning.

Point 3:   *Who, whose, whom,* and *which* can also be used to ask questions. When they are used in this way, they are called *interrogative* pronouns:

> *Who* murdered the secret agent?
> *Whose* fingerprints were on the bloodstained knife?
> To *whom* have the detectives been talking?
> *Which* suspect is going to confess?

Note: In informal usage, *who* is generally used instead of *whom* as an interrogative pronoun. Informally, we can say or write, ''*Who* are you rooting for in the game?'' or ''*Who* did the teacher fail?'' More formal usage would call for *whom:* ''*Whom* are you rooting for in the game?'' ''*Whom* did the teacher fail?''

Point 4:   *Who* and *whom* are used differently. *Who* is a subject pronoun. Use *who* as the subject of a verb:

> Let's see *who* will be teaching the course.

Whom is an object pronoun. Use *whom* as the object of a verb or a preposition:

> Dr. Kelsey is the teacher *whom* I like best.
> I haven't decided for *whom* I will vote.

You may want to review the material on subject and object pronouns on pages 104–106.

Here is an easy way to decide whether to use *who* or *whom*. Find the first verb after the place where the *who* or *whom* will go. See if it already has a subject. If it does have a subject, use the object pronoun *whom*. If there is no subject, give it one by using the subject pronoun *who*. Notice how *who* and *whom* are used in the sentences that follow:

> I don't know *who* sideswiped my car.
> The suspect *whom* the police arrested finally confessed.

In the first sentence, *who* is used to give the verb *sideswiped* a subject. In the second sentence, the verb *arrested* already has a subject, *police*. Therefore, *whom* is the correct pronoun.

Practice 1

Underline the correct pronoun in each of the following sentences.

1. Alexandre Dumas, (who, which) wrote *The Three Musketeers,* once fought a sword duel in which his pants fell down.
2. The power failure, (who, which) caused the stage to go black, happened during the singer's performance of ''You Light Up My Life.''
3. The football coach wasn't very encouraging toward Mark, (who, whom) he advised to get extra health insurance.
4. A national animal-protection society honored a high school student (who, whom) refused to dissect a frog in her biology class.
5. Several of the students (who, which) were taking College Survival Skills dropped out before the end of the semester.

Practice 2

Write five sentences using *who, whose, whom, which,* and *that.*

_____

_____

_____

_____

_____

POSSESSIVE PRONOUNS

Possessive pronouns show ownership or possession.

Clyde shut off the engine of *his* motorcycle.
The keys are *mine*.

Here is a list of possessive pronouns:

Possessive Pronouns	
my, mine	our, ours
your, yours	your, yours
his	their, theirs
her, hers	
its	

Points to Remember about Possessive Pronouns

Point 1:   A possessive pronoun *never* uses an apostrophe. (See also page 170.)

Incorrect	Correct
That coat is *hers'*.	That coat is *hers*.
The card table is *theirs'*.	The card table is *theirs*.

Point 2:   Do not use any of the following nonstandard forms to show possession.

Incorrect	Correct
I met a friend of *him*.	I met a friend of *his*.
Can I use *you* car?	Can I use *your* car?
Me sister is in the hospital.	*My* sister is in the hospital.
That magazine is *mines*.	That magazine is *mine*.

Practice

Cross out the incorrect pronoun form in each of the sentences that follow. Write the correct form in the space at the left.

_____My_____   **Example**   Me car has broken down again.

_____   1. Is this pocketbook hers'?

_____   2. That pile of books you knocked over is mines.

_____   3. Those running shoes are ours'.

_____   4. It took that dog six months to learn it's name.

_____   5. The store owners asked they employees to work until 9 P.M.

DEMONSTRATIVE PRONOUNS

Demonstrative pronouns point to or single out a person or thing. There are four demonstrative pronouns:

> **Demonstrative Pronouns**
>
> this   these
> that   those

Generally speaking, *this* and *these* refer to things close at hand; *that* and *those* refer to things farther away.

> Is anyone using *this* spoon?
> I am going to throw away *these* magazines.
> I just bought *that* white Volvo at the curb.
> Pick up *those* toys in the corner.

Note: Do not use *them, this here, that there, these here,* or *those there* to point out. Use only *this, that, these,* or *those.*

Incorrect	*Correct*
Them tires are badly worn.	*Those* tires are badly worn.
This here book looks hard to read.	*This* book looks hard to read.
That there candy is delicious.	*That* candy is delicious.
Those there squirrels are pests.	*Those* squirrels are pests.

Practice 1

Cross out the incorrect form of the demonstrative pronoun and write the correct form in the space provided.

_____Those_____   **Example**   Them clothes need washing.

_____   1.   This here waitress will take your order.

_____   2.   Them sunglasses make you look really sharp.

_____   3.   These here phones are out of order.

_____   4.   Them flash cubes won't fit my camera.

_____   5.   I didn't know that there gun was loaded.

Practice 2

Write four sentences using *this, that, these,* and *those*.

_____

_____

_____

_____

REFLEXIVE PRONOUNS

Reflexive pronouns are pronouns that refer to the subject of a sentence. Here is a list of reflexive pronouns:

Reflexive Pronouns	
myself	ourselves
yourself	yourselves
himself	themselves
herself	
itself	

Sometimes a reflexive pronoun is used for emphasis:

You will have to wash the dishes *yourself.*
We *ourselves* are willing to forget the matter.
The president *himself* turns down his living room thermostat.

Points to Remember
about Reflexive Pronouns

Point 1:   In the plural *-self* becomes *-selves.*

Lola washes *herself* in Calgon bath oil.
They treated *themselves* to a Bermuda vacation.

Point 2:   Be careful that you do not use any of the following incorrect forms as reflexive pronouns.

Incorrect	*Correct*
He believes in *hisself.*	He believes in *himself.*
We drove the children *ourself.*	We drove the children *ourselves.*
They saw *themself* in the fun house mirror.	They saw *themselves* in the fun house mirror.
I'll do it *meself.*	I'll do it *myself.*

Practice

Cross out the incorrect form of the reflexive pronoun and write the correct form in the space at the left.

themselves   **Example**   She believes that God helps those who help ~~themself.~~

_____   1.   We painted the kitchen ourself.

_____   2.   The mayor hisself spoke to the striking bus drivers.

_____   3.   Marian's sons don't like being left by theirselves in the house.

_____   4.   You must get the tickets yourselfs.

_____   5.   Bill and I cooked the dinner ourself.

Review Test I

Underline the correct word in the parentheses.

Example   Terry and (I, me) have already seen the movie.

1. It looks as if (this, this here) tape recorder is out of order.
2. I exercise twice as much as (she, her), and I'm in worse shape.
3. The only thing for Jack and (I, me) to eat was cold rice.
4. That folding umbrella you just picked up is (our's, ours).
5. Since Paula and (he, him) are engaged, we should give them a party.
6. Why do our parents always embarrass (we, us) kids by showing those old home movies?
7. The manager (hisself, himself) plans to take a cut in salary.
8. They knew the stolen clock radios were (theirs, their's), but they couldn't prove it.
9. If you put (them, those) vegetables in the microwave oven, they'll defrost in a few minutes.
10. My nephews couldn't stop giggling after they saw (theirselves, themselves) in their Halloween costumes.

Review Test 2

Underline the correct word in the parentheses.

1. I asked the dentist's receptionist for appointments for my sister and (I, me).
2. I can't tell if (them, those) potatoes are cooked all the way through or not.
3. Since the fault is (yours, your's), you owe me the cost of the repairs.
4. When the will was read, my cousin and (me, I) had inherited a thousand dollars each.
5. After we finished figuring out our income taxes, we rewarded (ourself, ourselves) and the kids with a trip to the shopping mall.
6. Mike's car had (its, it's) antenna broken off while it was parked outside the bowling alley.
7. Nothing bothers (he, him) more than having to make extra trips to the hardware store after he's started to fix something.

8. (This, This here) town needs a tough sheriff.

9. Since I take better notes than (he, him), we studied from mine for the exam.

10. In small claims court, the judges (themself, themselves) decide the cases and award the damages.

Review Test 3

On separate paper, write sentences that use each of the following words or word groups correctly.

Example   Peter and him   *The coach suspended Peter and him.*

1. you and I
2. yours
3. Kathy and me
4. Leon and he
5. the neighbors and us
6. taller than I
7. yourselves
8. with Ralph and him
9. those
10. Lisa and them

Adjectives
and
Adverbs

INTRODUCTORY PROJECT

Write in an appropriate word to complete each of the sentences below.

1. The teenage years were a _____ time for me.

2. The mechanic listened _____ while I described my car problem.

3. Basketball is a _____ game than football.

4. My brother is the _____ person in our family.

Now see if you can complete the following sentences.

> The word inserted in the first sentence is an (adjective, adverb); it describes the word *time*.
>
> The word inserted in the second sentence is an (adjective, adverb); it ends in the two letters _____ and describes the word *listened*.
>
> The word inserted in the third sentence is a comparative adjective; it is preceded by *more* or ends in the two letters _____.
>
> The word inserted in the fourth sentence is a superlative adjective; it is preceded by *most* or ends in the three letters _____.

Answers are on page 486.

Adjectives and adverbs are descriptive words. Their purpose is to make the meanings of the words they describe more specific.

ADJECTIVES

What Are Adjectives?

Adjectives describe nouns (names of persons, places, or things) or pronouns.

> Charlotte is a *kind* woman. (The adjective *kind* describes the noun *woman*.)
> He is *tired*. (The adjective *tired* describes the pronoun *he*.)

Adjectives usually come before the word they describe (as in *kind woman*). But they also come after forms of the verb *be* (*is, are, was, were,* and so on). Less often, they follow verbs such as *feel, look, smell, sound, taste, appear, become,* and *seem.*

> That bureau is *heavy*. (The adjective *heavy* describes the bureau.)
> The children seem *restless*. (The adjective *restless* describes the children.)
> These pants are *itchy*. (The adjective *itchy* describes the pants.)

Using Adjectives to Compare

For most *short* adjectives, add *-er* when comparing two things and *-est* when comparing three or more things.

> I am *taller* than my brother, but my father is the *tallest* person in the house.
> The farm market sells *fresher* vegetables than the corner store, but the *freshest* vegetables are the ones grown in my own garden.

For most *longer* adjectives (two or more syllables), add *more* when comparing two things and *most* when comparing three or more things.

> Backgammon is *more enjoyable* to me than checkers, but chess is the *most enjoyable* game of all.
> My mother is *more talkative* than my father, but my grandfather is the *most talkative* person in the house.

Points to Remember about Adjectives

Point 1: Be careful that you do not use both an *-er* ending and *more,* or both an *-est* ending and *most.*

Incorrect	Correct
Football is a *more livelier* game than baseball.	Football is a *livelier* game than baseball.
Tod Traynor was voted the *most likeliest* to succeed in our high school class.	Tod Traynor was voted the *most likely* to succeed in our high school class.

Point 2: Pay special attention to the following four words, each of which has irregular forms.

	Comparative (Two)	Superlative (Three or More)
bad	worse	worst
good, well	better	best
little	less	least
much, many	more	most

Practice I

Fill in the comparative and superlative forms for the following adjectives. Two are done for you as examples.

	Comparative (Two)	Superlative (Three or More)
fast	*faster*	*fastest*
timid	*more timid*	*most timid*
kind		
ambitious		
generous		
fine		
likable		

Practice 2

Add to each sentence the correct form of the adjective in the margin.

Example   *bad*   The _____*worst*_____ day of my life was the one when my house caught fire.

thick
1. I attempted to bite into the _____ sandwich I had ever seen.

lazy
2. Each perfect summer day was _____ than the last.

harsh
3. The judge pronounced the _____ sentence possible on the convicted robber.

flexible
4. My new hairbrush is _____ than my old one and doesn't pull out as many hairs.

bad
5. I felt even _____ after I had taken the anti-motion sickness pills.

good
6. The _____ seats in the stadium are completely sold out.

little
7. I'm looking for a cereal with _____ sugar than "Candy Flakes."

vulnerable
8. The body's central trunk is _____ to frostbite than the hands and feet.

wasteful
9. Many people throughout the world feel that Americans are the _____ people on earth.

shiny
10. My hair looked _____ than usual after I began taking vitamins.

ADVERBS

What Are Adverbs?

Adverbs describe verbs, adjectives, or other adverbs. They usually end in *-ly*.

> Charlotte spoke *kindly* to the confused man. (The adverb *kindly* describes the verb *spoke*.)
>
> The man said he was *completely* alone in the world. (The adverb *completely* describes the adjective *alone*.)
>
> Charlotte listened *very* sympathetically to his story. (The adverb *very* describes the adverb *sympathetically*.)

A Common Mistake
with Adjectives and Adverbs

Perhaps the most common mistake that people make with adjectives and adverbs is to use an adjective instead of an adverb after a verb.

Incorrect	Correct
Tony breathed *heavy*.	Tony breathed *heavily*.
I rest *comfortable* in that chair.	I rest *comfortably* in that chair.
She learned *quick*.	She learned *quickly*.

Practice

Underline the correct word in the parentheses.

1. She walked (hesitant, hesitantly) into the room.
2. I could have won the match (easy, easily) if I had concentrated more.
3. After turning the motorcycle (sharp, sharply), Marilyn tried to regain her balance.
4. The bus stopped (abrupt, abruptly), and the passengers were thrown forward.
5. The candidate campaigned too (aggressive, aggressively), and the voters turned against him.
6. The man talked (regretful, regretfully) about the chances he had missed.
7. The instructor spoke so (quick, quickly) that we gave up taking notes.
8. The students eat so (messy, messily) that the cafeteria must be cleaned twice a day.
9. The boy looked (envious, enviously) at his brother's new cowboy boots.
10. Maureen worked (terrible, terribly) hard at her job, yet she managed to find time for her children.

Well and *Good*

Two words often confused are *well* and *good*. *Good* is an adjective; it describes nouns. *Well* is usually an adverb; it describes verbs. *Well* (rather than *good*) is also used when referring to a person's health.

Here are some examples:

I became a *good* swimmer. (*Good* is an adjective describing the noun *swimmer*.)

For a change, two-year-old Tommy was *good* during the church service. (*Good* is an adjective describing Tommy and comes after *was,* a form of the verb *be.*)

Maryann did *well* on that exam. (*Well* is an adverb describing the verb *did.*)

I explained that I wasn't feeling *well*. (*Well* is used in reference to health.)

Practice

Write *well* or *good* in the sentences that follow.

1. I think I've done _____ on the first quiz.
2. Our young son is a _____ chess player.
3. The neighbors said they knew the suspect _____.
4. We need a _____ quarterback for our team.
5. I knew I wasn't doing _____ in math class.

Review Test I

Underline the correct word in the parentheses.

1. I knew she wasn't feeling (good, well) when I saw her put her head in her hands.
2. It is (better, best) for me now to be in school than to have a full-time job.
3. The mother pressed the baby against her shoulder and crooned (soft, softly) in his ear.
4. After the two-week camping trip, Donna gazed (grateful, gratefully) at her warm bathroom and clean towels.
5. That show is the (dullest, most dullest) one on television.
6. Squirming (restless, restlessly) in the seat next to her date, Carol felt uneasy during the violent movie scene.
7. My sister is the (kinder, kindest) of the four children in our family.
8. Clutching a bag of corn chips, the boy stood in the supermarket aisle and looked (imploring, imploringly) at his mother.
9. He had done (good, well) on the first test, so he decided not to study for the next one.
10. Peering (suspicious, suspiciously) at the can of corn, the woman peeled back the new price label that had been stuck over the old one.

Review Test 2

Write a sentence that uses each of the following adjectives and adverbs correctly.

1. nervous _____

2. nervously _____

3. good _____

4. well _____

5. careful _____

6. carefully _____

7. angry _____

8. angrily _____

9. quiet _____

10. quietly _____

Misplaced
Modifiers

INTRODUCTORY PROJECT

Because of misplaced words, each of the sentences below has more than one possible meaning. In each case, see if you can explain both the intended meaning and the unintended meaning.

1. The farmers sprayed the apple trees wearing masks.

    Intended meaning: _____

    Unintended meaning: _____

2. The woman reached out for the faith healer who had a terminal disease.

    Intended meaning: _____

    Unintended meaning: _____

Answers are on page 486.

WHAT MISPLACED MODIFIERS ARE
AND HOW TO CORRECT THEM

Misplaced modifiers are words that, because of awkward placement, do not describe the words the writer intended them to describe. Misplaced modifiers often confuse the meaning of a sentence. To avoid them, place words as close as possible to what they describe.

Misplaced Words	Correctly Placed Words
They could see the Goodyear blimp *sitting on the front lawn.* (The *Goodyear blimp* was sitting on the front lawn?)	Sitting on the front lawn, they could see the Goodyear blimp. (The intended meaning—that the Goodyear blimp was visible from the front lawn—is now clear.)
We had a hamburger after the movie, *which was too greasy for my taste.* (The *movie* was too greasy for your taste?)	After the movie, we had a hamburger, which was too greasy for my taste. (The intended meaning—that the hamburger was greasy—is now clear.)
Our phone *almost* rang fifteen times last night. (The phone *almost rang* fifteen times, but in fact did not ring at all?)	Our phone rang almost fifteen times last night. (The intended meaning—that the phone rang a little under fifteen times—is now clear.)

Other single-word modifiers to watch out for include *only, even, hardly, nearly,* and *often.* Such words should be placed immediately before the word they modify.

Practice I

Underline the misplaced word or words in each sentence. Then rewrite the sentence, placing related words together and thereby making the meaning clear.

Example   Anita returned the hamburger to the supermarket that was spoiled.

Anita returned the hamburger that was spoiled to the

supermarket.

1. We noticed several dead animals driving along the wooded road.

_____

2. Bobbi envisioned the flowers that would bloom in her mind.

_____

3. I watched my closest friends being married in my tuxedo.

_____

4. Sue Ellen carried her new coat on her arm which was trimmed with fur.

_____

5. We just heard that all major highways were flooded on the radio.

_____

6. Fresh-picked blueberries almost covered the entire kitchen counter.

_____

7. Betty licked the homemade peach ice cream making sounds of contentment.

_____

8. The salesman confidently demonstrated the vacuum cleaner with a grin.

_____

9. Gena is delivering singing telegrams dressed in a top hat and tails.

_____

10. The local drama group needs people to build scenery badly.

_____

Practice 2

Rewrite each sentence, adding the *italicized* words. Make sure that the intended meaning is clear and that two different interpretations are not possible.

Example   I borrowed a pen for the essay test. (Insert *that ran out of ink.*)

For the essay test, I borrowed a pen that ran out of ink.

1. I opened my mouth for the dentist. (Insert *with a pounding heart.*)

    _____

    _____

2. Newspapers announced that the space shuttle pilots had landed. (Insert *all over the world.*)

    _____

    _____

3. Newborn kangaroos crawl into their mothers' pouches. (Insert *which resemble blind, naked worms.*)

    _____

    _____

4. Bruce Springsteen's latest album has sold five million copies. (Insert *almost.*)

    _____

    _____

5. Joanne proudly deposited the fifty dollars she had earned typing term papers. (Insert *in her savings account.*)

    _____

    _____

Review Test 1

Write *M* for *misplaced* or *C* for *correct* in the space to the left of each sentence.

_____   1. Books don't sell well in the bookstores with hard covers.

_____   2. Books with hard covers don't sell well in the bookstores.

_____   3. Marilyn went to the door to let in the plumber wearing her nightgown.

_____   4. Wearing her nightgown, Marilyn went to the door to let in the plumber.

_____   5. Fred spent nearly three hours in the doctor's office.

_____   6. Fred nearly spent three hours in the doctor's office.

___M___   7. I spent three days in a hospital watching TV reruns recovering from surgery.

___C___   8. Recovering from surgery, I spent three days in a hospital watching TV reruns.

_____   9. Paula searched through the closet for something to wear on her date.

_____   10. Paula searched for something to wear on her date through the closet.

_____   11. Nick and Fran found six boxes of pictures of their vacation in the attic.

_____   12. Nick and Fran found six boxes of pictures in the attic of their vacation.

_____   13. In the attic, Nick and Fran found six boxes of pictures of their vacation.

_____   14. Mrs. Westcott mistakenly put the milk container which was leaking in the refrigerator.

___M___   15. Mrs. Westcott mistakenly put the milk container in the refrigerator which was leaking.

_____   16. Susie whispered a silent prayer before the exam began under her breath.

_____   17. Susie whispered a silent prayer under her breath before the exam began.

_____   18. Under her breath, Susie whispered a silent prayer before the exam began.

_____   19. On the patio, we ate roast beef sandwiches dripping with gravy.

_____   20. We ate roast beef sandwiches on the patio dripping with gravy.

● Review Test 2

Underline the five misplaced modifiers in the passage below. Then correct them in the spaces provided on the next page.

The tired hikers almost slept for ten hours in the trail shelter. Then Rick awakened and hurried out of his cot when he saw a black spider looking out of the corner of his eye. At this point, his brother Hal woke up with a start and sneezed several times. Because Hal was coming down with a cold, Rick agreed to prepare the breakfast. He first fetched a canteen of orange juice from a nearby stream which had cooled overnight. Next, he started a fire and set about boiling water for coffee and frying up some bacon and eggs. Meanwhile, Hal sniffled, sipped some orange juice, and waited by the fire for a cup of coffee wearing a heavy sweatshirt and gloves. After both had eaten, Rick was ready to plan another day's hiking. But Hal was interested only in hiking to the bus on the nearby highway that could drop him a block from his house.

1. _____
   _____
   _____

2. _____
   _____
   _____

3. _____
   _____
   _____

4. _____
   _____
   _____

5. _____
   _____
   _____

Dangling
Modifiers

INTRODUCTORY PROJECT

Because of dangling words, each of the sentences below has more than one possible meaning. In each case, see if you can explain both the intended meaning and the unintended meaning.

1. Munching leaves from a tall tree, the children were fascinated by the eighteen-foot-tall giraffe.

   Intended meaning: _____

   Unintended meaning: _____

2. Arriving home after ten months in the service, the neighbors threw a block party for Michael.

   Intended meaning: _____

   Unintended meaning: _____

Answers are on page 487.

WHAT DANGLING MODIFIERS ARE AND HOW TO CORRECT THEM

A modifier that opens a sentence must be followed immediately by the word it is meant to describe. Otherwise, the modifier is said to be *dangling,* and the sentence takes on an unintended meaning. For example, in the sentence

> While sleeping in his backyard, a Frisbee hit Bill on the head.

the unintended meaning is that the *Frisbee* was sleeping in his backyard. What the writer meant, of course, was that *Bill* was sleeping in his backyard. The writer should have placed *Bill* right after the modifier:

> While sleeping in his backyard, *Bill* was hit on the head by a Frisbee.

The sentence could also be corrected by placing the subject within the opening word group:

> While *Bill* was sleeping in his backyard, a Frisbee hit him on the head.

Other sentences with dangling modifiers follow. Read the explanations of why they are dangling and look carefully at the ways they are corrected.

Dangling	*Correct*
Having almost no money, my survival depended on my parents. (*Who* has almost no money? The answer is not *survival* but *I.* The subject *I* must be added.)	Having almost no money, *I* depended on my parents for survival. *Or:* Since *I* had almost no money, I depended on my parents for survival.
Riding his bike, a German shepherd bit Tony's ankle. (*Who* is riding the bike? The answer is not *German shepherd,* as it unintentionally seems to be, but *Tony.* The subject *Tony* must be added.)	Riding his bike, *Tony* was bitten on the ankle by a German shepherd. *Or:* While *Tony* was riding his bike, a German shepherd bit him on the ankle.
When trying to lose weight, all snacks are best avoided. (*Who* is trying to lose weight? The answer is not *snacks* but *you.* The subject *you* must be added.)	When trying to lose weight, *you* should avoid all snacks. *Or:* When *you* are trying to lose weight, avoid all snacks.

These examples make clear two ways of correcting a dangling modifier. Decide on a logical subject and do one of the following:

1 Place the subject *within* the opening word group:

Since *I* had almost no money, I depended on my parents for survival.

Note: In some cases an appropriate subordinating word such as *since* must be added, and the verb may have to be changed slightly as well.

2 Place the subject right *after* the opening word group:

Having almost no money, *I* depended on my parents for survival.

Sometimes even more rewriting is necessary to correct a dangling modifier. What is important to remember is that a modifier must be placed as close as possible to the word that it modifies.

Practice 1

Rewrite each sentence to correct the dangling modifier. Mark the one sentence that is correct with a *C*.

1. Foaming at the mouth, the dog warden had the stray put to sleep.

   _____

   _____

2. Kicked carelessly under the bed, Marian finally found her slippers.

   _____

   _____

3. Rusty with disuse, I tried out the old swing set. *that was*

   _____

   _____

4. Having given up four straight hits, the manager decided to replace his starting pitcher.

   _____

   _____

5. Having frozen on the vines, the farmers lost their entire tomato crop.

_____

_____

6. While I was pouring out the cereal, a coupon fell into my bowl of milk.

_____

_____

7. Dancing on their hind legs, the audience cheered wildly as the elephants paraded by.

_____

_____

8. Burned beyond all recognition, Martha took the overdone meat loaf from the oven.

_____

_____

9. Tattered, faded, and hanging in shreds, we decided to replace the dining room wallpaper.

_____

_____

10. When sealed in plastic, a person can keep membership cards clean.

_____

_____

Practice 2

Complete the following sentences. In each case, a logical subject should follow the opening words.

Example   Checking the oil stick, *I saw that my car was a quart low.* _____

1. Since going back to school, _____

2. After finishing an eight-hour shift, _____

3. While playing the radio, _____

4. Before learning how to drive, _____

5. At the age of eight, _____

Review Test 1

Write *D* for *dangling* or *C* for *correct* in the space to the left of each sentence. Remember that the opening words are a dangling modifier if they are not followed immediately by a logical subject.

_____ 1. Yellowed with age, my grandmother could hardly read the old newspaper clipping.

_____ 2. My grandmother could hardly read the old newspaper clipping that was yellowed with age.

_____ 3. Tired and exasperated, the fight we had was inevitable.

_____ 4. Since we were tired and exasperated, the fight we had was inevitable.

_____ 5. After signing the repair contract, I had second thoughts.

_____ 6. After signing the repair contract, second thoughts made me uneasy.

_____ 7. At the age of twelve, several colleges had already accepted the boy genius.

_____ 8. At the age of twelve, the boy genius had already been accepted by several colleges.

_____ 9. While setting up the board, several game pieces were missing.

_____ 10. While setting up the board, we noticed that several game pieces were missing.

_____ 11. Walking to class, a gorgeous white Corvette sped by me at sixty miles an hour.

_____ 12. As I was walking to class, a gorgeous white Corvette sped by me at sixty miles an hour.

_____ 13. While waiting for the dentist to see her, Vicky became more nervous.

_____ 14. While waiting for the dentist to see her, Vicky's nervousness increased.

_____ 15. While she was waiting for the dentist to see her, Vicky became more nervous.

_____ 16. Protected with slipcovers, my mother lets us put our feet on the living room furniture.

_____ 17. My mother lets us put our feet on the living room furniture, since it is protected with slipcovers.

_____ 18. Packed tightly in a tiny can, Fran had difficulty removing the anchovies.

_____ 19. Since they were packed tightly in a tiny can, Fran had difficulty removing the anchovies.

_____ 20. Packed tightly in a tiny can, the anchovies were difficult for Fran to remove.

Review Test 2

Underline the five dangling modifiers in the following passage. Then correct them in the spaces provided below.

For years, students have been using the same methods of cheating on exams. One tried-and-true technique is the casual glance. Pretending to stare thoughtfully out the window, peripheral vision will be used to look at another student's paper. Another all-time favorite method, the pencil or pen drop, requires a helper. Dropping a pen and then diving for it, ''Number seventeen'' (or the number of some other question) is whispered. Then, making a similar pen drop, the answer is whispered by the helper. The most elaborate system, though, is writing up cheat sheets. Tucked up a shirtsleeve, pages of textbook material are condensed into tiny scraps of paper. No matter how smooth a cheater's style is, however, the time-tested methods are often ineffective. Having been a student at one time, the same ones are probably familiar to the instructor.

1. _____

_____

2. _____

_____

3. _____

_____

4. _____

_____

5. _____

_____

Faulty Parallelism

INTRODUCTORY PROJECT

Read aloud each pair of sentences below. Write a check mark beside the sentence that reads more smoothly and clearly and sounds more natural.

Pair 1

I use my TV remote control to change channels, to adjust the volume, and for turning the set on and off.

I use my TV remote control to change channels, to adjust the volume, and to turn the set on and off.

Pair 2

One option the employees had was to take a cut in pay; the other was longer hours of work.

One option the employees had was to take a cut in pay; the other was to work longer hours.

Pair 3

The refrigerator has a cracked vegetable drawer, one of the shelves is missing, and a strange freezer smell.

The refrigerator has a cracked vegetable drawer, a missing shelf, and a strange freezer smell.

Answers are on page 487.

135

PARALLELISM EXPLAINED

Words in a pair or a series should have a parallel structure. By balancing the items in a pair or a series so that they have the same structure, you will make your sentences clearer and easier to read. Notice how the parallel sentences that follow read more smoothly than the nonparallel ones.

Nonparallel (Not Balanced)	*Parallel (Balanced)*
Fran spends her free time reading, listening to music, and she works in the garden.	Fran spends her free time reading, listening to music, and working in the garden. (A balanced series of *-ing* words: *reading, listening, working.*)
After the camping trip I was exhausted, irritable, and wanted to eat.	After the camping trip I was exhausted, irritable, and hungry. (A balanced series of descriptive words: *exhausted, irritable, hungry.*)
My hope for retirement is to be healthy, to live in a comfortable house, and having plenty of money.	My hope for retirement is to be healthy, to live in a comfortable house, and to have plenty of money. (A balanced series of *to* verbs: *to be, to live, to have.*)
Nightly, Fred puts out the trash, checks the locks on the doors, and the burglar alarm is turned on.	Nightly, Fred puts out the trash, checks the locks on the doors, and turns on the burglar alarm. (Balanced verbs and word order: *puts out the trash, checks the locks, turns on the burglar alarm.*)

Balanced sentences are not a skill you need to worry about when you are writing first drafts. But when you rewrite, you should try to put matching words and ideas into matching structures. Such parallelism will improve your writing style.

Practice 1

The unbalanced part of each sentence is *italicized.* Rewrite this part so that it matches the rest of the sentence.

Example   In the afternoon, I changed two diapers, ironed several shirts, and *was watching* soap operas. _____ *watched* _____

1. As the home team scored the winning touchdown, the excited fans screamed, cheered, and *pennants were waved.*

   _____

2. Would you prefer to go for a walk outside or *staying indoors?*

   _____

3. Before Pete could assemble the casserole, he had to brown the meat, dice the vegetables, and *a cream sauce had to be made.*

   _____

4. Please feed the dog, *the heat must be turned down,* and lock the doors.

   _____

5. That restaurant specializes in *hamburgers that are overdone,* wilted salads, and stale pastries.

   _____

6. The old Ford sputtered, *was coughing,* and finally stopped altogether.

   _____

7. The hospital patients can sometimes be cranky, *make a lot of demands,* and ungrateful.

   _____

8. After eating a whole pizza, *two milk shakes,* and sampling a bag of chips, Jerome was still hungry.

   _____

9. As soon as she gets up, she starts the coffee machine, turns on the radio, and *a frozen waffle is put into the toaster.*

   _____

10. The boss told Vern that he had only two options: to work harder or *leaving the company.*

   _____

Practice 2

Complete the following statements. The first two parts of each statement are parallel in form; the part that you add should be parallel in form as well.

Example   Three things I like about myself are my sense of humor, my thought-
fulness, and *my self-discipline.*

1. The movie was terrible: the scenery was fake, the plot was ridiculous, and

    _____ .

2. My New Year's resolutions were to lose weight, to stop smoking, and

    _____ .

3. The people in the long checkout line flipped through magazines, stared at the
    cashier, or _____ .

4. During my first day as a waitress, I learned how to fold napkins, how to use
    the coffee machine, and _____ .

5. My best friend is honest, dependable, and _____ .

Review Test I

Cross out the unbalanced part of each sentence. Then rewrite the unbalanced part
so that it matches the other item or items in the sentence.

Example   I enjoy watering the grass and to work in the garden.
              working

1. The traffic cop blew his whistle, was waving his hands, and nodded to the
    driver to start moving.

    _____

2. Mike's letter of application was smudged, improperly spaced, and it had
    wrinkles.

    _____

3. Nick spoke vividly and with force at the student government meeting.

    _____

4. I like Barry Manilow; Mick Jagger is preferred by my sister.

_____

5. Darkening skies, branches that were waving, and scurrying animals signaled the approaching storm.

_____

6. The pitcher wiped his brow, straightened his cap, and he was tugging at his sleeve.

_____

7. The driving instructor told me to keep my hands on the wheel, to drive defensively, and the use of caution at all times.

_____

8. The customer made choking noises, turned red, and was pointing to his throat.

_____

9. My sister eats spaghetti without sauce, cereal without milk, and doesn't put mustard on hot dogs.

_____

10. The scratches on my car's hood were caused by rocks hitting it, people who sat on it, and cats jumping on it.

_____

Review Test 2

On separate paper, write five sentences of your own that use parallel structure. Each sentence should contain three items in a series. Do not use the same format for each sentence.

Review Test 3

There are six nonparallel parts in the following passage. The first is corrected for you as an example; find and correct the other five.

Consumers have several sources of information they can use in the never-ending war against poor services and <u>merchandise that is shoddy</u>. For one thing, consumers can take advantage of the Better Business Bureau. If you plan to contract the Fly-By-Night Company to paint your house or the replacement of siding, you should first phone your local Better Business Bureau to learn about any complaints against that company. Second, consumers can refer to helpful information available from the U.S. Government Printing Office. You can learn, for instance, how to buy a house, shopping for health insurance, or protect yourself from auto repair rip-offs. Finally, careful buyers can turn to *Consumer Reports,* an independent magazine and one which is nonprofit, that tests and rates a wide range of consumer products. For example, if you are thinking about buying a certain car, *Consumer Reports* will give you information on its comfort level, safety features, fuel economy, and record for repair. If consumers remember to look before they leap and are taking advantage of the above sources of information, they are more likely to get a fair return on their hard-earned dollars.

1. *shoddy merchandise* _____

2. _____

3. _____

4. _____

5. _____

6. _____

Section 2: Mechanics

Paper Format

INTRODUCTORY PROJECT

Check the paper opening below that seems clearer and easier to read.

A

	Finding Faces
	It takes just a little imagination to find faces in the
	objects around you. For instance, clouds are sometimes
	shaped like faces. If you lie on the ground on a partly

B

	"finding faces"
	It takes just a little imagination to find faces in the objects
	around you. For instance, clouds are sometimes shaped like
	faces. If you lie on the ground on a partly cloudy day, cha-
	nces are you will be able to spot many well-known faces

What are four reasons for your choice?

_____

_____

_____

_____

Answers are on page 487.

PAPER GUIDELINES

Here are guidelines to follow in preparing a paper for an instructor.

1 Use full-sized theme or typewriter paper, 8½ by 11 inches.

2 Leave wide margins (1 to 1½ inches) all around the paper. In particular, do not crowd the right-hand or bottom margin. This white space makes your paper more readable; also, the instructor has room for comments.

3 If you write by hand:

   Use a blue or black pen (*not* a pencil).

   Be careful not to overlap letters and not to make decorative loops on letters.

   On narrow-ruled paper, write on every other line.

   Make all your letters distinct. Pay special attention to *a, e, i, o,* and *u*—five letters that people sometimes write illegibly.

   Keep your capital letters clearly distinct from your small letters. You may even want to print all capital letters.

4 Center the title of your paper on the first line of the first page. Do not put quotation marks around the title or underline the title. Capitalize all the major words in a title, including the first word. Short connecting words within a title, such as *of, for, the, in,* and *to,* are not capitalized.

5 Skip a line between the title and the first line of your text. Indent the first line of each paragraph about five spaces (half an inch) from the left-hand margin.

6 Make commas, periods, and other punctuation marks firm and clear. Leave a slight space after each period. When you type, leave a double space after a period.

7 If you break a word at the end of a line, break only between syllables (see page 207). Do not break words of one syllable.

8 Put your name, date, and course number where your instructor asks for them.

Also keep in mind these important points about the title and the first sentence of your paper:

9 The title should be several words that tell what the paper is about. It should usually *not* be a complete sentence. For example, if you are writing a paper about your jealous sister, the title could simply be "My Jealous Sister."

10 Do not rely on the title to help explain the first sentence of your paper. The first sentence must be independent of the title. For instance, if the title of your paper is "My Jealous Sister," the first sentence should *not* be, "She has been this way as long as I can remember." Rather, the first sentence might be, "My sister has always been a jealous person."

Practice 1

Identify the mistakes in format in the following lines from a student theme. Explain the mistakes in the spaces provided. One mistake is described for you as an example.

	"Too small to fight back"
	Until I was ten years old, I was at the mercy of my
	parents. Because they were bigger than I was, they cou-
	ld decide when we were going out, where we were going,
	and how long it would take to get there. I especially hated
	the long weekend trips that we would take even during

1. *Do not break words of one syllable (could).*
2. _____
3. _____
4. _____
5. _____
6. _____

Practice 2

As already stated, a title should tell in several words what a paper is about. Often a title can be based on the sentence that expresses the main idea of a paper.

Following are five main-idea sentences from student papers. Write a suitable and specific title for each paper, basing the title on the main idea.

Example   *Aging Americans as Outcasts*
Our society treats aging Americans as outcasts in many ways.

1. Title: _____

I will never forget my first-grade teacher.

2. Title: _____

The first year of college was the hardest year of my life.

3. Title: _____

My father has a wonderful sense of humor.

4. Title: _____

There are several ways that Americans could conserve energy.

5. Title: _____

In the past few years I have become concerned about the amount of violence in movies.

Practice 3

In four of the five examples below, the writer has mistakenly used the title to help explain the first sentence. But as has already been stated, you must *not* rely on the title to help explain your first sentence.

Rewrite the four sentences so that they stand independent of the title. Write *Correct* under the one sentence that is independent of the title.

Example   Title: Flunking an Exam

First sentence: I managed to do this because of several bad habits.

Rewritten: *I managed to flunk an exam because of several bad habits.*

1. Title: Lack of Communication
First sentence: This is often the reason why a relationship comes to an end.

Rewritten: _____

_____

2. Title: Educational TV Programs
First sentence: They are in trouble today for several reasons.

Rewritten: _____

_____

3. Title: My First Day of College
First sentence: My first day of college was the most frustrating day of my life.

Rewritten: _____

_____

4. Title: The Worst Vacation I Ever Had
   First sentence: It began when my brother suggested that we rent a large van and drive to Colorado.

   Rewritten: _____

   _____

5. Title: Professional Athletes
   First sentence: Most of them have been pampered since grade school days.

   Rewritten: _____

   _____

Review Test

Use the space provided below to rewrite the following sentences from a student paper, correcting the mistakes in format.

	"my first Blind Date"
	It is an occasion I will not easily forget. I was only thirt-
	een and had not gone out very much at all, but since I was
	so young, it hardly mattered. Then, one day, my mother
	came back from her appointment at the hairdresser's, smiling
	from ear to ear. She informed me that I was going out on

Capital Letters

INTRODUCTORY PROJECT

You probably know a good deal about the uses of capital letters. Answering the questions below will help you check your knowledge.

1. Write the full name of a person you know: _Lori Anne Hines_

2. In what city and state were you born? _Torrance_ _____

3. What is your present street address? _____

4. Name a country where you want to travel for a "fling": _____

5. Name a school that you attended: _____

6. Give the name of a store where you buy food: _____

7. Name a company where you or anyone you know works: _____

8. What day of the week gives you the best chance to relax? _____

9. What holiday is your favorite? _____

10. What brand of toothpaste do you use? _____

11. Give the brand name of a candy or chewing gum you like: _____

12. Name a song or a television show you enjoy: _____

13. Write the title of a magazine or newspaper you read: _____

Items 14–16: Three capital letters are needed in the example below. Underline the words you think should be capitalized. Then write them, capitalized, in the spaces provided.

on Super Bowl Sunday, my roommate said, "let's buy some snacks and invite a few friends over to watch the game." i knew my plans to write a term paper would have to be changed.

14. _____   15. _____   16. _____

Answers are on page 488.

MAIN USES OF CAPITAL LETTERS

Capital letters are used with:

1   The first word in a sentence or direct quotation
2   Names of persons and the word *I*
3   Names of particular places
4   Names of days of the week, months, and holidays
5   Names of commercial products
6   Titles of books, magazines, articles, films, television shows, songs, poems, stories, papers that you write, and the like
7   Names of companies, associations, unions, clubs, religious and political groups, and other organizations

Each use is illustrated on the pages that follow.

First Word in a Sentence or Direct Quotation

Our company has begun laying people off.
The doctor said, "This may hurt a bit."
"My husband," said Martha, "is a light eater. When it's light, he starts to eat."

Note: In the third example above, *My* and *When* are capitalized because they start new sentences. But *is* is not capitalized, because it is part of the first sentence.

Names of Persons and the Word *I*

At the picnic, I met Tony Curry and Lola Morrison.

Names of Particular Places

After graduating from Gibbs High School in Houston, I worked for a summer at a nearby Holiday Inn on Clairmont Boulevard.

But: Use small letters if the specific name of a place is not given.

After graduating from high school in my hometown, I worked for a summer at a nearby hotel on one of the main shopping streets.

Names of Days of the Week, Months, and Holidays

This year Memorial Day falls on the last Thursday in May.

But: Use small letters for the seasons—summer, fall, winter, spring.

In the early summer and fall, my hay fever bothers me.

Names of Commercial Products

The consumer magazine rates highly Cheerios breakfast cereal, Howard Johnson's ice cream, and Jif peanut butter.

But: Use small letters for the *type* of product (breakfast cereal, ice cream, peanut butter, or whatever).

Titles of Books, Magazines, Articles, Films, Television Shows, Songs, Poems, Stories, Papers That You Write, and the Like

My oral report was on *The Diary of a Young Girl,* by Anne Frank.

While watching *The Young and the Restless* on television, I thumbed through *Cosmopolitan* magazine and *The New York Times.*

Names of Companies, Associations, Unions, Clubs, Religious and Political Groups, and Other Organizations

A new bill before Congress is opposed by the National Rifle Association.

My wife is Jewish; I am Roman Catholic. We are both members of the Democratic Party.

My parents have life insurance with Prudential, auto insurance with Allstate, and medical insurance with Blue Cross and Blue Shield.

Practice

Cross out the words that need capitals in the sentences that follow. Then write the capitalized forms of the words in the space provided. The number of spaces tells you how many corrections to make in each case.

Example   Rhoda said, "~~why~~ should I bother to *eat* this ~~hershey~~ bar? I should just apply it directly to my hips."   _Why_   _Hershey_

1. My sister, a greeting card addict, sends cards on the fourth of july and veterans' day.

   _____   _____   _____   _____

2. My lazy brother George said, "when I get the urge to exercise, i lie down until it goes away."

   _____   _____

3. When Steve's toyota ran out of gas on the long island expressway, he hitched a ride to the nearest filling station.

   _____   _____   _____   _____

4. According to the latest issue of *TV guide, sixty minutes* is still the most popular show in its time slot.

   _____   _____   _____

5. Alberta opened an account at the First national bank in order to get the free general electric clock radio offered to new depositors.

   _____   _____   _____   _____

6. Teresa works part time at the melrose diner and takes courses at the Taylor business institute.

   _____   _____   _____   _____

7. In a story by Ray Bradbury called "a sound of thunder," tourists of the future can travel back in time to observe living dinosaurs.

   _____   _____   _____

8. Stacy, whose ambition is to be a hairdresser, studies at the pacific school of cosmetology.

   _____   _____   _____

9. Last night there was a fire at the sears store on ninth street.

   _____   _____   _____

10. For breakfast, I mixed a glass of tang and fried some swift's bacon-flavored strips.

    _____   _____

OTHER USES OF CAPITAL LETTERS

Capital letters are also used with:

1   Names that show family relationships
2   Titles of persons when used with their names
3   Specific school courses
4   Languages
5   Geographic locations
6   Historical periods and events
7   Races, nations, and nationalities
8   Opening and closing of a letter

Each use is illustrated on the pages that follow.

Names That Show Family Relationships

Aunt Fern and Uncle Jack are selling their house.
I asked Grandfather to start the fire.
Is Mother feeling better?

But: Do not capitalize words like *mother, father, grandmother, grandfather, uncle, aunt,* and so on when they are preceded by *my* or another possessive word.

My aunt and uncle are selling their house.
I asked my grandfather to start the fire.
Is my mother feeling better?

Titles of Persons When Used with Their Names

I wrote an angry letter to Senator Blutt.
Can you drive to Dr. Stein's office?
We asked Professor Bushkin about his attendance policy.

But: Use small letters when titles appear by themselves, without specific names.

I wrote an angry letter to my senator.
Can you drive to the doctor's office?
We asked our professor about his attendance policy.

Specific School Courses

My courses this semester include Accounting I, Introduction to Data Processing, Business Law, General Psychology, and Basic Math.

But: Use small letters for general subject areas.

This semester I'm taking mostly business courses, but I have a psychology course and a math course as well.

Languages

Lydia speaks English and Spanish equally well.

Geographic Locations

I lived in the South for many years and then moved to the West Coast.

But: Use small letters in giving directions.

Go south for about five miles and then bear west.

Historical Periods and Events

One essay question dealt with the Battle of the Bulge in World War II.

Races, Nations, Nationalities

The census form asked whether I was African American, Native American, Hispanic, or Asian.
Last summer I hitchhiked through Italy, France, and Germany.
The city is a melting pot for Koreans, Vietnamese, and Mexican Americans.

But: Use small letters when referring to *whites* or *blacks*.

Both whites and blacks supported our mayor in the election.

Opening and Closing of a Letter

Dear Sir: Sincerely yours,

Dear Madam: Truly yours,

Note: Capitalize only the first word in a closing.

Practice

Cross out the words that need capitals in the following sentences. Then write the capitalized forms of the words in the spaces provided. The number of spaces tells you how many corrections to make in each case.

1.   Last year uncle harry had a hair transplant; the doctor inserted little plugs of real hair into his scalp.

   _____   _____

2.   Before school started this fall, my little boy begged for some new bic pens and a snoopy lunch box.

   _____   _____

3.   I wrote to congressman hughes about my problem but received only a form letter in reply.

   _____   _____

4.   A teenage native American girl guided the explorers Lewis and Clark on their journey to the west coast.

   _____   _____   _____

5.   I signed up for a course called introduction to astronomy after my original choice, general biology, closed out early.

   _____   _____   _____   _____

UNNECESSARY USE OF CAPITALS

Practice

Many errors in capitalization are caused by adding capitals where they are not needed. Cross out the incorrectly capitalized words in the following sentences and write the correct forms in the spaces provided. The number of spaces tells you how many corrections to make in each sentence.

1. In our High School, the vice-Principal was in charge of Discipline.

    _____   _____   _____   _____

2. My Father settled in to watch his favorite *Twilight Zone* rerun, the one in which a man sitting in a plane sees a weird Creature out on the Wing.

    _____   _____

3. A group called Project Bigfoot offers a thousand-dollar reward to anyone finding the Skull, Hair, or Bones of the legendary Bigfoot.

    _____   _____   _____

4. In Salt Lake City, Utah, there is a Monument to the sea gulls that saved the first Settlers' crops by eating a Plague of Locusts.

    _____   _____   _____   _____   _____

5. "My brand-new Motorcycle was crushed by a Tractor-Trailer in the Motel parking lot," moaned Gene.

    _____   _____   _____   _____

Review Test I

Cross out the words that need capitals in the following sentences. Then write the capitalized forms of the words in the spaces provided. The number of spaces tells you how many corrections to make in each sentence.

Example   During halftime of the ~~saturday~~ afternoon football game, my sister said, "~~let's~~ get some hamburgers from ~~wendy's~~ or put a pizza in the oven."

    *Saturday*_____   *Let's*_____   *Wendy's*_____

1. Jeannie put a johnny mathis record on her stereo, and the outside world faded away.

    _____   _____

2. After uncle Bruce returned from his trip to florida, he showed us endless slides of the everglades and miami Zoo.

    _____   _____   _____   _____

3. As grandma turned on the *wheel of fortune* show, we slipped out of the living room and began a serious game of monopoly in the den.

    _____   _____   _____   _____

4. This saint patrick's day, the local school band is going to march down fifth avenue.

_____   _____   _____   _____   _____

5. Jackie yelled, "you kids have seen that episode of *star trek* at least fifteen times!"

_____   _____   _____

6. Last spring, in my introduction to anthropology course, we had to start fires without using matches or flints.

_____   _____

7. After he watched the miss america contest on television, Norman dreamed that miss texas wanted to make him king for a day.

_____   _____   _____   _____

8. In namibia, a country in africa, a small herd of elephants survives in an area where it hasn't rained for five years.

_____   _____

9. During our visit to the west coast, we ate dinner on the *queen Mary,* the old british luxury liner docked in Long Beach.

_____   _____   _____   _____

10. "Since last september," said Dave, "i've been repossessing cars for a collection agency. I've had to collect everything from a small toyota to a rolls-royce."

_____   _____   _____   _____   _____

Review Test 2

On separate paper, write:

- Seven sentences demonstrating the seven main uses of capital letters
- Eight sentences demonstrating the eight other uses of capital letters

Numbers and Abbreviations

INTRODUCTORY PROJECT

Write a check mark beside the item in each pair that you think uses numbers correctly.

I finished the exam by 8:55, but my grade was only 65 percent. _____

I finished the exam by eight-fifty-five, but my grade was only sixty-five percent. _____

9 people are in my biology lab, but there are 45 in my lecture group. _____

Nine people are in my biology lab, but there are forty-five in my lecture group. _____

Write a check mark beside the item in each pair that you think uses abbreviations correctly.

Both of my bros. were treated by Dr. Lewis after the mt. climbing accident. _____

Both of my brothers were treated by Dr. Lewis after the mountain climbing accident. _____

I spent two hrs. finishing my Eng. paper and handed it to my teacher, Ms. Peters, right at the deadline. _____

I spent two hours finishing my English paper and handed it to my teacher, Ms. Peters, right at the deadline. _____

Answers are on page 488.

155

NUMBERS

Rule 1: Spell out numbers that take no more than two words. Otherwise, use numerals—the numbers themselves.

> Last year Tina bought nine new records.
> Ray struck out fifteen batters in Sunday's softball game.

But

> Tina now has 114 records in her collection.
> Already this season Ray has recorded 168 strikeouts.

You should also spell out a number that begins a sentence:

> One hundred fifty first-graders throughout the city showed flu symptoms today.

Rule 2: Be consistent when you use a series of numbers. If some numbers in a sentence or paragraph require more than two words, then use numbers themselves throughout the selection.

> This past spring, we planted 5 rhodos, 15 azaleas, 50 summersweet, and 120 myrtle around our house.

Rule 3: Use numbers to show dates, times, addresses, percentages, exact sums of money, and parts of a book.

> John Kennedy was killed on November 22, 1963.
> My job interview was set for 10:15. (*But:* Spell out numbers before *o'clock.* For example: The time was then changed to eleven o'clock.)
> Janet's new address is 118 North 35 Street.
> Almost 40 percent of my meals are eaten at fast-food restaurants.
> The cashier rang up a total of $18.35. (*But:* Round amounts may be expressed as words. For example: The movie has a five-dollar admission charge.)
> Read Chapter 6 in your math textbook and answer questions 1 to 5 on page 250.

Practice

Use the three rules to make the corrections needed in these sentences.

1. Vince's new girlfriend lives only 5 blocks away from him.

2. My dog is 8 years old—that's 56 in people years.

3. The box office opens at ten-thirty in the morning.

4. However, some people have been waiting in line since 5 o'clock.

5. About sixty-five percent of the typical human body is water.

6. In order to speak one word, a human being uses 72 muscles.

7. I liked the good old days when Lincoln's Birthday always fell on February twelfth.

8. At the fire fighters' fund-raising breakfast, six hundred sausages, 450 fried eggs, 900 pancakes, and eighty packets of Alka-Seltzer were sold.

9. Two weeks after she died on November third, nineteen-ninety-two, we heard that Mrs. Miller had left $2,500 to her pet canary.

10. My little brother got a notice from the library that his copy of *The 3 Musketeers* was 2 weeks overdue.

ABBREVIATIONS

While abbreviations are a helpful time-saver in note-taking, you should avoid most abbreviations in formal writing. Listed below are some of the few abbreviations that can acceptably be used in compositions. Note that a period is used after most abbreviations.

1 Mr., Mrs., Ms., Jr., Sr., Dr. when used with proper names:

 Mr. Rollin   Ms. Peters   Dr. Coleman

2 Time references:

 A.M. or a.m.   P.M. or p.m.   B.C. or A.D.

3 First or middle initial in a name:

T. Alan Parker   Linda M. Evans

4 Organizations, technical words, and trade names known primarily by their initials:

ABC   CIA   UNESCO   GM   STP   LTD

Practice

Cross out the words that should not be abbreviated and correct them in the spaces provided.

1. My mother can't go into a dept. store without making an impulse purch.

   —————————   —————————

2. Driving along Rt. 90 in Fla., we saw armadillos along the roadside.

   —————————   —————————

3. The fattest man who ever lived in Amer. weighed over nine hundred lbs. and was buried in a piano crate.

   —————————   —————————

4. This Swiss army knife has everything from a pr. of scissors to a six-in. ruler.

   —————————   —————————

5. The first appt. my eye dr., Dr. C. I. Glass, could give me was for early next mo.

   —————————   —————————   —————————

6. After I study in the lib. for fifteen min., I get bored and open a mag.

   —————————   —————————   —————————

7. Only a tsp. of watery Fr. dressing was sprinkled over the limp lettuce salad.

   —————————   —————————

8. Sally lost her lic. when she was arrested for driv. on the wrong side of the rd.

   —————————   —————————   —————————

9. How can I be expected to fin. my assign. by 9 P.M. if there isn't one ball-pt. pen in the house?

   —————————   —————————   —————————

10. The *CBS Evening News* suggested that if we don't approve of the new speed lim., we should let our state sen. or rep. know.

    —————————   —————————

Review Test

Cross out the mistake or mistakes in numbers and abbreviations and correct them in the spaces provided.

1. The Liberty Bell cracked several yrs. after the Amer. Revolution.

   _____   _____

2. The power failure happened at exactly five-twenty A.M. and lasted for almost 2 hours.

   _____   _____

3. I mailed my letter at the p.o. on Grant and Carter Sts.

   _____   _____

4. Little Danny's insect collection includes seventeen grasshoppers, eight moths, and 148 fireflies.

   _____   _____

5. I didn't have time to study for my chem. test because I had to study for my Span. final.

   _____   _____

6. I arrive at the Hartford Ins. Build. at 8 o'clock every morning.

   _____   _____   _____

7. How can I write a 3-page paper on a poem that's only 14 lines long?

   _____   _____

8. Every Mon. morning I wake up wishing it was Fri.

   _____   _____

9. Juan found a great bargain today—a wool jacket and 2 pairs of pants for ninety dollars and ninety-nine cents.

   _____   _____

10. This is the 3rd time since New Year's that I've tried to lose 10 lbs.

   _____   _____   _____

Section 3: Punctuation

End Marks

A sentence always begins with a capital letter. It always ends with a period, a question mark, or an exclamation point.

PERIOD (.)

Use a period after a sentence that makes a statement.

More single parents are adopting children.
It has rained for most of the week.

Use a period after most abbreviations.

Mr. Brady	B.A.	Dr. Ballard
Ms. Peters	A.M.	Tom Ricci, Jr.

QUESTION MARK (?)

Use a question mark after a *direct* question.

When is your paper due?
How is your cold?
Tom asked, "When are you leaving?"
"Why doesn't everyone take a break?" Rosa suggested.

Do not use a question mark after an *indirect* question (a question not in the speaker's exact words).

She asked when the paper was due.
He asked how my cold was.
Tom asked when I was leaving.
Rosa suggested that everyone take a break.

EXCLAMATION POINT (!)

Use an exclamation point after a word or sentence that expresses strong feeling.

Come here!
Ouch! This pizza is hot!
That truck just missed us!

Note: Be careful not to overuse exclamation points.

Practice

Add a period, question mark, or exclamation point, as needed, to each of the following sentences.

1. Why do shoelaces always snap when there are no spares in the house

2. My father throws out most of his mail without even opening it

3. Look out for the escaped tiger

4. Is $47.50 your absolutely final offer for the lawn mower

5. After working in the sun all day, Jerry felt as dry as a potato chip

6. The ad read, ''Do you want to be a millionaire without working ''

7. For a prank, the boys ran out of the water yelling, ''Shark ''

8. Edward had the nerve to ask if my blond hair came out of a bottle

9. While Marian was rinsing the dishes, her class ring fell down the drain

10. ''The end is near,'' said the wild-eyed man in the street as he passed out leaflets

 **Review Test**

Add a period, a question mark, or an exclamation point, as needed, to each of the following sentences.

1. Why do these mashed potatoes have a green cast to them
2. The group which donates the most blood wins free T-shirts
3. Watch out so you don't step in that broken glass
4. The artist throws buckets of paint at a huge canvas on the wall
5. Did you know that Gail has a twin brother
6. There's the man who stole my wallet
7. The dinosaurs in that movie looked like overgrown lizards
8. Have you read the new book by Stephen King
9. All that remained after the car accident was a blood stain
10. Be careful not to run over that turtle on the highway

Apostrophe

1. You're the kind of person who believes he's going to be a big success without doing any hard work, but the world doesn't work that way.

   What is the purpose of the apostrophe in *You're, he's,* and *doesn't?*

   _____

   _____

2. the eagle's nest
   Fred's feet
   my mother's briefcase
   the children's drawings
   Babe Ruth's bat

   What is the purpose of the *'s* in all the examples above?

   _____

   _____

3. The piles of old books in the attic were starting to decay. One book's spine had been gnawed away by mice.
   Two cars were stolen yesterday from the mall parking lot. Another car's antenna was ripped off.

   In the pairs of sentences above, why is the *'s* used each time in the second sentence but not in the first?

   _____

   _____

Answers are on page 489.

The two main uses of the apostrophe are:

1   To show the omission of one or more letters in a contraction
2   To show ownership or possession

Each use is explained on the pages that follow.

APOSTROPHE IN CONTRACTIONS

A contraction is formed when two words are combined to make one word. An apostrophe is used to show where letters are omitted in forming the contraction. Here are two contractions:

> have + not = haven't (the *o* in *not* has been omitted)
>
> I   + will = I'll (the *wi* in *will* has been omitted)

The following are some other common contractions:

I + am	= I'm		it + is	= it's
I + have	= I've		it + has	= it's
I + had	= I'd		is + not	= isn't
who + is	= who's		could + not	= couldn't
do + not	= don't		I + would	= I'd
did + not	= didn't		they + are	= they're
let + us	= let's		there + is	= there's

Note: The combination *will* + *not* has an unusual contraction: *won't*.

Practice 1

Combine the following words into contractions. One is done for you.

they + will	=	*they'll*	they + are	=	_____
should + not	=	_____	can + not	=	_____
does + not	=	_____	who + is	=	_____
is + not	=	_____	would + not	=	_____
will + not	=	_____	are + not	=	_____

Practice 2

Write the contraction for the words in parentheses.

Example   He (could not) _____ *couldn't* _____ come.

1. When you hear the whistle blow, (you will) _____ know (it
    is) _____ quitting time.

2. Because he (had not) _____ studied the owner's manual, he
    (could not) _____ figure out how to start the power mower.

3. There (is not) _____ a rug in this house that (does not)
    _____ have stains on it.

4. (I am) _____ fine in the morning if (I am) _____
    left alone.

5. (Where is) _____ the idiot (who is) _____
    responsible for leaving the front door wide open?

Note: Even though contractions are common in everyday speech and in written
dialogue, usually it is best to avoid them in formal writing.

Practice 3

Write five sentences using the apostrophe in different contractions.

1. _____
2. _____
3. _____
4. _____
5. _____

Four Contractions to Note Carefully

Four contractions that deserve special attention are *they're, it's, you're,* and *who's.*
Sometimes these contractions are confused with the possessive words *their, its,
your,* and *whose.* The following chart shows the difference in meaning between
the contractions and the possessive words.

Contractions	*Possessive Words*
they're (means *they are*)	their (means *belonging to them*)
it's (means *it is* or *it has*)	its (means *belonging to it*)
you're (means *you are*)	your (means *belonging to you*)
who's (means *who is*)	whose (means *belonging to whom*)

Note: Possessive words are explained further on page 170.

Practice

Underline the correct form (the contraction or the possessive word) in each of the following sentences. Use the contraction whenever the two words of the contraction (*they are, it is, you are, who is*) would also fit.

1. (It's, Its) the rare guest who knows when (it's, its) time to go home.
2. If (they're, their) going to bring (they're, their) vacation pictures, I'm leaving.
3. (You're, Your) a difficult kind of person because you always want (you're, your) own way.
4. I don't know (who's, whose) fault it was that the window got broken, but I know (who's, whose) going to pay for it.
5. Unless (it's, its) too much trouble, could you make it (you're, your) business to find out (who's, whose) been throwing garbage in my yard?

APOSTROPHE TO SHOW
OWNERSHIP OR POSSESSION

To show ownership or possession, we can use such words as *belongs to, owned by,* or (most commonly) *of.*

the knapsack *that belongs to* Lola
the house *owned by* my mother
the sore arm *of* the pitcher

But the apostrophe plus *s* (if the word does not end in *-s*) is often the quickest and easiest way to show possession. Thus we can say:

Lola's knapsack
my mother's house
the pitcher's sore arm

Points to Remember

1   The *'s* goes with the owner or possessor (in the examples given, *Lola, mother,* and *pitcher*). What follows is the person or thing possessed (in the examples given, *knapsack, house,* and *sore arm*). An easy way to determine the owner or possessor is to ask the question ''Whom does it belong to?'' In the first example, the answer to the question ''Whom does the knapsack belong to?'' is *Lola.* Therefore, the *'s* goes with *Lola.*

2   In handwriting, there should always be a break between the word and the *'s*.

Yes   No

Practice 1

Rewrite the italicized part of each of the sentences listed below, using the *'s* to show possession. Remember that the *'s* goes with the owner or possessor.

Examples   *The motorcycle owned by Clyde* is a frightening machine.
                  Clyde's motorcycle
                  _____

                  The roommate of my brother is a sweet and friendly person.
                  My brother's roommate
                  _____

1. *The rifle of the assassin* failed to fire.

   _____

2. The playboy spent *the legacy of his mother* within six months.

   _____

3. *The throat of Mark* tightened when the doorbell rang.

   _____

4. The new salesman took *the parking space of Sam.*

   _____

5. *The hat of the chef* fell into the pea soup.

   _____

6. A big man wearing sunglasses stayed near *the wife of the president.*

   _____

7. *The hand of the mugger* closed over the victim's mouth.

_____

8. The *briefcase of Harry* was still there, but the documents were gone.

_____

9. *The shoulder bag of Sandy* had vanished from her locker.

_____

10. *The leash of the dog* was tangled around a fire hydrant.

_____

Practice 2

Underline the word in each sentence that needs an *'s*. Then write the word correctly in the space below. One is done for you as an example.

1. Julie is always upset after one of her <u>ex-husband</u> visits.

   ex-husband's

2. My instructor worst habit is leaving her sentences unfinished.

   _____

3. The astrologer predictions were all wrong.

   _____

4. Ellen jeans were so tight that she had to lie flat in order to zip them.

   _____

5. The lemonade bitter flavor assaulted my taste buds.

   _____

6. My sister life is like a soap opera.

   _____

7. Brian gold wedding band slid into the garbage disposal.

   _____

8. Sue ten-year-old Volvo is still dependable.

   _____

9. We didn't believe any of Uncle Charles stories.

   _____

10. The hypnotist piercing eyes frightened Kelly.

   _____

Practice 3

Add an *'s* to each of the following words to make them the possessors or owners of something. Then write sentences using the words. Your sentences can be serious or playful. One is done for you as an example.

1. Cary _____ *Cary's* _____

   Cary's hair is bright red.

2. friend _____

   _____

3. cashier _____

   _____

4. teammate _____

   _____

5. brother _____

   _____

Apostrophe versus Possessive Pronouns

Do not use an apostrophe with possessive pronouns. They already show ownership. Possessive pronouns include *his, hers, its, yours, ours,* and *theirs.*

Correct	*Incorrect*
The bookstore lost its lease.	The bookstore lost its' lease.
The racing bikes were theirs.	The racing bikes were theirs'.
The change is yours.	The change is yours'.
His problems are ours, too.	His' problems are ours', too.
His skin is more tanned than hers.	His' skin is more tanned than hers'.

Apostrophe versus Simple Plurals

When you want to make a word plural, just add an *s* at the end of the word. Do *not* add an apostrophe. For example, the plural of the word *movie* is *movies,* not *movie's* or *movies'*. Look at this sentence:

When Sally's cat began catching birds, the neighbors called the police.

The words *birds* and *neighbors* are simple plurals, meaning more than one bird, more than one neighbor. The plural is shown by adding *-s* only. (More information about plurals starts on page 217.) On the other hand, the *'s* after *Sally* shows possession—that Sally owns the cat.

Practice

In the space provided under each sentence, add the one apostrophe needed and explain why the other words ending in *s* are simple plurals.

Example   Sarahs yard is full of gophers.

Sarahs: _Sarah's, meaning "yard of Sarah"_

gophers: _simple plural meaning more than one gopher_

1. Phil thinks that the diners hamburgers taste better than sirloin steaks.

   diners: _____

   hamburgers: _____

   steaks: _____

2. San Franciscos cable cars can go up hills at a sixty-degree angle.

   San Franciscos: _____

   cars: _____

   hills: _____

3. My twelve-year-old brothers collection of baseball cards is in six shoe boxes.

   brothers: _____

   cards: _____

   boxes: _____

4. Only women shaped like toothpicks look decent in this years fashions.

   toothpicks: _____

   year: _____

   fashions: _____

5. Pedros blood pressure rose when he drove around the mall for twenty minutes and saw that there were no parking spaces.

Pedros: _____

minutes: _____

spaces: _____

6. The write-ups of Ellens promotion made her coworkers jealous.

write-ups: _____

Ellens: _____

coworkers: _____

7. My sons backyard fort is made from pieces of scrap lumber, old nails, and spare roof shingles.

sons: _____

pieces: _____

nails: _____

shingles: _____

8. The mayors double-talk had reporters scratching their heads and scribbling in their notebooks.

mayors: _____

reporters: _____

heads: _____

notebooks: _____

9. Two cuts over the boxers left eye prompted the referee to stop the fight after six rounds.

cuts: _____

boxers: _____

rounds: _____

10. As rock music blared over the cafeterias loudspeakers, Theresa tried to study for her exams.

cafeterias: _____

loudspeakers: _____

exams: _____

Apostrophe with Plural Words Ending in -s

Plurals that end in -s show possession simply by adding the apostrophe, rather than an apostrophe plus s.

Both of my *neighbors'* homes have been burglarized recently.
The many *workers'* complaints were ignored by the company.
All the *campers'* tents were damaged by the hailstorm.

Practice

In each sentence, cross out the one plural word that needs an apostrophe. Then write the word out correctly, with the apostrophe, in the space provided.

Example   My two ~~bosses~~ tempers are much the same: explosive.
bosses'

1. Little Bobby wanted to look in all the mall stores windows.

   _____

2. Why are all my friends problems easier to solve than my own?

   _____

3. Dad hopes that the Dallas Cowboys new quarterback will get them into the Super Bowl.

   _____

4. The students insect collections were displayed in a glass case.

   _____

5. The poll showed that the voters wish was to replace all the politicians in office.

   _____

Review Test I

In each sentence, cross out the two words that need apostrophes. Then write the words correctly in the spaces provided.

1. That restaurants menu hasnt changed its selections since ten years ago.

   _____   _____

2. Steve doesnt begin writing his papers until the day before theyre due.

   _____   _____

3. My fathers habit is never to root for a team until he thinks its going to lose.

   _____   _____

4. The toddler knocked his mothers sewing box onto the floor; then, he dropped her calculator into the dogs water bowl.

   _____   _____

5. Part of Stans nursing training consists of a stint in the local hospitals trauma center.

   _____   _____

6. "Youre daring someone to steal that camera if you carry it to the rock concert," warned Tinas dad.

   _____   _____

7. Ever since my sister passed her drivers test, she keeps asking for the keys to our parents car.

   _____   _____

8. The department store wouldnt exchange Carols birthday gift since pierced earrings cannot be returned.

   _____   _____

9. I use Sids dry-cleaning service because he will clean anyones American flag free.

   _____   _____

10. When little Dannys cut was being stitched up, he asked the doctor why he didnt use a sewing machine.

    _____   _____

Review Test 2

Rewrite the following sentences, changing the underlined words into either (1) a contraction or (2) a possessive.

1. I wanted to buy the house of my uncle but could not get a mortgage.

   _____

   _____

2. The issue of this week of the *National Enquirer* features the diet of a Hollywood starlet on which she lost fifteen pounds in three days.

   _____

   _____

3. The programs of next week always look better than what is on now.

   _____

   _____

4. The tires of the car are as smooth as the eggs of a hen.

   _____

   _____

5. The voice of the instructor boomed in the ears of Marie as she sat in the front row.

   _____

   _____

Quotation Marks

Read the following scene and underline all the words enclosed within quotation marks. Your instructor may also have you dramatize the scene, with one person reading the narration and two persons acting the two speaking parts—Clyde and Sam. The two speakers should imagine the scene as part of a stage play and try to make their words seem as real and true-to-life as possible.

At a party that Clyde and Charlotte recently had, Clyde got angry at a guy named Sam who kept bothering his wife. "Listen, man," Clyde said, "what's this thing you have for my wife? There are lots of other chicks at this party."

"Be cool," Sam said. "Charlotte is a very sweet person. I enjoy talking with her."

"I'm saying it just one more time," Clyde said. "Lay off my wife, or get the blazes out of my party."

Sam, a mean hunk of a man, just looked at Clyde and grinned. "You've got good booze here. Why should I leave? Come on, Charlotte," he said, taking her arm. "Let's sit by the window."

Clyde went to his basement and was back a minute later holding a two-by-four. "I'm giving you a choice," Clyde said. "Leave by the door or I'll slam you out the window."

Sam left by the door.

1. On the basis of the above selection, what is the purpose of quotation marks?

   _____

2. Do commas and periods that come after a quotation go inside or outside the quotation marks?

   _____

Answers are on page 490.

The two main uses of quotation marks are as follows. Each use is explained here.

1   To set off the exact words of a speaker or writer
2   To set off the titles of short works

QUOTATION MARKS TO SET OFF THE WORDS OF A SPEAKER OR WRITER

Use quotation marks when you want to show the exact words of a speaker or writer:

''Who left the cap off the toothpaste?'' Lola demanded.
(Quotation marks set off the exact words that Lola spoke.)

Ben Franklin wrote, ''Keep your eyes wide open before marriage, half shut afterward.''
(Quotation marks set off the exact words that Ben Franklin wrote.)

''You're never too young,'' Aunt Fern told me, ''to have a heart attack.''
(Two pairs of quotation marks are used to enclose the aunt's exact words.)

Maria complained, ''I look so old some days. Even makeup doesn't help. I feel as though I'm painting a corpse!''
(Note that the end quotes do not come until the end of Maria's speech. Place quotation marks before the first quoted word of a speech and after the last quoted word. As long as no interruption occurs in the speech, do not use quotation marks for each new sentence.)

Punctuation Hint: In the four examples above, notice that a comma sets off the quoted part from the rest of the sentence. Also observe that commas and periods at the end of a quote always go *inside* quotation marks.

Complete the following statements, which explain how capital letters, commas, and periods are used in quotations. Refer to the four examples as guides.

- Every quotation begins with a _____ letter.
- When a quotation is split (as in the sentence about Aunt Fern), the second part does not begin with a capital letter unless it is a _____ sentence.
- _____ are used to separate the quoted part of a sentence from the rest of the sentence.
- Commas and periods that come at the end of a quote go _____ quotation marks.

The answers are *capital, new, Commas,* and *inside.*

Practice I

Insert quotation marks where needed in the sentences that follow.

1. This is the tenth commercial in a row, complained Maureen.
2. The police officer said sleepily, I could really use a cup of coffee.
3. My boss asked me to step into his office and said, Joanne, how would you like a raise?
4. I'm out of work again, Miriam sighed.
5. I didn't know this movie was R-rated! Lorraine gasped.
6. Why does my dog always wait until it rains before he wants to go out? Clyde asked.
7. A sign over the box office read, Please form a single line and be patient.
8. Unless I run three miles a day, Marty said, my legs feel like lumpy oatmeal.
9. I had an uncle who knew when he was going to die, claimed Dan. The warden told him.
10. The unusual notice in the newspaper read, Young farmer would be pleased to hear from young lady with tractor. Send photograph of tractor.

Practice 2

Rewrite the following sentences, adding quotation marks where needed. Use a capital letter to begin a quote and use a comma to set off a quoted part from the rest of the sentence.

Example   I'm getting tired Sally said.
    "I'm getting tired," Sally said.

1. The officer said I'm giving you a ticket.

   _____

2. Please wait your turn the frantic clerk begged.

   _____

3. Phil yelled where's the Drano?

   _____

4. These directions don't make any sense Laura muttered.

   _____

5. Inside every fat person, someone once said, is a thin person struggling to get out.

   _____

   _____

Practice 3

1. Write three quotations that appear in the first part of a sentence.

   Example   _"Let's go shopping," I suggested._____

   a. _____

   b. _____

   c. _____

2. Write three quotations that appear at the end of a sentence.

   Example   _Bob asked, "Have you had lunch yet?"_____

   a. _____

   b. _____

   c. _____

3. Write three quotations that appear at the beginning and end of a sentence.

   Example   _"If the bus doesn't come soon," Mary said, "we'll freeze."_

   a. _____

   b. _____

   c. _____

Indirect Quotations

An indirect quotation is a rewording of someone else's comments rather than a word-for-word direct quotation. The word *that* often signals an indirect quotation.

Direct Quotation	*Indirect Quotation*
George said, ''My son is a daredevil.''	George said that his son is a daredevil.
(George's exact spoken words are given, so quotation marks are used.)	(We learn George's words *indirectly*, so no quotation marks are used.)
Carol's note to Arnie read, ''I'm at the neighbors'. Give me a call.''	Carol left a note for Arnie that said she would be at the neighbors' and he should give her a call.
(The exact words that Carol wrote in the note are given, so quotation marks are used.)	(We learn Carol's words *in*directly, so no quotation marks are used.)

Practice I

Rewrite the following sentences, changing words as necessary to convert the sentences into direct quotations. The first one is done for you as an example.

1. Lew asked Marian if she had had a bad day at work.
   Lew asked Marian, "Did you have a bad day at work?"
   _____

2. Marian exclaimed that it was the worst day of her life.
   _____
   _____

3. Lew said to tell him all about it.
   _____
   _____

4. Marian insisted that he wouldn't understand her job problems.
   _____
   _____

5. Lew said he would certainly try.
   _____
   _____

Practice 2

Rewrite the following sentences, converting each direct quotation into an indirect quotation. In each case you will have to add the word *that* or *if* and change other words as well.

Example   The barber asked Fred, ''Have you noticed how your hair is thinning?''

The barber asked Fred if he had noticed how his hair was

thinning.

1. He said, ''I need a vacation.''

   _____

   _____

2. Martha said, ''Purple is my favorite color.''

   _____

   _____

3. She asked the handsome stranger, ''Could I buy you a drink?''

   _____

   _____

4. My brother asked, ''Has anyone seen my frog?''

   _____

   _____

5. Fran complained, ''I married a man who falls asleep during horror movies.''

   _____

   _____

QUOTATION MARKS TO SET OFF
THE TITLES OF SHORT WORKS

Titles of short works are usually set off by quotation marks, while titles of long works are underlined. Use quotation marks to set off the titles of such short works as articles in books, newspapers, or magazines; chapters in a book; short stories, poems, and songs. On the other hand, you should underline the titles of books, newspapers, magazines, plays, movies, music albums, and television shows. See the examples below.

Note: In printed form the titles of long works are set off by italics—slanted type that looks *like this.*

Quotation Marks	*Underlines*
the article ''The Toxic Tragedy''	in the book Who's Poisoning America
the article ''New Cures for Headaches''	in the newspaper The New York Times
the article ''When the Patient Plays Doctor''	in the magazine Family Health
the chapter ''Connecting with Kids''	in the book Straight Talk
the story ''The Dead''	in the book Dubliners
the poem ''Birches''	in the book The Complete Poems of Robert Frost
the song ''Some Enchanted Evening''	in the album South Pacific
	the television show Hill Street Blues
	the movie Rear Window

Practice

Use quotation marks or underlines as needed.

1. My recently divorced sister refused to be in the talent show when she was told she'd have to sing Love Is a Many-Splendored Thing.

2. Disgusted by the constant dripping noise, Brian opened his copy of Handy Home Repairs to the chapter entitled Everything about the Kitchen Sink.

3. My little brother has seen the movie Star Wars at least eight times.

4. Before they bought new car tires, Nick and Fran studied the article Testing Tires in the February, 1993, issue of Consumer Reports.

5. Many people mistakenly think that Huckleberry Finn and The Adventures of Tom Sawyer are children's books only.

6. I just found out that the musical My Fair Lady is taken from a play by George Bernard Shaw called Pygmalion.

7. The ending of Shirley Jackson's story The Lottery really surprised me.

8. I sang the song Mack the Knife in our high school production of The Threepenny Opera.

9. Unless he's studied the TV Guide listings thoroughly, my father won't turn on his television.

10. Stanley dreamed that both Time and Newsweek had decided to use him in their feature article Man of the Year.

OTHER USES OF QUOTATION MARKS

Here are two more uses of quotation marks:

1   To set off special words or phrases from the rest of a sentence:

Many people spell the words ''all right'' as one word, ''alright,'' instead of correctly spelling them as two words.
I have trouble telling the difference between ''principal'' and ''principle.''

2   To mark off a quote within a quote. For this purpose, single quotes (') are used:

Ben Franklin said, ''The noblest question in the world is, 'What good may I do in it?' ''
''If you want to have a scary experience,'' Nick told Fran, ''read Stephen King's story 'The Mangler' in his book *Night Shift.*''

Review Test 1

Place quotation marks around the exact words of a speaker or writer in the sentences that follow.

1. Look at the dent in my car! Herb cried.
2. My mother always says to me, When in doubt, don't.
3. Franklin Roosevelt said, The only thing we have to fear is fear itself.
4. It's much too quiet in here, whispered Vince as he entered the library.
5. The sign on the manager's desk reads: I'd like to help you out. Which way did you come in?
6. Clutching his partner's hands in midair, the trapeze artist murmured, We've got to stop meeting like this.
7. I've got two tickets on the fifty-yard line! the scalper shouted as the fans filed into the stadium.
8. Looking at the fanatic football fan who had removed his shirt in subzero weather, Lonnie said, There's a guy whose elevator doesn't go to the top.
9. I can't believe it, he muttered. I put that hammer right there a minute ago, and now it's gone.
10. Why doesn't anyone ever get hungry at the beach? Dad asked. When we didn't answer, he explained, Because of all the sand which is there.

Review Test 2

1. Write a sentence in which you quote a favorite expression of someone you know. Identify the relationship of the person to you.

   Example   *My brother Sam often says after a meal, "That wasn't bad*
   _____

   at all."
   _____

   _____

   _____

   _____

2. Write a quotation that contains the words *Tony asked Lola.* Write a second quotation that includes the words *Lola replied.*

_____

_____

_____

3. Write a sentence that interests or amuses you from a book. Identify the title and author of the book.

Example   *Thoreau writes in Walden, "What a man thinks of himself,*

that is what determines, or rather indicates, his fate."

_____

_____

_____

4. Write a sentence that interests you from a newspaper. Identify the title and the author (if given) of the article.

_____

_____

_____

5. Write a sentence that interests you from a magazine. Identify the title and the author of the article.

_____

_____

_____

Review Test 3

Go through the comics section of a newspaper to find a comic strip that amuses you. Be sure to choose a strip in which two or more characters are speaking to each other. Write a full description that will enable people who have not read the comic strip to visualize it clearly and appreciate its humor. Describe the setting and action in each panel and enclose the words of the speakers in quotation marks.

Comma

Commas often (though not always) signal a minor break or pause in a sentence. Each of the six pairs of sentences below illustrates one of six main uses of the comma. Read each pair of sentences aloud and place a comma wherever you feel a slight pause occurs.

1. a. Joel watched the eleven o'clock news a movie a *Honeymooners* rerun and the station sign-off.
    b. Please endorse your check write your account number on the back and fill out a deposit slip.
2. a. Even though I was safe indoors I shivered at the thought of the bitter cold outside.
    b. To start the car depress the accelerator and then turn the ignition key.
3. a. The opossum an animal much like the kangaroo carries its young in a pouch.
    b. George Derek who was recently arrested was a high school classmate of mine.
4. a. I had enrolled in the course during pre-registration but my name did not appear on the class list.
    b. A police cruiser blocked the busy intersection and an ambulance pulled up on the sidewalk near the motionless victims.
5. a. Emily said ''Why is it so hard to remember your dreams the next day?''
    b. ''After I left the interview'' said David ''I couldn't remember a word I had said.''
6. a. Mike has driven over 1500000 accident-free miles in his job as a long-distance trucker.
    b. The Gates Trucking Company of 1800 Industrial Highway Jersey City New Jersey gave Mike an award on January 26 1994 for his superior safety record.

Answers are on page 491.

SIX MAIN USES OF THE COMMA

Commas are used mainly as follows:

1   To separate items in a series
2   To set off introductory material
3   On both sides of words that interrupt the flow of thought in a sentence
4   Between two complete thoughts connected by *and, but, for, or, nor, so, yet*
5   To set off a direct quotation from the rest of a sentence
6   For certain everyday material

You may find it helpful to remember that the comma often marks a slight pause, or break, in a sentence. These pauses or breaks occur at the points where the six main comma rules apply. Sentence examples for each of the comma rules are given on the following pages; read these sentences aloud and listen for the minor pauses or breaks that are signaled by commas.

However, you should keep in mind that commas are far more often overused than underused. As a general rule, you should *not* use a comma unless a given comma rule applies or unless a comma is otherwise needed to help a sentence read clearly. A good rule of thumb is that ''when in doubt'' about whether to use a comma, it is often best to ''leave it out.''

After reviewing each of the comma rules that follow, you will practice adding commas that are needed and omitting commas that are not needed.

1   Comma between Items in a Series

Use a comma to separate items in a series.

Magazines, paperback novels, and textbooks crowded the shelves.

Hard-luck Sam needs a loan, a good-paying job, and a close friend.

Pat sat in the doctor's office, checked her watch, and flipped nervously through a magazine.

Lola bit into the ripe, juicy apple.

More and more people entered the crowded, noisy stadium.

Note: A comma is used between two descriptive words in a series only if *and* inserted between the words sounds natural. You could say:

Lola bit into the ripe *and* juicy apple.
More and more people entered the crowded *and* noisy stadium.

But notice in the following sentences that the descriptive words do not sound natural when *and* is inserted between them. In such cases, no comma is used.

The model wore a light sleeveless blouse. (''A light *and* sleeveless blouse'' doesn't sound right, so no comma is used.)
Dr. Van Helsing noticed two tiny puncture marks on his patient's neck. (''Two *and* tiny puncture marks'' doesn't sound right, so no comma is used.)

Practice 1

Place commas between items in a series.

1. Shelley packed tennis rackets a volleyball and a first-aid kit in the car.
2. Marty never reads anything in the paper except the comics the sports page and the personals.
3. On the Johnsons' lawn are a cement birdbath two stone deer a flagpole and a plastic daisy.

Practice 2

In each sentence, cross out the one comma that is not needed. Add the one comma that is needed between items in a series.

1. A metal tape measure, a pencil a ruler, and a hammer dangled, from the carpenter's pockets.
2. The fortune-teller uncovered the crystal ball peered into it, and began, to predict my future.
3. That hairdresser is well-known, for her frizzy perms butchered haircuts, and brassy hair colorings.

2   Comma after Introductory Material

Use a comma to set off introductory material.

Fearlessly, Lola picked up the slimy slug.

Just to annoy Tony, she let it crawl along her arm.

Although I have a black belt in karate, I decided to go easy on the demented bully who had kicked sand in my face.

Mumbling under her breath, the woman picked over the tomatoes.

Note: If the introductory material is brief, the comma is sometimes omitted. In the activities here, you should include the comma.

Practice I

Place commas after introductory material.

1. With shaking hands the frightened baby-sitter dialed the police emergency number.
2. During the storm snow drifted through cracks in the roof of the cabin.
3. Ashamed to ask for help Betty glanced around nervously at the other students to see how they were filling out the computer questionnaire.

Practice 2

In each sentence, cross out the one comma that is not needed. Add the one comma that is needed after introductory material.

1. In order to work at that fast-food restaurant you have to wear a cowboy hat and six-guns. In addition, you have to shout "Yippee!" every time, someone orders the special Western-style double burger.
2. Barely awake, the woman slowly rocked, her crying infant. While the baby softly cooed the woman fell asleep.
3. When I painted the kitchen, I remembered to cover the floor with newspapers. Therefore I was able to save the floor from looking, as if someone had thrown confetti on it.

3 Comma around Words
Interrupting the Flow of Thought

Use a comma on both sides of words that interrupt the flow of thought in a sentence.

The car, cleaned and repaired, is ready to be sold.
Martha, our new neighbor, used to work as a bouncer at Rexy's Tavern.
Taking long walks, especially after dark, helps me sort out my thoughts.

Usually you can ''hear'' words that interrupt the flow of thought in a sentence. However, if you are not sure if certain words are interrupters, remove them from the sentence. If it still makes sense without the words, you know that the words are interrupters and that the information they give is nonessential. Such nonessential information is set off with commas. In the following sentence,

Susie Hall, who is my best friend, won a new car in the *Reader's Digest* sweepstakes.

the words *who is my best friend* are extra information, not needed to identify the subject of the sentence, *Susie Hall*. Put commas around such nonessential information. On the other hand, in the sentence

The woman who is my best friend won a new car in the *Reader's Digest* sweepstakes.

the words *who is my best friend* supply essential information that we need to identify the woman. If the words were removed from the sentence, we would no longer know which woman won the sweepstakes. Commas are not used around such essential information.

Here is another example:

The Shining, a novel by Stephen King, is the scariest book I've ever read.

Here the words *a novel by Stephen King* are extra information, not needed to identify the subject of the sentence, *The Shining*. Commas go around such nonessential information. On the other hand, in the sentence

Stephen King's novel *The Shining* is the scariest book I've ever read.

the words *The Shining* are needed to identify the novel. Commas are not used around such essential information.

Most of the time you will be able to ''hear'' words that interrupt the flow of thought in a sentence and will not have to think about whether the words are essential or nonessential.*

Practice 1

Add commas to set off interrupting words.

1. This all-purpose kitchen gadget ladies and gentlemen sells for only $19.98!
2. Tigers because they eat people do not make good house pets.
3. A practical joker had laid a dummy its straw-filled ''hands'' tied with rope across the railroad tracks.

Practice 2

In each sentence, cross out the one comma that is not needed. Add the comma that is needed to complete the setting off of interrupting words.

1. My brother, who likes only natural foods would rather eat a soybean patty, than a cheeseburger.
2. That room with its filthy rug, and broken dishwasher, is the nicest one in the building.
3. My aunt who claims she is an artist, painted her living room ceiling, to look like the sky at midnight.

4 Comma between Complete Thoughts Connected by a Joining Word

Use a comma between two complete thoughts connected by *and, but, for, or, nor, so, yet.*

My parents threatened to throw me out of the house, so I had to stop playing the drums.

The polyester bed sheets had a gorgeous design, but they didn't feel as comfortable as plain cotton sheets.

The teenage girls walked the hot summer streets, and the teenage boys drove by in their shined-up cars.

---

* Some instructors refer to nonessential or extra information that is set off by commas as a *nonrestrictive clause*. Essential information that interrupts the flow of thought is called a *restrictive clause*. No commas are used to set off a restrictive clause.

Notes

a   The comma is optional when the complete thoughts are short:

Hal relaxed but Bob kept working.
The soda was flat so I poured it away.
We left school early for the furnace broke down.

b   Be careful not to use a comma in sentences having *one* subject and a *double* verb. The comma is used only in sentences made up of two complete thoughts (two subjects and two verbs). In the sentence

Mary lay awake that stormy night and listened to the thunder crashing.

there is only one subject (*Mary*) and a double verb (*lay* and *listened*). No comma is needed. Likewise, the sentence

The quarterback kept the ball and plunged across the goal line for a touchdown.

has only one subject (*quarterback*) and a double verb (*kept* and *plunged*); therefore, no comma is needed.

Practice

Place a comma before a joining word that connects two complete thoughts (two subjects and two verbs). Remember, do *not* place a comma within sentences that have only one subject and a double verb. If a sentence is correct, mark it with a *C*.

1. Vince has to make sixty sandwiches an hour or he'll lose his job at Burgerland.
2. The doctor assured me that my back was fine but it still felt as rigid as an iron rod.
3. That new video store gets the latest releases and it provides free popcorn for customers who rent two or more movies.
4. This new electric typewriter is much easier to use than my old manual but it makes just as many spelling errors.
5. Carol and Barbara pulled the volleyball net as tight as they could and then lashed it to a convenient pair of trees.
6. Ralph refuses to pay rent to his parents and will not do any chores at home.
7. Frieda wore a pair of wooden clogs while housecleaning and the people in the apartment next door could hear her clomping up and down the stairs.

8. William kept the cookie in his mouth until its chocolate coating melted and then he crunched the naked wafer into bits.

9. My little sister loves to call strangers on the telephone but she hangs up as soon as anyone answers.

10. Gregory plans to make a million dollars by the time he's twenty-five and then write a book about his experiences.

5   Comma with Direct Quotations

Use a comma to set off a direct quotation from the rest of a sentence.

> "Please take a number," said the deli clerk.
> Fred told Martha, "I've just signed up for a Dale Carnegie course."
> "Those who sling mud," a famous politician once said, "usually lose ground."
> "Reading this book," complained Stan, "is about as interesting as watching paint dry."

Note: Commas and periods at the end of a quotation go inside quotation marks. See also page 177.

Practice 1

Add commas to set off quotations from the rest of the sentence.

1. Frowning, the clerk asked "Do you have a driver's license and two major credit cards for identification?"

2. In my high school yearbook, my best friend wrote "2 Good 2 B 4 Gotten."

3. "The only thing that man couldn't talk his way out of " said Richie "is a coffin."

Practice 2

In each sentence, cross out the one comma that is not needed. Add the comma that is needed to set off a quotation from the rest of the sentence.

1. "Could you spare a quarter," the boy asked passersby, in the mall "for a video game?"

2. "Man does not live by words alone " wrote Adlai Stevenson, "despite the fact, that sometimes he has to eat them."

3. "That actress," said Vicki "has promoted everything, from denture cleaner to shoelaces."

6 Comma with Everyday Material

Use a comma with certain everyday material as shown in the following sections.

Persons Spoken To

I think, Sally, that you should go to bed.
Please turn down the stereo, Mark.
Please, sir, can you spare a dollar?

Dates

Our house was burglarized on December 28, 1993, and two weeks later on January 11, 1994.

Addresses

Lola's sister lives at 342 Red Oak Drive, Los Angeles, California 90057.

Note: No comma is used before the zip code.

Openings and Closings of Letters

Dear Marilyn,	Sincerely,
Dear John,	Truly yours,

Note: In formal letters, a colon is used after the opening:

Dear Sir:
Dear Madam:

Numbers

Government officials estimate that Americans spend about 785,000,000 hours a year filling out federal forms.

UNNECESSARY USE OF COMMAS

Remember that if no clear rule applies for using a comma, it is usually better not to use a comma. As stated earlier, "when in doubt, leave it out." Following are some typical examples of unnecessary commas.

Incorrect

Sharon told me, that my socks were different colors.
(A comma is not used before *that* unless the flow of thought is interrupted.)

The union negotiations, dragged on for three days.
(Do not use a comma between a simple subject and verb.)

I waxed all the furniture, and cleaned the windows.
(Use a comma before *and* only with more than two items in a series or when *and* joins two complete thoughts.)

Sharon carried, the baby into the house.
(Do not use a comma between a verb and its object.)

I had a clear view, of the entire robbery.
(Do not use a comma before a prepositional phrase.)

Practice

Cross out the one comma that does not belong in each sentence. Do not add any commas.

1. A new bulletproof material has been developed, that is very lightweight.
2. The vet's bill included charges, for a distemper shot.
3. Since the firehouse, is directly behind Ken's home, the sound of its siren pierces his walls.
4. Hard sausages, and net-covered hams hung above the delicatessen counter.
5. The students in the dance class, were dressed in a variety of bright tights, baggy sweatshirts, and woolly leg warmers.
6. A woman in the ladies' room asked me, if she could borrow a safety pin.
7. Telephone books, broken pencils, and scraps of paper, littered the reporter's desk.
8. The frenzied crowd at the game cheered, and whistled.
9. Splitting along the seams, the old mattress spilled its stuffing, on the ground.
10. To satisfy his hunger, Enrique chewed on a piece of dry, rye bread.

Review Test I

Insert commas where needed. In the space provided under each sentence, summarize briefly the rule that explains the use of the comma or commas.

1. During the sudden downpour people covered their heads with folded newspapers.

   _____

2. Sheila's sister always stopped her from buying expensive items by saying ''You have champagne taste and a beer budget.''

   _____

3. The damp musty shadowy cellar was our favorite playground.

   _____

4. My favorite pillow a sad specimen leaking chunks of foam is over ten years old.

   _____

5. Mary Ann started work as a file clerk on June 21 1993 and quit on June 22.

   _____

6. George agreed to sit in the window seat but he kept his eyes tightly shut during the takeoff and landing.

   _____

7. The massive fullback his uniform torn and bloodied hobbled back to the huddle.

   _____

8. Martin Luther King wrote ''A man can't ride on your back unless it's bent.''

   _____

9. If you want to avoid that run-down feeling you should look both ways before crossing the street.

   _____

10. My brother who is a practical joker once put a plastic shark in our bathtub.

    _____

Review Test 2

1. Write a sentence telling of three items you want to get the next time you go to the store. _____

    _____

    _____

2. Write a sentence that describes three things you would like to get done this week. _____

    _____

3. Write two sentences, starting the first one with *If I found a hundred-dollar bill* and the second one with *Also*. _____

    _____

    _____

    _____

4. Write two sentences describing how you relax after getting home from school or work. Start the first sentence with *After* or *When*. Start the second sentence with *Next*. _____

    _____

    _____

    _____

5. Write a sentence about a selfish or generous person you know. Use the words *a selfish person* or *a generous person* right after his or her name.

    _____

    _____

6. Write a sentence that tells something about your favorite magazine or television show. Use the words *which is my favorite magazine* or *which is my favorite television show* after the name of the magazine or show.

    _____

    _____

7. Write two complete thoughts about foods you enjoy. Use *and* to join the two complete thoughts. _____

    _____

8. Write two complete thoughts about a person you know. The first thought should tell of something you like about the person. The second thought should tell of something you don't like. Join the thoughts with *but*.

_____

_____

_____

9. Invent something that Lola might say to Tony. Use the words *Lola said* in the sentence. _____

_____

10. Write a remark that you made to someone today. Use the words *I said* somewhere in the middle of the sentence. _____

_____

Review Test 3

On separate paper, write six sentences, with each sentence demonstrating one of the six main comma rules.

Other Punctuation Marks

INTRODUCTORY PROJECT

Each of the sentences below needs one of the following punctuation marks:

     ;   —   -   ( )   :

See if you can insert the correct mark in each case.

1. The following singers were nominated by the Grammy Awards Committee for Best Male Artist Randy Travis, Bruce Springsteen, Luther Vandross, Phil Collins, and Michael Bolton.
2. A life size statue of her cat adorns the living room of Diana's penthouse.
3. Sigmund Freud, the pioneer psychoanalyst 1856–1939, was a habitual cocaine user.
4. As children, we would put pennies on the railroad track we wanted to see what they would look like after being run over by a train.
5. The stuntwoman was battered, broken, barely breathing but alive.

Answers are on page 492.

COLON (:)

The colon is a mark of introduction. Use the colon at the end of a complete statement to do the following:

1   Introduce a list.

My little brother has three hobbies: playing video games, racing his Hot Wheels cars all over the floor, and driving me crazy.

2   Introduce a long quotation.

Janet's paper was based on a passage from George Eliot's novel *Middlemarch:* ''If we had a keen vision and feeling of all ordinary human life, it would be like hearing the grass grow and the squirrel's heart beat, and we should die of that roar which lies on the other side of silence. As it is, the quickest of us walk about well wadded with stupidity.''

3   Introduce an explanation.

There are two ways to do this job: the easy way and the right way.

Two minor uses of the colon are after the opening in a formal letter (*Dear Sir or Madam:*) and between the hour and the minute when writing the time (*The bus will leave for the game at 11:45*).

Practice

Place colons where needed.

1. A comedian once defined mummies as follows Egyptians who are pressed for time.
2. The manager boasted that his restaurant was full of good things good food, good selections, and good prices.
3. In her book *The Plug-In Drug,* Marie Winn describes the effect of television on family life ''By its domination of the time families spend together, it destroys the special quality that distinguishes one family from another, a quality that depends to a great extent on what a family *does,* what special rituals, games, recurrent jokes, familiar songs, and shared activities it accumulates.''

SEMICOLON (;)

The semicolon signals more of a pause than the comma alone but not quite the full pause of a period. Use a semicolon to do the following:

1   Join two complete thoughts that are not already connected by a joining word such as *and, but, for,* or *so.*

   The chemistry lab blew up; Professor Thomas was fired.
   I once stabbed myself with a pencil; a black mark has been under my skin ever since.

2   Join two complete thoughts that include a transitional word such as *however, otherwise, moreover, furthermore, therefore,* or *consequently.*

   I cut and raked the grass; moreover, I weeded the lawn.
   Sally finished typing the paper; however, she forgot to bring it to class.

Note: The first two uses of the semicolon are treated in more detail on pages 44–45.

3   Separate items in a series when the items themselves contain commas.

   This fall I won't have to work on Labor Day, September 7; Veterans' Day, November 11; or Thanksgiving Day, November 26.
   At the final Weight Watchers' meeting, prizes were awarded to Sally Johnson, for losing 20 pounds; Irving Ross, for losing 26 pounds; and Betty Mills, the champion loser, who lost 102 pounds.

Practice

Place semicolons where needed.

1.   Be sure to plug up all unused electrical outlets otherwise, your toddler might get a severe shock.
2.   In the old horror movie, the incredible shrinking man battled a black widow spider he finally speared it with a straight pin.
3.   Having nothing better to do, Laurie watched the *Today* show from 7:00 to 9:00 A.M. a rerun of *Marcus Welby, M.D.,* from 9:00 to 10:00 and soap operas from 12:30 to 4:00 P.M.

DASH (—)

A dash signals a degree of pause longer than a comma but not as complete as a period. Use the dash to set off words for dramatic effect.

> I suggest—no, I insist—that you stay for dinner.
> The prisoner walked toward the electric chair—grinning.
> A meaningful job, a loving wife, and a car that wouldn't break down all the time—these are the things he wanted in life.

Practice

Place dashes where needed.

1. Our dishwasher doesn't dry very well the glasses look as if they're crying.

2. After I saw two museums, three monuments, and the governor's mansion, there was only one other place I wanted to see my hotel room.

3. I hoped no, I prayed that the operation would be successful.

HYPHEN (-)

Use a hyphen in the following ways:

1 With two or more words that act as a single unit describing a noun.

> The society ladies nibbled at the deep-fried grasshoppers.
> A white-gloved waiter then put some snails on their table.

Your dictionary will often help when you are unsure about whether to use a hyphen between words.

2 To divide a word at the end of a line of writing or typing.

> Although it had begun to drizzle, the teams decided to play the championship game that day.

Notes

a Always divide a word between syllables. Use your dictionary (see page 207) to be sure of correct syllable divisions.

b Do not divide words of one syllable.

c Do not divide a word if you can avoid dividing it.

Practice

Place hyphens where needed.

1. Al's Auto Agency is a first rate place to buy a brand new car.
2. Nick and Fran dream of someday replacing their worn out rugs with wall to wall carpeting in every room.
3. "What's a great looking guy like you doing in a two bit place like this?" she asked.

PARENTHESES ( )

Use parentheses to do the following:

❙ Set off extra or incidental information from the rest of a sentence.

The chapter on drugs in our textbook (pages 142–178) contains some frightening statistics.
The normal body temperature of a cat (101 to 102°) is 3° higher than the temperature of its owner.

2 Enclose letters or numbers that signal items in a series.

Three steps to follow in previewing a textbook are to (1) study the title, (2) read the first and last paragraphs, and (3) study the headings and subheadings.

Note: Do not use parentheses too often in your writing.

Practice

Add parentheses where needed.

1. The high ticket prices twenty to fifty dollars made Vince think twice about going to the rock concert.
2. In the last election the April primary , only 20 percent of the eligible voters showed up at the polls.
3. When you come to take the placement test, please bring with you 1 two sharpened pencils and 2 an eraser.

Review Test I

At the appropriate spot, place the punctuation mark shown in the margin.

Example ; The singles dance was a success; I met several people I wanted to see again.

: 1. Fascinated, Greg read two unusual recipes in *The Joy of Cooking* roasted saddle of moose and woodchuck smothered with onions.

— 2. Sam's Pizza Heaven is advertising a Friday-night special on lasagna all you can eat for $2.99.

- 3. Very few older cars have front wheel drive.

( ) 4. The sign on my instructor's office door read, "Available only during office hours 2 to 4 P.M."

: 5. In *Walden,* Thoreau wrote "I went to the woods because I wished to live deliberately, to front only the essential facts of life, and see if I could not learn what it had to teach, and not, when I came to die, discover that I had not lived."

; 6. Mosquitoes prefer to bite children rather than adults they are also more attracted to blonds than to brunettes.

— 7. Please go to the Seven-Eleven it's that little store in the middle of the next block and get a carton of Tab.

- 8. We can't afford to see first run movies anymore.

( ) 9. Four hints for success in taking exams are 1 review your notes the night before, 2 be on time for the exam, 3 sit in a quiet place, and 4 read all directions carefully before you begin to write.

; 10. My neighbor's boxer, Dempsey, is a great watchdog in fact, he can sit on my porch and watch me for hours.

Review Test 2

On separate paper, write two sentences for each of the following punctuation marks: colon, semicolon, dash, hyphen, parentheses.

Section 4: Word Use

Dictionary Use

Answers are on page 492–493.

INTRODUCTORY PROJECT

The dictionary is an indispensable tool, as will be apparent if you try to answer the following questions *without* using the dictionary.

1. Which one of the following words is spelled incorrectly?

    fortutious   macrobiotics   stratagem

2. If you wanted to hyphenate the following word correctly, at which points would you place the syllable divisions?

    h i e r o g l y p h i c s

3. What common word has the sound of the first *e* in the word *chameleon?*

4. Where is the primary accent in the following word?

    o c t o g e n a r i a n

5. What are two separate meanings of the word *earmark?*

    _____

    _____

Your dictionary is a quick and sure authority on all these matters: spelling, syllabication, pronunciation, and word meanings. And as the chapter ahead will show, it is also a source for many other kinds of information.

Answers are on page 492–493.

The dictionary is a valuable tool. To take advantage of it, you need to understand the main kinds of information that a dictionary gives about a word. Look at the information provided for the word *dictate* in the following entry from the *American Heritage Dictionary,* paperback edition.*

Spelling and syllabication   Pronunciation   Part of speech

Meanings
Etymology

dic•tate (dĭk′tāt′, dĭk-tāt′) *v.* **-tat•ed, -tat•ing.**
1. To say or read aloud for transcription.
2. To prescribe or command with authority.
—*n.* (dĭk′tāt′). An order; directive. [< Lat. *dictare.*] **—dic•ta′tion** *n.*

Other form of the word

SPELLING

The first bit of information, within the boldface **(heavy type)** entry itself, is the spelling of *dictate*. You probably already know the spelling of *dictate,* but if you didn't, you could find it by pronouncing the syllables in the word carefully and then looking it up in the dictionary.

Use your dictionary to correct the spelling of the following words:

responsable _____	delite _____
thorogh _____	duble _____
akselerate _____	carefull _____
finaly _____	luckyer _____
refiree _____	dangrous _____
shizophrenic _____	accomodate _____
prescripshun _____	envalope _____
hankercheif _____	prenatel _____
marryed _____	progres _____
alright _____	jeneric _____
fotographer _____	excelent _____
krucial _____	persue _____

* © 1983 Houghton Mifflin Company. Reprinted by permission from *American Heritage Dictionary of the English Language,* Paperback Edition.

SYLLABICATION

The second bit of information that the dictionary gives, also within the boldface entry, is the syllabication of *dic•tate*. Note that a dot separates each syllable (or part) of the word.

Use your dictionary to mark the syllable divisions in the following words. Also indicate how many syllables are in each word.

c o n t r a c t   (_____ syllables)

m a g n e t i c   (_____ syllables)

d e h u m a n i z e   (_____ syllables)

s e n t i m e n t a l i z e   (_____ syllables)

Noting syllable divisions will enable you to *hyphenate* a word: divide it at the end of one line of writing and complete it at the beginning of the next line. You can correctly hyphenate a word only at a syllable division, and you may have to check your dictionary to make sure of the syllable divisions for a particular word.

PRONUNCIATION

The third bit of information in the dictionary entry is the pronunciation of *dictate:* (dĭk′tāt′) or (dĭk-tāt′). You already know how to pronounce *dictate,* but if you did not, the information within the parentheses would serve as your guide. Use your dictionary to complete the following pronunciation exercises.

Vowel Sounds

You will probably use the pronunciation key in your dictionary mainly as a guide to pronouncing different vowel sounds (*vowels* are the letters *a, e, i, o,* and *u*). Here is the pronunciation key that appears on every other page of the paperback *American Heritage Dictionary:*

> ă pat ā pay â care ä father ĕ pet ē be ĭ pit ī tie î pier ŏ pot ō toe ô paw, for oi noise ŏŏ took o͞o boot ou out th thin *th* this ŭ cut û urge yo͞o abuse zh vision ə about, item, edible, gallop, circus

This key tells you, for example, that the short *a* is pronounced like the *a* in *pat,* the long *a* is like the *a* in *pay,* and the short *i* is like the *i* in *pit.*

Now look at the pronunciation key in your own dictionary. The key is probably located in the front of the dictionary or at the bottom of every page. What common word in the key tells you how to pronounce each of the following sounds?

ĕ _____   ō _____

ī _____   ŭ _____

ŏ _____   o͞o _____

(Note that a long vowel always has the sound of its own name.)

The Schwa (ə)

The symbol ə looks like an upside-down e. It is called a *schwa,* and it stands for the unaccented sound in such words as *about, item, edible, gallop,* and *circus.* More approximately, it stands for the sound *uh*—like the *uh* that speakers sometimes make when they hesitate in their speech. Perhaps it would help to remember that *uh,* as well as ə, could be used to represent the schwa sound.

Here are three of the many words in which the sound appears: *socialize* (sō′shə līz or sō′shuh līz); *legitimate* (lə jĭt′ə mĭt or luh jĭt′uh mĭt); *oblivious* (ə blĭv′ē əs or uh blĭv′ē uhs). Open your dictionary to any page, and you will almost surely be able to find three words that make use of the schwa in the pronunciation in parentheses after the main entry. Write three such words and their pronunciations in the following spaces:

1. _____

2. _____

3. _____

Accent Marks

Some words contain both a primary accent, shown by a heavy stroke (′), and a secondary accent, shown by a lighter stroke (′). For example, in the word *vicissitude* (vĭ sĭs′ĭ to͞od′), the stress, or accent, goes chiefly on the second syllable (sĭs′), and to a lesser extent on the last syllable (to͞od′).

Use your dictionary to add stress marks to the following words:

soliloquy (sə lĭl ə kwē)   inventory (in vən tôr ē)

diatribe (dī ə trīb)   marmalade (mär mə lād)

rheumatism (ro͞o mə tĭz əm)   recognition (rek eg nish ən)

representation (rĕp rĭ zĕn tā shən)   monumental (mŏn yə men tl)

Full Pronunciation

Use your dictionary to write out the full pronunciation (the information given in parentheses) for each of the following words:

1. germane _____
2. jettison _____
3. juxtapose _____
4. catastrophic _____
5. alacrity _____
6. exacerbate _____
7. sporadic _____
8. cacophony _____

9. intrepid _____
10. oligarchy _____
11. raucous _____
12. temerity _____
13. forensic _____
14. megalomania _____
15. perpetuity _____

Now practice pronouncing each word. Use the pronunciation key in your dictionary as an aid to sounding out each syllable. Do *not* try to pronounce a word all at once; instead, work on mastering *one syllable at a time.* When you can pronounce each of the syllables in a word successfully, then say them in sequence, add the accent, and pronounce the entire word.

OTHER INFORMATION ABOUT WORDS

Parts of Speech

The dictionary entry for *dictate* includes the abbreviation *v.* This means that the meanings of *dictate* as a verb will follow. The abbreviation *n.* is then followed by the meaning of *dictate* as a noun.

At the front of your dictionary, you will probably find a key that will explain the meanings of abbreviations used in the dictionary. Use the key to fill in the meanings of the following abbreviations:

pl. = _____

sing. = _____

adj. = _____

adv. = _____

Principal Parts of Irregular Verbs

Dictate is a regular verb and forms its principal parts by adding *-d, -d,* and *-ing* to the stem of the verb. When a verb is irregular, the dictionary lists its principal parts. For example, with *begin* the present tense comes first (the entry itself, *begin*). Next comes the past tense (*began*), and then the past participle (*begun*)—the form of the verb used with such helping words as *have, had,* and *was.* Then comes the present participle (*beginning*)—the *-ing* form of the word.

Look up the principal parts of the following irregular verbs and write them in the spaces provided. The first one has been done for you.

Present	Past	Past Participle	Present Participle
see	*saw*	*seen*	*seeing*
go			
ride			
speak			

Plural Forms of Irregular Nouns

The dictionary supplies the plural forms of all irregular nouns (regular nouns form the plural by adding *-s* or *-es*). Give the plurals of the following nouns:

crisis	_____
library	_____
phenomenon	_____
variety	_____

Note: See page 217 for more information about plurals.

Meanings

When a word has more than one meaning, its meanings are numbered in the dictionary, as with the verb *dictate.* In many dictionaries, the most common meanings are presented first. The introductory pages of your dictionary will explain the order in which meanings are presented.

Use the sentence context to try to explain the meaning of the underlined word in each of the following sentences. Write your definition in the space provided. Then look up and record the dictionary meaning of the word. Be sure to select the meaning that fits the word as it is used in the sentence.

1. The insurance company compensated Jean for the two weeks she missed work.

   Your definition: _____

   Dictionary definition: _____

2. Howard is in excellent condition from running two miles a day.

   Your definition: _____

   Dictionary definition: _____

3. The underworld chief attained power by liquidating his competitors.

   Your definition: _____

   Dictionary definition: _____

Etymology

Etymology refers to the history of a word. Many words have origins in foreign languages, such as Greek (abbreviated Gk in the dictionary) or Latin (L). Such information is usually enclosed in brackets and is more likely to be present in a hardbound desk dictionary than in a paperback one. A good desk dictionary will tell you, for example, that the word *cannibal* derives from the name of the man-eating tribe, the Caribs, that Christopher Columbus discovered on Cuba and Haiti.

Good desk dictionaries include the following:

The American Heritage Dictionary
The Random House College Dictionary
Webster's New Collegiate Dictionary
Webster's New World Dictionary

See if your dictionary says anything about the origins of the following words.

derrick _____

_____

berserk _____

_____

boycott _____

_____

chauvinism _____

_____

Usage Labels

As a general rule, use only standard English words in your writing. If a word is not standard English, your dictionary will probably give it a usage label such as *informal, nonstandard, slang, vulgar, obsolete, archaic,* or *rare.*

Look up the following words and record how your dictionary labels them. Remember that a recent hardbound desk dictionary will always be the best source of information about usage.

fink _____

push (a noun meaning *persevering energy*) _____

dander (meaning *temper*) _____

ain't _____

gross out (meaning *to fill with disgust*) _____

Synonyms

A *synonym* is a word that is close in meaning to another word. Using synonyms helps you avoid unnecessary repetition of the same word in a paper. A paperback dictionary is not likely to give you synonyms for words, but a good desk dictionary will. (You might also want to own a *thesaurus,* a book that lists synonyms and antonyms. An *antonym* is a word approximately opposite in meaning to another word.)

Consult a desk dictionary that gives synonyms for the following words, and write some of the synonyms in the spaces provided.

frighten _____

giant _____

insane _____

Review Test

Items 1–5: Use your dictionary to answer the following questions.

1. How many syllables are in the word *magnanimous?* _____

2. Where is the primary accent in the word *detrimental?* _____

3. In the word *tractable,* the second *a* is pronounced like
   a. short *a.*
   b. long *a.*
   c. short *i.*
   d. schwa.

4. In the word *officiate,* the second *i* is pronounced like
   a. short *i.*
   b. long *i.*
   c. long *e.*
   d. schwa.

5. In the word *sedentary,* the first *e* is pronounced like
   a. short *e.*
   b. long *e.*
   c. short *i.*
   d. schwa.

Items 6–10: There are five misspelled words in the following sentence. Cross out each misspelled word and write the correct spelling in the spaces provided below.

Our physicle education instructer, Mrs. Stevens, constently tells us that people who exersize every day have a more positive atitude toward life than people who never work out.

6. _____

7. _____

8. _____

9. _____

10. _____

Spelling Improvement

INTRODUCTORY PROJECT

See if you can circle the word that is misspelled in each of the following pairs:

akward	*or*	awkward
exercise	*or*	exercize
business	*or*	buisness
worried	*or*	worryed
shamful	*or*	shameful
begining	*or*	beginning
partys	*or*	parties
sandwichs	*or*	sandwiches
heroes	*or*	heros

Answers are on page 493.

Poor spelling often results from bad habits developed in the early school years. With work, such habits can be corrected. If you can write your name without misspelling it, there is no reason why you can't do the same with almost any word in the English language. Following are seven steps you can take to improve your spelling.

STEP 1: USING THE DICTIONARY

Get into the habit of using the dictionary. When you write a paper, allow yourself time to look up the spelling of all the words you are unsure about. Do not underestimate the value of this step just because it is such a simple one. By using the dictionary, you can probably make yourself a 95 percent better speller.

STEP 2: KEEPING A PERSONAL SPELLING LIST

Keep a list of words you misspell and study those words regularly. Use the chart on the inside front cover of this book as a starter. When you accumulate additional words, you may want to use a back page of your English notebook.

Hint: When you have trouble spelling long words, try to break each word down into syllables and see whether you can spell the syllables. For example, *misdemeanor* can be spelled easily if you can hear and spell in turn its four syllables: *mis-de-mean-or*. The word *formidable* can be spelled easily if you hear and spell in turn its four syllables: *for-mi-da-ble*. Remember, then: try to see, hear, and spell long words in terms of their syllable parts.

STEP 3: MASTERING COMMONLY CONFUSED WORDS

Master the meanings and spellings of the commonly confused words on pages 228–242. Your instructor may assign twenty words for you to study at a time and give you a series of quizzes until you have mastered all the words.

STEP 4: USING ELECTRONIC AIDS

There are three electronic aids that may help your spelling. First, many *electronic typewriters* on the market today will beep automatically when you misspell or mistype a word. They include built-in dictionaries that will then give you the correct spelling. Smith-Corona, for example, has a series of portable typewriters with an "Auto-Spell" feature that start at around $150 at discount stores.

Second, a *computer with a spell-checker* will identify incorrect words and suggest correct spellings. If you know how to write on a computer, you will have no trouble learning how to use the spell-check feature.

Third, *electronic spell-checkers* are pocket-size devices that look much like the pocket calculators you may carry to your math class. They are the latest example of how technology can help the learning process. Electronic spellers can be found in the typewriter or computer section of any discount store, at prices in the $100 range. The checker has a tiny keyboard. You type out the word the way you think it is spelled, and the checker quickly provides you with the correct spelling of related words. Some of these checkers even *pronounce* the word aloud for you.

STEP 5: UNDERSTANDING BASIC SPELLING RULES

Explained briefly here are three rules that may improve your spelling. While exceptions sometimes occur, these rules hold true most of the time.

1   ***Change y to i.***   When a word ends in a consonant plus *y,* change *y* to *i* when you add an ending.

try   + ed = tried   marry + es   = marries
worry + es = worries   lazy   + ness = laziness
lucky + ly = luckily   silly + est = silliest

2   ***Final silent e.***   Drop a final *e* before an ending that starts with a vowel (the vowels are *a, e, i, o,* and *u*).

hope + ing = hoping   sense + ible = sensible
fine + est = finest   hide   + ing = hiding

Keep the final *e* before an ending that starts with a consonant.

use + ful = useful   care   + less = careless
life + like = lifelike   settle + ment = settlement

3 **Doubling a final consonant.** Double the final consonant of a word when all the following are true:

a The word is one syllable or is accented on the last syllable.
b The word ends in a single consonant preceded by a single vowel.
c The ending you are adding starts with a vowel.

sob + ing = sobbing	big + est = biggest
drop + ed = dropped	omit + ed = omitted
admit + ing = admitting	begin + ing = beginning

Practice

Combine the following words and endings by applying the three rules above.

1. carry + ed = _____
2. revise + ing = _____
3. study + es = _____
4. wrap + ing = _____
5. horrify + ed = _____

6. permit + ed = _____
7. glide + ing = _____
8. angry + ly = _____
9. rebel + ing = _____
10. grudge + es = _____

STEP 6: UNDERSTANDING PLURALS

Most words form their plurals by adding -s to the singular.

Singular	Plural
blanket	blankets
pencil	pencils
street	streets

Some words, however, form their plurals in special ways, as shown in the rules that follow.

1 Words ending in -s, -ss, -z, -x, -sh, or -ch usually form the plural by adding -es.

kiss	kisses	inch	inches
box	boxes	dish	dishes

2 Words ending in a consonant plus *y* form the plural by changing *y* to *i* and adding *-es.*

party	parties	county	counties
baby	babies	city	cities

3 Some words ending in *f* change the *f* to *v* and add *-es* in the plural.

leaf	leaves	life	lives
wife	wives	yourself	yourselves

4 Some words ending in *o* form their plurals by adding *-es.*

potato	potatoes	mosquito	mosquitoes
hero	heroes	tomato	tomatoes

5 Some words of foreign origin have irregular plurals. When in doubt, check your dictionary.

antenna	antennae	crisis	crises
criterion	criteria	medium	media

6 Some words form their plurals by changing letters within the word.

man	men	foot	feet
tooth	teeth	goose	geese

7 Combined words (words made up of two or more words) form their plurals by adding *-s* to the main word.

brother-in-law	brothers-in-law
passerby	passersby

Practice

Complete these sentences by filling in the plural of the word at the left.

crash 1. In driver training school, Bea covered her eyes during the film showing bloody car _____.

match 2. Leon collects packs of _____ from hotels and restaurants.

doily 3. Lace _____ are pinned to the arms of Aunt Agatha's chairs.

cross 4. The jeweled _____ in the museum display case were priceless.

dozen 5. At the base of the rotten oak were _____ of sucker shoots.

potato 6. Sherry tossed five _____ into the pot.

twenty 7. I dug deep in my pocket and pulled out two _____ to pay for the groceries.

wife 8. Three of the sheik's _____ emerged from the long limousine.

passerby 9. Several _____ stopped to listen to the street musician.

medium 10. The candidate said that the print and electronic _____ had not paid enough attention to his campaign.

STEP 7: MASTERING A BASIC WORD LIST

Make sure you can spell all the words in the following list. They are some of the words used most often in English. Again, your instructor may assign twenty words for you to study at a time and give you a series of quizzes until you have mastered the words.

ability	always	attention	40	bottom
absent	although	awful		breathe
accident	among	awkward		building
across	angry	balance		business
address	animal	bargain		careful
advertise	another	beautiful		careless
advice	20 answer	because		cereal
after	anxious	become		certain
again	apply	before		change
against	approve	begin		cheap
all right	argue	being		chief
almost	around	believe		children
a lot	attempt	between		church

	cigarette	100	house		only		something
	clothing		however		operate		soul
	collect		hundred		opportunity		started
	color		hungry		original		state
	comfortable		important		ought		straight
	company		instead		pain		street
	condition		intelligence		paper	200	strong
60	conversation		interest		pencil		student
	daily		interfere		people		studying
	danger		kitchen		perfect		success
	daughter		knowledge		period		suffer
	decide		labor		personal		surprise
	death		language		picture		teach
	deposit		laugh	160	place		telephone
	describe		leave		pocket		theory
	different		length		possible		thought
	direction		lesson		potato		thousand
	distance		letter		president		through
	doubt		listen		pretty		ticket
	dozen		loneliness		problem		tired
	during	120	making		promise		today
	each		marry		property		together
	early		match		psychology		tomorrow
	earth		matter		public		tongue
	education		measure		question		tonight
	either		medicine		quick		touch
	English		middle		raise	220	travel
80	enough		might		ready		truly
	entrance		million		really		understand
	everything		minute		reason		unity
	examine		mistake		receive		until
	exercise		money		recognize		upon
	expect		month		remember		usual
	family		morning	180	repeat		value
	flower		mountain		restaurant		vegetable
	foreign		much		ridiculous		view
	friend		needle		said		visitor
	garden		neglect		same		voice
	general		newspaper		sandwich		warning
	grocery		noise		send		watch
	guess	140	none		sentence		welcome
	happy		nothing		several		window
	heard		number		shoes		would
	heavy		ocean		should		writing
	height		offer		since		written
	himself		often		sleep		year
	holiday		omit		smoke	240	yesterday

Review Test

Items 1–8:   Use the three spelling rules to spell the following words.

1. date   + ing   = _____
2. hurry   + ed   = _____
3. drive   + able = _____
4. try   + es   = _____
5. swim   + ing   = _____
6. guide   + ed   = _____
7. happy   + est   = _____
8. bare   + ly   = _____

Items 9–14:   Circle the correctly spelled plural in each pair.

9. gooses   geese
10. richs   riches
11. heros   heroes
12. wolfs   wolves
13. pantries   pantrys
14. lifes   lives

Items 15–20:   Circle the correctly spelled word (from the basic word list) in each pair.

15. dout   doubt
16. written   writen
17. a lot   alot
18. exercize   exercise
19. origenal   original
20. anser   answer

Omitted Words and Letters

INTRODUCTORY PROJECT

Some people drop small connecting words such as *of, and,* or *in* when they write. They may also drop the *-s* endings of plural nouns. See if you can find the six places in the passage below where letters or words have been dropped. Supply whatever is missing.

Two glass bottle of apple juice lie broken the supermarket aisle. Suddenly, a toddler who has gotten away from his parents appears at the head of the aisle. He spots the broken bottles and begins to run toward them. His chubby body lurches along like wind-up toy and his arm move excitedly up and down. Luckily, alert shopper quickly reacts to the impending disaster and blocks the toddler's path. Then the shopper waits with crying, frustrated little boy until his parents show up.

Answers are on page 493.

Be careful not to leave out words or letters when you write. The omission of words like *a, an, of, to,* or *the* or the *-s* ending needed on nouns or verbs may confuse and irritate your readers. They may not want to read what they regard as careless work.

FINDING OMITTED WORDS AND LETTERS

Finding omitted words and letters, like finding many other sentence-skills mistakes, is a matter of careful proofreading. You must develop your ability to look carefully at a page to find places where mistakes may exist.

The exercises here will give you practice in finding omitted words and omitted *-s* endings on nouns. Another section of this book (pages 53–55) gives you practice in finding omitted *-s* endings on verbs.

Omitted Words

Practice

Add the missing word (*a, an, the, of,* or *to*) as needed.

Example   Some people regard television as ∧*a* tranquilizer that provides temporary

relief from ∧*the* pain and anxiety ∧*of* modern life.

1. In the rest room, Jeff impatiently rubbed his hands under mechanical dryer, which blew out feeble puffs cool air.

2. On February 10, 1935, *The New York Times* reported that eight-foot alligator had been dragged out of city sewer by three teenage boys.

3. Gene dressed up as stuffed olive for Halloween by wearing green plastic garbage bag and a red knitted cap.

4. Mrs. Hanson nearly fainted when she opened health insurance bill and saw enormous rate increase.

5. At 4 A.M., all-night supermarket where I work hosts assortment of strange shoppers.

6. With loud hiss, inflated beach ball suddenly shrank to size of orange.

7. The boiling milk bubbled over the sides the pot, leaving a gluey white film on stove top.

8. Susan turned the answer page of the crossword book, pretended herself that she hadn't, and turned back to her puzzle.

9. In order avoid stepping on the hot blacktop of parking lot, the barefoot boy tiptoed along the cooler white lines.

10. The messy roommates used hubcaps for ashtrays scribbled graffiti on their own bathroom walls.

The Omitted -s Ending

The plural form of regular nouns usually ends in -s. One common mistake that some people make with plurals is to omit this -s ending. People who drop the ending from plurals when speaking also tend to do it when writing. This tendency is especially noticeable when the meaning of the sentence shows that a word is plural.

> Ed and Mary pay two hundred dollar a month for an apartment that has only two room.

The -s ending has been omitted from *dollars* and *rooms*.

The activities that follow will help you correct the habit of omitting the -s endings from plurals.

Practice 1

Add -s endings where needed.

Example   Bill beat me at several game˄ of darts.

1. Can you really get fifteen shave from one of those razor blade?

2. With perfect timing, the runner's powerful leg glided smoothly over a dozen hurdle.

3. One of the strangest fad of the 1950s was the promotion of chocolate-covered ant by candy manufacturers.

4. Because pet owner abandoned them, small bands of monkey are now living in southern Florida.

5. The photographer locked themselves in steel cages in order to film great white shark in their underwater environment.

6. The breeze blew dandelion spore and dry brown leave through the air.

7. Jim made twelve circular cage from chicken wire and set them around his growing tomato plant.

8. The special this week is three pound of grape for eighty-nine cent.

9. The rope sole on my summer shoe have begun to disintegrate.

10. The skinny man ordered two double cheeseburger and three vanilla shake.

Practice 2

Write sentences that use plural forms of the following pairs of words.

Example   girl, bike   *The little girls raced their bikes down the street.*

1. paper, grade _____

_____

2. pillow, bed _____

_____

3. sock, shoe _____

_____

4. day, night _____

_____

5. game, ball _____

_____

Note: People who drop the -*s* ending on nouns also tend to omit endings on verbs. Pages 53–55 will help you correct the habit of dropping endings on verbs.

Review Test I

In each of the following sentences, two small connecting words are needed. Write them in the spaces provided, and write a caret (^) at each place in the sentence where a connecting word should appear.

_____   1.   Suffering from horrible head cold, Susan felt as though she were trying breathe under water.
_____

_____   2.   Because he forgot the key his padlock, Al asked gym attendant to saw the lock off his locker.
_____

_____   3.   The store made mistake when it sent me a letter saying that I hadn't paid any my bills for six months.
_____

_____   4.   The children laughed with delight when small dog jumped on circus clown's back.
_____

_____   5.   Dr. Marini recommends that my grandfather drink one glass wine every day to stimulate appetite and improve his circulation.
_____

Review Test 2

Add the two -s endings needed in each sentence.

1.   The whites of Sam's eyes were red from broken blood vessel, and his forehead was a mass of purple bruise.

_____   _____

2.   Ray has held five different job in four different cities in the past two year.

_____   _____

3.   I've been to several specialist, but I still don't know what's causing these terrible headache.

_____   _____

4.   Laurie watched with dread as a bulldozer began knocking down tree and shrub in the patch of woods next door.

_____   _____

5.   Vince was driving eighty mile an hour when two police car stopped him.

_____   _____

Commonly Confused Words

INTRODUCTORY PROJECT

Circle the five words that are misspelled in the following passage. Then see if you can write their correct spellings in the spaces provided.

If your a resident of a temperate climate, you may suffer from feelings of depression in the winter and early spring. Scientists are now studying people who's moods seem to worsen in winter, and there findings show that the amount of daylight a person receives is an important factor in ''seasonal depression.'' When a person gets to little sunlight, his mood darkens. Its fairly easy to treat severe cases of seasonal depression; the cure involves spending a few hours a day in front of full-spectrum fluorescent lights that contain all the components of natural light.

1. _____

2. _____

3. _____

4. _____

5. _____

Answers are on page 493.

HOMONYMS

The commonly confused words shown below are known as *homonyms;* they have the same sounds but different meanings and spellings. Complete the activities for each set of words, and check off and study the words that give you trouble.

Common Homonyms

all ready	pair	threw
already	pear	through
brake	passed	to
break	past	too
		two
coarse	peace	
course	piece	wear
		where
hear	plain	
here	plane	weather
		whether
hole	principal	
whole	principle	whose
		who's
its	right	
it's	write	your
		you're
knew	than	
new	then	
know	their	
no	there	
	they're	

---

all ready   completely prepared
already   previously; before

We were *all ready* to go, for we had eaten and packed *already* that morning.

Fill in the blanks: Sally has ___already___ phoned them twice to ask if they'll be ___all ready___ to go by nine o'clock.

Write sentences using *all ready* and *already.*

_____

_____

brake   stop
break   come apart

Dot slams the *brake* pedal so hard that I'm afraid I'll *break* my neck in her car.

Fill in the blanks: I hit the ____*brake*____ pedal so hard that my car spun around on the slick highway; luckily, there was a ____*break*____ in the traffic at that point.

Write sentences using *brake* and *break.*

_____

_____

coarse   rough
course   part of a meal; a school subject; direction; certainly (with *of*)

During the *course* of my career as a waitress, I've dealt with some very *coarse* customers.

Fill in the blanks: As her final project in the weaving ____*course*____, Maria made a tablecloth out of ____*coarse*____ fibers in shades of blue.

Write sentences using *coarse* and *course.*

_____

_____

hear   perceive with the ear
here   in this place

If I *hear* another insulting ethnic joke *here,* I'll leave.

Fill in the blanks: Do you want to ____*hear*____ about what happened to the last visitors who stayed ____*here*____ at the count's castle?

Write sentences using *hear* and *here.*

_____

_____

hole   empty spot
whole entire

If there is a *hole* in the tailpipe, I'm afraid we will have to replace the *whole* exhaust assembly.

Fill in the blanks: He walked the ＿＿＿＿＿＿＿＿＿＿ way, despite the ＿＿＿＿＿＿＿＿＿＿ in the sole of his right shoe.

Write sentences using *hole* and *whole.*

＿＿＿＿＿＿＿＿＿＿＿＿＿＿＿＿＿＿＿＿＿＿＿＿＿＿＿＿＿＿＿＿＿＿＿＿

＿＿＿＿＿＿＿＿＿＿＿＿＿＿＿＿＿＿＿＿＿＿＿＿＿＿＿＿＿＿＿＿＿＿＿＿

its   belonging to it
it's shortened form for *it is* or *it has*

The kitchen floor has lost *its* shine because *it's* been used as a roller skating rink by the children.

Fill in the blanks: ＿＿＿＿＿＿＿＿＿＿ foolish to wear your flimsy jacket with ＿＿＿＿＿＿＿＿＿＿ thin hood in this downpour.

Write sentences using *its* and *it's.*

＿＿＿＿＿＿＿＿＿＿＿＿＿＿＿＿＿＿＿＿＿＿＿＿＿＿＿＿＿＿＿＿＿＿＿＿

＿＿＿＿＿＿＿＿＿＿＿＿＿＿＿＿＿＿＿＿＿＿＿＿＿＿＿＿＿＿＿＿＿＿＿＿

knew past tense of *know*
new   not old

We *knew* that the *new* television comedy would be canceled quickly.

Fill in the blanks: Mary ＿＿＿＿＿＿＿＿ that a ＿＿＿＿＿＿＿＿ color set would tempt the children to spend more hours parked in front of the TV.

Write sentences using *knew* and *new.*

＿＿＿＿＿＿＿＿＿＿＿＿＿＿＿＿＿＿＿＿＿＿＿＿＿＿＿＿＿＿＿＿＿＿＿＿

＿＿＿＿＿＿＿＿＿＿＿＿＿＿＿＿＿＿＿＿＿＿＿＿＿＿＿＿＿＿＿＿＿＿＿＿

know   to understand
no   a negative

    I never *know* who might drop in even though *no* one is expected.

Fill in the blanks: Now that we _____ how the movie ends—
thanks to you—there will be _____ pleasure in watching it.

Write sentences using *know* and *no.*

_____

_____

pair   set of two
pear   a fruit

    The dessert consisted of a *pair* of thin biscuits topped with vanilla ice cream
and poached *pear* halves.

Fill in the blanks: This _____ of infant overalls has a _____
embroidered on the bib.

Write sentences using *pair* and *pear.*

_____

_____

passed   went by; succeeded in; handed to
past   time before the present; by, as in ''I drove past the house.''

    After Edna *passed* the driver's test, she drove *past* all her friends' houses
and honked the horn.

Fill in the blanks: As his mother _____ around her traditional
Christmas cookies, Terry remembered all the times in the _____
when he had left some of those very cookies on a plate for Santa Claus.

Write sentences using *passed* and *past.*

_____

_____

peace   calm
piece   part

The *peace* of the little town was shattered when a *piece* of a human body was found in the town dump.

Fill in the blanks: I won't give you any _____ unless you share that _____ of coconut cake with me.

Write sentences using *peace* and *piece*.

_____

_____

plain   simple
plane   aircraft

The *plain* box contained a very expensive model *plane* kit.

Fill in the blanks: The black-and-silver _____ on the runway looked exotic next to the _____ ones surrounding it.

Write sentences using *plain* and *plane.*

_____

_____

principal   main; a person in charge of a school; amount of money borrowed
principle   law or standard

My *principal* goal in child rearing is to give my daughter strong *principles* to live by.

Fill in the blanks: The _____ sport at our high school, basketball, was coached by a man whose guiding _____ was team play.

Write sentences using *principal* and *principle.*

_____

_____

Note: It might help to remember that the *e* in *principle* is also in *rule*—the meaning of *principle*.

right   correct; opposite of *left*; something to which one is entitled
write   what you do in English

It is my *right* to refuse to *write* my name on your petition.

Fill in the blanks: As I rested my fractured _____ arm on his desk, I asked the doctor to _____ out a prescription for a painkiller.

Write sentences using *right* and *write.*

_____

_____

than   used in comparisons
then   at that time

I glared angrily at my boss, and *then* I told him our problems were more serious *than* he suspected.

Fill in the blanks: Frankenstein's monster played peacefully with the little girl; _____ he was chased by the villagers, who were more hysterical _____ stampeding turkeys.

Write sentences using *than* and *then.*

_____

_____

Note: It might help to remember that *then* (the word spelled with an *e*) is a tim*e* signal (*time* also has an *e*).

their   belonging to them

there   at that place; a neutral word used with verbs like *is, are, was, were, have,* and *had*

they're   the shortened form of *they are*

The tenants *there* are complaining because *they're* being cheated by *their* landlords.

Fill in the blanks: _____ has been an increase in burglaries in _____ neighborhood, so _____ planning to install an alarm.

Write sentences using *their, there,* and *they're.*

_____

_____

_____

threw   past tense of *throw*

through   from one side to the other; finished

When a character in a movie *threw* a cat *through* the window, I had to close my eyes.

Fill in the blanks: As he picked _____ the clothes in the dryer, he _____ the still-damp towels aside.

Write sentences using *threw* and *through.*

_____

_____

to   verb part, as in *to smile;* toward, as in "I'm going to heaven."
too overly, as in "The pizza was too hot"; also, as in "The coffee was hot, too."
two the number 2

> Lola drove *to* the store *to* get some ginger ale. (The first *to* means *toward;* the second *to* is a verb part that goes with *get.*)
> The sport jacket is *too* tight; the slacks are tight, *too.* (The first *too* means *overly;* the second *too* means *also.*)
> The *two* basketball players leapt for the jump ball. (2)

Fill in the blanks: I don't know how _____ such different people were attracted _____ each other and made a happy marriage, _____.

Write sentences using *to, too,* and *two.*

_____

_____

_____

wear   to have on
where in what place

> I work at a nuclear reactor, *where* one must *wear* a radiation-detection badge at all times.

Fill in the blanks: At the restaurant _____ I work, the waiters _____ cowboy hats and Western snap-front shirts.

Write sentences using *wear* and *where.*

_____

_____

weather   atmospheric conditions
whether   if it happens that; in case; if

Because of the *weather,* it's not certain *whether* the game will be played.

Fill in the blanks: The _____ vane was once a valuable agricultural tool, indicating _____ to plant now or wait till a later time.

Write sentences using *weather* and *whether.*

_____

_____

whose   belong to whom
who's   shortened form for *who is* and *who has*

The man *who's* the author of the latest diet book is a man *whose* ability to cash in on the latest craze is well known.

Fill in the blanks: The substitute teacher, _____ lack of experience was obvious, asked, "_____ the person who threw that spitball?"

Write sentences using *whose* and *who's.*

_____

_____

your   belonging to you
you're   shortened form of *you are*

Since *your* family has a history of heart disease, *you're* the kind of person who should take extra health precautions.

Fill in the blanks: I may not like _____ opinion, but _____ certainly entitled to express it in this class.

Write sentences using *your* and *you're.*

_____

_____

OTHER WORDS FREQUENTLY CONFUSED

Following is a list of other words that people frequently confuse. Complete the activities for each set of words, and check off and study the ones that give you trouble.

Commonly Confused Words			
a	among	desert	learn
an	between	dessert	teach
accept	beside	does	loose
except	besides	dose	lose
advice	can	fewer	quiet
advise	may	less	quite
affect	clothes	former	though
effect	cloths	latter	thought

a   Both *a* and *an* are used before other words to mean, approximately, *one*.
an

Generally you should use *an* before words starting with a vowel (*a, e, i, o, u*):

   an absence   an exhibit   an idol   an offer   an upgrade

Generally you should use *a* before words starting with a consonant (all other letters):

   a pen   a ride   a digital clock   a movie   a neighbor

Fill in the blanks: In _____ instant, he realized that _____ diamond-patterned snake was slithering over his shoe.

Write sentences using *a* and *an.*

_____

_____

accept receive; agree to
except exclude; but

If I *accept* your advice, I'll lose all my friends *except* you.

Fill in the blanks: The crowd couldn't _____ the judges' decision; _____ for some minor mistakes, Jones had clearly won the fight.

Write sentences using *accept* and *except.*

_____

_____

advice noun meaning *opinion*
advise verb meaning *to counsel, to give advice*

Jake never listened to his parents' *advice,* and he ended up listening to a cop *advise* him of his rights.

Fill in the blanks: I asked a plumber to _____ me, since the _____ in the do-it-yourself book has been disastrous.

Write sentences using *advice* and *advise.*

_____

_____

affect verb meaning *to influence*
effect verb meaning *to bring about something;* a noun meaning *result*

My sister Sally cries for *effect,* but her act no longer *affects* us.

Fill in the blanks: A dangerous flooding _____ is created when the full moon _____s the tides in the spring.

Write sentences using *affect* and *effect.*

_____

_____

among implies three or more
between implies only two

> We selfishly divided the box of candy *between* the two of us rather than *among* all the members of the family.

Fill in the blanks: _____ the heads of lettuce in the bin was one with a large insect nestled _____ the wrapper and the outer leaf.

Write sentences using *among* and *between*.

_____

_____

beside along the side of
besides in addition to

> Fred sat *beside* Martha. *Besides* them, there were ten other people at the Tupperware party.

Fill in the blanks: _____ the broken leg, he suffered a deep cut _____ his mouth.

Write sentences using *beside* and *besides*.

_____

_____

can refers to the ability to do something
may refers to permission or possibility

> If you *can* work overtime on Saturday, you *may* take Monday off.

Fill in the blanks: Although that mole _____ be removed, it _____ be better to leave it alone.

Write sentences using *can* and *may*.

_____

_____

clothes   articles of dress
cloths   pieces of fabric

I tore up some old *clothes* to use as polishing *cloths.*

Fill in the blanks: Maxine used inexpensive dust ___*cloths*___ to make ___*clothes*___ for her daughter's doll.

Write sentences using *clothes* and *cloths.*

_____

_____

desert   a stretch of dry land; to abandon one's post or duty
dessert   last part of a meal

Don't *desert* us now; order a sinful *dessert* along with us.

Fill in the blanks: Guests began to ___*desert*___ the banquet room after the strawberry shortcake ___*dessert*___ had been cleared away.

Write sentences using *desert* and *dessert.*

_____

_____

does   form of the verb *do*
dose   specific amount of medicine

Martha *does* not realize that a *dose* of brandy is not the best medicine for the flu.

Fill in the blanks: If this ___*dose*___ of cough syrup ___*does*___ its work, I'll be able to give my speech.

Write sentences using *does* and *dose.*

_____

_____

fewer   used with things that can be counted
less   refers to amount, value, or degree

I missed *fewer* classes than Rafael, but I wrote *less* effectively than he did.

Fill in the blanks: Larry took _____ chances after the accident; he was _____ sure of his driving ability.

Write sentences using *fewer* and *less.*

_____

_____

former   refers to the first of two items named
latter   refers to the second of two items named

I turned down both a job at a service station and a job as a shipping clerk; the *former* involved irregular hours and the *latter* offered very low pay.

Fill in the blanks: She eats lots of raisins and strawberries; the _____ contain iron and the _____ are rich in vitamin C.

Write sentences using *former* and *latter.*

_____

_____

Note: Be sure to distinguish *latter* from *later* (meaning *after some time*).

learn   to gain knowledge
teach   to give knowledge

After Roz *learns* the new dance, she is going to *teach* it to me.

Fill in the blanks: If little Beth can _____ sign language, we can _____ her parents how to communicate with her.

Write sentences using *learn* and *teach.*

_____

_____

loose   not fastened; not tight-fitting
lose   misplace; fail to win

   I am afraid I'll *lose* my ring: it's too *loose* on my finger.

Fill in the blanks: When he discovered that his pet turtles had gotten

_____, he worried that he might _____ some of
them.

Write sentences using *loose* and *lose*.

_____

_____

quiet   peaceful
quite   entirely; really; rather

   After a busy day, the children were not *quiet,* and their parents were *quite* tired.

Fill in the blanks: Bobby couldn't keep _____ about the scholarship

his daughter had won; it was really _____ an honor.

Write sentences using *quiet* and *quite.*

_____

_____

though   despite the fact that
thought   past tense of *think*

   Though I enjoyed the dance, I *thought* the cover charge of ten dollars was
   too high.

Fill in the blanks: _____ everyone claimed the silvery object was

an airplane, I _____ it was a UFO.

Write sentences using *though* and *thought.*

_____

_____

INCORRECT WORD FORMS

Following is a list of incorrect word forms that people sometimes use in their writing. Complete the activities for each word, and check off and study the words that give you trouble.

Some Incorrect Word Forms

being that	could of	would of
can't hardly	must of	irregardless
couldn't hardly	should of	

---

being that   Incorrect! Use *because* or *since*.

I'm going to bed now ~~being that~~ I must get up early tomorrow.
(because)

Correct the following sentences.

1. Being that the boss heard my remark, I doubt if I'll get the promotion.

2. I'll have more cake, being that my diet is officially over.

3. Peter knows a lot about cars, being that his dad is a mechanic.

can't hardly   Incorrect! Use *can hardly* or *could hardly*.
couldn't hardly

Small store owners ~~can't~~ hardly afford to offer large discounts.
(can)

Correct the following sentences.

1. They couldn't hardly see the drive-in movie screen through the fog.

2. I can't hardly keep from laughing when I watch that show.

3. We couldn't hardly wait to see her face when she walked into the surprise party.

could of   Incorrect! Use *could have, must have, should have, would have.*
must of
should of
would of

I should ~~of~~ *have* applied for a loan when my credit was good.

Correct the following sentences.

1. Thelma must of painted the walls by herself.

2. I should of left the tip on the table.

3. I would of been glad to help if you had asked politely.

4. No one could of predicted that accident.

irregardless   Incorrect! Use *regardless.*

~~Irregardless~~ *Regardless* of what anyone says, he will not change his mind.

Correct the following sentences.

1. Irregardless of what anybody else does, I'm wearing jeans to the meeting.

2. Irregardless of the weather, the parade will go on as scheduled.

3. Irregardless of what my parents say, I will continue to see Elena.

Review Test 1

These sentences check your understanding of *its, it's; there, their, they're; to, too, two;* and *your, you're.* Underline the correct word in the parentheses. Rather than guess, look back at the explanations of the words when necessary.

1. As I walked (to, too, two) the car, I stepped in the freshly laid cement that (to, too, two) workers had just smoothed over.
2. (Its, It's) safe (to, too, two) park (your, you're) car over (there, their, they're).
3. "(Your, You're) wearing (your, you're) shoes on the wrong feet," Carla whispered to her little sister.
4. (There, Their, They're) are more secrets about (there, their, they're) past than (there, their, they're) willing to share.
5. The (to, too, two) of us plan to go to (your, you're) party, (to, too, two).
6. (Its, It's) been a long time since (your, you're) car has had (its, it's) carburetor checked.
7. (To, Too, Two) get into the dance, (your, you're) friend will have to pay (to, too, two) dollars.
8. (Its, It's) a shame that (your, you're) being laid off from your job (there, their, they're).
9. (Its, It's) rumored that the team has lost (its, it's) best pitcher for the rest of the season.
10. (There, Their, They're) is a mistake on (there, their, they're) check, so they are speaking (to, too, two) the manager.

Review Test 2

The sentences that follow check your understanding of a variety of commonly confused words. Underline the correct word in the parentheses. Rather than guess, look back at the explanations of the words when necessary.

1. My sister is better at math (than, then) I am, but I (right, write) more easily.
2. I was (all ready, already) (to, too, two) sign up for (your, you're) (coarse, course) when I discovered it had (all ready, already) closed.

3. He is the kind of person who (accepts, excepts) any (advice, advise) he is given, even if (its, it's) bad.

4. I (know, no) you want to (hear, here) the (hole, whole) story.

5. (There, Their, They're) is no (plain, plane) paper in the house, only a (pair, pear) of lined pads.

6. Our team got a real (brake, break) when Pete's pop fly fell (among, between) (to, too, two) infielders for a base hit.

7. I (can't hardly, can hardly) (hear, here) the instructor in that (coarse, course) without making (a, an) effort.

8. If (your, you're) going to have (desert, dessert), pick something with (fewer, less) calories than chocolate cheesecake.

9. Looking (threw, through) his front window, Fred could see a (pair, pear) of squirrels getting (there, their, they're) food ready for the cold (weather, whether) to come.

10. When I (learn, teach) you to drive a stick-shift car, we'll go (to, too, two) a (quiet, quite) country road where (there, their, they're) won't be much traffic.

Review Test 3

On separate paper, write short sentences using the ten words shown below.

there	too (meaning *also*)
past	affect
then	its
advise	who's
you're	break

Effective Word Choice

Answers are on page 494.

INTRODUCTORY PROJECT

Put a check beside the sentence in each pair that you feel makes more effective use of words.

1. After the softball game, we wolfed down a few burgers and drank a couple of brews. _____

   After the softball game, we ate hamburgers and drank beer. _____

2. A little birdie told me you're getting married next month. _____

   Someone told me you're getting married next month. _____

3. The personality adjustment inventories will be administered on Wednesday.

   _____

   Psychological tests will be given on Wednesday. _____

4. The referee in the game, in my personal opinion, made the right decision in the situation. _____

   I think the referee made the right decision. _____

Now see if you can circle the correct number in each case:

Pair (1, 2, 3, 4) contains a sentence with slang; pair (1, 2, 3, 4) contains a sentence with a cliché; pair (1, 2, 3, 4) contains a sentence with pretentious words; and pair (1, 2, 3, 4) contains a wordy sentence.

Answers are on page 494.

Choose your words carefully when you write. Always take the time to think about your word choices, rather than simply using the first word that comes to mind. You want to develop the habit of selecting words that are appropriate and exact for your purposes. One way you can show sensitivity to language is by avoiding slang, clichés, pretentious words, and wordiness.

SLANG

We often use slang expressions when we talk because they are so vivid and colorful. However, slang is usually out of place in formal writing. Here are some examples of slang expressions:

> The party was a *real horror show.*
> I don't want to *lay a guilt trip* on you.
> Our boss is not *playing with a full deck.*
> Dad *flipped out* when he learned that Jan had *totaled* the car.

Slang expressions have a number of drawbacks. They go out of date quickly, they become tiresome if used excessively in writing, and they may communicate clearly to some readers but not to others. Also, the use of slang can be an evasion of the specific details that are often needed to make one's meaning clear in writing. For example, in "The party was a real horror show," the writer has not provided the specific details about the party necessary for us to understand the statement clearly. Was it the setting, the food and drink (or lack of same), the guests, the music, the hosts, the writer, or what that made the party such a dreadful experience? In general, then, you should avoid the use of slang in your writing. If you are in doubt about whether an expression is slang, it may help to check a recently published hardbound dictionary.

Practice

Rewrite the following sentences, replacing the italicized slang words with more formal ones.

Example   My friend had *wheels,* so we decided to *cut out* of the *crummy* dance.
We decided to use my friend's car to leave the boring dance.

1.   The scene in the *flick* where Rocky ate six raw eggs *grossed me out.*

_____

_____

2. *Ex-cons* have a hard time adjusting after leaving the *slammer.*

    _____

    _____

3. Manny *whipped right through* the multiple-choice questions, but the essay section *threw him for a loop.*

    _____

    _____

4. The professional assassin *wasted* over twenty victims before someone *ratted* on him.

    _____

    _____

5. That book on suicide is *heavy;* it really *bent me out of shape.*

    _____

    _____

CLICHÉS

Clichés are expressions that have been worn out through constant use. Some typical clichés are listed below.

Common Clichés	
all work and no play	saw the light
at a loss for words	short but sweet
better late than never	sigh of relief
drop in the bucket	singing the blues
easier said than done	taking a big chance
had a hard time of it	time and time again
in the nick of time	too close for comfort
in this day and age	too little, too late
it dawned on me	took a turn for the worse
it goes without saying	under the weather
last but not least	where he (*or* she) is coming
make ends meet	from
on top of the world	word to the wise
sad but true	work like a dog

Clichés are common in speech but make your writing seem tired and stale. Also, they are often an evasion of the specific details that you must work to provide in your writing. You should, then, avoid clichés and try to express your meaning in fresh, original ways.

Practice 1

Underline the cliché in each of the following sentences. Then substitute specific, fresh words for the trite expression.

Example   My parents supported me through some <u>trying times.</u>
               *rough years*_____

1.   Salespeople who are rude make my blood boil.

    _____

2.   Vince has been down in the dumps ever since his girlfriend broke up with him.

    _____

3.   That new secretary is one in a million.

    _____

4.   We decided to hire a hall and roll out the red carpet in honor of our parents' silver wedding anniversary.

    _____

5.   The minute classes let out for the summer, I feel free as a bird.

    _____

Practice 2

Write a short paragraph describing the kind of day you had yesterday. Try to put as many clichés as possible into your writing. For example, "I had a long hard day. I had a lot to get done, and I kept my nose to the grindstone." By making yourself aware of clichés in this way, you should lessen the chance that they will appear in your writing.

PRETENTIOUS WORDS

Some people feel that they can improve their writing by using fancy and elevated words rather than more simple and natural words. They use artificial and stilted language that more often obscures their meaning than communicates it clearly.

Here are some unnatural-sounding sentences:

The football combatants left the gridiron.
His instructional technique is a very positive one.
At the counter, we inquired about the arrival time of the aircraft.
I observed the perpetrator of the robbery depart from the retail establishment.

The same thoughts can be expressed more clearly and effectively by using plain, natural language, as below:

The football players left the field.
He is a good teacher.
At the counter, we asked when the plane would arrive.
I saw the robber leave the store.

Following is a list of some other inflated words and the simple words that could replace them.

Inflated Words	Simpler Words
component	part
delineate	describe
facilitate	help
finalize	finish
initiate	begin
manifested	shown
subsequent to	after
to endeavor	to try
transmit	send

Practice

Cross out the two artificial words in each sentence. Then substitute clear, simple language for the artificial words.

Example Sally was ~~terminated~~ from her ~~employment~~.

<u>Sally was fired from her job.</u>

1. I do not comprehend that individual's behavior.

_____

2. He eradicated all the imperfections in his notes.

_____

3. She contemplated his utterance.

_____

4. The police officer halted the vehicle.

_____

5. Inez told the counselor about her vocational aspirations.

_____

WORDINESS

Wordiness—using more words than necessary to express a meaning—is often a sign of lazy or careless writing. Your readers may resent the extra time and energy they must spend when you have not done the work needed to make your writing direct and concise.

Here are examples of wordy sentences:

At this point in time in our country, the amount of violence seems to be increasing every day.

I called to the children repeatedly to get their attention, but my shouts did not get any response from them.

Omitting needless words improves these sentences:

Violence is increasing in our country.

I called to the children repeatedly, but they didn't respond.

Here is a list of some wordy expressions that could be reduced to single words.

Wordy Form	Short Form
a large number of	many
a period of a week	a week
arrive at an agreement	agree
at an earlier point in time	before
at the present time	now
big in size	big
due to the fact that	because
during the time that	while
five in number	five
for the reason that	because
good benefit	benefit
in every instance	always
in my own opinion	I think
in the event that	if
in the near future	soon
in this day and age	today
is able to	can
large in size	large
plan ahead for the future	plan
postponed until later	postponed
red in color	red
return back	return

Practice

Rewrite the following sentences, omitting needless words.

Example   Starting as of the month of June, I will be working at the store on a full-time basis.

As of June, I will be working at the store full time.

1. In light of the fact that I am a vegetarian, I don't eat meat.

2. On Tuesday of last week, I started going to college classes on a full-time basis.

   _____

3. On account of the fact that all my money is gone and I am broke, I can't go to the movies.

   _____

4. I repeated over and over again that I refused to go under any circumstances, no matter what.

   _____

5. Regardless of what I say, regardless of what I do, my father is annoyed by my words and behavior.

   _____

Review Test 1

Certain words are italicized in the following sentences. In the space provided, identify whether the words are slang (*S*), clichés (*C*), or pretentious words (*PW*). Then replace them with more effective words.

_____ 1. The sight of the car crash *sent chills down my spine.*

   _____

_____ 2. That garbage *receptacle* is *at maximum capacity.*

   _____

_____ 3. The *old geezer* kept his *choppers* in a glass on the nightstand.

   _____

_____ 4. The town *cheapskate* finally *cashed in his chips* and left all his money to charity.

   _____

_____ 5. I left work ten minutes early and made it home *in no time flat.*

   _____

_____ 6. Phyllis *lamented* her grandmother's *demise.*

   _____

_____ 7. The pitcher *hurled* the *sphere* toward the batter.

   _____

_____ 8. When she got her first paycheck, Joanne was *sitting on top of the world.*

   _____

_____   9. After studying for three hours, we *packed it in* and *cruised over* to the pizza parlor.

_____

_____   10. Last year's popular television star turned out to be *a flash in the pan.*

_____

Review Test 2

Rewrite the following sentences, omitting needless words.

1. Before I woke up this morning, while I was still asleep, I had a dream about an airline disaster in which a plane crashed.

_____

_____

2. Trish lifted up the empty suitcase, which had nothing in it, and tossed it onto the unmade bed covered with messy sheets and blankets.

_____

_____

3. While he glared at me with an unfriendly face, I just sat there silently, not saying a word.

_____

_____

4. Whereas some people feel that athletes are worth their salaries, I feel that the value of professional sports players in this country is vastly overrated moneywise.

_____

_____

5. I don't like reading the historical type of novel because this kind of book is much too long and, in addition, tends to be boring and uninteresting.

_____

_____

Reinforcement of the Skills

Part Two

INTRODUCTION

To reinforce the sentence skills presented in Part One, this part of the book—Part Two—provides mastery tests, combined mastery tests, proofreading tests, and editing tests. There are four *mastery tests* for each of the skills where errors occur most frequently and two *mastery tests* for each of the remaining skills. A series of *combined mastery tests* will measure your understanding of important related skills. *Editing* and *proofreading tests* offer practice in finding and correcting one kind of error in a brief passage. *Combined editing tests* then offer similar practice—except that each of these passages contains a variety of mistakes. Both the editing and the proofreading tests will help you become a skillful editor and proofreader. All too often, students can correct mistakes in practice sentences but are unable to do so in their own writing. They must learn to look carefully for sentence-skills errors and to make close checking a habit.

Appendix C at the end of the book provides progress charts that will help you keep track of your performance on these tests.

Mastery Tests

Mastery Test I

Draw one line under the subjects and two lines under the verbs. Cross out prepositional phrases as necessary to help find subjects. (Be sure to underline all the parts of a verb. Also, remember that you may find more than one subject and one verb in a sentence.)

1. My cat sleeps on the radiator.
2. An opened bag of lemon cookies hung over the edge of the shelf.
3. Margie and Paul walked hand in hand into the haunted house.
4. Those early Beatles records have become collectors' items.
5. Twenty people crammed themselves into the tiny elevator.
6. The truck driver got out his jumper cables and attached them to the battery of my car.
7. The man in the gorilla suit is my brother.
8. Vince always watches football on television but almost never goes to a game.
9. Unable to find his parents in the supermarket, Billy sat down and cried.
10. She opened the book, placed her finger at the top of the page, and began to speed-read.

Score: Number correct _____ × 10 = _____%

SUBJECTS AND VERBS

 Mastery Test 2

Draw one line under the subjects and two lines under the verbs. Cross out prepositional phrases as necessary to help find subjects. (Be sure to underline all the parts of a verb. Also, remember that you may find more than one subject and one verb in a sentence.)

1. Nancy burned her arm on the charcoal grill.
2. I always keep a first-aid kit in the trunk of my car.
3. He has been looking for that book for at least a week.
4. The new office manager was hired on Tuesday and fired on Wednesday.
5. My grandfather is often troubled by arthritis.
6. Cheryl and her sister found a ten-dollar bill in the wastebasket.
7. Fred ran across the porch and tripped on a loose board.
8. Those violent cartoons on Saturday-morning television are too scary for small children.
9. All the leftover Christmas decorations just went on sale at half price.
10. Bonnie and Clyde strode into the bank, waved their guns, and told everyone to lie down on the floor.

Score: Number correct _____ × 10 = _____%

SUBJECTS AND VERBS

 Mastery Test 3

Draw one line under the subjects and two lines under the verbs. Cross out prepositional phrases as necessary to help find subjects. (Be sure to underline all the
parts of a verb. Also, remember that you may find more than one subject and
one verb in a sentence.)

1. Tom reads the sports pages every morning.
2. The name of that woman just flew out of my head.
3. Our dog whined pitifully during the violent thunderstorm.
4. That screen has at least twenty holes and needs to be replaced.
5. Her problems are starting to sound like TV reruns.
6. Three copies of that book have been stolen from the library.
7. The little girl with pigtails did graceful cartwheels in the yard.
8. My sixth-grade teacher never could understand my questions.
9. We bought a broken floor lamp at our neighbor's garage sale and then could
   not decide what to do with it.
10. The mud slides, flooded roads, and washed-out bridges were caused by last
    week's heavy rains.

Score: Number correct _____ × 10 = _____%

SUBJECTS AND VERBS

 ### Mastery Test 4

Draw one line under the subjects and two lines under the verbs. Cross out prepositional phrases as necessary to help find subjects. (Be sure to underline all the parts of a verb. Also, remember that you may find more than one subject and one verb in a sentence.)

1. A low whistle suddenly pierced the silence.
2. Liz had spread her beach towel over the hot sand.
3. At the health food bar, Bob was sipping a strawberry-coconut milk shake.
4. Our old car has been repaired only three times in the last four years.
5. Annabelle's skin turned bright orange from the indoor tanning lotion.
6. Marsha and Ann begged their parents for permission to go to the rock concert.
7. The officer dismounted his motorcycle, walked over to me, and asked for my license and registration.
8. Bananas, skim milk, and bran buds were the ingredients in the breakfast drink.
9. I listened to all the candidate's promises but did not believe a single one.
10. A doctor and nurse walked into the room, pulled down Mike's covers, and ordered him to roll over.

Score: Number correct _____ × 10 = _____%

SENTENCE FRAGMENTS

Mastery Test 1

Each word group in the student paragraph below is numbered. In the space provided, write *C* if a word group is a complete sentence; write *frag* if it is a fragment. You will find ten fragments in the paragraph.

1. _____
2. _____
3. _____
4. _____
5. _____
6. _____
7. _____
8. _____
9. _____
10. _____
11. _____
12. _____
13. _____
14. _____
15. _____
16. _____
17. _____
18. _____
19. _____
20. _____

¹One of my favorite dishes to cook and eat is chili. ²The hotter the better. ³First, I chop onion, garlic, and sweet red and green peppers into small cubes. ⁴While I fry the vegetables in one pan. ⁵I brown some lean ground beef in another pan. ⁶Then combine the two mixtures. ⁷And add a can of shiny red kidney beans. ⁸Next, I decide what kind of seasonings to use. ⁹In addition to chili powder, hot pepper flakes, and Tabasco sauce. ¹⁰I sometimes add unusual ingredients. ¹¹Like molasses, cinnamon, chocolate, beer, red wine, or raisins. ¹²Stirring the bubbling pot and inhaling the spicy aromas. ¹³I occasionally taste the mixture to make sure it's good. ¹⁴I cook the chili over a low flame for as long as possible. ¹⁵To give the flavors time to mellow and blend together. ¹⁶Also, longer cooking time produces spicier chili. ¹⁷My chili has been known to burn people's tongues and cause beads of perspiration to form on their brows. ¹⁸And has made friends reach desperately for a glass of water. ¹⁹However, no one has ever complained. ²⁰Or forgotten to ask for a second helping.

Score: Number correct _____ × 5 = _____%

SENTENCE FRAGMENTS

 ## Mastery Test 2

Underline the fragment in each item. Then make whatever changes are needed to turn the fragment into a sentence.

Example   In grade school, I didn't want to wear glasses. ~~And~~ $\overset{a}{A}$nd avoided having to get them by memorizing the Snellen eye chart.

1. Nita's sons kept opening and closing the refrigerator door. To see just when the little light inside went out.

2. Even though there are a million pigeons in the city. You never see a baby pigeon. It makes you wonder where they are hiding out.

3. Frank likes to get to work early. And spread papers all over his desk. Then he looks too busy to be given any more work.

4. Brenda's doctor warned her to cut out sweets. Especially ice cream and candy.

5. Dragging her feet in the paper slippers. The patient shuffled along the corridor. She hugged the wall closely as nurses and visitors bustled past her.

6. The children ignored the sign. That the lifeguard had posted. They raced around on the slick cement bordering the pool.

7. Pete flunked out of college. After only two semesters. The only thing he could pass was a football.

8. My neighbors' dog likes to borrow things. Today, I saw him trotting away from my back steps. Carrying one of my gardening shoes in his mouth.

9. Since cooking with a small toaster oven saves energy. I bought one to use for small meals and snacks.

10. My cousin sends me funny cards. Such as the one with a picture of a lion hanging on to a parachute. It says, ''Just thought I'd drop you a lion.''

Score: Number correct _____ × 10 = _____%

SENTENCE FRAGMENTS

Mastery Test 3

Underline the fragment in each item. Then make whatever changes are needed to turn the fragment into a sentence.

1. As Robert twisted the front doorknob. It came off in his hand. He regretted the day he had bought the house as a "do-it-yourself special."

2. Large, spiky plants called *Spanish spears* bordered the path. The leaves brushed against my legs. And left little slash marks on my ankles.

3. Tim stockpiles canned and dried foods in his basement. In case of emergency. Some of his Campbell's soup is eight years old.

4. At the amusement park, we piled into a boat shaped like a hollowed-out log. Then, gripping the boat's sides and screaming in fear. We plunged through clouds of spray down a water-filled chute.

5. At the lumberyard, Clarence loaded his compact car. With ten-foot planks of raw pine. The car's open hatchback bounced and vibrated as he drove away.

6. Before the newly painted parking stripes had dried. Cars had begun driving over them. As a result, the lot was crisscrossed with pale white lines.

7. My father used to take me to ball games. He would always bring along a newspaper. To read between innings.

8. When Vince goes on vacation, he fills the bathtub with an inch of water. Then puts his houseplants in the tub. This way, they don't die of thirst.

9. Terry carries her portable tape player everywhere she goes. For example, to the bookstore. She can't survive for ten minutes without her favorite songs.

10. The perfect shell glittered on the ocean bottom. The diver lifted it off the sand. And placed it in the bag hanging from his shoulder.

Score: Number correct _____ × 10 = _____%

SENTENCE FRAGMENTS

 Mastery Test 4

Underline and then correct the ten fragments in the following passage.

This summer, I discovered that nature offers some surprises to people. Who take the time to look and listen. After I began an exercise program of walking quickly a half hour a day. I soon slowed down because the world around me was so interesting. For one thing, becoming aware of the richness of the bird and animal life around me. I saw a robin with strands of newspaper in his mouth. And realized it was building a nest in a nearby tree. A family of quail exploded from hiding as I skirted a brushy field. I began to connect the bird songs I heard with individual birds. For instance, I now know the lonely call of a mourning dove. And the happy buzz of a chickadee. After it rained. I discovered that creatures I have never seen live in my neighborhood. In the mud beside my walking paths were various tracks. Among them, paws, hooves, and scaly feet. I also found that little dramas were taking place all the time. And that there are some grim moments in nature. I saw a swarm of maggots covering a dead mouse. I also came upon a fat snake spread across the path. I prodded it with a stick. To see if it would move. It shocked me by coughing up an entire frog. My walks have taught me that there is a great deal to discover. When I open my eyes and ears.

Score: Number correct _____ × 10 = _____%

RUN-ONS

Mastery Test I

In the spaces provided, write *R-O* beside run-on sentences and *C* for sentences that are punctuated correctly. Some of the run-ons have no punctuation between the two complete thoughts; others have only a comma.

Correct each run-on by using (1) a period and a capital letter, (2) a comma and a joining word, or (3) a semicolon. Do not use the same method of correction in each sentence.

Examples

___R-O___ I applied for the job, ^*but* I never got called in for an interview.

___R-O___ Carla's toothache is getting worse, *S* she should go to a dentist soon.

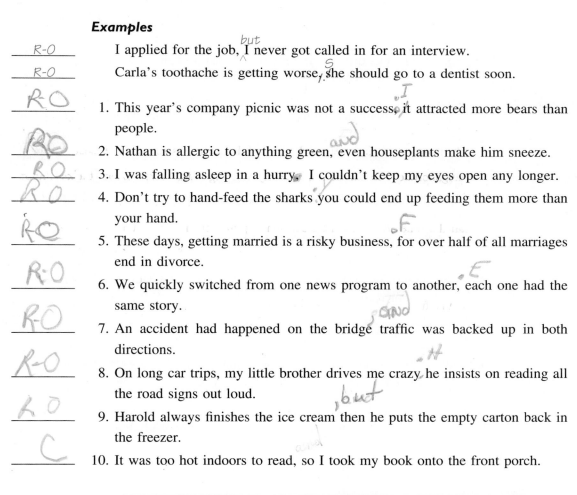

___R O___ 1. This year's company picnic was not a success, *.I* it attracted more bears than people.

___R O___ 2. Nathan is allergic to anything green, *and* even houseplants make him sneeze.

___R O___ 3. I was falling asleep in a hurry, I couldn't keep my eyes open any longer.

___R O___ 4. Don't try to hand-feed the sharks *;* you could end up feeding them more than your hand.

___R O___ 5. These days, getting married is a risky business, *.F* for over half of all marriages end in divorce.

___R-O___ 6. We quickly switched from one news program to another, *.E* each one had the same story.

___R-O___ 7. An accident had happened on the bridge *;and* traffic was backed up in both directions.

___R-O___ 8. On long car trips, my little brother drives me crazy *.H* he insists on reading all the road signs out loud.

___R O___ 9. Harold always finishes the ice cream *,but* then he puts the empty carton back in the freezer.

___C___ 10. It was too hot indoors to read, so I took my book onto the front porch.

Score:	Number correct _____	× 10 =	_____%

RUN-ONS

 ## Mastery Test 2

Correct the run-on in each sentence by using subordination. Choose from among the following dependent words:

after	because	if	until
although	before	since	when
as	even though	unless	while

Example   The bus drivers are on strike, I had to walk to work today.

Because the bus drivers are on strike, I had to walk to work today.

1. I work for about two hours on my homework I then spend about an hour watching television.

   After I work for about two hours on my homework, I then spend about an hour watching TV

2. Sheets of heavy rain were pounding against my car windshield, I pulled over to the side of the road.

   Because ... windshield, I

3. A bus pulled away slowly from the curb an elderly woman ran after it, waving her hand for it to stop.

   While

4. Our apartment gets really cold at night the landlord refuses to turn up the heat.

   Although ... night, the

5. The little boy was struggling with the top of the candy bag, it suddenly tore open and spilled M&Ms all over the floor.

   As ... bag, it

Score: Number correct _____ × 20 = _____%

RUN-ONS

Mastery Test 3

In the spaces provided, write *R-O* for run-on sentences and *C* for sentences that are punctuated correctly. Some of the run-ons have no punctuation between the two complete thoughts; others have only a comma.

Correct each run-on by using (1) a period and capital letter, (2) a comma and a joining word, or (3) a semicolon. Do not use the same method of correction in each sentence.

___RO___   1. Stanley waited in the long bank line, every minute seemed like an hour.

___RO___   2. Vandals had stripped the abandoned Buick, then they set it on fire.

___RO___   3. The little boy stared at his empty cone there was a puddle of mint chocolate chips at his feet.

___RO___   4. Bored, Rita sat at her desk she made a necklace out of paper clips and a tepee out of pencils.

___C___   5. I made sure not to put any syrup in Herbie's sundae, for his mother had mentioned that he was allergic to chocolate.

___R-O___   6. Using a handkerchief, the detective picked up the telephone receiver he was being careful not to smudge the fingerprints.

___C___   7. Nick ordered metallic paint for his new Chevette, also he had a racing stripe painted along each side.

___RO___   8. Ray's horoscope for last Monday said he would rise to great heights, that was the day he began work as an elevator operator.

___C___   9. The line outside the movie theater was wrapped around the corner, so we walked along the line hoping to see someone we knew.

___RO___ 10. Lana tossed the trumpet case into the backseat, she had twenty minutes to get to rehearsal.

Score: Number correct _____ × 10 = _____%

RUN-ONS

 ## Mastery Test 4

Correct the run-on in each sentence by using subordination. Choose from among the following dependent words:

after	before	unless
although	even though	until
as	if	when
because	since	while

1. Flora carried heavy trays all day long her feet felt like hundred-pound lead weights.

   Since . . . . long, her

2. The young woman paced anxiously the laundry circled lazily in the dryer.

   anxiously, while the

3. The musician strummed his most popular song the crowd waved cigarette lighters and chanted the words along with him.

   When . . . . song, the

4. That man has a million-dollar company he prefers to wear a stained T-shirt and torn jeans.

   Even though that . . . company, he

5. I finished writing the paper for my English class I started reading and taking notes on a chapter in my psychology text.

   when I . . . class, I

Score: Number correct _____ × 20 = _____%

STANDARD ENGLISH VERBS

Mastery Test 1

Underline the correct words in the parentheses.

1. "Jim doesn't work," my father (claim, claims). "He just (push, pushes) pencils."
2. Because my engine (leak, leaks) oil, I (park, parks) my car in the street rather than in the driveway.
3. Perspiration (drip, dripped) off Tom's forehead as he (mix, mixed) sand into the new cement.
4. Every time our upstairs neighbor (do, does) his workout, we hear him grunt as he (lift, lifts) his barbells.
5. Elaine (were, was) so famished that she (swallow, swallowed) the mouthful of hamburger without chewing it.
6. Uncle Arthur, who (is, be) as bald as a grapefruit, buys every new hair-growing preparation he (have, has) heard about on television.
7. You (frighten, frightened) me to death a minute ago when I (turn, turned) around and saw you standing in the doorway.
8. Before Sharon (take, takes) a bath, she (unplug, unplugs) the phone.
9. Why is it that whenever I (drop, drops) my toast, it (fall, falls) on the buttered side?
10. I just (finish, finished) reading a horror story about some creatures from outer space who (invade, invades) earth disguised as video games.

Score: Number correct _____ × 5 = _____%

STANDARD ENGLISH VERBS

Mastery Test 2

Cross out the nonstandard verb form and write the correct form in the space provided.

seems   **Example**   The job offer seem too good to be true.

_____   1. Charlie break into a rash when he eats strawberries.

_____   2. It feel strange to get up when it is still dark out.

_____   3. Before he showed the movie, Carlos thread the film through the reels of the projector.

_____   4. The driver of the huge moving van do a double take as a tiny VW passed him on the turnpike.

_____   5. The bartender flattered my aunt when he ask her to prove she was of drinking age.

_____   6. As Vince strolled casually into the singles bar, he unbutton the top three buttons of his sports shirt.

_____   7. I intends to pay all my bills the minute I obtain some extra cash.

_____   8. He's so lazy that if opportunity knock, he'd say no one was at home.

_____   9. Whenever we see my sister and her family coming down the front walk, we pretends we aren't at home.

_____   10. Pete have an antique car that looks like an overturned bathtub.

Score: Number correct _____ × 10 = _____%

STANDARD ENGLISH VERBS

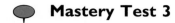 **Mastery Test 3**

Part 1:   Fill in each blank with the appropriate standard verb form of *be, have,* or *do* in the present or past tense.

A small town in New England _____ the best kind of dogcatcher—
1

the kind who _____ not want to hurt an animal. In this town, it
2

_____ the law to shoot on sight dogs that _____ running
3   4

loose. It turned out that the local police _____ not want to enforce this
5

law, so they asked the dogcatcher. He answered, "I _____ never shot
6

a dog in my life, and I _____ not going to start shooting them now."
7

Instead, he _____ seen on several occasions picking up stray dogs and
8

putting them in his car to return them to their homes. He _____ often
9

taken dogs to his own house until he can find their owners. This man _____
10

certainly worthy of being called a dog's best friend.

Part 2:   Fill in each blank with the appropriate form of the regular verb shown in parentheses. Use the present or past tense as needed.

Ed's mother always (*clip*) _____ the cents-off coupons from the
1

newspaper and (*save*) _____ them for him. Every time he (*visit*)
2

_____, his mother (*refuse*) _____ to let him go without
3   4

those little pieces of paper that advertise "12¢ off on 3 cans" or "Save 35¢ on large

economy size." Last week, she even (*hand*) _____ him some coupons
5

for dog food, although he has never (*own*) _____ a dog in his life.
6

Whenever he (*remember*) _____ to take some of her coupons to the
7

market, they have usually already (*expire*) _____. But he never (*turn*)
8

_____ them down, because he (*know*) _____ that his
9   10

mother's coupons are her way of saying, "I love you."

Score: Number correct _____ × 5 = _____%

STANDARD ENGLISH VERBS

Mastery Test 4

Part 1:   Fill in each blank with the appropriate standard verb form of *be, have,* or *do* in the present or past tense.

My grandmother _____ an eccentric character. She

_____ the idea that my name was Joe (which it _____
  2   3

not), and she insisted on calling me that. She _____ also a miser;
                                                                                4

she _____ not hide money, though, only candy. Under her bed
        5

_____ a suitcase full of spearmint leaves and licorice. Once, when she
        6

thought she _____ alone, I saw her count the candy pieces and then put
                                7

them back. I'll never forget one thing she _____. When I brought my
                                                                          8

girlfriend home for the first time, Grandma _____ sure we were married;
                                                                                  9

she kept asking us if we _____ any children yet.
                                              10

Part 2:   Fill in each blank with the appropriate form of the regular verb shown in parentheses. Use the present or past tense as needed.

A funny thing (*happen*) _____ recently at the Port Authority Bus
                                          1

Terminal in New York City. This terminal (*serve*) _____ 168,000 riders
                                                                                    2

every day, so commuters (*expect*) _____ all sorts of delays. In fact,
                                                            3

someone who (*ride*) _____ a bus can spend the first twenty minutes of
                              4

the trip just waiting in line to buy a ticket. To reward these long-suffering commuters,

the Port Authority (*ask*) _____ a sculptor to create a statue in their
                                    5

honor. When the statue (*arrive*) _____, it (*turn*) _____
                                                6   7

out to be three cast bronze commuters waiting in line. Then the statues were (*place*)

_____ in front of a gate, and a few commuters actually (*line*)
        8

_____ up behind the bronze figures. "The line (*seem*)
        9

_____ to be moving about as fast as usual," one commuter said.
        10

> *Score:*   Number correct _____ × 5 = _____%

IRREGULAR VERBS

Mastery Test 1

Underline the correct word in the parentheses.

1. My girlfriend and I (saw, seen) a bad car accident yesterday.
2. Tina (weared, wore) her favorite jeans until the patches were paper-thin.
3. Fran (hurt, hurted) her hand when she tried to open the mayonnaise jar.
4. That new Cutlass (cost, costed) more than I was willing to pay.
5. We should have (took, taken) the dog to the vet sooner.
6. Ralph has (drawed, drawn) blueprints for the cabin he hopes to build.
7. Sharon (sended, sent) Mike their divorce papers in the mail.
8. Ever since Betty (became, become) a supervisor, she hasn't talked to us.
9. Art (catched, caught) pneumonia when he went camping in the mountains.
10. I (knew, knowed) the answer—I just couldn't think of it.
11. I must have (drove, driven) around the development for half an hour looking for my brother's new house.
12. Within a month, the baby had (grew, grown) two inches and gained three pounds.
13. Before my grandfather died, he (gave, given) me his gold pocket watch and Army medals.
14. That gray-haired lumberjack has (arose, arisen) every day at dawn for the past fifty years.
15. When I heard that my car still hadn't been repaired, I (lost, losted) my temper.
16. As soon as you have (ate, eaten) all your ice cream, you may have some spinach.
17. Shelley (choose, chose) soft pink shag carpeting for her bedroom.
18. After raking the leaves, Julio (lay, laid) down under a tree and fell sound asleep.
19. The dummy (sang, sung) in a clear voice, but the ventriloquist's lips never moved.
20. Valerie had (rode, ridden) the roller coaster five times before she started complaining that everything was going around in circles.

> *Score:*   Number correct _____ × 5 = _____%

IRREGULAR VERBS

Mastery Test 2

Cross out the incorrect verb form. Write the correct form in the space provided.

_____ 1. Vince sweared loudly when the wasp stung him.

_____ 2. I bited down hard on a caramel and lost a filling.

_____ 3. As the car groaned and lurched from side to side, we realized that Lamont had never drove a manual shift before.

_____ 4. Because Fran had throwed away the sales slip, she couldn't take the frying pan back to Sears.

_____ 5. Though the runner slided head first, he was still tagged out at home plate.

_____ 6. Barry rung the bell for fifteen minutes and then decided that no one was home.

_____ 7. After I ran three miles in ninety-degree heat, I drunk a whole quart of iced tea.

_____ 8. Lenny hided his daughter's Christmas present so well that he couldn't find it.

_____ 9. If I had knew better, I would never have left my car door unlocked.

_____ 10. Maria broke her engagement but kept all the wedding presents.

Score: Number correct _____ × 10 = _____%

IRREGULAR VERBS

🖊 Mastery Test 3

Write in the space provided the correct form of the verb shown in the margin.

teach   1. When I was little, my parents _____ me how to find my way
home if I got lost.

lend   2. My best friend _____ me ten dollars so I could buy Dad a
birthday gift.

build   3. It took Andy eight months before his garage was finally _____.

wear   4. I used to fidget in class so much that I _____ a hole in my
trousers.

write   5. Susie has read every romance novel Barbara Cartland has _____.

fall   6. Frowning, the building inspector stood where the grocery store's sign had

_____.

see   7. We _____ the other car coming, but we couldn't stop in time.

send   8. Rita and Marvin _____ telegrams to their families saying that
they were eloping.

speak   9. I don't think he's heard a single word I have _____.

sleep   10. I must have _____ twelve hours before I finally woke up.

| Score: Number correct _____ × 10 = _____% |

IRREGULAR VERBS

Mastery Test 4

Write in the space provided the correct form of the verb shown in the margin.

burst   1. As soon as little Davy stuck a pin in the balloon, it _____.

go   2. When the alarm rang, Fred shut it off and _____ back to sleep.

bring   3. Yesterday, my cousin _____ over his entire baseball card collection.

hurt   4. You really _____ my feelings when you told me you didn't like my new outfit.

keep   5. Whenever she rode in a car, my mother _____ reminding the driver when a turn was coming up or a light was changing.

shake   6. After the collision, we were badly _____ up, but we had no broken bones.

spend   7. Stanley _____ a fortune on fishing equipment, but all he ever caught was a cold.

shrink   8. When she saw the giant tomato reaching for her in her dream, Amy _____ back in horror.

buy   9. Because stick shifts made her nervous, Cecilia _____ a car with automatic transmission.

stick   10. Why do I always get _____ with taking the car for its inspection?

Score: Number correct _____ × 10 = _____%

SUBJECT-VERB AGREEMENT

Mastery Test I

Underline the correct verb in the parentheses. Note that you will first have to determine the subject in each sentence. To help find subjects in certain sentences, you may find it helpful to cross out prepositional phrases.

1. The shelves in my bedroom closet (is, are) jammed with my sister's left-over belongings.
2. The toy trucks and Lincoln logs on the kitchen floor (belongs, belong) to my four-year-old niece.
3. Each of those custard pies (looks, look) gooey.
4. There (goes, go) Mario on his way to the bowling alley.
5. Annabelle and her sister (intends, intend) to compete in the next Miss America pageant.
6. Everyone in my family (plans, plan) to be at my parents' fiftieth wedding anniversary celebration.
7. Mary and her mother (is, are) going to Weight Watchers.
8. (Does, Do) your roof leak when it rains hard?
9. Either Elaine or Ray (is, are) working overtime this week.
10. Anything (is, are) likely to happen at one of Harold's parties.
11. The carton filled with roofing tiles (was, were) too heavy for me to lift.
12. Most of the game show hosts on television (looks, look) alike.
13. Not only loud talking but also loud clothes (gives, give) me a headache.
14. Here (is, are) the questions that will be on next week's assignment.
15. Sleeping in the doorway of the run-down building (was, were) two shopping-bag women.
16. All the letters on that poster (glows, glow) in the dark.
17. One of my sisters (plans, plan) to learn karate this summer.
18. Neither the plumber nor his helpers (works, work) on weekends.
19. When (is, are) your sister and her four children coming for a visit?
20. Everyone watching a cowboy movie (knows, know) who the good guys are.

Score: Number correct _____ × 5 = _____%

SUBJECT-VERB AGREEMENT

Mastery Test 2

In the space provided, write the correct form of the verb shown in the margin.

comes, come   1. All the wrinkles in a drip-dry shirt _____ out with a cool iron.

Is, Are   2. _____ all the bracelets Toshiko wears made of real gold?

does, do   3. Alcoholic beverages and allergy pills _____ not make a good combination.

was, were   4. No one _____ willing to take the blame for the spilled paint.

is, are   5. Under the sofa _____ a year's supply of dust.

was, were   6. Neither of the jackets I was looking for _____ in the closet.

sees, see   7. Phyllis and Eve _____ better with contact lenses than they saw with glasses.

is, are   8. Three of the books Sandy borrowed from the library _____ overdue.

was, were   9. A complete list of complaints and demands _____ read at the beginning of the tenants' meeting.

is, are   10. At the intersection of Pleasant Grove Lane and Valley View Road _____ the future location of the new shopping mall.

Score: Number correct _____ × 10 = _____%

SUBJECT-VERB AGREEMENT

Mastery Test 3

Cross out the incorrect form of the verb. In addition, underline the subject that goes with the verb. Then write the correct form of the verb in the space provided. Mark the one sentence that is correct with a *C*.

_____ 1. There is some unpleasant surprises among this month's bills.

_____ 2. Those piles of dirty laundry does not belong to me.

_____ 3. The lilies that we planted last year has grown to over six feet tall.

_____ 4. My counselor and my English instructor has agreed to write job recommendations for me.

_____ 5. Everyone in my neighborhood under the age of ten believe in Santa Claus.

_____ 6. Neither Gale nor Jerry plans to look for a job this summer.

_____ 7. Many gas stations on that highway stays open all night.

_____ 8. The mayor, along with the council members, are helping carry sandbags for flood control.

_____ 9. Lying across all the lanes of the highway were a jackknifed tractor-trailer.

_____ 10. Emil's parents, who have been seeing a marriage counselor, has decided to get a divorce.

> *Score:* Number correct _____ × 10 = _____%

SUBJECT-VERB AGREEMENT

Mastery Test 4

Cross out the incorrect form of the verb. In addition, underline the subject that goes with the verb. Then write the correct form of the verb in the space provided. Mark the one sentence that is correct with a *C*.

_____ 1. At the back of my mother's closet hang an old-fashioned muskrat fur coat with padded shoulders.

_____ 2. Anyone who punches in late more than once get an official warning from the personnel department.

_____ 3. Many pages of Naomi's diary contains R-rated material.

_____ 4. His toy soldiers and stamp collection is the only things that mean anything to him.

_____ 5. Leaning against the lamppost with his hands in his pockets were a dangerous-looking character.

_____ 6. When I was seven, being alone in the house and hearing the walls creak in the wind were the scariest things in my life.

_____ 7. Something seem odd about Uncle Neil this evening; he's remembering everything people are saying.

_____ 8. The plastic trash bags that never bursts on TV always break in my kitchen.

_____ 9. Thick white fur and black skin acts like a greenhouse, trapping heat and keeping a polar bear warm in the coldest weather.

_____ 10. When is Lew and Marian going to return the camping equipment they borrowed from us?

Score: Number correct _____ × 10 = _____%

CONSISTENT VERB TENSE

Mastery Test I

In each item, one verb must be changed so that it agrees in tense with the other verbs. Cross out the inconsistent verb and write the correct form in the space provided.

_____   1. Before the toothbrush was invented, people wipe their teeth with a rag that had chalk on it.

_____   2. When I drive to my 8:30 A.M. class, I always stopped at Ben's Bagel Bakery and get an onion bagel and cream cheese.

_____   3. I stepped on a horseshoe crab at the beach and discover it had sky-blue blood.

_____   4. Sally washes her permanent-press curtains and hung them on the rods while they were still wet.

_____   5. While Ray is dieting, he avoids submarine sandwiches, turned down Danish pastry, and passes up chocolate milk shakes.

_____   6. Leo enjoyed his first airplane flight, although the trip frightens him so much at first that he held on to the armrests.

_____   7. Whenever I smoked more than ten cigarettes a day, my eyes burn and my hands start to shake.

_____   8. Dawn reached for the economy brand of ketchup but finds that it cost as much as the national brand.

_____   9. For my sociology project, I went to a laundromat, observe the people there, and took notes on their behavior.

_____   10. Mrs. Frank sat wearily on her suitcase and stared off into space as the bus pulls into the station.

> *Score:*   Number correct _____ × 10 = _____%

CONSISTENT VERB TENSE

Mastery Test 2

In each item, one verb must be changed so that it agrees in tense with the other verbs. Cross out the inconsistent verb and write the correct form in the space provided.

_____ 1. After I got my promotion, my friends collect a hundred dollars, hired a hall, and threw a party in my honor.

_____ 2. Every year when Christmas comes and we trim the tree, we argued about who gets to put the silver angel at the top.

_____ 3. When the strike finally ends and the teachers went back to work, everyone rejoiced except the students.

_____ 4. Aunt Esther, who collects antique bottles, visits every garage sale in the neighborhood and poked around in people's attics for hidden treasures.

_____ 5. Leon decided to become a CIA agent, so he purchases a trench coat and began speaking in whispers whenever he was in public.

_____ 6. Everything was strangely peaceful on our street; not a person was in sight and not a car is moving.

_____ 7. When I wake up with a hangover, my head pounds, my eyes looked like road maps, and my teeth itch.

_____ 8. I was really nervous before my first date. I comb my hair a dozen times and looked in the mirror over and over to make sure my false eyelashes hadn't come unglued.

_____ 9. At Thanksgiving, we consume a twenty-pound turkey and three kinds of pie for dessert. Then, everyone collapsed on the floor and moans in agony.

_____ 10. My little brother borrowed my dad's toolbox so he could play home repairman. Then he fixes all the kitchen chairs by removing the screws that held them together.

Score: Number correct _____ × 10 = _____%

PRONOUN REFERENCE, AGREEMENT, AND POINT OF VIEW

🍭 **Mastery Test 1**

Underline the correct word in the parentheses.

1. Each of my daughters had to get (her, their) own lunch before leaving for school.
2. Bob needed his writing folder from the file cabinet, but he couldn't find (it, the folder).
3. In our office we have to work for six months before (we, you) get a raise.
4. Shoppers seem to like the new store because (you, they) rarely have to wait in line.
5. Although I liked my math teacher, I never really understood (it, math).
6. The bellhop discovered that someone had left (his, their) expensive suit in one of the hotel closets.
7. If you want to lose weight by exercising, (one, you) should begin with a sensible program of light workouts.
8. Every player on the Rangers' bench pulled on (his, their) helmet and jumped onto the ice as soon as the fight broke out.
9. John's neighbor just called to tell him that someone had just parked in (his, John's) spot.
10. Whenever I go to that post office, (they, the clerks) act as if I'm troubling them when I ask for stamps.

Score: Number correct _____ × 10 = _____%	

PRONOUN REFERENCE, AGREEMENT, AND POINT OF VIEW

Mastery Test 2

In the spaces provided, write *PE* for sentences that contain pronoun errors. Write *C* for the three sentences that use pronouns correctly. Then cross out each pronoun error and write a correction above it.

_____PE_____   ***Example***   Each of the boys explained ~~their~~ his project.

_____   1. Drew told his boss that he needed more time to finish the report.

_____   2. Each musician carried his or her own instrument onto the bus.

_____   3. In this course, people can sit in class for weeks before the instructor calls on them.

_____   4. Harold refuses to take his children to amusement parks because he doesn't like them.

_____   5. Everyone who parks on that street has had their car windows smashed.

_____   6. Carl says he has problems taking lecture notes because they all talk too fast.

_____   7. I hate standing in bakery lines where you have to take a number.

_____   8. "Anyone even suspected of cheating," warned the instructor at the boys' school, "forfeits his chance of passing this test."

_____   9. The ace pilots flew in formation over the crowded stadium, which was breathtaking.

_____   10. He avoids foods that might give you heartburn.

Score: Number correct _____ × 10 = _____%

PRONOUN REFERENCE, AGREEMENT, AND POINT OF VIEW

Mastery Test 3

In the spaces provided, write *PE* for sentences that contain pronoun errors. Write *C* for the two sentences that use pronouns correctly. Then cross out each pronoun error and write a correction above it.

_____ 1. Pam called Ellen to tell her that the instructor had read her paper to the class.

_____ 2. Danny's favorite Christmas toy is the robot you must wind up.

_____ 3. Neither contestant answered her bonus question about the Civil War battles correctly.

_____ 4. Jesse won't go for the job interview because he says they hire only college graduates.

_____ 5. If you send in your ticket order in advance, one can be sure of getting good seats.

_____ 6. With rain in the forecast, just about everybody in the stadium had an umbrella by their side.

_____ 7. The old man asked me to move my suitcase off the bench so he could sit on it.

_____ 8. Sally is really a generous person, but she keeps it hidden.

_____ 9. Whenever we take our children on a trip, we have to remember to bring snacks and toys to keep them occupied.

_____ 10. One of the men in our cab company just got their license revoked.

Score: Number correct _____ × 10 = _____%

PRONOUN REFERENCE, AGREEMENT, AND POINT OF VIEW

Mastery Test 4

In the spaces provided, write *PE* for sentences that contain pronoun errors. Write *C* for the sentence that uses pronouns correctly. Then cross out each pronoun error and write a correction above it.

_____   1. After Erica put the candles on her twin sons' birthday cakes, the dog ate them.

_____   2. None of the women in the class was eager to have their presentation put on videotape.

_____   3. The cheeseburgers we were served were so thick that you could hardly bite into them.

_____   4. The citizens protested at City Hall because they had raised taxes for the second year in a row.

_____   5. Tina knew Ed was still angry, but he wouldn't talk about it.

_____   6. Bill asked Spencer to try out his new motorbike.

_____   7. Carol was told to sign on the dotted line with her ballpoint pen, but she couldn't find it.

_____   8. Either the dog or the cat had spilled water from its dish all over the kitchen floor.

_____   9. Davy complained to his brother that he always got asked to walk the puppy.

_____   10. The grounder took a bad hop and bounced over the shortstop's head; this resulted in two runs scoring.

Score: Number correct _____ × 10 = _____%

PRONOUN TYPES

 Mastery Test I

Underline the correct word in the parentheses.

1. (Them, Those) doves nest in our cedar tree every year.
2. I suspect those dirty dishes are (yours, your's).
3. Horror movies don't scare my friends and (I, me) one bit.
4. The four boys finally had the house all to (themself, themselves).
5. Laura and (I, me) have been engaged for over three years.
6. (That, That there) woman is a helicopter pilot.
7. Without asking for permission, (he, him) and Nelson began cutting up the cake.
8. My new Buick got (its, it's) first scratch when I parked too close to a fence.
9. Bernie decided to buy (hisself, himself) a reward for sticking to his diet for one solid month.
10. The plumber showed Elaine and (I, me) the corroded lead pipes under the sink.
11. Terry's foul-shooting percentage isn't as good as (mine, mines).
12. Lonnie needs some sleep right now more than he needs (we, us).
13. Maria is taking more courses this semester than (I, me).
14. I don't understand how (this, this here) formula is used.
15. Does anyone know how (those, them) screens got torn?
16. Any friend of the Newtons is a friend of (our's, ours).
17. The team members (theirselves, themselves) are selling candy door to door.
18. I wish (those, those there) babies would stop crying.
19. When you're finished with the radio, return it to either Roberta or (I, me).
20. Those power tools are (hers, hers').

Score: Number correct _____ × 5 = _____%

PRONOUN TYPES

 Mastery Test 2

Cross out the incorrect pronoun in each sentence and write the correct form in the space provided.

_____ 1. If we offered Michael and she some money, would they accept it?

_____ 2. Every one of those there courses is filled.

_____ 3. We caught a lot more fish than them.

_____ 4. Them mountains in the distance are the Catskills.

_____ 5. Lenny hisself decided to confess to the robbery.

_____ 6. My dog and me usually eat our meals at the same time.

_____ 7. Our station wagon can hold more people than their's.

_____ 8. These here boots will hurt you until they're fully broken in.

_____ 9. This will be the first time in weeks we've had dinner by ourself.

_____ 10. Those garden tools of your's are getting rusty.

_____ 11. The sweaters Gloria knitted for Ron and I came out two sizes too small.

_____ 12. Every girl at the party wore jeans except Michelle and I.

_____ 13. The chief showed we rookie fire fighters what to do when an alarm sounded.

_____ 14. You can't park here because this here space is reserved for the supervisor.

_____ 15. Are these binoculars her's?

_____ 16. Brenda and him have nothing to discuss.

_____ 17. Of all my grandchildren, Chris and him wear me out the fastest.

_____ 18. Check the pockets of that there bathrobe for your glasses.

_____ 19. His bicycle had its' tires slashed overnight.

_____ 20. They've decided to repair the engine by themself.

Score: Number correct _____ × 5 = _____%

ADJECTIVES AND ADVERBS

Mastery Test I

Part I: Cross out the incorrect adjectival or adverbial form in each sentence. Then write the correct form in the space provided.

1. Clark runs good for a person who's thirty pounds overweight.

   _____

2. The car's brakes were acting strange, so the mechanic checked the fluid.

   _____

3. The girls sang beautiful, but the faulty microphones spoiled the show.

   _____

4. That actor's inexperience is real obvious.

   _____

5. Pam tiptoed careful past the guest room, not wanting to wake the sleeping children.

   _____

Part 2: Cross out the error in comparison in each sentence. Then write the correct form in the space provided.

6. The ad tried to prove which model's hair was the most glossiest by using a light meter.

   _____

7. My sister does more well on standardized tests than I do.

   _____

8. The longer Luis waited in line at the bank, the impatienter he got.

   _____

9. My awkwardest moment came when I tried to introduce my wife to my boss and forgot both their names.

   _____

10. This has been the most productivest session we've had yet.

   _____

Score: Number correct _____ × 10 = _____%

ADJECTIVES AND ADVERBS

⬤ Mastery Test 2

Part 1: Cross out the incorrect adjectival or adverbial form in each sentence. Then write the correct form in the space provided.

1. Sherry ate quick so she wouldn't miss the beginning of the early show.

   _____

2. Bruce decided he wasn't feeling good enough to bowl for the team.

   _____

3. I had a terrible high fever and a deep cough.

   _____

4. Vince makes friends easy because he is so sure of himself.

   _____

5. Paul gripped the handle tight and told them to let the mechanical bull loose.

   _____

Part 2: Add to each sentence the correct form of the word in the margin.

loud
6. During the spring thunderstorm, each booming clap of thunder was _____ than the preceding one.

tired
7. After doing fifty push-ups, I was _____ than I had been in years.

cheap
8. You'll need binoculars if you sit in the _____ seats in the stadium.

bad
9. The _____ clashes of the war occurred in the hot jungles of some small South Pacific islands.

little
10. This semester, I'm making _____ money at my after-school job, but I have more free time.

Score: Number correct _____ × 10 = _____%

MISPLACED MODIFIERS

Mastery Test I

Underline the misplaced word or words in each sentence. Then rewrite the sentence, placing related words together and making the meaning clear.

1. Leroy stepped on the worm without shoes on.

   _____

   _____

2. Scott purchased an expensive ticket from a scalper that turned out to be a fake.

   _____

   _____

3. I watched a woman board a bus wearing a dress that was several sizes too small.

   _____

   _____

4. A tray of doughnuts had been placed on the counter which smelled delicious.

   _____

   _____

5. The student tried to study in the noisy library with great concentration.

   _____

   _____

6. Craig was spotted by a teacher cheating on an examination.

   _____

   _____

7. I stayed at the cabin window watching the bear in my pajamas.

   _____

   _____

8. Tri Lee almost read the whole psychology assignment in two hours.

   _____

   _____

Score: Number correct _____ × 12.5 = _____%

MISPLACED MODIFIERS

Mastery Test 2

Underline the misplaced word or words in each sentence. Then rewrite the sentence, placing related words together and making the meaning clear.

1. I bought the used car from a friend with a bad exhaust system.

   _____

2. The news featured a handicapped man who played basketball in a wheelchair with no legs.

   _____

   _____

3. Our neighbor received a reward for returning the puppy to its family which had been missing for a week.

   _____

   _____

4. We saw a commercial for a company that promises to remodel any bathroom on television.

   _____

   _____

5. The hungry lions crept up behind the big game hunter who had fallen asleep without making a sound.

   _____

   _____

6. Marian watched her sons toss a baseball back and forth through her living room picture window.

   _____

   _____

7. We were notified that we had won a trip to Disney World by telegram.

   _____

8. I woke up this morning thinking I had a paper due in a cold sweat.

   _____

Score: Number correct _____ × 12.5 = _____%

DANGLING MODIFIERS

Mastery Test 1

Underline the dangling modifier in each sentence. Then rewrite the sentence, correcting the dangling modifier.

1. Being made of clear glass, the children kept bumping into the sliding door.

   _____

   _____

2. Still green, Helen put the tomato in sunlight to ripen.

   _____

3. Though somewhat warped, my grandfather still enjoys playing his record collection from the forties.

   _____

   _____

4. Having turned crispy and golden, I removed the chicken from the pan.

   _____

5. Bigger than ever, Aunt Clara predicted that this year's watermelon entry would win first prize at the county fair.

   _____

   _____

6. After changing the bait, the fish started to bite.

   _____

7. Coming home without a job, the comedies on television only made Helen feel depressed.

   _____

   _____

8. Having rehearsed his speech several times, Nick's presentation to the staff went smoothly.

   _____

   _____

Score: Number correct _____ × 12.5 = _____%

DANGLING MODIFIERS

Mastery Test 2

Underline the dangling modifier in each sentence. Then rewrite the sentence, correcting the dangling modifier.

1. Being too heavy to lift, Jo asked Bob to help her move the sofa.

   _____

2. Parched and dry, the ice-cold Coke soothed my throat.

   _____

3. Clutching a handful of silver and a portable TV set, our neighbor's watchdog surprised a burglar.

   _____

   _____

4. Living in a tent for two weeks, the camping trip made us appreciate hot showers and dry towels.

   _____

   _____

5. Thrown on the floor in a heap, we could not tell if the clothes were clean or dirty.

   _____

   _____

6. Afraid to look his father in the eye, Danny's head remained bowed.

   _____

7. Straining at the leash, I could see my neighbor's Great Dane getting ready for his walk.

   _____

   _____

8. While lying in bed with a cold, my cat jumped on me and curled up on my stomach.

   _____

   _____

Score: Number correct _____ × 12.5 = _____%

PARALLELISM

 Mastery Test I

The unbalanced part of each sentence is italicized. Rewrite this part so that it matches the rest of the sentence.

1. The bus squealed, grunted, and then *there was a hiss* as it shifted gears.

   _____

2. *With grace* and skillfully, Charles took aim and tossed a quarter into the basket at the toll booth.

   _____

3. Sue beats the blues by taking a hot bubble bath, cuddling up in a cozy quilt, and *eats her favorite snack.*

   _____

4. They didn't want a black-and-white set, but *a color set couldn't be afforded.*

   _____

5. We stayed at a country inn and dined on tender steak, baked Idaho potatoes, and *vegetables that were homegrown.*

   _____

6. When she learned she had won the gymnastic contest, Jackie gasped, screamed, and *all teammates were kissed by her.*

   _____

7. I avoid camping because I don't like to eat half-cooked food, sleep on rocks and twigs, or *the biting of insects.*

   _____

8. Make sure you have proofread your paper, stapled it, and *there are numbers on the pages* before you turn it in.

   _____

9. Unless you are either very noisy or *persist,* you won't wake me up.

   _____

10. Kerry uses his roller skates to get to school, to go to the store, and *for going to football practice.*

   _____

Score: Number correct _____ × 10 = _____%

PARALLELISM

 Mastery Test 2

Draw a line under the unbalanced part of each sentence. Then rewrite the unbalanced part so that it matches the other items in the sentence.

1. Stanley was so hungry he could have eaten a horse—roasted, broiled, or in a stew.

_____

2. In the last game, Julio had one single, a two-base hit, and one triple.

_____

3. Bill told us to help ourselves from the buffet and that we could fix our own drinks in the kitchen.

_____

4. My grandfather must have foods that are easy to cook and digestible.

_____

5. The awards show was filled with splashy dance numbers, film clips that were boring, and long-winded speeches.

_____

6. My driving instructor told me to keep both hands on the wheel, to use caution at all times, and don't take my eyes off the road.

_____

7. Nan sucked in her stomach, stopped breathing, and was trying to pull the zipper up again.

_____

8. Phil was so sick that all he was good for was lying in bed and to look up at the ceiling.

_____

9. When she gets very angry, Gale works off her anger by cleaning out her desk drawers, windows getting washed, or scrubbing the bathtub.

_____

10. The movie about the "mad slasher" was violent, it caused shock, and demeaning to women.

_____

Score: Number correct _____ × 10 = _____%

CAPITAL LETTERS

Mastery Test I

Cross out the two capitalization errors in each of the following sentences. Then write the corrections in the spaces provided.

_____   1. My Sister Tanya is studying french this semester.
_____

_____   2. Bill Cosby's comedy routine focused on his childhood in philadelphia and
_____   his exploits at Temple university.

_____   3. I ordered a Big Mac, and the counterperson said, ''you're at Burger king,
_____   you know.''

_____   4. Alice found two milky way wrappers and a peach pit in the shag rug.
_____

_____   5. The Frank Sinatra version of ''my way'' was blasting from the diner's
_____   jukebox.

_____   6. I traded in my kodak for an olympus camera with a telephoto lens.
_____

_____   7. As soon as mrs. Werner pulled into the gas station, the children headed for
_____   the pepsi machine.

_____   8. Rita always breaks her New year's resolutions long before Valentine's day.
_____

_____   9. Terry said, ''did you read the _National Enquirer_ story about the woman who
_____   was locked in an Attic for forty-seven years?''

_____   10. My little brother really annoyed dr. Thompson when he asked him if his
_____   Malpractice insurance was paid up.

Score: Number correct _____ × 5 = _____%

CAPITAL LETTERS

Mastery Test 2

Cross out the two capitalization errors in each of the following sentences. Then write the corrections in the spaces provided.

_____ 1. I fed my plants with miracle-gro so often that they died from overeating.

_____

_____ 2. It would take eighteen hours to drive to chicago, so Brad suggested that we stay one night in a Holiday inn.

_____

_____ 3. Every fourth of july, my dog howls when he hears the fireworks.

_____

_____ 4. "it's so dull in this town," said Joe, "that sometimes we go down to the shoprite store just to watch them restock the toothpaste."

_____

_____ 5. The tigers played well in Florida but started losing when they got back to detroit.

_____

_____ 6. To curb her impulse buying, Nancy cut up her visa and J. C. penney charge cards.

_____

_____ 7. During the argument, my brother accused me of needing scope and I told him to buy some right Guard.

_____

_____ 8. On his way to california, the hitchhiker rode in a moving van, a 1962 ford, and a 1993 Cadillac.

_____

_____ 9. Because I hadn't gotten the new *TV guide,* I didn't know whether *monday Night at the Movies* would be worth watching.

_____

_____ 10. The red Cross poster urged, "have a heart and give blood."

_____

Score: Number correct _____ × 5 = _____%

CAPITAL LETTERS

Mastery Test 3

Cross out the two capitalization errors in each of the following sentences. Then write the corrections in the spaces provided.

_____
_____
1. ''with friends like you, George,'' said Pat, ''a person doesn't need Enemies.''

_____
_____
2. Every payday, we treat ourselves to dinner at a Steak house on baltimore Pike.

_____
_____
3. Bill bought three Lottery tickets and a pack of gum at marv's News.

_____
_____
4. When my Aunt was pregnant, she craved raw green Peppers sprinkled with salt.

_____
_____
5. Next to my neighbor's german shepherd, my toy poodle looks like a Mosquito.

_____
_____
6. Every time I buy a box of wheat thins, the price goes up three cents.

_____
_____
7. Kelly almost fell over backwards trying to see the top of the world trade Center.

_____
_____
8. When my issue of _time_ arrives, i turn to the ''People'' section first.

_____
_____
9. An infielder for the terrible New York mets team of 1962 once hit a Triple and was called out because he forgot to touch first base.

_____
_____
10. The prentices, who live in the next Apartment, have a new baby that cries all the time.

_____

Score: Number correct _____ × 5 = _____%

CAPITAL LETTERS

Mastery Test 4

Cross out the two capitalization errors in each of the following sentences. Then write the corrections in the spaces provided.

_____ 1. Maxine begins classes at the university of miami this fall.
_____

_____ 2. My Grandmother starts buying Christmas presents in august.
_____

_____ 3. The press conference was carried live on all three Networks the evening
_____   before thanksgiving.

_____ 4. The disk jockey promised to play a complete side of the Beatles' album *abbey*
_____   *road* after the commercial.

_____ 5. The history professor announced that there would be a quiz on Friday about
_____   the revolutionary war.

_____ 6. "I've just gotten a request," said the disk jockey, "to play some elton john
_____   for the night crew at McNeil Industries."

_____ 7. I suddenly realized my lunch consisted of an english muffin, swiss cheese,
_____   and German potato salad.

_____ 8. Last Summer, we drove to San Francisco in our chevy van.
_____

_____ 9. A tractor-trailer loaded with Chemicals had flipped over at the intersection
_____   of Oakdale and Cherry streets.

_____ 10. I ordered two corned beef sandwiches and a pound of Cole slaw from the
_____   dee-lish Delicatessen.

Score: Number correct _____ × 5 = _____%

NUMBERS AND ABBREVIATIONS

Mastery Test I

Cross out the mistake in numbers or abbreviations in each sentence and correct it in the space provided.

_____ 1. *Consumer Reports* rated 2 of twelve brands of bacon it tested as "unacceptable."

_____ 2. When the air cond. broke down, the supermarket employees packed shaved ice around the dairy products.

_____ 3. After her husband died in eighteen sixty-one, Queen Victoria went into mourning for twenty-five years.

_____ 4. One pg. of the science textbook showed the stone tools of prehistoric people.

_____ 5. I managed to fit the entire contents of my apt. into the back of my brother's station wagon.

_____ 6. The team of six bank robbers got away with less than 1,000 dollars.

_____ 7. The telephone book lists one hundred and nine Richard Browns and 41 Dick Browns.

_____ 8. The six of us left Cleveland in a camper and headed for Daytona Beach, Fla.

_____ 9. On page 122 of the tax guide is a sample form showing a typical joint return filed by a couple with 4 dependents.

_____ 10. By 9:30, every student in my ten o'clock psychology class was already in the examination rm.

Score: Number correct _____ × 10 = _____%

NUMBERS AND ABBREVIATIONS

Mastery Test 2

Cross out the mistake in numbers or abbreviations in each sentence and correct it in the space provided. Mark the one sentence that is correct with a *C*.

_____ 1. As soon as Ginny finishes 6 months of work, she will get one week's paid vacation.

_____ 2. Tonight, I have to read two chaps. in my English textbook.

_____ 3. The new puppy chewed the wooden legs on our dining rm. chairs.

_____ 4. Sherry answered 16 of the twenty test questions correctly.

_____ 5. There's a smudge on page seventy-three that looks like chocolate syrup and one on page 90 that looks like coffee.

_____ 6. The Pres. waved to the crowd as he left on the flight to California.

_____ 7. When the astronauts landed on the moon in nineteen sixty-nine, they had traveled over 244,000 miles.

_____ 8. If I go without a cigarette for several hrs., I begin to feel nervous.

_____ 9. Half of all the people in the United States live in just eight of the fifty states.

_____ 10. The flight from San Juan, Puerto Rico, to N. Y. was delayed for over three hours.

Score: Number correct _____ × 10 = _____%

END MARKS

 ## Mastery Test I

Add a period, question mark, or exclamation point, as needed, to each of the following sentences.

Note: End marks always go *inside* the quotation marks that appear in some sentences.

1. Andy wondered if he would look better if he shaved off his beard
2. ''My hand's as swollen as a baseball glove,'' moaned Kelly
3. Suddenly, someone yelled, ''Get off that wet cement ''
4. During the electrical storm, the nervous mother asked all her children to put on their rubber sneakers
5. When Rob woke up, his tongue felt as though it were wearing a wooly sock
6. ''How many people here believe in ESP?'' the speaker asked
7. If I pay for the gas, will you do all the driving
8. Hurry, grab the fire extinguisher
9. Florence slammed the phone down and yelled, ''Don't call me again ''
10. Audrey asked, ''Is the dinosaur the biggest animal that ever lived ''
11. Sylvia wondered if she would ever see Sam again
12. On a bet, Bruce ate a shot glass full of horseradish
13. I yelled as my spoon touched something squishy in the coffee cup
14. The TV evangelist exclaimed to his audience, ''If you've been born again, raise your hand ''
15. Why does the same pair of jeans cost more in the women's department than in the men's
16. Do snakes really shed their skins all in one piece
17. Would someone give me a hand with this window
18. Three different people have asked me for a match already
19. Will you please save my seat for me
20. In the movies, it seems that only two minutes after a woman goes into labor, someone shouts, ''It's a boy ''

Score: Number correct _____ × 5 = _____%

END MARKS

 ## Mastery Test 2

Add a period, question mark, or exclamation point, as needed, to each of the following sentences.

Note: End marks always go *inside* the quotation marks that appear in some sentences.

1. The coach screamed ''That runner was safe ''
2. ''For someone so wrapped up in himself,'' Dora snapped, ''Steve makes a pretty small package ''
3. The stereo ad asked, ''Are you ready for wall-to-wall sound ''
4. When she goes out, Edith worries about what her children are watching on TV
5. The teenagers in the back row threw Milk Duds at the people in front
6. The headline in the yellowing old newspaper read, ''Horsecar Strikes Pedestrian ''
7. ''I can't believe you gave my favorite jacket to the Salvation Army '' Nick yelled.
8. When did our instructor say the paper would be due
9. Please fill up the tank and check the oil
10. It's strange that no one has ever told Vince that he needs to use mouthwash
11. Ken put the money in a safe place and then couldn't find it
12. Little Debbie asked her mother, ''If I don't keep my dentist appointment, will my teeth fall out ''
13. I was told I could pick up this suit Wednesday afternoon
14. Can we stop for lunch soon
15. The zookeeper yelled, ''Close the cage ''
16. He wondered whether the mail had arrived yet
17. I wish my boss would stop looking over my shoulder and asking when the project will be done
18. Fred remarked, ''Can this be the same hotel we stayed at five years ago ''
19. Jan, expecting the glass door to open automatically, got a painful surprise
20. He is afraid of only two things: snakes and the IRS

Score: Number correct _____ × 5 = _____%

APOSTROPHE

 Mastery Test 1

Cross out the word in each sentence that needs an apostrophe. Then write the word correctly in the space provided.

1. She is nobodys fool when money is involved.

   _____

2. The ducks beak had been taped shut.

   _____

3. That was Ronnies third car accident this year.

   _____

4. A hawks wings beat faster when it is about to dive at its prey.

   _____

5. The safecrackers eyes gleamed as the lock clicked open.

   _____

6. My dentists worst habit is asking me questions when my mouth is stuffed with cotton.

   _____

7. Its been estimated that the typical American consumes one hundred pounds of white sugar a year.

   _____

8. When the insurance companys check arrived, I ran to the bank.

   _____

9. The doctors waiting room was stuffy and crowded.

   _____

10. The resorts policy is to give a partial refund if the weather is poor.

    _____

Score: Number correct _____ × 10 = _____%

APOSTROPHE

Mastery Test 2

In the space provided under each sentence, add the one apostrophe needed and explain why the other word ending in *s* is a simple plural.

Example   Joans hair began to fall out two days after she dyed it.

Joans: _____ *Joan's, meaning "the hair belonging to Joan"* _____

days: _____ *simple plural meaning more than one day* _____

1. The elderly womans long, knotty fingers show a lifetime of wear.

   womans: _____

   fingers: _____

2. Studies show that a rooms color can affect our moods.

   rooms: _____

   moods: _____

3. Kens homework is not yet done because of the two football games on TV today.

   Kens: _____

   games: _____

4. The raccoons tracks led from a hole in the backyard fence to our garbage can.

   raccoons: _____

   tracks: _____

5. In my mothers picture collection, my grandparents posed against a backdrop of painted scenery.

   mothers: _____

   grandparents: _____

Score: Number correct _____ × 10 = _____%

APOSTROPHE

Mastery Test 3

In each sentence two apostrophes are missing or are used incorrectly. Cross out the two errors and write the corrections in the spaces provided.

1. I cant understand why our neighbors disturb the evenings quiet with their electronic bug zapper.

   _____   _____

2. My sisters habit of tying up the phone for hours' drives my parents crazy.

   _____   _____

3. I wonder whos responsible for making childrens clothes so expensive.

   _____   _____

4. The gunslinger barged through the saloons swinging door's.

   _____   _____

5. Qualifying for the Olympic's is the amateur athletes crowning achievement.

   _____   _____

6. The stores photographer used a variety of antics' to get the children to smile.

   _____   _____

7. While her mother paid the clerk, Michelle wandered over to the supermarkets gum-ball machine's.

   _____   _____

8. The suspect couldnt have committed the crime, for his shoe size did not match the burglars footprints.

   _____   _____

9. At twelve oclock, the factorys whistle blows, and the shift changes.

   _____   _____

10. Dewdrops' glistened on the bicycles vinyl seat.

    _____   _____

Score: Number correct _____ × 5 = _____%

APOSTROPHE

 Mastery Test 4

In each sentence two apostrophes are missing or are used incorrectly. Cross out the two errors and write the corrections in the spaces provided.

1. Sandys brown eyes filled with tears as she listened to Jims explanation.

   _____   _____

2. My sons toys were strewn all over the Greenfields driveway.

   _____   _____

3. Mikes Saint Bernard has a custom-built shelter as big as a childs playhouse.

   _____   _____

4. Monday mornings *Press* omitted several popular comic strip's.

   _____   _____

5. Stans behavior at the Bradleys party surprised everyone.

   _____   _____

6. When the jurys verdict was announced, both defendants' looked stunned.

   _____   _____

7. When Franks phone bill comes in, hes likely to rip it into little pieces.

   _____   _____

8. Helens mistake was to trust the strength of the fraying hammock in her fathers yard.

   _____   _____

9. Two fire fighter's rushed into the burning building to rescue the familys pet dog.

   _____   _____

10. When she cant handle her two toddlers, Madge takes them to her mothers house.

    _____   _____

Score: Number correct _____ × 5 = _____%

QUOTATION MARKS

Mastery Test 1

Place quotation marks or underlines where needed.

1. The lifeguard shouted, No ball playing in the water!

2. Sally insisted in a loud voice, I'm not really overweight, I'm just six inches too short.

3. If today were a blackboard, Barry said, I'd erase it and start over.

4. In her diet book, Miss Piggy advises, Never eat anything at one sitting that you can't lift.

5. Something is wrong with my radio, Fred said to the mechanic. It won't work unless the windshield wipers are turned on.

6. You creep! Zella yelled to the tailgater behind her. I've got small children in this car!

7. The first chapter in the book How to Train Your Dog is entitled Training the Master.

8. Why do I skydive? the elderly man repeated to the news reporter. Well, I guess because I'm terrible at checkers.

9. I'll only warn you this time, said the officer. But next time you'd better drive more slowly or be prepared to open your wallet.

10. When I was a child, said Cindy, I thought that if you swallowed a watermelon seed, a watermelon would grow in your stomach.

Score: Number correct _____ × 10 = _____%

QUOTATION MARKS

Mastery Test 2

Place quotation marks or underlines where needed.

1. Darlene said, To err is human. That's why I do it so much.

2. At breakfast, Terry said, I'll trade the sports section and a piece of bacon for the comics.

3. Danny's second-grade teacher asked, How many months have twenty-eight days?

4. All twelve of them, Danny answered.

5. And the winner, announced the host, is Miss Mexico!

6. I'm not hungry, said Bertha. I'm starved.

7. The bumper sticker on the car ahead of us read, If you get any closer, introduce yourself.

8. Where are you going? asked Carrie sarcastically. A Halloween party?

9. If you guys don't start hustling, warned the coach, you're going to see football scholarships start vanishing into thin air.

10. The episode entitled Finding a Voice on the television series Nova describes how some people with cerebral palsy are now speaking through the use of computers that have artificial voices.

Score: Number correct _____ × 10 = _____%	

QUOTATION MARKS

🖋 Mastery Test 3

Place quotation marks or underlines where needed.

1. Minds are like parachutes, the teacher said. They work only when they're open.

2. If you refrigerate candles before using them, said the household hints book, they'll last longer and won't drip.

3. In Psychology Today magazine, the author of the article called The Techniques of the Artful Salesman suggests that successful salespeople almost hypnotize their customers.

4. When I wake up in the morning, said Fran, I sometimes have dream hangovers. For several hours, I can't shake the emotions I felt in my dream.

5. My insomnia is terrible these days, said Stan. I can't even sleep on the job.

6. I turned the radio up when Elvis Presley's classic song Blue Suede Shoes came on.

7. I read a horror story entitled Children of the Kingdom, in which giant slugs that eat people live in the sewers of New York City.

8. As the miser was taking a walk, a robber pressed a gun into his ribs and demanded, Your money or your life!

9. Take my life, said the miser. I'm saving my money for my old age.

10. The sign on Carl's desk reads, In the rat race, only the rats win.

Score: Number correct _____ × 10 = _____%

QUOTATION MARKS

Mastery Test 4

Place quotation marks or underlines where needed.

1. When I saw Raiders of the Lost Ark, my father said, it reminded me of the old adventure serials we watched in the thirties and forties.

2. Before she asked her boss for a raise, Nadine said timidly, Are you in a good mood, Mr. Huff?

3. The newspaper headline read, Good Humor Man Slays Ten.

4. The driver leaned out and handed two dollars to the toll collector, saying, I'm paying for the car behind me, too.

5. Did you know, he said to the expectant mother, that it now costs $85,000 to raise a child to the age of eighteen?

6. The TV announcer warned, The latest figures indicate there will be a billion cars on the road by the year 2000. So if you want to cross the street, you'd better do it now.

7. My six-year-old nephew stared at me and asked, How did you break your kneecap with that big, heavy cast on your leg?

8. I never go back on my word, he promised. I might just go around it a little, though.

9. After Kay read a book called Chocolate: The Consuming Passion, she ran out and bought six Hershey bars.

10. Reassuring me that my diseased elm would recover, the tree surgeon said, Don't worry. Its bark is worse than its blight.

Score: Number correct _____ × 10 = _____%

COMMA

Mastery Test 1

Add commas where needed. Then refer to the box below and write, in the space provided, the letter of the comma rule that applies in each sentence.

a. Between items in a series	d. Between complete thoughts
b. After introductory material	e. With direct quotations
c. Around interrupters	f. With everyday material

1. Rita makes her studying more bearable by having plenty of Triscuits pretzels and peanut-filled M&Ms close by.

2. Because Jim is the company's top salesperson he receives special attention from the boss.

3. "You look different" said Lily. "Have you lost weight?"

4. My Uncle Al who is hard of hearing always asks me to repeat what I just said.

5. "I really appreciate the ride" the hitchhiker said. "A hundred cars must have passed me."

6. My little sister loves to ride on the back of my motorcycle but my parents worry about her falling off.

7. I have to pay $8,250 by June 30 1996 before I officially own my car.

8. Little Danny emptied his piggy bank and sorted the nickels dimes and quarters into three shiny piles.

9. Huddled under a large piece of plastic we waited out the rain delay in the ball game.

10. The vacationing boys slept in the car that night for they'd spent too much on meals and souvenirs.

Score: Number correct _____ × 10 = _____%

COMMA

 Mastery Test 2

Add commas where needed. Then refer to the box below and write, in the space provided, the letter of the comma rule that applies in each sentence.

a. Between items in a series	d. Between complete thoughts
b. After introductory material	e. With direct quotations
c. Around interrupters	

_____ 1. As the noisy jet flew directly overhead the framed photographs on the wall jumped and rattled.

_____ 2. Pete marinated the mild sweet purple-tinged onions in oil vinegar and parsley flakes.

_____ 3. Bill's college expenses and dormitory rent both increased this semester so he works nights at a pizza parlor.

_____ 4. The photo contest offered a prize for the best picture of a family pet a baby or a flower.

_____ 5. Boris a man I didn't trust had a smile as hard and cold as a car grille.

_____ 6. Trailing a cloud of choking cologne the teenage girls entered the school dance.

_____ 7. "I've decided to get married" Teresa announced.

_____ 8. Lisa stopped in her tracks turned around and screamed when she realized she was being followed.

_____ 9. Despite the two cheeseburgers already under his belt Mike ordered a fried chicken platter and a chocolate shake.

_____ 10. An industrious janitor heedless of the lecture still in progress began disconnecting the microphones.

Score: Number correct _____ × 10 = _____%

COMMA

 **Mastery Test 3**

Add commas where needed. Then refer to the box below and write, in the space provided, the letter of the comma rule that applies in each sentence.

a. Between items in a series	d. Between complete thoughts
b. After introductory material	e. With direct quotations
c. Around interrupters	f. With everyday material

_____ 1. My friend Tina lives at 333 Virginia Avenue Atlantic City.

_____ 2. I went to her house one night recently and the two of us watched television for several hours.

_____ 3. Tina who is always hungry suggested we go to Tony's Grill for a pizza.

_____ 4. Along with about a dozen other cars I parked in a tiny lot with a ''No Parking'' sign.

_____ 5. I believed foolishly enough that my car would be safe there.

_____ 6. We had our pizza left the restaurant and returned to the lot.

_____ 7. A 1975 Chevy and a tow truck were parked on the lot but my Honda and all the other cars had vanished.

_____ 8. After walking twenty blocks back to Tina's house I called the towing company.

_____ 9. A recorded voice said ''Come to 26 Texas Avenue tomorrow morning with seventy-five dollars in cash.''

_____ 10. Whenever Tina craves pizza I now buy a frozen pie at the local Seven-Eleven store.

Score: Number correct _____ × 10 = _____%

COMMA

 ## Mastery Test 4

Add commas where needed. Then refer to the box below and write, in the space provided, the letter of the comma rule that applies in each sentence.

---

a. Between items in a series	d. Between complete thoughts
b. After introductory material	e. With direct quotations
c. Around interrupters	

_____ 1. Matt's first car a 1960 Chevy Impala had enormous tail fins.

_____ 2. Fran called down from upstairs ''Could you turn the TV down?''

_____ 3. The broken-down farm housed a swaybacked horse a blind cow and two lame chickens.

_____ 4. In Phil's job as toll collector he takes quarters from over 5,500 drivers every day.

_____ 5. In the middle of the love scene two little boys in the audience began to giggle.

_____ 6. The combination of milk stains peanut butter splotches and jelly smears made the toddler's face look like a finger painting.

_____ 7. Though public transportation saves her money Dotty prefers driving to work.

_____ 8. ''Better to keep your mouth shut and be thought a fool'' my father always says ''than to open it and remove all doubt.''

_____ 9. The fried eggs as they sizzled in the rusty iron skillet began to turn red.

_____ 10. The road map must have been out of date for the highway it showed no longer existed.

Score: Number correct _____ × 10 = _____%

OTHER PUNCTUATION MARKS

Mastery Test 1

At the appropriate spot (or spots), insert the punctuation mark shown in the margin.

;   1. There are several ways to save money on your grocery bills for example, never go shopping on an empty stomach.

:   2. There are only two ways to get there hike or hitch a ride.

—   3. ''The cooking at this restaurant,'' said the dissatisfied customer, ''lacks just one thing good taste.''

-     4. Pete's over the shoulder catch brought the crowd to its feet.

( )   5. Call your local office of the IRS Internal Revenue Service if you think you're entitled to a refund.

—   6. Annabelle gave Harold back his engagement ring without the diamond.

:   7. That new ice cream place has the weirdest flavors blueberry cheesecake, pineapple, bubble gum, and Oreo cookie.

—   8. Some teenage boys there they go around the corner just stole that man's wallet.

-     9. I'm waiting for the day when someone invents low calorie junk food.

;   10. In a study, people were asked who in their family got the most smiles and touches 44 percent said the family pet.

Score: Number correct _____ × 10 = _____%

OTHER PUNCTUATION MARKS

 Mastery Test 2

Add colons, semicolons, dashes, hyphens, or parentheses as needed. Each sentence requires only one of the five kinds of punctuation marks.

1. It's impossible for two blue eyed parents to have a brown-eyed child.
2. People watch more television than most of us realize the average set is on for over six hours a day.
3. My aunt loves giving blow by blow accounts of all her operations.
4. Electrical storms, inflation, and my little brother's jokes these are the things that bother me the most.
5. My car was losing power I asked a gas station attendant to check the battery.
6. To cure hiccups, try one of the following methods put a paper bag over your head, hold your breath, or eat a teaspoon of sugar.
7. A portion of the sociology text pages 150–158 deals with the changing roles of women.
8. My mother likes to listen to talk shows she feels less lonely if there's a conversation going on.
9. Our math instructor said ''Standard units of measurement used to be set by parts of the body; for example, King Henry I of England defined a yard as the distance from his nose to his outstretched thumb.''
10. From my second row seat at the movies, I could count the leading lady's eyelashes.

Score: Number correct _____ × 10 = _____%

DICTIONARY USE

🕳 **Mastery Test 1**

Items 1–5: Use your dictionary to answer the following questions.

1. How many syllables are in the word *incongruous?* _____

2. Where is the primary accent in the word *culmination?* _____

3. In the word *periphery,* the *i* is pronounced like
   a. long *i.*
   b. short *i.*
   c. long *e.*
   d. short *e.*

4. In the word *acquiesce,* the *i* is pronounced like
   a. long *i.*
   b. short *i.*
   c. long *e.*
   d. short *e.*

5. In the word *apostasy,* the first *a* is pronounced like
   a. long *a.*
   b. short *a.*
   c. short *o.*
   d. schwa.

Items 6–10: There are five misspelled words in the following sentence. Cross out each misspelled word and write in the correct spelling in the spaces provided.

Altho there were legal suits filed against him, the mayer decided to run for reelection, but the citazens of our town were not anxous to give him a second oportunity at public office.

6. _____   8. _____   10. _____

7. _____   9. _____

Score: Number correct _____ × 10 = _____%

DICTIONARY USE

 **Mastery Test 2**

Items 1–5:   Use your dictionary to answer the following questions.

1. How many syllables are in the word *pandemonium?* _____

2. Where is the primary accent in the word *unremitting?* _____

3. In the word *expatriate,* the *i* is pronounced like a
   a. long *i.*
   b. short *i.*
   c. long *e.*
   d. short *e.*

4. In the word *recapitulate,* the *i* is pronounced like a
   a. long *i.*
   b. short *i.*
   c. long *e.*
   d. short *e.*

5. In the word *frivolous,* the first *o* is pronounced like a
   a. long *o.*
   b. short *o.*
   c. short *u.*
   d. schwa.

Items 6–10:   There are five misspelled words in the following sentences. Cross out each misspelled word and write the correct spelling in the spaces provided.

We regreted that we could not attend your anniversery celabration. Our station wagon broke down on the freeway, leaving us with no means of transpertation.

6. _____   8. _____   10. _____

7. _____   9. _____

Score: Number correct _____ × 10 = _____%

SPELLING IMPROVEMENT

🗨 Mastery Test I

Use the three spelling rules to spell the following words.

1. palate + able = _____
2. silly + est = _____
3. fate + ful = _____
4. drag + ing = _____
5. plan + er = _____
6. healthy + ly = _____
7. cause + ing = _____
8. prefer + ed = _____

Circle the correctly spelled plural in each pair.

9. chiefs   chievs   12. candys   candies
10. sandwichs   sandwiches   13. vetos   vetoes
11. yourselfs   yourselves   14. supplys   supplies

Circle the correctly spelled word (from the basic word list) in each pair.

15. compeny   company   18. oppertunity   opportunity
16. hieght   height   19. restarant   restaurant
17. lonliness   loneliness   20. importent   important

Score: Number correct _____ × 5 = _____%

SPELLING IMPROVEMENT

 Mastery Test 2

Use the three spelling rules to spell the following words.

1. drip   + ed   = _____

2. merry   + ment = _____

3. escape   + ing   = _____

4. expel   + ed   = _____

5. finance   + ing   = _____

6. accuse   + er   = _____

7. happy   + ness   = _____

8. spite   + ful   = _____

Circle the correctly spelled plural in each pair.

9. indexs	indexes	12. babies	babys
10. echos	echoes	13. lifes	lives
11. gifts	giftes	14. scratchs	scratches

Circle the correctly spelled word (from the basic word list) in each pair.

15. temorrow	tomorrow	18. straght	straight
16. truely	truly	19. ready	readdy
17. vegtable	vegetable	20. condition	conditshun

Score: Number correct _____ × 5 = _____%

OMITTED WORDS AND LETTERS

Mastery Test 1

Part 1:   In the spaces provided, write in the two short connecting words needed in each sentence. Use carets (∧) within the sentences to show where these words belong.

_____   1. Returning her car, Sarah found she'd left the keys the ignition.
_____

_____   2. Tony has superstitious habit of dribbling the ball exactly six times before he
_____   shoots free throw.

_____   3. Carefully, Joanne pasted small strips correction tape over each typing mis-
_____   take on page.

_____   4. I know easy way to get an A in that course—just agree with everything
_____   instructor says.

_____   5. Andy dreaded tests he would have to undergo even more than operation
_____   itself.

Part 2:   Add the two -*s* endings needed in each sentence.

_____   6. Marcy ate an entire jar of olive and left a pile of pit on the coffee table.
_____

_____   7. Shards of green glass glittered on the pavement where those teenager had
_____   smashed a whole six-pack of empty beer bottle.

_____   8. Our supermarket's deli section sells tray of party cold cut.
_____

_____   9. Eddie's tight-fitting new shoes have worn hole in all his sock.
_____

_____   10. Those heavy rainstorm have flattened all my tomato plant.
_____

Score: Number correct _____ × 5 = _____%

OMITTED WORDS AND LETTERS

Mastery Test 2

Part 1:   In the spaces provided, write in the two short connecting words needed in each sentence. Use carets (∧) within the sentences to show where these words belong.

_____   1. This weekend, we're going replace all the shingles that have fallen off roof.
_____

_____   2. My favorite snacks this restaurant are the crispy baked-potato skins the marinated mushrooms.
_____

_____   3. The eyes of woman on billboard seemed to follow me as I drove by.
_____

_____   4. When I sat down, three quarters fell out of pants pocket and rolled under sofa.
_____

_____   5. My pet turtles live in large, galvanized tin tub in garage.
_____

Part 2:   Add the two *-s* endings needed in each sentence.

_____   6. After I had read several horror book, I began listening for weird sound.
_____

_____   7. I love to eat exotic dessert, but my husband likes only vanilla ice cream cone.
_____

_____   8. All the neighbor comment on my mother's garden of roses and daffodil.
_____

_____   9. I slowed the car when I noticed a pair of kitchen chair that had been set out along with three garbage can.
_____

_____   10. The old man sold me two bag of cookie from a homemade stand in front of his house.
_____

> *Score:*   Number correct _____ × 5 = _____%

COMMONLY CONFUSED WORDS

Mastery Test I

For each sentence, underline the correct word in each set of parentheses.

1. When (you're, your) looking for the (right, write) career, it's helpful to talk to other people about their jobs.
2. Carol keeps a special (pair, pear) of (lose, loose) trousers with tough patches on the knees to wear while gardening.
3. (There, Their, They're) the (right, write) size, but these screws still don't fit.
4. "It's a matter of (principal, principle)," the editor said. "I won't print anything unless it's the (hole, whole) truth."
5. By twenty (passed, past) eight o'clock, I was (all ready, already) for my ten o'clock interview.
6. We went (through, threw) the entrance to the amusement park haunted house and were met by (to, too, two) scary-looking creatures.
7. We all (past, passed) the midterm exam, (accept, except) for the student who had shown up for only three classes.
8. I (can hardly, can't hardly) see (through, threw) my windshield, since it's covered with squashed bugs and grit.
9. (Weather, Whether) or not Duane (loses, looses) his license depends on the outcome of the court hearing.
10. The tragic (affect, effect) of one car's faulty (brakes, breaks) was a six-car pileup.

Score: Number correct _____ × 5 = _____%

COMMONLY CONFUSED WORDS

 Mastery Test 2

For each sentence, underline the correct word in each set of parentheses.

1. We were expected to (know, no) the (principals, principles) of photosynthesis for the biology test.
2. (You're, Your) the first professor to ask me to (right, write) a sixty-page term paper.
3. I took a (coarse, course) in speed-reading and can now read (to, too, two) books in the time it once took to read one.
4. "It's (all ready, already) eight o'clock, and nobody's (hear, here) yet," Fran complained.
5. I ate so much that I was (quiet, quite) full before (desert, dessert) arrived.
6. (Among, Between) the three of us, we (though, thought) we could scrape up enough money for a large pizza.
7. You (should of, should have) saved the last (peace, piece) of chicken for me.
8. At the back of my (cloths, clothes) closet, I discovered a (pair, pear) of old, mildewed sneakers.
9. (Whose, Who's) willing to sit (beside, besides) me in the back seat?
10. The (plain, plane) truth is that (fewer, less) Americans feel financially secure these days.

Score: Number correct _____ × 5 = _____%

COMMONLY CONFUSED WORDS

Mastery Test 3

Cross out the two mistakes in usage in each sentence. Then write the correct words in the spaces provided.

_____ 1. Dose anyone know who's glasses these are?
_____

_____ 2. Your a lot taller then I was when I was your age.
_____

_____ 3. Nancy went too the mall for one item but came home with a armful of packages.
_____

_____ 4. I told my brother that he should except my advise on all matters.
_____

_____ 5. With his fingers, Gene attempted to brake off a piece of the crusty, course bread.
_____

_____ 6. In August 1945, a lone plain passed over the city of Hiroshima. Than a living
_____   hell began for the city's inhabitants.

_____ 7. Marilyn, a housewife whose returning to college, has been excepted in the
_____   medical technicians' program.

_____ 8. We divided the huge hero sandwich, with it's layers of salami and cheese,
_____   between the three of us.

_____ 9. Irregardless of the rumors, nobody could of guessed that the business
_____   would close.

_____ 10. Their go the obnoxious fans who through bottles onto the field.
_____

Score: Number correct _____ × 5 = _____%

COMMONLY CONFUSED WORDS

Mastery Test 4

Cross out the two mistakes in usage in each sentence. Then write the correct words in the spaces provided.

_____.

_____

1. As soon as my jeans get to tight, I know its time to cut out junk food.

_____

_____

2. I must of read the assignment five times, but I couldn't hardly make any sense out of it.

_____

_____

3. After we drove passed the same diner for the third time, we new we were lost.

_____

_____

4. I put my paycheck under my pillow, being that I was afraid I was going to loose it.

_____

_____

5. As the wind blew threw the rafters, we wondered weather or not the old boathouse would survive the storm.

_____

_____

6. I couldn't decide on which of the too costumes to where to the party.

_____

_____

7. Knew desserts are being created all over the world by the careless destruction of trees.

_____

_____

8. The plane brown pears in the fruit bowl are sweeter then they look.

_____

_____

9. Although I could here it's pitiful cries, I couldn't reach the animal caught under the caved-in shed.

_____

_____

10. Before I took this writing coarse, I would brake into a cold sweat every time I picked up a pen.

Score: Number correct _____ × 5 = _____%

EFFECTIVE WORD CHOICE

Mastery Test I

Certain words are italicized in the following sentences. In the spaces at the left, identify whether those words are slang (*S*), clichés (*C*), or pretentious words (*PW*). Then, in the spaces below, replace the words with more effective diction.

_____ 1. After she received an A, Barbara was *walking on air* for the rest of the day.

_____

_____ 2. A *wheeler-dealer* salesman sold Jim a *lemon*.

_____   _____

_____ 3. Robert's *rain garment* was *saturated*.

_____   _____

_____ 4. He is inhumane to *members of the animal kingdom.*

_____

_____ 5. I have a lot of studying to do, but *my brain is out to lunch.*

_____

_____ 6. After moving the furniture, James lay down on the couch and *went out like a light.*

_____

_____ 7. My parents *hit the roof* when they saw the dented car.

_____

_____ 8. If I had known you were *hard up,* I would have lent you the *dough.*

_____   _____

_____ 9. I *extinguished my smoking material* before the *aircraft* took off.

_____   _____

_____ 10. Darlene gave the collection agency a *buzz* and asked to speak to the *head honcho.*

_____   _____

Score: Number correct _____ × 10 = _____%

EFFECTIVE WORD CHOICE

Mastery Test 2

Certain words are italicized in the following sentences. In the spaces at the left, identify whether those words are slang (*S*), clichés (*C*), or pretentious words (*PW*). Then, in the spaces below, replace the words with more effective diction.

_____ 1. The professor *perceived* that the students *had a negative response to the idea.*

_____   _____

_____ 2. The movie was *a total downer.*

_____

_____ 3. At nursery school, my child is learning to *interact in a positive manner* with her *peers.*

_____   _____

_____ 4. Carlos felt *like a fish out of water* at the party.

_____

_____ 5. I talked to my daughter until I was *blue in the face,* but my words *went in one ear and out the other.*

_____   _____

_____ 6. Leon *stuffed his face with* so many *munchies* that he felt sick.

_____   _____

_____ 7. Charlene *asserted* that her story was not a *fabrication.*

_____   _____

_____ 8. I tried to *sack out* for a while, but some *yo-yo* kept calling my number by mistake.

_____   _____

_____ 9. Teresa grabbed the rolls out of the oven *in the nick of time.*

_____

_____ 10. *Keep your mitts off* me or you'll get a *knuckle sandwich.*

_____   _____

> *Score:*   Number correct _____ × 10 = _____%

EFFECTIVE WORD CHOICE

Mastery Test 3

The following sentences include examples of wordiness. Rewrite the sentences in the spaces provided, omitting needless words.

1. Because of the fact that a time span of only five seconds separates the lightning from the thunder, we may safely conclude that the storm is directly overhead.

   _____

   _____

2. After his long twelve-mile hike, Mike was so exhausted that when he walked into his living room, he staggered.

   _____

   _____

3. My mouth dropped open in amazement when I heard the startling news that Tim had just had a nervous breakdown last month.

   _____

   _____

4. Julia was convinced in her heart that she was doing the very best thing for both of them when she returned Clark's ring.

   _____

   _____

5. A sad-eyed mournful-looking little dog, no bigger than a puppy, followed my son home and walked behind him into the house.

   _____

   _____

Score: Number correct _____ × 20 = _____%

EFFECTIVE WORD CHOICE

Mastery Test 4

The following sentences include examples of wordiness. Rewrite the sentences in the spaces provided, omitting needless words.

1. My outgrown closet is filled to bursting with piles of useless junk that I no longer need.

   _____

   _____

2. The leaky faucet that wouldn't stop dripping annoyed and bothered me all night long.

   _____

   _____

3. If you are having difficulties with your schoolwork and are not keeping up with your assignments, you should budget your time so that you stick to a schedule.

   _____

   _____

4. The main idea that I am trying to get across in this essay is that no driver of a motor vehicle should be permitted to drive in excess of the speed limit of fifty-five miles per hour.

   _____

   _____

5. When we looked as if we didn't believe him, Frank got upset and indignant and insisted that his story was a true incident that had really happened.

   _____

   _____

Score: Number correct _____ × 20 = _____%

Combined Mastery Tests

SENTENCE FRAGMENTS AND RUN-ONS

🗩 Combined Mastery Test I

Each of the word groups below is numbered. In the space provided, write *C* if a word group is a complete sentence, *F* if it is a fragment, and *R-O* if it is a run-on.

1. _____
2. _____
3. _____
4. _____
5. _____
6. _____
7. _____
8. _____
9. _____
10. _____
11. _____
12. _____
13. _____
14. _____
15. _____
16. _____
17. _____
18. _____
19. _____
20. _____

[1]A few years ago, an experiment was conducted in Germany. [2]To determine how dependent people are on their television sets. [3]The researchers chose 184 volunteers these people were paid to give up watching television for one year. [4]During the first months of the experiment. [5]Most of the subjects did not suffer any ill effects. [6]Or complain that they were missing anything important. [7]The volunteers said they had more free time, and they were grateful for the extra hours. [8]Spending them on reading, paying attention to their children, or visiting friends. [9]Another month went by, suddenly things took a turn for the worse. [10]The subjects became tense and restless. [11]In addition, quarreled frequently with other family members. [12]Their tension continued until the subjects were permitted to watch television again. [13]Nobody in the experiment survived an entire year without television, in fact, the longest anyone lasted was five months. [14]As soon as the television sets were turned on again. [15]The symptoms of anxiety disappeared. [16]This experiment suggests a conclusion. [17]Which would be dangerous to ignore. [18]Television is habit-forming it may be even more habit-forming than cigarettes or drugs. [19]Perhaps the little screen should carry a warning label. [20]Which says, "Caution—This Product May Be Hazardous to Your Health."

Score: Number correct _____ × 5 = _____%

SENTENCE FRAGMENTS AND RUN-ONS

Combined Mastery Test 2

In the space provided, indicate whether each item below contains a fragment (*F*) or a run-on (*R-O*). Then correct the error.

_____ 1. With mounting horror, Elena looked at the anxiously awaited snapshots. Which had just been developed. Not one picture had turned out.

_____ 2. Doug tried to grasp his new soft contact lens it was like trying to pick up a drop of water. The slippery little lens escaped from his fingers again and again.

_____ 3. Wearing huge, bright-blue sunglasses with gold wires. The new instructor strolled into class. One student whispered that she looked like a human dragonfly.

_____ 4. Because Sandy carried a large shoulder bag when she went shopping. Store security guards regarded her with suspicion. They had been trained to watch out for shoplifters with extra-large purses.

_____ 5. I watched my sister, a cleanliness fanatic, put away the produce. First she washed all the bananas and oranges, then she rubbed the onions with a towel.

_____ 6. The crowd became silent. Then, while the drums rolled. The acrobat attempted a triple somersault in midair.

_____ 7. Irene peeled off the itchy wool knee socks, she stared at the vertical red ridges the tight socks had left on the tender skin. With a sigh, she massaged her sore shins.

_____ 8. Although they sip nectar for energy. Butterflies never eat anything substantial. They have no need to because their bodies don't grow. Their only function is to mate.

_____ 9. When he smelled the acrid odor, Lee rushed to the kitchen. He popped up the smoking bread something was still aflame in the toaster's crumb tray.

_____ 10. Joanne painted her fingernails with pale-pink nail polish. And put a slightly deeper shade of pink on her toenails. Her fingertips and toes looked as if they were blushing.

Score:	Number correct _____ × 10 = _____%

VERBS

Combined Mastery Test I

Each sentence contains a mistake involving (1) standard English or irregular verb forms, (2) subject-verb agreement, or (3) consistent verb tense. Cross out the incorrect verb and write the correct form in the space provided.

_____ 1. The razor-sharp coral had tore a hole in the hull of the flimsy boat.

_____ 2. The signs in the park warns that litterers will be fined.

_____ 3. I cringe in embarrassment every time I started my car because its broken exhaust makes it sound like a hot rod.

_____ 4. Somebody in the dorm keep the radio on all night long.

_____ 5. Mike wants to overcome his shyness but hesitated to meet new people because he fears he won't have anything interesting to say.

_____ 6. Each of my professors expect a term paper to be turned in before the holidays.

_____ 7. The judge reminded the witness that she had swore to tell the truth.

_____ 8. There were a heavy load of soggy clothes to be washed when Janet got home from camp.

_____ 9. Sue type the final word and fell back in her chair; her report was finally finished.

_____ 10. Someone called Elaine at the office to tell her that her son had been bit by a stray dog.

Score:	Number correct _____	× 10 =	_____%

VERBS

 ## Combined Mastery Test 2

Each sentence contains a mistake involving (1) standard English or irregular verb forms, (2) subject-verb agreement, or (3) consistent verb tense. Cross out the incorrect verb and write the correct form in the space provided.

_____ 1. Karen searched for the fifty-dollar bill she had hid in the thick book.

_____ 2. After I leave the dentist's office, my jaw and mouth feels numb.

_____ 3. After he stirred the thick paint for several minutes, Walt reels backward as the strong fumes made his head spin.

_____ 4. My nephew must have grew a foot since I last saw him.

_____ 5. Hovering overhead at the scene of the accident was several traffic helicopters.

_____ 6. When the nurse gave him the injection, Alfonso felt as if a huge bee had just stinged him.

_____ 7. When I caught my little boy pulling the dog's ears, I sat him down and talk to him about being kind to animals.

_____ 8. McDonald's has selled enough hamburgers to reach to the moon.

_____ 9. When he noticed Helen holding only a quart of milk, the man ahead of her in the checkout line motions for Helen to take his place.

_____ 10. Leaping out of the patrol car was two police officers with their guns drawn.

Score: Number correct _____ × 10 = _____%	

PRONOUNS

● Combined Mastery Test I

Choose the sentence in each pair that uses pronouns correctly. Write the letter of that sentence in the space provided.

_____ 1. a. If someone wants to try out for the women's softball team, they should go to the practice field today after class.
        b. If someone wants to try out for the women's softball team, she should go to the practice field today after class.

_____ 2. a. At the hardware store, they told me I would need specially treated lumber to build an outdoor deck.
        b. At the hardware store, the clerks told me I would need specially treated lumber to build an outdoor deck.

_____ 3. a. Those greedy squirrels ate all the sunflower seeds in the bird feeder.
        b. Them greedy squirrels ate all the sunflower seeds in the bird feeder.

_____ 4. a. Each of the student waiters had to write a report about their employment experience.
        b. Each of the student waiters had to write a report about his employment experience.

_____ 5. a. We liked the price of the house, but you would have to do too much work to make it livable.
        b. We liked the price of the house, but we would have to do too much work to make it livable.

Score: Number correct _____ × 20 = _____%

PRONOUNS

Combined Mastery Test 2

In the spaces provided, write *PE* for each of the nine sentences that contain pronoun errors. Write *C* for the sentence that uses pronouns correctly. Then cross out each pronoun error and write the correction in the space provided.

_____   1. Bobby, Earl, and me are studying for the math test together.

_____   2. Someone in the women's aerobics class complained that their back was sore.

_____   3. If I fail the final exam, does that mean that you automatically fail the course?

_____   4. Each of the twins had her name printed on her sweatshirt.

_____   5. I enjoy my word processing work, but you tend to have eyestrain by the end of the day.

_____   6. When Juanita got her job as a waitress, they told her she would have to buy her own uniforms.

_____   7. Tom read the paper while eating his lunch and then threw the rest of it away.

_____   8. At the minicar racetrack, I proved that my reaction time was quicker than her's.

_____   9. If anyone walks to the cafeteria, will they bring me a cup of coffee?

_____   10. Since I've been up until two o'clock the last few nights and feel fine, I'm convinced that you need only six hours of sleep.

Score: Number correct _____ × 10 = _____%

FAULTY MODIFIERS AND PARALLELISM

Combined Mastery Test I

In the spaces provided, indicate whether each sentence contains a misplaced modifier (*MM*), a dangling modifier (*DM*), or faulty parallelism (*FP*). Then correct the error in the space under the sentence.

_____ 1. Before she went to bed, Sue brushed her teeth, took out her contact lenses, and was setting the alarm for six o'clock.

_____

_____ 2. After enjoying the fabulous meal, the bill dampened our spirits.

_____

_____ 3. Carmen read an article about exploring outer space in the dentist's office.

_____

_____ 4. While watching my favorite show, the smoke detector emitted a whistle.

_____

_____ 5. The wind blew over the card table, and the cups and plates were scattered.

_____

_____ 6. Backfiring and stalling, we realized that the car needed a tune-up.

_____

_____

_____ 7. Being left-handed, scissors seem upside down to me.

_____

_____ 8. A month ago, the Wallaces moved into the house next door from Ohio.

_____

_____ 9. I found an antique necklace in the old carton worn by my grandmother.

_____

_____ 10. The salesperson said we could pay for the furniture with cash, a credit card, or writing a check.

_____

Score: Number correct _____ × 10 = _____%

FAULTY MODIFIERS AND PARALLELISM

Combined Mastery Test 2

In the spaces provided, indicate whether each sentence contains a misplaced modifier (*MM*), a dangling modifier (*DM*), or faulty parallelism (*FP*). Then correct the error in the space under the sentence.

_____ 1. Working in her vegetable garden, a bee stung Debbie on the shoulder.

_____

_____ 2. Our boss is smart and with plenty of dedication but coldhearted.

_____

_____ 3. Mr. Harris said he would be leaving the company during the meeting.

_____

_____ 4. The delivery boy placed the pizza on the couch with anchovies.

_____

_____ 5. Covered with wavy lines, the technician suggested that our computer monitor needed adjusting.

_____

_____

_____ 6. Twisted in several places, Karl straightened out the garden hose.

_____

_____ 7. As I waited, the secretary typed, filed, and was talking on the telephone.

_____

_____ 8. Holly saw a dress she was dying to wear in the department store window.

_____

_____ 9. Weighing three tons, my neighbor pays an added registration fee for his truck.

_____

_____

_____ 10. While sitting in the traffic jam, I almost read the entire newspaper.

_____

Score: Number correct _____ × 10 = _____%

CAPITAL LETTERS
AND PUNCTUATION

💬 Combined Mastery Test I

Each of the following sentences contains an error in capitalization or punctuation. Refer to the box below and write, in the space provided, the letter identifying the error. Then correct the error.

a. missing capital	c. missing quotation marks
b. missing apostrophe	d. missing comma

_____ 1. The elevator was stuck for more than an hour but all the passengers stayed calm.

_____ 2. ''When I step onto dry land after weeks at sea, said the sailor, ''I feel as if I'm standing on a sponge.''

_____ 3. He doesn't talk about it much, but my uncle has been a member of alcoholics Anonymous for ten years.

_____ 4. My parents always ask me where Im going and when I'll be home.

_____ 5. Whenever Phil eats peanuts he leaves a pile of shells in the ashtray.

_____ 6. In the schools ''food band,'' the children used pumpkins for drums and bags of pretzels for shakers.

_____ 7. ''Stop making a fool of yourself,'' said Emily, and put that sword back on the wall.''

_____ 8. The sweating straining horses neared the finish line.

_____ 9. The children a costumed horde of Halloween pirates and hoboes, fanned out through the neighborhood.

_____ 10. I decided to drink a glass of milk rather than order a pepsi.

Score: Number correct _____ × 10 = _____%

CAPITAL LETTERS
AND PUNCTUATION

Combined Mastery Test 2

Each of the following sentences contains an error in capitalization or punctuation. Refer to the box below and write, in the space provided, the letter identifying the error. Then correct the error.

a.	missing capital	c.	missing quotation marks
b.	missing apostrophe	d.	missing comma

_____ 1. She had never seen anyone put mustard catsup, and mayonnaise on French fries.

_____ 2. The schools janitor received nothing but a plaque for his loyal service.

_____ 3. "Using these chopsticks," said Wayne, "is like trying to eat soup with a fork.

_____ 4. Some people don't know that manhattan is an island.

_____ 5. Wanting to make a good impression Bill shaved twice before his date.

_____ 6. Crumpled sheets of paper and a spilled bottle of bayer aspirin littered Laurie's desk.

_____ 7. "German," said the history instructor, came within one vote of being named the official language of the United States."

_____ 8. My mothers checks are printed with pictures of endangered wild animals.

_____ 9. Feeling brave and silly at the same time Art volunteered to go onstage and help the magician.

_____ 10. My Uncle Tyrone fought in the Battle of the Bulge during World war II.

_____

Score: Number correct _____ × 10 = _____%

WORD USE

🗨 Combined Mastery Test I

Each of the following sentences contains a mistake identified in the left-hand margin. Underline the mistake and then correct it in the space provided.

Slang

1. At 50 percent off, this suit is a real steal.

_____

Wordiness

2. Although Loretta was on a reducing diet to lose weight, she splurged on some ice cream.

_____

Cliché

3. Ken knew his friends would be green with envy when they saw his new car.

_____

Pretentious language

4. We must complete the decision-making process.

_____

Adverb error

5. I tied the knot slow, making sure it wouldn't come loose again.

_____

Error in comparison

6. I felt more thirstier than I ever had in my life.

_____

Confused word

7. "Its the tallest building in the world," the guide said.

_____

Confused word

8. There parking the car in one of those enclosed garages.

_____

Confused word

9. He's the center who's teammates throw him the ball every time.

_____

Confused word

10. If you keep your wallet sticking out of a rear pocket, your bound to lose it to a pickpocket.

_____

Score: Number correct _____ × 10 = _____%

WORD USE

 ## Combined Mastery Test 2

Each of the following sentences contains a mistake identified in the left-hand margin. Underline the mistake and then correct it in the space provided.

Slang

1. After his workout at the gym, Paul was too wiped out to cook dinner.

_____

Wordiness

2. I asked the attendant at the gas station to fill up my tank with gas as far as possible.

_____

Cliché

3. I try to turn the other cheek instead of getting angry.

_____

Pretentious language

4. Next fall, I plan to matriculate at a nearby college.

_____

Adverb error

5. Esther hadn't been feeling good ever since the buffet lunch.

_____

Error in comparison

6. Sharon was more happier after she quit her job.

_____

Confused word

7. Charles knew he was all ready late for the interview, so he ran up the steps.

_____

Confused word

8. Michael's principle fault is his tendency to lose his temper.

_____

Confused word

9. The rabbi tried to advice the confused teenager.

_____

Confused word

10. Before the operation, the surgeon will carefully study you're x-rays.

_____

Score: Number correct _____ × 10 = _____%

Editing and Proofreading Tests

The passages in this section can be used in either of two ways:

1   As Editing Tests: Each test consists of three passages (A, B, and C), and each passage contains a number of mistakes involving a single sentence skill. For example, the first passage (on page 349) contains five sentence fragments. Your instructor may ask you to proofread this passage (A) to locate the five fragments. Spaces are provided for you to indicate which word groups are fragments. Your instructor may also have you correct the errors, either in the text itself or on separate paper. Depending on how you do, you may also be asked to edit the second and third passages (B and C) for fragments.

Twelve skills are covered in all. Here is a list of the skill areas:

Test 1	Sentence fragments
Test 2	Run-ons (fused sentences)
Test 3	Run-ons (comma splices)
Test 4	Standard English verbs
Test 5	Irregular verbs
Test 6	Misplaced and dangling modifiers
Test 7	Faulty parallelism
Test 8	Capital letters
Test 9	Apostrophes
Test 10	Quotation marks
Test 11	Commas
Test 12	Commonly confused words

2 *As Guided Composition Activities:* To give you added practice, your instructor may ask you to do more than correct the mistakes in each passage. You may be asked to rewrite the passage, correcting it for sentence-skills mistakes *and also* copying the rest of the passage perfectly. Should you miss one mistake or make even one error in copying (for example, omitting a word, dropping a verb ending, misspelling a word, or misplacing an apostrophe), you may be asked to rewrite a different passage that deals with the same skill.

Here is how you would proceed. You would start with sentence fragments, rewriting the first passage, proofreading your paper carefully, and then showing it to your instructor. He or she will check it quickly to see that all the fragments have been corrected and that no copying mistakes have been made. If the passage is error-free, the instructor will mark and initial the appropriate box in the progress chart on pages 498–499 and you can move on to run-ons.

If even a single mistake is made, the instructor may question you briefly to see if you recognize and understand it. (Perhaps he or she will put a check beside the line in which the mistake appears, and then ask if you can correct it.) You may then be asked to write the second passage covering a particular skill. If necessary, you will keep working on that skill and rewrite the third passage as well (and perhaps even repeat the first and second passages).

You will complete the program in guided composition when you successfully work through all twelve skills. Completing the twelve skills will strengthen your understanding of the skills, increase your ability to transfer the skills to actual writing situations, and markedly improve your proofreading ability.

In working on the passages, note the following points:

a For each skill, you will be told the number of mistakes that appear in the passages. If you have trouble finding the mistakes, turn back and review the pages in this book that explain the skill.

b Here is an effective way to go about correcting a passage. First, read it over quickly. Look for and mark off mistakes in the skill area involved. For example, in your first reading of a passage that has five fragments, you might locate and mark only three fragments. If so, reread the passage carefully to find the remaining errors. Finally, make notes in the margin about how to correct each mistake. Only at this point should you begin to rewrite the passage.

c Be sure to proofread with care after you finish a passage. Go over your writing word for word, looking for careless errors. Remember that you may be asked to do another passage involving the same skill if you make even one mistake.

Test 1: Sentence Fragments

Mistakes in each passage: 5

Passage A

^{1}My best friend Linda recently bought a dog. ^{2}A German shepherd named Hindenburg which likes getting into fights. ^{3}In fact, Hindenburg wins every fight that he gets into. ^{4}One day, Linda was walking her new dog. ^{5}When she saw a man coming toward her with a big dog of his own. ^{6}The dog had a long tail and very short legs. ^{7}As soon as Hindenburg noticed the other dog, he went after it. ^{8}And began to snarl and to nip at its tail. ^{9}Being positive her dog would win, Linda did not interfere and let the fight continue. ^{10}Soon Hindenburg was bleeding from ear to ear. ^{11}The other dog was at his throat and was getting ready. ^{12}To finish him off with one savage bite of his sharp teeth. ^{13}Linda panicked and yelled at the man to pull his dog away. ^{14}Then she asked him what kind of dog it was. ^{15}"That's not an ordinary dog," Linda insisted. ^{16}"You're absolutely right," the man replied. ^{17}"Before he got his nose job. ^{18}He was an alligator."

Word groups with fragments: _____   _____   _____   _____   _____

Passage B

^{1}It is the year 2090. ^{2}You want to buy something to read. ^{3}Instead of entering a store filled with neatly shelved paperbacks and hardbacks. ^{4}You walk into a room that resembles an electronics factory. ^{5}Offering you a catalog of titles. ^{6}The robot salesperson asks you to choose the "books" you wish to purchase. ^{7}Then, after consulting the master computer. ^{8}Your salesperson records the entire contents of each selected work on a tiny crystal. ^{9}As small as a pea. ^{10}At home, you can insert the crystal into a mechanical "reader," which will read the work aloud. ^{11}(A choice of voices is, of course, available.) ^{12}Or, you can use an optical reader. ^{13}That flashes the "book's" contents, a page at a time, on a plastic sheet.

Word groups with fragments: _____   _____   _____   _____   _____

Passage C

¹Walter won't admit that he is out of a job. ²Last month, Walter was laid off by the insurance company. ³Where he had been working as a salesperson. ⁴But Walter hasn't told anyone. ⁵And continues to go downtown every morning. ⁶Waiting at the bus stop with his newspaper folded under his arm and his briefcase on the sidewalk beside him. ⁷He looks at his watch as if he were worried about being late. ⁸When he gets downtown. ⁹Walter goes to an arcade. ¹⁰He plays video games for an hour or two. ¹¹Then he visits the public library. ¹²To lose himself in the latest spy novel. ¹³At five o'clock, Walter catches the bus for home. ¹⁴His newspaper is still folded under his arm. ¹⁵He has not opened the paper to look at the want ads. ¹⁶I feel sorry for Walter, but I understand his desire to live in a fantasy world.

Word groups with fragments: _____ _____ _____ _____ _____

Test 2: Run-Ons (Fused Sentences)

Mistakes in each passage: 5

Passage A

¹People do funny things when they get on an elevator. ²They try to move into a corner or against a wall. ³They all face forward their hands are kept in front or at their sides. ⁴Most of all, they avoid eye contact with the other passengers, preferring to stare at the floor numbers. ⁵Nobody teaches these people how to behave on an elevator however, everyone seems to obey the same rules. ⁶Psychologists have one theory about elevator behavior which they feel explains these actions. ⁷Elevators are small, enclosed spaces they force people into contact with one another. ⁸The contact is a violation of a person's ''personal space'' this is the invisible shield we all carry with us. ⁹We get nervous when a stranger stands too close to us we want to put that invisible shield back. ¹⁰Therefore, an elevator isn't the place to try to get to know someone.

Sentences with run-ons: _____   _____   _____   _____   _____

Passage B

¹How would you like to live in the most expensive part of New York City without paying any rent? ²Recently, a fifty-five-year-old man did just that he set up residence on a thirty-five-foot-long traffic island in the middle of East River Drive. ³His furniture was made from storage crates his stove was an oil drum. ⁴His only protection from the weather was the elevated highway overhead. ⁵People waved to him as they drove by some even donated food and beer. ⁶Local television stations soon began to feature this unusual resident. ⁷He was pictured relaxed and reading a book the traffic streamed by on both sides of him. ⁸Social workers wanted to put him in a city shelter he refused, saying it was a pigpen. ⁹Finally, the police took him away, but not before he had become a hero. ¹⁰He had achieved the ultimate American dream; for a little while, he had beaten the system.

Sentences with run-ons: _____   _____   _____   _____   _____

Passage C

[1]Many common expressions have interesting origins one of these is the phrase "the real McCoy." [2]In fact, the real McCoy was not really named McCoy he was a farmer's son from Indiana named Norman Selby who got tired of farming and left home around 1890. [3]One year later, he began a boxing career, using the name Kid McCoy soon he was fighting every month. [4]He was willing to meet any opponent anywhere in the country. [5]He soon had a long string of victories most of them were knockouts. [6]A number of other fighters began calling themselves "Kid McCoy," thinking the name would get them more boxing matches and more money. [7]However, on March 24, 1899, the Kid defeated another great champion the fight lasted twenty rounds and cost the Kid three broken ribs. [8]In his report of the fight, the *San Francisco Examiner*'s sportswriter wrote, "Now you've seen the real McCoy!" [9]From then on, people have said "the real McCoy" whenever they have meant something is not a fake.

Sentences with run-ons: _____ _____ _____ _____ _____

Test 3: Run-Ons (Comma Splices)

Mistakes in each passage: 5

Passage A

[1]One evening, a group of friends got together for a dinner party, after dinner they began telling stories. [2]As the evening wore on, the stories got wilder and wilder. [3]Some of the stories involved unusual scientific experiments, others were about strange creatures, such as werewolves and vampires. [4]The friends competed to see who could tell the most exciting story. [5]In the group was a young woman named Mary, who had recently been married. [6]When Mary went to bed that night, she had a frightening dream. [7]In her dream, a hideous monster came to life, she saw it bending over her. [8]The next morning, Mary told her dream to her new husband, Percy, he persuaded her to write it down. [9]After he read her account, Percy was so impressed that he urged her to expand it into a book. [10]The novel that Mary Shelley finally wrote, *Frankenstein,* is probably the most famous horror story of all time, hundreds of monster movies have been inspired by it.

Sentences with run-ons: _____ _____ _____ _____ _____

Passage B

[1]One of the coldest, snowiest, windiest places on earth is not in the Himalayas or the Arctic, it is on Mount Washington in the pleasant state of New Hampshire. [2]The top of this rather small mountain experiences hurricane-force winds, they slice through human beings like razors. [3]The world's highest wind speed was recorded on the mountain one April day in 1934, that speed was 231 miles per hour! [4]Snow is always possible, even in summer. [5]Supercooled fog, called *rime,* hugs the mountain, there is almost no visibility 55 percent of the time. [6]At least sixty people have lost their lives on Mount Washington in the last hundred years. [7]However, people continue to climb to the top, some take the auto route, open only in the summer. [8]The more foolish attempt to climb the mountain at other times of the year. [9]A warning sign on the mountain reads, ''People don't die on this mountain. They perish.''

Sentences with run-ons: _____ _____ _____ _____ _____

Passage C

[1] During the days of the Old West, the Wells Fargo Company came to dread Black Bart. [2] This outlaw repeatedly robbed company stagecoaches of gold. [3] Surprisingly, Bart didn't appear on horseback, wear a black mask, or fire a pistol. [4] Instead, he would choose a spot where the ground was marked with fresh hoofprints, then he would hide in the bushes, waiting for the stagecoach. [5] After the robbery, the sheriff's men would mistakenly race off after someone else's horse, Bart would simply walk away. [6] Bart always carried an unloaded shotgun or a pistol-sized stick, also, he set up branches and broomsticks in the shadows behind him to look like he had partners holding guns. [7] After a decade of successful holdups, Black Bart was caught. [8] He wasn't gunned down or cornered, he was found because he dropped his handkerchief at the scene of the crime, and the laundry mark on the handkerchief was traced to him. [9] Five years later, Bart was released from prison, the Wells Fargo Company immediately experienced another series of robberies. [10] The only way Wells Fargo could stop Black Bart was to offer him a company pension of $200 a month. [11] Bart accepted the offer and promptly retired from crime.

Sentences with run-ons: _____ _____ _____ _____ _____

Test 4: Standard English Verbs

Mistakes in each passage: 5

Passage A

[1]Did you ever wonder how trainers get porpoises to do all those tricks, like leaping over a high bar or jumping through a hoop? [2]Wild porpoises are first taught to eat fish from their trainer's hand. [3]When the animal accept a fish, the trainer blows a whistle. [4]The porpoise associate the whistle with ''correct'' behavior. [5]Once the porpoise touch a human hand to get a fish, it will touch other things, like a red target ball. [6]For example, the trainer will hold the ball high above the water while leaning over a kind of pulpit. [7]Seeing the ball, the porpoise leap out of the water; it knows it will be rewarded with a fish. [8]A hoop can then be substituted for a ball, and the porpoise's behavior can be ''shaped'' so it will jump through the hoop. [9]If the porpoise miss the hoop by jumping too low, the fish reward is withheld. [10]The intelligent mammal will associate ''no fish'' with ''wrong'' behavior; very quickly, the porpoise will be leaping gracefully through the center of the hoop.

Sentences with nonstandard verbs: _____   _____   _____   _____   _____

Passage B

[1]1The scenes of flood damage on the network news tonight were horrible. [2]Two weeks of steady, heavy rains had raise the waters of several Midwestern rivers past the levels of their banks, and they had overflow onto the surrounding houses and fields. [3]Extensive damage had resulted, with some buildings actually torn from their foundations and suck helplessly into the swirling flood waters. [4]Here and there a rooftop could be seen as it float by with one or two frightened survivors clinging to it. [5]Many people's lives had been disrupted, and many millions of dollars' worth of damage had been cause. [6]It would be several days yet until the waters receded. [7]They say that ''into every life some rain must fall,'' but no one could have predicted all this.

Sentences with nonstandard verbs (write the number of a sentence twice if it contains two nonstandard verbs):

_____   _____   _____   _____   _____

Passage C

¹I read an odd item in the newspaper about a pet snail that nearly frighten its owner to death. ²Actually, the owner did not even know that he had been keeping a pet. ³The snail, which was very fancy, had been varnish and made into an ornament. ⁴Its owner had bought the snail at a gift shop and place it on his desk. ⁵Apparently the snail was not really dead but had been seal into hibernation by the varnish and was just asleep. ⁶Three years later, when its owner accidentally knock the ornament off his desk, chipping the varnish, the snail woke up. ⁷It began moving across the desk as the owner was writing a letter and startled him so much that he jumped out of his chair. ⁸The owner is feeding his former ornament on cabbage before taking it back to the seashore where it belongs.

Sentences with nonstandard verbs: _____   _____   _____   _____   _____

Test 5: Irregular Verbs

Mistakes in each passage: 10

Passage A

^{1}Vince choosed a job as a supermarket cashier because he liked people. ^{2}After what happened yesterday, though, he isn't so sure. ^{3}First, after he had rang up her entire order, a woman throwed a handful of coupons at him. ^{4}Then she give him a hard time when he shown her that a few had expired. ^{5}She begun making nasty comments about stupid supermarket help. ^{6}The next person in line thought Vince had put the eggs on the bottom and would not leave until Vince had took everything out of the bag and repacked it. ^{7}Later, two teenagers fighted with Vince over the price of a bag of M&Ms, saying that it could never have rose so high in one week. ^{8}Vince gone home in a terrible mood, wondering how he would ever force himself to come in the next day.

Sentences with irregular verbs (write the number of a sentence twice if it contains two irregular verbs):

_____   _____   _____   _____   _____

_____   _____   _____   _____   _____

Passage B

^{1}One winter my Siamese cat catched the flu. ^{2}She was only a kitten then, and she had never slowed down for a minute until the day she begun sneezing. ^{3}Then she creeped over to a corner of the living room and set perfectly still, looking at us through sad saucer eyes that constantly oozed tears. ^{4}For three days, she ate almost nothing and drunk much more water than usual—a sure sign of illness. ^{5}I finally taked her to the vet, who prescribed a thick pink medicine that had to be feeded to her three times a day by eyedropper. ^{6}This was easier said than did; more medicine got onto the furniture and me than into the cat. ^{7}What finally cured her, I think, was the electric blanket I had just buyed for my own bed. ^{8}She climbed onto it, I turned it on, and it keeped her warm until her flu went away.

Sentences with irregular verbs (write the number of a sentence twice if it contains two irregular verbs):

_____   _____   _____   _____   _____

_____   _____   _____   _____   _____

Passage C

¹A college professor has wrote a book about what he calls ''urban legends.'' ²These are folktales that have spreaded all over the country. ³They usually have a moral to teach or touch on a basic fear holded by many Americans. ⁴In one of the more gruesome legends, a young couple parked on a lovers' lane heared a report on their car radio about a one-armed killer stalking the area. ⁵The couple leaved; after they gotten home, they seen a bloody hook hanging on the car's door handle. ⁶The moral of this urban legend? ⁷Don't park on lovers' lanes! ⁸In another story, a man finded pieces of fried rat mixed in with his take-out fried chicken. ⁹The professor has sayed that this story is related to the American consumer's fear of being contaminated with some dreadful substance. ¹⁰No one can find a factual basis for any of these stories, although many tellers have swore they are true.

Sentences with irregular verbs (write down the number of a sentence twice or more if it contains two or more irregular verbs):

_____   _____   _____   _____   _____

_____   _____   _____   _____   _____

Test 6: Misplaced and Dangling Modifiers

Mistakes in each passage: 5

Passage A

¹Bob had always dreamed of winning the lottery. ²Then he won the million-dollar jackpot. ³After winning, dramatic changes took place in Bob's life. ⁴At the plant where Bob worked, his coworkers told him he should give up his job to someone who really needed it. ⁵They started snubbing him. ⁶Bob quit. ⁷At school, Bob's kids had their pockets turned inside out—at knifepoint. ⁸Phone calls disturbed his family at all hours that included pleas for money, insults, and threats. ⁹Bob arranged for an unlisted number. ¹⁰His closest friend came by, to ask for a new car. ¹¹Bob told him to leave the house in an angry voice. ¹²The friendship was over. ¹³Next, Bob had a serious disagreement over how to use the money with his wife. ¹⁴Suspicious that people just wanted to use him, Bob made no new friends. ¹⁵Strangers drove up to Bob's house, parked in front, and stared. ¹⁶Then the house was robbed. ¹⁷Having moved since then, their new house has a high wire fence with a burglar alarm. ¹⁸Asked whether or not he would like to win the lottery again, Bob answers, "What—and repeat the nightmare?"

Sentences with misplaced modifiers: _____ _____ _____

Sentences with dangling modifiers: _____ _____

Passage B

¹Are you experiencing car trouble? ²Is your transmission acting up or your muffler rattling? ³By tuning in to your radio, help can be found. ⁴A Sunday-evening program has become popular all over the country which mixes serious car advice with humor. ⁵The show began in Boston when a radio station invited a number of mechanics to take live calls on car problems. ⁶Although expecting a large group, only Tom and Ray showed up. ⁷Tom and Ray are two brothers who had opened a garage that had liked fixing cars in their spare time. ⁸The response to the show was so great that it became a weekly event. ⁹Tom and Ray take all car questions that the audience asks with no advance preparation. ¹⁰They delight listeners with their wit, their down-to-earth philosophy, and their good car sense.

Sentences with misplaced modifiers: _____ _____ _____

Sentences with dangling modifiers: _____ _____

Passage C

¹Humans have used certain animals to carry heavy loads for thousands of years. ²The ox, the elephant, the donkey, and the mule are examples of these "beasts of burden." ³Although having a reputation for being stubborn at times, people find that these animals normally work very hard for long hours. ⁴One beast of burden, however, refuses to be overworked. ⁵The llama, a South American animal much like the camel, has very definite ideas of what it's willing to do. ⁶Knowing just how much it can carry comfortably, an extra half pound placed on its back will cause it to sit down and refuse to budge. ⁷In addition, the llama will carry a burden only a certain distance. ⁸Sitting down in the middle of the road, nothing will convince it to continue after it travels twenty miles. ⁹Sometimes its owner tries to prod the llama after the animal has decided to quit with a stick. ¹⁰When it is annoyed in this fashion, the llama has an unusual way of striking back. ¹¹It puckers its lips and spits in its owner's face.

Sentences with misplaced modifiers: ——— ———
Sentences with dangling modifiers: ——— ——— ———

Test 7: Faulty Parallelism

Mistakes in each passage: 5

Passage A

¹For the 10 percent of the American population that is left-handed, life is not easy. ²Using a pair of scissors or to write in a spiral notebook can be very difficult. ³The scissors and the notebook are two items designed for right-handers. ⁴Also, have you ever seen a "southpaw" take notes or writing an exam at one of those right-handed half-desks? ⁵The poor "lefty" has to twist like a yoga devotee or in the style of a circus acrobat in order to reach the paper. ⁶But a recent study proves that being left-handed can be psychologically damaging as well as tax a person physically. ⁷A survey of 2,300 people showed that 20 percent more left-handers than right-handers smoked. ⁸Could lefties smoke to relieve the tension or forgetting the problems of living in a right-handed world?

Sentences with faulty parallelism:

_____   _____   _____   _____   _____

Passage B

¹Some people today are "survivalists." ²These people, because they fear some great disaster in the near future (like economic collapse or nuclear war), are preparing for a catastrophe. ³Hoarding food, stockpiling weapons, and the achievement of self-sufficiency are some of the activities of survivalists. ⁴In Arkansas, for example, one group has built a mountain fortress to defend its supplies and staying safe. ⁵Arkansas, the group feels, is the best place to be for several reasons: it is an unlikely target for nuclear attack; it offers plentiful supplies of food and water; a good climate. ⁶Some Americans feel that the attitude of survivalists is selfish and greed. ⁷These people say that such a philosophy turns society into a "dog-eat-dog" race for life. ⁸Other people believe that after a nuclear war, the world, with radiation and where there would be disease, wouldn't be worth living in.

Sentences with faulty parallelism:

_____   _____   _____   _____   _____

Passage C

¹Doing your own painting is easy, inexpensive, and you will enjoy it, if you know what you're doing. ²First, you must properly prepare the surface you are going to paint. ³This means removing dirt, rust, or mildew. ⁴Also, you should get rid of loose paint and to fill any cracks with spackling compound. ⁵Primers or sealers should be used on bare wood or over stains. ⁶Another important rule to follow is to buy the right amount of paint. ⁷Some painters guess how much paint they need and are failing to measure accurately. ⁸Then they might buy too little or an excessive amount of paint for the job. ⁹The result is making an extra trip to the hardware store or to have a lot of paint left over. ¹⁰Finally, before you begin to paint, read the directions on the container. ¹¹These hints will save you time and money.

Sentences with faulty parallelism:

_____   _____   _____   _____   _____

Test 8: Capital Letters

Mistakes in each passage: 10

Passage A

¹Last november, joanne fisher put her turkey in the oven and drove into town to see the thanksgiving day parade. ²Parking downtown was almost impossible. ³Joanne saw the sign warning visitors not to park on the private lot at Tenth street, but she thought that since it was a holiday, nobody would mind. ⁴When she returned after the parade, her datsun was missing. ⁵It had been towed to a lot in a faraway section of the city. ⁶When Joanne finally got to the lot, the owner insisted on a cash payment and refused to accept a check for fifty dollars. ⁷Joanne lost her temper and screamed, "all right, go ahead and call the police, but I'm going to drive out of here!" ⁸A police car arrived immediately, and Joanne had visions of spending the next month in jail. ⁹But the officer, sgt. Roberts of the Sixteenth precinct, agreed to cash her check so she could pay the fine. ¹⁰Joanne was delighted until she got home and found that her turkey had burned to a crisp.

Sentences with missing capitals (write the number of a sentence as many times as it contains capitalization mistakes):

_____   _____   _____   _____   _____

_____   _____   _____   _____   _____

Passage B

¹Some seventh-graders in a pittsburgh school have gone into the candy-making business. ²It all started one january when a parent showed the children how to make chocolates. ³the first week, the children made 775 chocolate-covered pretzels and sold the entire batch. ⁴Then the frick foundation, a charitable organization, donated $2,100. ⁵With this money, the students bought candy molds and began taking orders for $800 worth of easter candy. ⁶They also produced red heart lollipops for Valentine's day. ⁷The children have even gotten good at packaging their products. ⁸They proudly tell their parents, "we are learning how to keep our own financial records!" ⁹They are now planning a line of candies for Christmas, to be delivered by their own Santa claus. ¹⁰It is good to hear that one school in america has experienced the sweet smell of success.

Sentences with missing capitals (write the number of a sentence as many times as it contains capitalization mistakes):

_____   _____   _____   _____   _____

_____   _____   _____   _____   _____

Passage C

[1]Loretta never realized how expensive it was going to be to have a baby. [2]Before the birth, Loretta visited dr. willis, her obstetrician, eleven times. [3]After her baby was born, a multiple-page bill from valley hospital arrived. [4]There were charges, not only from Loretta's own doctor, but also from a Dr. David, the anesthesiologist, and a Dr. Ripley, the hospital pediatrician. [5]After she had brought the baby home, Loretta found herself visiting the supermarket more often. [6]She loaded her cart with boxes of expensive pampers, dozens of cans of enfamil formula, and lots of smaller items like johnson's baby powder and oil. [7]Loretta realized that she would have to return to her job at richmond insurance company if she was going to make ends meet.

Sentences with missing capitals (write the number of a sentence as many times as it contains capitalization mistakes):

_____ _____ _____ _____ _____

_____ _____ _____ _____ _____

Test 9: Apostrophes

Mistakes in each passage: 10

Passage A

¹Two Minnesota brothers, Ed and Norman, are engaged in a war. ²It all started when Eds wife gave him a pair of pants that didnt fit. ³Ed wrapped up the pants and put them under Normans Christmas tree. ⁴When Norman opened the box, he recognized the unwanted pants. ⁵The next year, he gave them back to Ed, sealed in a heavy carton tied with knotted ropes. ⁶The War of the Pants was on. ⁷Each year, on one of the brothers birthdays, or on Christmas, the dreaded pants reappear. ⁸The war has escalated, however, with each brother trying to top the others pants delivery of the previous year. ⁹Two years ago, Norman bought an old safe, put the pants in it, welded it shut, and delivered it to Eds house. ¹⁰Somehow, Ed retrieved the pants (one of the wars rules is that the pants must not be damaged). ¹¹Last year, Ed went to an auto junkyard. ¹²The pants were placed in an ancient Fords backseat, and the car went through the huge auto crusher. ¹³On his birthday, Norman found a four-foot square of smashed metal on his doorstep; he knew it could only be Eds doing and the pants must be inside. ¹⁴Norman is still trying to get at the pants and prepare next years ''topper.''

Sentences with missing apostrophes (write the number of a sentence twice if it contains two missing apostrophes):

_____   _____   _____   _____   _____

_____   _____   _____   _____   _____

Passage B

¹If youre going to visit someone in the hospital, dont be gloomy. ²Other peoples problems wont help someone whos sick to feel better. ³But you dont have to limit yourself to ''safe'' topics like todays weather. ⁴You can even discuss the patients condition, as long as neither of you gets upset. ⁵Also, dont stay too long. ⁶Patients are usually weak and cant talk for long periods. ⁷Leave before the patient gets tired.

Sentences with missing apostrophes (write the number of a sentence twice if it contains two missing apostrophes):

_____   _____   _____   _____   _____

_____   _____   _____   _____   _____

Passage C

¹Sometimes I wish the telephone hadnt been invented. ²When I come home after class or work, all Im interested in is lying down for an hours nap. ³Typically, five minutes after Ive closed my eyes, the phone rings. ⁴Someone Ive never met is trying to sell me a subscription to *Newsweek*. ⁵Or I may have just begun to mix up some hamburger when I hear the phones insistent ringing. ⁶It wont stop, so I wipe the ground meat off my hands and run to answer it. ⁷Yesterday, when this happened, it was my mothers best friend. ⁸Shed found some clothes in her attic. ⁹And she wanted to know if I could use an old evening gown. ¹⁰Even if its someone I want to talk to, the phone call always seems to come at a bad time.

Sentences with missing apostrophes (write the number of a sentence twice if it contains two missing apostrophes):

_____ _____ _____ _____ _____

_____ _____ _____ _____ _____

Test 10: Quotation Marks

Quotation marks needed in each passage: 10 pairs

Passage A

¹ Tony and Lola were driving home from the movies when they saw a man staggering along the street. ² I wonder if he's all right, Tony said.

³ Let's stop and find out, Lola suggested. ⁴ They caught up to the man, who was leaning against a tree.

⁵ Are you OK? Lola asked. ⁶ Is there anything we can do?

⁷ There's nothing the matter, the man answered. ⁸ I guess I had a few too many after work. ⁹ Now I can't seem to find my front door.

¹⁰ Tony steadied the man and asked, Do you live anywhere near here?

¹¹ He responded, Yes, if this is Forrest Avenue, I live at 3619.

¹² Tony and Lola walked the man to his door, where he fumbled in his pockets, took out a key, and began to stab wildly with it at the lock.

¹³ Let me hold your key, and I'll let you in, Tony offered.

¹⁴ The man refused, saying, Oh, no, I'll hold the key—you hold the house.

Sentences or sentence groups with missing quotation marks:

—— —— —— —— ——

—— —— —— —— ——

Passage B

¹ When Martin found a large dent in his new Datsun, he took it back to the agency. ² We can fix that, the smiling mechanic said. ³ Just leave it for a few days.

⁴ Martin waited three days and then called. ⁵ Is my car ready yet? he asked.

⁶ Not yet, the mechanic said. ⁷ Try the end of the week.

⁸ The following Monday, Martin called again. ⁹ Is my car ready?

¹⁰ The mechanic sounded apologetic. ¹¹ Not yet. ¹²We'll have it Friday for sure.

¹³ On Friday, when Martin picked up his car, he noticed a new cigarette burn in the upholstery. ¹⁴ We'll fix that, but it takes a week to match the material, the manager said.

¹⁵ Martin took the bus home, fuming. ¹⁶ A few minutes later, the phone rang.

¹⁷ It was the mechanic. ¹⁸ You left your owner's card here. ¹⁹ Want us to mail it?

²⁰ Martin said, You may as well keep it. ²¹ You're using the car more than I am.

Sentences or sentence groups with missing quotation marks:

—— —— —— —— ——

—— —— —— —— ——

Passage C

¹ Fran put aside her books to answer the phone. ² Hello, she said.

³ Hey, Fran, take a break, said Nick. ⁴ There's a great party going on here. ⁵ Why don't you come over?

⁶ Fran hesitated. ⁷ She was tired and bored; the party was tempting. ⁸ She felt like a cartoon character with a devil perched on one shoulder and an angel on the other.

⁹ Go to the party, the devil said. ¹⁰ Forget this studying.

¹¹ Stay home, the angel whispered, or you'll regret it tomorrow.

¹² Interrupting Fran's thoughts, Nick urged, Oh, come on, you can cram when you get home.

¹³ Fran felt an imaginary stab from the devil's pitchfork. ¹⁴ I want to, Nick, she said. ¹⁵ Then she gave in to the imaginary angel. ¹⁶ But I can't. ¹⁷ I really have to pass this test.

Sentences or sentence groups with missing quotation marks:

_____ _____ _____ _____ _____

_____ _____ _____ _____ _____

Test 11: Commas

Mistakes in each passage: 10

Passage A

¹Frank has a hard time studying so he plays little games to get himself to finish his assignments. ²He will begin by saying to himself "Whenever I finish an assignment I'll give myself a prize." ³Frank has all kinds of prizes; his favorites are watching a detective show on television drinking a cold beer or spending an hour with his girlfriend. ⁴Of course too many of these rewards will mean that Frank won't get much else done. ⁵So Frank uses other strategies. ⁶He will for example set the stove timer for one hour. ⁷Then he will work at the kitchen table until the timer buzzes. ⁸Also he puts a paper clip on every tenth page of the book he is studying. ⁹As soon as he reaches the clip he can take a five-minute break.

Sentences with missing commas (write the number of a sentence as many times as it contains comma mistakes):

_____   _____   _____   _____   _____

_____   _____   _____   _____   _____

Passage B

¹You've probably heard of Robinson Crusoe but there is an even stranger story of shipwreck and survival. ²In 1757 a Scottish whaling ship sank in the icy polar seas of the Arctic. ³Only one man Bruce Gordon survived. ⁴Without food or shelter Gordon spent his lonely first night huddled on the ice. ⁵The next day the whaling ship—upside-down—rose to the surface of the sea and lodged tightly in the ice floes. ⁶Gordon using some of the shipwreck debris managed to break into a cabin window. ⁷He survived for a year in the freezing world of the upside-down ship by using some stored coal to build a fire. ⁸Eventually Bruce Gordon was rescued by a band of Eskimo hunters. ⁹After living for more than five years in the native village the shipwrecked sailor finally made it back to Scotland.

Sentences with missing commas (write the number of a sentence as many times as it contains comma mistakes):

_____   _____   _____   _____   _____

_____   _____   _____   _____   _____

Passage C

[1] When Janice gets bored with her secretarial job she has a whole assortment of things to do to pass the time until five o'clock. [2] First of all she cleans out her desk. [3] Desk drawers she has found contain all sorts of hidden treasure. [4] Janice found her old diary the gold chain bracelet she had gotten for Christmas and two unread murder mysteries the last time she ''cleaned house.'' [5] Another thing Janice likes to do is read the company directory. [6] She looks through all the names of the junior executives and she picks out three she'd like to meet at the next company picnic. [7] In the secretaries' lounge Janice can make a cup of coffee read the job opportunities on the bulletin board or talk to a coworker about what she is going to do after work. [8] These little pleasures help Janice keep her sanity.

Sentences with missing commas (write the number of a sentence as many times as it contains comma mistakes):

——— ——— ——— ——— ———

——— ——— ——— ——— ———

Test 12: Commonly Confused Words

Mistakes in each passage: 10

Passage A

¹Did you know that until May 5 of every year, your not really working for yourself? ²A group in Washington, D.C., has learned that it takes workers an average of four months and four days to earn enough to pay there taxes. ³The group found in it's study that taxes eat up 34 percent of all the income in the United States. ⁴So, if workers used they're entire income for taxes, they would not be threw paying them until May. ⁵Being that May 5 is the first day people really work for themselves, the study group has some advise. ⁶It would like a bill past naming May 5 ''Tax Freedom Day.'' ⁷On that day, you would give yourself a brake, irregardless of how hard you worked. ⁸For, from May 5 on, you would finally be your own boss.

Sentences with commonly confused words (write the number of a sentence twice if it contains two commonly confused words):

_____ _____ _____ _____ _____

_____ _____ _____ _____ _____

Passage B

¹Did you ever daydream about writing you're life story? ²Do you think that your life is to dull, or you can't right? ³Anyone's life story is filled with fascinating events, and writing them down in the best way you know can give you a sense of accomplishment and, perhaps, leave a valuable inheritance to your family. ⁴The first thing to do is to buy a lose-leaf notebook. ⁵Each page of the book should be titled with a significant milestone in your life—from your first dog to your proudest moment. ⁶You should than jot down a few key words in the book whenever a memory comes back to you. ⁷The idea is *not* to begin with ''I was born . . .'' and try to write a chronological history of your hole life. ⁸Just delve into your passed at random; one memory will trigger another. ⁹It will become quiet easy after a while. ¹⁰Its also important to write in your own language. ¹¹Plane, honest writing is the goal.

Sentences with commonly confused words (write the number of a sentence twice if it contains two commonly confused words):

_____ _____ _____ _____ _____

_____ _____ _____ _____ _____

Passage C

[1]When Nick and Fran got there phone bill, they new something was wrong. [2]They couldn't figure out why the new bill was over seven dollars more then the old one. [3]Then Nick saw the long-distance charges. [4]There were ten calls listed too the town of Rosemont, several hundred miles away. [5]"But we don't no anybody in Rosemont," Fran protested. [6]"Wear is Rosemont, anyway? [7]Besides, no one would have such a ridiculous phone number as 123-456-7890." [8]Suddenly, they though of their twin sons, who were just learning how to count. [9]They must of been playing with the push buttons on the dial. [10]This turned out to be the write solution to the mystery of Nick and Fran's phone bill. [11]Now the twins know they can't afford to let their fingers do the walking. [12]And Nick and Fran expect less long-distance charges from now on.

Sentences with commonly confused words (write the number of a sentence twice if it contains two commonly confused words):

_____ _____ _____ _____ _____

_____ _____ _____ _____ _____

Combined Editing Tests

EDITING FOR
SENTENCE-SKILLS MISTAKES

The twelve editing tests in this section will give you practice in finding a variety of sentence-skills mistakes. People often find it hard to edit their own writing carefully. They have put so much work into their writing, or so little, that it's almost painful for them to look at the paper one more time. You may have to simply *force* yourself to edit. Remember that eliminating sentence-skills mistakes will improve an average paper and help ensure a high grade for a good paper. Further, as you get into the habit of editing your papers, you will get into the habit of using the sentence skills consistently. They are a basic part of clear and effective writing.

The first two tests check your understanding of the correct format to use when writing and handing in a paper. The remaining tests check your ability to identify a variety of sentence-skills mistakes, especially sentence fragments and run-ons. In tests 3 through 8, the places where errors occur have been underlined; your job is to identify each error. In the last tests, 9 through 12, you must locate as well as identify the errors. Use the progress chart on page 500 to keep track of your performance on these tests.

Combined Editing Test I

Identify the five mistakes in paper format in the student paper on the opposite page. From the box below, choose the letters that describe the five mistakes and write those letters in the spaces provided.

---

a. The title should not be underlined.

b. The title should not be set off in quotation marks.

c. There should not be a period at the end of a title.

d. All the major words in a title should be capitalized.

e. The title should just be several words and not a complete sentence.

f. The first line of a paper should stand independent of the title.

g. A line should be skipped between the title and the first line of the paper.

h. The first line of a paper should be indented.

i. The right-hand margin should not be crowded.

j. Hyphenation should occur only between syllables.

---

1. _____   2. _____   3. _____   4. _____   5. _____

	"Noise in quiet places"
	The quietest places make the most noise. A library is one exam-
	ple. If you crinkle a bag of potato chips in a quiet library, people
	will stare at you as if you lit a firecracker under their feet. But
	you could drop a food tray in a noisy cafeteria and nobody would
	pay much attention to you. Then, there's the cough in church. A
	muffled cough bounces off the stained glass windows like a sonic
	boom. But you could cough up a storm at a rock concert and not
	one head would turn. Finally, elevators are hushed places. If you
	ask someone for the time in an elevator, everyone will look at his
	or her watch. Ask the same question on a busy city street, and
	chances are that no one will hear you. It takes a quiet place for
	sound to be really heard.

Combined Editing Test 2

Identify the five mistakes in paper format in the student paper on the opposite page. From the box below, choose the letters that describe the five mistakes and write those letters in the spaces provided.

---

   a.   The title should not be underlined.

   b.   The title should not be set off in quotation marks.

   c.   There should not be a period at the end of a title.

   d.   All the major words in a title should be capitalized.

   e.   The title should just be several words and not a complete sentence.

   f.   The first line of a paper should stand independent of the title.

   g.   A line should be skipped between the title and the first line of the paper.

   h.   The first line of a paper should be indented.

   i.   The right-hand margin should not be crowded.

   j.   Hyphenation should occur only between syllables.

---

1. _____   2. _____   3. _____   4. _____   5. _____

"Bus Travel."

It is the worst way to get to work or school in the morning. First, the weather is unpredictable. Many bus stops are not sheltered, and the rider must wait in rain, cold, and heat. Another unpleasant thing about bus riding is the wait. It seems that buses are on time only when you're running late. Next, there is the matter of having exact change. If you try to enter without the right change, the driver looks at you as if your hair is on fire. Last, there's the problem of finding a seat. The elderly folks are saving seats for their friends, and most people look as if they will bite your nose if you sit next to them. Chances are that the only seat open will be next to a strange-smelling person with a wild look in his eye.

Combined Editing Test 3

Identify the sentence-skills mistakes at the underlined spots in the selection that follows. From the box below, choose the letter that describes each mistake and write it in the space provided. The same mistake may appear more than once. In one case, there is no mistake.

a. sentence fragment	e. incorrect end mark
b. run-on	f. missing apostrophe
c. dropped verb ending	g. missing comma
d. misplaced modifier	h. no mistake

When I was little, I really hate visiting Aunt Martha. She was my fathers sister and
¹ ²
had never married. Since she had no children of her own, she didnt know what to do
³
with me. I remember the sofa in her living room, which was dark brown. And filled with
⁴ ⁵
horsehair. Every time I sat on it, I got stabbed by the stuffing. I had to plump up the
cushion when I got up otherwise, she would frown at me. She would sit opposite me with
⁶
a stiff smile on her face and ask me what I was learning in school or if I had been good?
⁷ ⁸
Things that I didn't want to talk about. I couldn't wait to say goodbye plump up her
⁹ ¹⁰
awful sofa, and escape.

1. _____   3. _____   5. _____   7. _____   9. _____

2. _____   4. _____   6. _____   8. _____   10. _____

Combined Editing Test 4

Identify the sentence-skills mistakes at the underlined spots in the selection that follows. From the box below, choose the letter that describes each mistake and write it in the space provided. The same mistake may appear more than once. In one case, there is no mistake.

a. sentence fragment	f. missing capital letter
b. run-on	g. missing quotation marks
c. dropped verb ending	h. missing comma
d. irregular verb mistake	i. no mistake
e. dangling modifier	

In the unending war of people versus machines, a blow was <u>striked</u> by a man in
<u>pennsylvania</u> who had a run-in with an automatic banking machine. At about ten o'clock
one night, he approached the machine to make a withdrawal. After he inserted his <u>card</u>
the machine spit it back at him. The same thing then <u>happen</u> a second time. He put
his card in <u>again, this</u> time the machine kept the card. <u>And did not give him the money</u>
he had requested. By now the customer was totally disgusted. <u>Hitting the machine with</u>
<u>all his strength,</u> the card still did not come back. This was the last <u>straw he</u> grabbed a
metal trash <u>can and</u> proceeded to beat up the machine. Unfortunately, the machine still
had his card, and the man was later arrested and charged with causing $2,500 worth of
damage. He didn't mind. "I've been ripped off so <u>often,</u> he said, "that it was time for
me to get even."

1. _____   3. _____   5. _____   7. _____   9. _____

2. _____   4. _____   6. _____   8. _____   10. _____

Combined Editing Test 5

Identify the sentence-skills mistakes at the underlined spots in the selection that follows. From the box below, choose the letter that describes each mistake and write it in the space provided. The same mistake may appear more than once. In one case, there is no mistake.

a. sentence fragment	f. mistake in subject-verb agreement
b. run-on	g. irregular verb mistake
c. omitted word	h. no mistake
d. misplaced modifier	
e. missing capital letter	

If you were asked name our most dangerous insects or animals, which ones
                    ‾‾‾‾‾‾‾‾‾‾
                         1
would you list? You might jot down black widow spiders, rattlesnakes, and scorpions.

Just to list a few. However, our Public Enemy Number One is the bee, more people die
‾‾‾‾‾‾‾‾‾‾‾‾‾‾‾‾   ‾‾‾‾‾‾‾‾‾
       2   3
from bee and wasp stings every year than are killed by animals. Not too long ago in

Camden, new Jersey, over twenty-seven people were took to hospitals who had been
        ‾‾‾   ‾‾‾‾   ‾‾‾‾‾‾‾‾‾‾‾‾
         4   5
stung by a runaway swarm of bees. The bees, which had escaped from a hive that had
‾‾‾‾
  6
fallen off a truck, was maddened by what they thought was an attack on their hive and
                   ‾‾‾
                    7
would have destroyed anyone who came near them. If there is no threat to their hive.
                               ‾‾‾‾   ‾‾‾‾‾‾‾‾‾‾‾‾‾‾‾‾‾‾‾‾‾‾‾‾‾‾‾‾‾‾
                                8   9
Bees will usually not sting, for once they lose their stingers, they die. Wasps and yellow

jackets, however, is able to sting repeatedly with no danger to themselves. For that 1
                  ‾‾
                  10
percent of the population allergic to insect stings, such attacks can be fatal.

1. _____   3. _____   5. _____   7. _____   9. _____

2. _____   4. _____   6. _____   8. _____   10. _____

Combined Editing Test 6

Identify the sentence-skills mistakes at the underlined spots in the selection that follows. From the box below, choose the letter that describes each mistake and write it in the space provided. The same mistake may appear more than once. In one case, there is no mistake.

a.	sentence fragment	e.	mistake in parallelism
b.	run-on	f.	apostrophe mistake
c.	irregular verb mistake	g.	missing comma
d.	inconsistent verb tense	h.	no mistake

As she walked into the dimly lit room. Julie was more nervous than usual. This was
<u>   </u>
                    1
the first time she had ever <u>went</u> to a singles bar, and she wasn't sure how she should
                            2
behave. She stood near the back <u>wall and</u> waited for her <u>eyes'</u> to adjust to the darkness.
                                 3   4
In a minute or so, she could see what was going on. Several women were sipping drinks
at the <u>bar, nearby,</u> unattached men were whispering and glancing at the women. Seated
       5
at small <u>tables pairs</u> of men and women were talking animatedly and <u>smiled</u> at each other.
         6   7
They looked as if they were having a good time. Julie <u>watches</u> for a few minutes and
                                                       8
then went to find the <u>ladies</u> room. Joining the singles scene, she <u>thought could</u> wait just
                       9   10
a little longer.

1. _____   3. _____   5. _____   7. _____   9. _____

2. _____   4. _____   6. _____   8. _____   10. _____

Combined Editing Test 7

Identify the sentence-skills mistakes at the underlined spots in the selection that follows. From the box below, choose the letter that describes each mistake and write it in the space provided. The same mistake may appear more than once. In one case, there is no mistake.

a.	sentence fragment	e.	dangling modifier
b.	run-on	f.	mistake in parallelism
c.	mistake in pronoun reference	g.	missing comma
d.	mistake in subject-verb agreement	h.	missing quotation marks
		i.	no mistake

A clerk who works in a computerized office was complaining to me the other day about how impersonal his workplace has become. "It's just not the same," he <u>insisted</u>[1] "as it was before <u>they</u>[2] put in all the new <u>systems.</u>[3] One of the things that really bother him <u>are</u>[4] the computer terminal on which he has to type his figures. <u>Cold and impersonal,</u>[5] he finds it much more threatening than the typewriter he used before the managers decided to modernize. He also misses the walls and shelf he had in his old office. <u>Before the department was reorganized as an open office without partitions.</u>[6] Now he <u>don't</u>[7] have any place to put his trophies and the pictures of his <u>family, he</u>[8] feels vulnerable out <u>there</u>[9] in the open where everyone can see him. The new office may be more streamlined and <u>with efficiency,</u>[10] but something is definitely missing—perhaps the feeling that it is a place where people can be people.

1. _____ 3. _____ 5. _____ 7. _____ 9. _____

2. _____ 4. _____ 6. _____ 8. _____ 10. _____

Combined Editing Test 8

Identify the sentence-skills mistakes at the underlined spots in the selection that follows. From the box below, choose the letter that describes each mistake and write it in the space provided. The same mistake may appear more than once. In one case, there is no mistake.

a. sentence fragment	e. apostrophe mistake
b. run-on	f. missing comma
c. mistake in parallelism	g. dropped -*ly* ending
d. missing capital letter	(adverb mistake)
	h. no mistake

What would you do if you were driving to work during the morning rush hour and you saw a family of geese blocking the road? The adult <u>canada</u> goose and her goslings
1

had been standing on the west side of River Drive, looking at the water on the other side. When a slight break in traffic <u>occurred the</u> mother started across. Traffic <u>slowed brakes</u>
2   3

squealed, and all the babies except one made it to the other side. That one stood right in the middle of the highway. <u>Blocking one of the lanes.</u> Meanwhile, the mother goose
4

honked <u>helpless</u> from the safety of the riverbank. Not a single car moved as all the
5

<u>driver's</u> waited for the gosling to cross. <u>Then, just</u> as one driver opened his door to get
6   7

out and rescue the little <u>one the</u> mother gave a deafening <u>honk, the</u> gosling quickly
8   9

hurried over to join her. The drivers restarted their motors and <u>were continuing</u> on their
10

way, proud, perhaps, that they had helped save a life.

1. _____   3. _____   5. _____   7. _____   9. _____

2. _____   4. _____   6. _____   8. _____   10. _____

Combined Editing Test 9

Locate and correct the twenty sentence-skills mistakes in the following passage. The mistakes are listed in the box below. As you locate each mistake, write the number of the word group containing it. Use the spaces provided.

---

3 sentence fragments ____

____ ____

2 run-ons ____ ____

3 irregular verb mistakes ____

____ ____

1 dangling modifier ____

1 missing comma after a quotation

____

4 missing apostrophes ____

____ ____ ____

6 missing quotation marks ____

____ ____ ____ ____ ____

---

[1]Our infant daughter was a happy, pleasant child until she reached the age of two. [2]Then, she begun having tantrums—and not just any tantrums. [3]No, Jennifer would thrash on the floor, knock her head against the wall, and let out a bloodcurdling scream that pierced our eardrums like an ice pick. [4]Consulting our child-care books, the decision was made to ignore the screams, Jennifers attempts to capture our attention might then stop. [5]Have you ever tried to ignore a toddler whose howls and moans make the walls shake? [6]We had to think of something before Jennifer drove us to a pair of padded cells, it was then that I came up with a notion of a "screaming place." [7]The next time that Jennifer started the low, siren-like wail that preceded a full-fledged scream. [8]I carried her to the downstairs bathroom. [9]I said, Jennifer, this is your screaming place. [10]Its small, so youll hear your screams nice and loud. [11]You can roll around on the soft carpet. [12]You can even get a drink if your throat feels dry. [13]Jennifer comed barreling out of the bathroom in about ten seconds—screaming—and I gently pushed her back in. [14]When she came out the next time, she had stopped screaming. [15]After a few more episodes like this. [16]Jennifer's tantrums started to subside. [17]Apparently, the private screaming place wasnt as much fun as the more public parts of the house. [18]I knew my system had triumphed when, one day, I passed Jennifer's room and heard some muffled moans. [19]I poked my head in the door. [20]And asked her why she was crying. [21]"I'm not crying, Daddy," she said. [22]"Brownie's crying." [23]Brownie is the name of Jennifer's teddy bear. [24]But where is Brownie? I asked. [25]Jennifer walked over to the closet and opened it, revealing a rather lonely stuffed bear. [26]He's in his screaming place she replied.

Combined Editing Test 10

Locate and correct the twenty sentence-skills mistakes in the following passage. The mistakes are listed in the box below. As you locate each mistake, write the number of the word group containing it. Use the spaces provided.

---

4 sentence fragments ____ ____   1 dangling modifier ____

____ ____   3 apostrophe mistakes

2 run-ons ____ ____   ____ ____ ____

2 dropped verb endings   2 mistakes in parallelism

____ ____   ____ ____

2 irregular verb mistakes   4 missing capital letters

____ ____   ____ ____ ____ ____

---

[1]In 1940, an unusual young man was buried. [2]In a custom-built, ten-foot-long casket. [3]The young man needed such a gigantic casket because he himself was a giant. [4]He was just a shade under nine feet tall. [5]And weighed almost five hundred pounds. [6]Robert Wadlow, an american born in 1918, lived a tragic, pain-filled life. [7]Weighing eight pounds, Robert's mother had given birth to a normal infant. [8]But by the age of five, Robert stood over five feet tall. [9]His exceptional growth never stopped he grew three inches every year until he died. [10]Because a human's internal organs cant support an excessively large body. [11]Robert was doomed to an early death. [12]Just before he died, he was fitted with ankle braces to help support his enormous weight. [13]One of the braces cut into an ankle, triggering an infection that overload his already strained nervous system.

[14]The wadlow familys reaction to Robert's plight was an intelligent and loving one. [15]They refuse to let him be exploited, turning down offers from freak shows and greedy promoters. [16]Robert's parents attempted to give him a normal life they encouraged him to read, to join the boy scouts, and playing sports. [17]When the company that made Robert's shoes offered to employ him as a traveling representative. [18]Mr. Wadlow drove his son more than 300,000 miles, all over the United States, on behalf of the shoe company. [19]The Wadlows helped Robert to stay cheerful and avoiding the depression and gloom he could so easily have sinked into. [20]Robert's life is an example of tremendous courage and persistence in the face of incredible handicap's.

Combined Editing Test 11

Locate and correct the twenty sentence-skills mistakes in the following passage. The mistakes are listed in the box below. As you locate each mistake, write the number of the word group containing it. Use the spaces provided.

4 sentence fragments ____ ____ ____ ____	2 missing commas after introductory words ____ ____
2 run-ons ____ ____	
4 irregular verb mistakes ____ ____ ____ ____	2 missing commas around an interrupter ____ ____
1 mistake in subject-verb agreement ____	3 clichés ____ ____ ____
2 mistakes in parallelism ____ ____	

¹Everyone suffer from an occasional bad mood, but I get down in the dumps more often than other people. ²As a result I've developed a list of helpful hints for dealing with depression, one thing I've learned to do is to keep a mood diary. ³About four times a day, I jot down a one-word description of my mood at that moment—sad, tired, frustrated, happy, and so on. ⁴Then I ask myself questions like, ''What event preceded this mood? ⁵Have I just ate a lot of junk food or drank a lot of coffee? ⁶Have I felt this way before?'' ⁷After keeping this diary for a while. ⁸I've began to see patterns to my moods. ⁹I've found for example that consuming a lot of salty foods like chips or pretzels makes me feel tense. ¹⁰Another mood-controlling hint that I've took is to exercise every day. ¹¹Exercise seems to prevent depression, it also helps me to sleep better. ¹²Any type of exercise works, including jogging, dancing, and even just to walk around the block. ¹³I can also overcome depression by giving myself a small treat at those times my spirits are under the weather. ¹⁴For instance, going to a movie, listening to a record album, or a new shirt. ¹⁵Finally, I try not to go to sleep in a bad mood. ¹⁶I find that I will probably wake up in the same mood I fell asleep in. ¹⁷Before getting into bed I'll do some relaxation techniques. ¹⁸Like deep breathing or stretching exercises. ¹⁹Or, I'll soak in a hot tub. ²⁰Which seems to pull the tension out of my muscles. ²¹If I still feel miserable, I try to keep my chin up, for no bad mood lasts forever.

Combined Editing Test 12

Locate and correct the twenty sentence-skills mistakes in the following passage. The mistakes are listed in the box below. As you locate each mistake, write the number of the word group containing it. Use the spaces provided.

---

4 sentence fragments ____

____ ____ ____

1 run-on ____

4 dropped verb endings

____ ____ ____ ____

1 mistake in subject-verb
agreement ____

1 mistake in pronoun
agreement ____

1 missing comma between
complete thoughts ____

2 missing commas
around an interrupter

____ ____

3 missing capital letters

____ ____ ____

3 apostrophe mistakes

____ ____ ____

---

[1]A former advertising copywriter named paul stevens explain in a book called *I Can Sell You Anything* how advertisers use "weasel words" to persuade people to buy. [2]Weasel words are slippery, sneaky words that may not really mean what they imply. [3]Some of them make you believe things that have never been stated. [4]For example, the weasel words *help* and *like*. [5]How many ads can you think of that include the phrases *helps stop, helps prevent,* or *helps fight?* [6]A toothpaste manufacturer couldnt possibly say that their product "stops cavities forever" so that weasel word *helps* is put in front of the claim. [7]Now the ad sound impressive. [8]But doesn't actually guarantee anything. [9]The same is true of *like*. [10]If a household cleanser claims that it clean "like a white tornado." [11]Are you impressed? [12]The image of the powerful, dirt-sucking whirlwind has gripped your mind. [13]However if you think about it a tornado springing out of a bottle is clearly impossible. [14]then there is the weasel words that don't have any particular meaning. [15]Words like *taste, flavor,* and *good looks* are all base on subjective standards. [16]That vary with each individual. [17]The truth is that every cigarette in the world can "taste best," every car manufacturer can claim the "most advanced styling." [18]Theres just no scientific way to measure qualities like these. [19]Advertisers, using weasel words, manipulate language to win the trust (and the cash) of consumer's.

Sentence Variety Through Combining Activities

INTRODUCTION

Part One of this book gives you practice in the skills needed to write clear sentences. Part Two helps you work on reinforcing those skills. The purpose of this part of the book—Part Three—is to provide you with methods for writing varied and interesting sentences. Through the technique of sentence combining, you will learn about the many different options for expressing a given idea. At the same time, you will develop a natural instinct and "ear" for choosing the option that sounds best in a particular situation. When you finish Part Three, you will be able to compose sentences that bring to your writing style a greater variety and ease. You will also be able to write sentences that express more complex thoughts.

How Sentence Combining Works: The combining technique used to help you practice various sentence patterns is a simple one. Two or more short sentences are given and then combined in a particular way. You are then asked to combine other short sentences in the same way. Here is an example:

- The diesel truck chugged up the hill.
- It spewed out black smoke.
  Spewing out black smoke, the diesel truck chugged up the hill.

The content of most sentences is given to you, so that you need not focus on *what* you will say; instead, you can concentrate on *how* to say it.

The sentence-combining activities are presented in a sequence of three sections. The first section describes the four traditional sentence patterns in English and explains the important techniques of coordination and subordination central to these patterns. The second section presents other patterns that can be used to add variety to writing. The third section provides a number of practice units in which you can apply the combining patterns you have learned as well as compose patterns of your own.

Four Traditional Sentence Patterns

Sentences in English are traditionally described as *simple*, *compound*, *complex*, or *compound-complex*. This section explains and offers practice in all four types of sentences. The section also describes coordination and subordination—the two central techniques you can use to achieve different kinds of emphasis in your writing.

THE SIMPLE SENTENCE

A simple sentence has a single subject-verb combination.

> Children play.
> The game ended early.
> My car stalled three times last week.
> The lake has been polluted by several neighboring streams.

A simple sentence may have more than one subject:

> Lola and Tony drove home.
> The wind and water dried my hair.

or more than one verb:

> The children smiled and waved at us.
> The lawn mower smoked and sputtered.

or several subjects and verbs:

> Manny, Moe, and Jack lubricated my car, replaced the oil filter, and cleaned the spark plugs.

Activity

On separate paper, write:

> Three sentences, each with a single subject and verb
> Three sentences, each with a single subject and a double verb
> Three sentences, each with a double subject and a single verb

In each case, underline the subject once and the verb twice. (See pages 10–11 if necessary for more information on subjects and verbs.)

THE COMPOUND SENTENCE

A compound, or ''double,'' sentence is made up of two (or more) simple sentences. The two complete statements in a compound sentence are usually connected by a comma plus a joining word (*and, but, for, or, nor, so, yet*).

A compound sentence is used when you want to give equal weight to two closely related ideas. The technique of showing that ideas have equal importance is called *coordination*.

Following are some compound sentences. Each sentence contains two ideas that the writer considers equal in importance.

> The rain increased, so the officials canceled the game.
> Martha wanted to go shopping, but Fred refused to drive her.
> Tom was watching television in the family room, and Marie was upstairs on the phone.
> I had to give up wood carving, for my arthritis had become very painful.

Activity 1

Combine the following pairs of simple sentences into compound sentences. Use a comma and a logical joining word (*and, but, for, so*) to connect each pair.

Note: If you are not sure what *and, but, for,* and *so* mean, review pages 41–43.

Example ● We hung up the print.

● The wall still looked bare.

We hung up the print, but the wall still looked bare.

1. ● I am studying computer science.

● My sister is majoring in communications.

_____

_____

2. ● The children started hitting each other.

● I made them turn off the TV.

_____

_____

3. ● Betsy put masking tape on her forehead at night.

● She wanted to stop wrinkles from forming.

_____

_____

4. ● The pizza was covered with salty anchovies and pepperoni.

● He picked up the salt shaker as usual.

_____

_____

5. ● She felt faint.

● She grabbed the metal lamppost.

_____

_____

Activity 2

On separate paper, write five compound sentences of your own. Use a different joining word (*and, but, for, or, nor, so, yet*) to connect the two complete ideas in each sentence.

THE COMPLEX SENTENCE

A complex sentence is made up of a simple sentence (a complete statement) and a statement that begins with a dependent word.* Here is a list of common dependent words:

Dependent Words

after	if, even if	when, whenever
although, though	in order that	where, wherever
as	since	whether
because	that, so that	which, whichever
before	unless	while
even though	until	who
how	what, whatever	whose

A complex sentence is used when you want to emphasize one idea over another in a sentence. Look at the following complex sentence:

Because I forgot the time, I missed the final exam.

The idea that the writer wants to emphasize here—*I missed the final exam*—is expressed as a complete thought. The less important idea—*Because I forgot the time*—is subordinated to the complete thought. The technique of giving one idea less emphasis than another is called *subordination.*

Following are other examples of complex sentences. In each case, the part starting with the dependent word is the less emphasized part of the sentence.

While Sue was eating breakfast, she began to feel sick.
I checked my money *before* I invited Tom for lunch.
When Jerry lost his temper, he also lost his job.
Although I practiced for three months, I failed my driving test.

---

* The two parts of a complex sentence are sometimes called an *independent clause* and a *dependent clause. A clause* is simply a word group that contains a subject and a verb. An *independent clause* expresses a complete thought and can stand alone. A *dependent clause* does not express a complete thought in itself and "depends on" the independent clause to complete its meaning. Dependent clauses always begin with a dependent or subordinating word.

Activity 1

Use logical dependent words to combine the following pairs of simple sentences into complex sentences. Place a comma after a dependent statement when it starts the sentence.

Examples
- I obtained a credit card.
- I began spending money recklessly.

  When I obtained a credit card, I began spending money recklessly.

- Alan dressed the turkey.
- His brother greased the roasting pot.

  Alan dressed the turkey while his brother greased the roasting pot.

1.
   - The movie disgusted Karen.
   - She walked out after twenty minutes.

   _____

   _____

2.
   - The house had been burglarized.
   - Dave couldn't sleep soundly for several months.

   _____

   _____

3.
   - My vision begins to fade.
   - I know I'd better get some sleep.

   _____

   _____

4.
   - The family would need a place to sleep.
   - Fred told the movers to unload the mattresses first.

   _____

   _____

5.
   - The hurricane hit the coast.
   - We crisscrossed our windows with strong tape.

   _____

   _____

Activity 2

Rewrite the following sentences, using subordination rather than coordination. Include a comma when a dependent statement starts a sentence.

Example The hair dryer was not working right, so I returned it.

Because the hair dryer was not working right, I returned it.

1. The muffler shop advertised same-day service, but my car wasn't ready for three days.

    _____

    _____

2. The high-blood-pressure pills produced dangerous side effects, so the government banned them.

    _____

    _____

3. Phil lopped dead branches off the tree, and Michelle stacked them into piles on the ground below.

    _____

    _____

4. Anne wedged her handbag tightly under her arm, for she was afraid of muggers.

    _____

    _____

5. Ellen counted the cash three times, but the total still didn't tally with the amount on the register tape.

    _____

    _____

Activity 3

Combine the following simple sentences into complex sentences. Omit repeated words. Use the dependent words *who, which,* or *that.* Use commas around the dependent statement only if it seems to interrupt the flow of thought in the sentence. (See also pages 190–191.)

Notes: The word *who* refers to persons. The word *which* refers to things. The word *that* refers to persons or things.

Examples   • Clyde picked up a hitchhiker.
              • The hitchhiker was traveling around the world.

Clyde picked up a hitchhiker who was traveling around the

world.

              • Larry is a sleepwalker.
              • Larry is my brother.

Larry, who is my brother, is a sleepwalker.

1.   • The boy was in a motorcycle accident.
     • The boy limps.

     _____

     _____

2.   • Joan is a champion weight lifter.
     • Joan is my neighbor.

     _____

     _____

3.   • The two screws were missing from the assembly kit.
     • The two screws held the bicycle frame together.

     _____

     _____

4.   • The letter is from my ex-wife.
     • The letter arrived today.

     _____

     _____

5.   • The tall hedge muffled the highway noise.
     • The hedge surrounded the house.

     _____

     _____

Activity 4

On separate paper, write eight complex sentences, using, in turn, the dependent words *unless, if, after, because, when, who, which,* and *that.*

THE COMPOUND-COMPLEX SENTENCE

A compound-complex sentence is made up of two (or more) simple sentences and one (or more) dependent statements. In the following examples, there is a solid line under the simple sentences and a dotted line under the dependent statements.

When the power line snapped, Jack was listening to the stereo, and Linda was reading in bed.

After I returned to school following a long illness, the math instructor gave me makeup work, but the history instructor made me drop her course.

Activity I

Read through each sentence to get a sense of its overall meaning. Then insert a logical joining word (*and, or, but, for,* or *so*) and a logical dependent word (such as *until, because, since, when,* or *although*).

1. _____ he had worked at the construction site all day, Tom decided not to meet his friends at the diner, _____ he was too tired to think.

2. _____ the projector broke for a second time, some people in the audience hissed, _____ others shouted for a refund.

3. Nothing could be done _____ the river's floodwaters receded, _____ the townspeople waited helplessly in the emergency shelter.

4. _____ you are sent damaged goods, the store must replace the items, _____ it must issue a full refund.

5. Sears had the outdoor grill I wanted, _____ the clerk wouldn't sell it to me _____ it was the floor sample.

Activity 2

On separate paper, write five compound-complex sentences.

REVIEW OF COORDINATION AND SUBORDINATION

Remember that coordination and subordination are ways of showing the exact relationship of ideas within a sentence. Through coordination we show that ideas are of equal importance. When we coordinate, we use the words *and, but, for, or, nor, so, yet.* Through subordination we show that one idea is less important than another. When we subordinate, we use dependent words like *when, although, since, while, because,* and *after.* A list of common dependent words is given on page 394.

Activity

Use coordination or subordination to combine the groups of simple sentences on the next pages into one or more longer sentences. Omit repeated words. Since a variety of combinations is possible, you might want to jot down several combinations on separate paper. Then read them aloud to find the combination that sounds best.

Keep in mind that the relationship among ideas in a sentence will often be clearer when subordination rather than coordination is used.

Example
- My car is not starting on cold mornings.
- I think the battery needs to be replaced.
- I already had it recharged once.
- I don't think it would help to charge it again.

Because my car is not starting on cold mornings, I think the battery needs to be replaced. I already had it recharged once, so I don't think it would help to charge it again.

Comma Hints

a   Use a comma at the end of a word group that starts with a dependent word (as in "Because my car is not starting on cold mornings, . . .").

b   Use a comma between independent word groups connected by *and, but, for, or, nor, so, yet* (as in "I already had it recharged once, so . . .").

1. • I needed butter to make the cookie batter.
   • I couldn't find any.
   • I used vegetable oil instead.

   _____

   _____

   _____

2. • Gina had worn glasses for fifteen years.
   • She decided to get contact lenses.
   • She would be able to see better.
   • She would look more glamorous.

   _____

   _____

   _____

3. • The children at the day-care center took their naps.
   • They unrolled their sleeping mats.
   • They piled their shoes and sneakers in a corner.

   _____

   _____

   _____

4. • Jack dialed the police emergency number.
   • He received a busy signal.
   • He dropped the phone and ran.
   • He didn't have time to call back.

   _____

   _____

   _____

5. • Louise disliked walking home from the bus stop.
   • The street had no overhead lights.
   • It was lined with abandoned buildings.

   _____

   _____

   _____

6. ● The rain hit the hot pavement.
   ● Plumes of steam rose from the blacktop.
   ● Cars slowed to a crawl.
   ● The fog obscured the drivers' vision.

   _____

   _____

   _____

   _____

7. ● His car went through the automated car wash.
   ● Harry watched from the sidelines.
   ● Floppy brushes slapped the car's doors.
   ● Sprays of water squirted onto the roof.

   _____

   _____

   _____

   _____

8. ● The pipes had frozen.
   ● The heat had gone off.
   ● We phoned the plumber.
   ● He couldn't come for two days.
   ● He had been swamped with emergency calls.

   _____

   _____

   _____

9. ● My car developed an annoying rattle.
   ● I took it to the service station.
   ● The mechanic looked under the hood.
   ● He couldn't find what was wrong.

   _____

   _____

   _____

   _____

10. ● The childproof cap on the aspirin bottle would not budge.
   ● The arrows on the bottleneck and cap were lined up.
   ● I pried the cap with my fingernails.
   ● One nail snapped off.
   ● The cap still adhered tightly to the bottle.

   _____

   _____

   _____

   _____

   _____

Other Patterns That Add Variety to Writing

This section gives you practice in other patterns or methods that can add variety and interest to your sentences. These patterns can be used with any of the four types of sentences already explained. Note that you will not have to remember the grammar terms that are often used to describe the patterns. What is important is that you practice the various patterns extensively, so that you increase your sense of the many ways available to you for expressing your ideas.

–ING WORD GROUPS

Use an *-ing* word group at some point in a sentence. Here are examples:

> The doctor, *hoping* for the best, examined the x-rays.
> *Jogging* every day, I soon raised my energy level.

More information about *-ing* words, also known as *present participles,* appears on page 89.

Activity 1

Combine each pair of sentences below into one sentence by using an *-ing* word and omitting repeated words. Use a comma or commas to set off the *-ing* word group from the rest of the sentence.

Example • The diesel truck chugged up the hill.
         • It spewed out smoke.
         Spewing out smoke, the diesel truck chugged up the hill.

         or *The diesel truck, spewing out smoke, chugged up the hill.*

1. • The sparrow tried to keep warm.
   • It fluffed out its feathers.

   _____

   _____

2. • I managed to get enough toothpaste on my brush.
   • I squeezed the tube as hard as I could.

   _____

   _____

3. • The janitor started up the enormous boiler.
   • He checked the glass-faced gauges.

   _____

   _____

4. • The runner set his feet into the starting blocks.
   • He stared straight ahead.

   _____

   _____

5. • The produce clerk cheerfully weighed bags of fruit and vegetables.
   • He chatted with each customer.

   _____

   _____

Activity 2

On separate paper, write five sentences of your own that contain *-ing* word groups.

–ED WORD GROUPS

Use an *-ed* word group at some point in a sentence. Here are examples:

Tired of studying, I took a short break.
Mary, *amused* by the joke, told it to a friend.
I opened my eyes wide, *shocked* by the red ''F'' on my paper.

More information about *-ed* words, also known as *past participles,* appears on page 89.

Activity

Combine each of the following pairs of sentences into one sentence by using an *-ed* word and omitting repeated words. Use a comma or commas to set off the *-ed* word group from the rest of the sentence.

Example   ● Tim woke up with a start.
　　　　　 ● He was troubled by a dream.
　　　　　 Troubled by a dream, Tim woke up with a start.

　　　　 or *Tim, troubled by a dream, woke up with a start.*

1. ● I dozed off.
 ● I was bored with the talk show.

   _____

2. ● The old dollar bill felt like tissue paper.
 ● It was crinkled with age.

   _____

3. ● The students acted nervous and edgy.
 ● They were crowded into a tiny, windowless room.

   _____

   _____

4. ● I waited for someone to open the door.
 ● I was loaded down with heavy bags of groceries.

   _____

   _____

5. ● Ron bought a green-striped suit.
 ● He was tired of his conservative wardrobe.

   _____

APPOSITIVES

Use appositives. An *appositive* is a word group that renames a noun (any person, place, or thing). Here is an example:

Rita, a good friend of mine, works as a police officer.

The word group *a good friend of mine* is an appositive that renames the word *Rita*.

Activity 1

Combine each of the following pairs of sentences into one sentence by using an appositive and omitting repeated words. Most appositives are set off by commas.

Example ● Alan Thorn got lost during the hiking trip.
            ● He is a former Eagle Scout.
            Alan Thorn, a former Eagle Scout, got lost during the hiking
            trip.

1. ● My uncle attends counseling sessions to cure his addiction.
   ● My uncle is a compulsive gambler.

   _____

   _____

2. ● Marie leafed through the *National Enquirer.*
   ● The *National Enquirer* is a weekly paper filled with sensational stories.

   _____

   _____

3. ● The porch carpet felt like hundreds of little needles.
   ● The porch carpet was a green plastic imitation of grass.

   _____

   _____

4. ● I could eat chocolate fudge ice cream at every meal.
   ● Chocolate fudge ice cream is my favorite food.

   _____

   _____

5. ● Ralph lives in my room.
    ● Ralph is my pet tarantula.

_____

_____

Activity 2

On separate paper, write five sentences of your own that contain appositives. Use commas as necessary to set the appositives off.

–LY OPENERS

Use a word ending in -ly to open a sentence. Here are examples:

Gently, he mixed the chemicals together.
Anxiously, the contestant looked at the game clock.
Skillfully, the quarterback rifled a pass to his receiver.

More information about -ly words, which are also known as _adverbs,_ appears on page 119.

Activity 1

On the following page are five pairs of sentences. Combine each pair into one sentence by starting with a word ending in -ly. Omit repeated words. Place a comma after the opening -ly word. Note the example below.

Example   ● I gave several yanks to the starting cord of the lawn mower.
              ● I was angry.

Angrily, I gave several yanks to the starting cord of the lawn mower.

1. ● Fran hung up on the telephone salesman.
   ● She was abrupt.

   _____

   _____

2. ● The thief slipped one of the watches into her coat sleeve.
   ● She was casual.

   _____

   _____

3. ● I tugged on my shoes and pants as the doorbell rang.
   ● I was swift.

   _____

   _____

4. ● The defense lawyer cross-examined the witnesses.
   ● He was gruff.

   _____

   _____

5. ● Estelle poked the corner of a handkerchief into her eye.
   ● She was careful.

   _____

   _____

Activity 2

On separate paper, write five sentences of your own that begin with *-ly* words.

TO OPENERS

Use a *to* word group to open a sentence. Here are examples:

To succeed in that course, you must attend every class.
To help me sleep better, I learned to quiet my mind through meditation.
To get good seats, we went to the game early.

The combination of *to* and a verb is also known as an *infinitive,* as explained on page 89.

Activity 1

Combine each of the following pairs of sentences into one sentence by starting with a *to* word group and omitting repeated words. Use a comma after the opening *to* word group.

Example   ●   I fertilize the grass every spring.

          ●   I want to make it greener.

          To make the grass greener, I fertilize it every spring.

1. ●   We set bricks on the ends of the picnic table.
   ●   We did this to anchor the flapping tablecloth.

   _____

   _____

2. ●   Darryl scraped the windshield with a plastic credit card.
   ●   He did this to break up the coating of ice.

   _____

   _____

3. ●   We gave our opponents a ten-point advantage.
   ●   We wanted to make the basketball game more even.

   _____

   _____

4. ●   I offered to drive the next five hundred miles.
   ●   I wanted to give my wife a rest.

   _____

   _____

5. ●   Fran added Hamburger Helper to the ground beef.
   ●   She did this to feed the unexpected guests.

   _____

   _____

Activity 2

On separate paper, write five sentences of your own that begin with *to* word groups.

PREPOSITIONAL PHRASE OPENERS

Use prepositional phrases as openers. Here are examples:

> *From the beginning,* I disliked my boss.
> *In spite of her work,* she failed the course.
> *After the game,* we went to a movie.

Prepositional phrases begin with words like *in, from, of, at, by,* and *with.* A list of common prepositions appears on page 13.

Activity 1

Combine each of the following groups of sentences into one sentence. First, omit repeated words. Then, start each sentence with a suitable prepositional phrase and place the other prepositional phrases in places that sound right. Generally you should use a comma after the opening prepositional phrase.

Example
- A fire started.
- It did this at 5 A.M.
- It did this inside the garage.

    At 5 A.M., a fire started inside the garage.

1.
- The old man wrote down my address.
- He did this on the bus.
- He did this with a stubby pencil.

_____

_____

2.
- Special bulletins interrupted regular programs.
- They did this during the day.
- The bulletins were about the astronauts' flight.

_____

_____

3.
- My clock radio turned itself on.
- It did this at 6:00 A.M.
- It did this with a loud blast.
- The loud blast was of rock music.

_____

_____

4. ● The security guard looked.
    ● He did this at the concert.
    ● He did this in Sue's pocketbook.
    ● He did this for concealed bottles.

    _____

    _____

5. ● A plodding turtle crawled.
    ● It did this on the highway.
    ● It did this toward the grassy shoulder of the road.

    _____

    _____

Activity 2

On separate paper, write five sentences of your own that begin with prepositional phrases and that contain at least one other prepositional phrase.

SERIES OF ITEMS

Use a series of items. Following are two of the many items that can be used in a series: adjectives and verbs.

Adjectives in Series

Adjectives are descriptive words. Here are examples:

The *husky young* man sanded the *chipped, weather-worn* paint off the fence.

Husky and *young* are adjectives that describe *man; chipped* and *weather-worn* are adjectives that describe *paint*. More information about adjectives appears on page 117.

Activity 1

Combine each of the following groups of sentences into one sentence by using adjectives in a series and omitting repeated words. Use commas between adjectives only when *and* inserted between them sounds natural.

Example
- I sewed a set of buttons onto my coat.
- The buttons were shiny.
- The buttons were black.
- The coat was old.
- The coat was green.

  I sewed a set of shiny black buttons onto my old green coat.

1.
   - The child gazed at the gift box.
   - The child was impatient.
   - The child was excited.
   - The gift box was large.
   - The gift box was mysterious.

   _____

   _____

2.
   - Juice spurted out of the caterpillar.
   - The juice was sticky.
   - The caterpillar was fuzzy.
   - The caterpillar was crushed.

   _____

   _____

3.
   - The car dangled from the crane.
   - The car was battered.
   - The crane was gigantic.
   - The crane was yellow.

   _____

   _____

4.
   - Patty squeezed her feet into the shoes.
   - Patty's feet were swollen.
   - Patty's feet were tender.
   - Patty's feet were sunburned.
   - The shoes were tight.

   _____

   _____

5.   ●   The cook flipped the hamburgers on the grill.
      ●   The cook was tall.
      ●   The cook was white-aproned.
      ●   The hamburgers were thick.
      ●   The hamburgers were juicy.
      ●   The grill was grooved.
      ●   The grill was metal.

_____

_____

Activity 2

On separate paper, write five sentences of your own that contain a series of adjectives.

Verbs in Series

Verbs are words that express action. Here are examples:

> In my job as a cook's helper, I *prepared* salads, *sliced* meat and cheese, and *made* all kinds of sandwiches.

Basic information about verbs appears on pages 10–11.

Activity 1

Combine each group of sentences on the next page into one sentence by using verbs in a series and omitting repeated words. Use a comma between verbs in a series.

Example   ●   In the dingy bar Sam shelled peanuts.
         ●   He sipped a beer.
         ●   He talked up a storm with friends.

In the dingy bar Sam shelled peanuts, sipped a beer, and talked up a storm with friends.

1. • The bank robber donned his gloves.
   • He twirled the lock.
   • He opened the door of the vault.

   _____

2. • Fans at the rock concert popped balloons.
   • They set off firecrackers.
   • They dropped bottles from the balcony.

   _____

3. • The doctor slid the needle into Gordon's arm.
   • She missed the vein.
   • She tried again.

   _____

4. • The magician walked over hot coals.
   • He lay on a bed of nails.
   • He stuck pins into his hands.

   _____

5. • The journalists surrounded the president.
   • They shouted questions.
   • They snapped pictures.

   _____

Activity 2

On separate paper, write five sentences of your own that use verbs in a series.

Note: The section on parallelism (pages 135–140) gives you practice in some of the other kinds of items that can be used in a series.

Sentence-Combining Exercises

This section provides a series of combining exercises. Each exercise consists of several groups of short sentences; the sentences in each group can be combined into one sentence. (Occasionally, however, you may decide that certain sentences are more effective if they are not combined.) The patterns you have already practiced will suggest ideas for combining the short sentences, but do not feel limited to these previous patterns. Use your own natural instinct to explore and compose a variety of sentence combinations. It will help if you write out possible combinations and then read them aloud. Choose the one that sounds best. You will gradually develop an ear for hearing the option that reads most smoothly and clearly and that sounds most appropriate in the context of surrounding sentences. As you continue to practice, you will increase your ability to write more varied, interesting, and sophisticated sentences.

Here is an example of a group of sentences and some possible combinations:

- Martha moved in the desk chair.
- Her moving was uneasy.
- The chair was hard.
- She worked at her assignment.
- The assignment was for her English class.

Martha moved uneasily in the hard desk chair, working at the assignment for her English class.

Moving uneasily in the hard desk chair, Martha worked at the assignment for her English class.

Martha moved uneasily in the hard desk chair as she worked at the assignment for her English class.

While she worked at the assignment for her English class, Martha moved uneasily in the hard desk chair.

Note: In combining groups of short sentences into one sentence, omit repeated words where necessary. Use separate paper.

1   Decline of the Family Dinner

- The family dinner is a memory.
- The dinner is old-fashioned.
- The memory is fading.

- People have changed.
- The changing is of the way they eat.
- They have done this in today's world.

- Both parents work.
- Neither is home to cook.
- The cooking is of an old-fashioned meal.

- There is no time to make a pot roast.
- There is no time to cook a chicken.
- There is no time to prepare a stew.

- The parents arrive home after five o'clock.
- They are tired.
- They do not want to cook.

- Alternatives are available.
- They are alternatives to cooking.

- One alternative is to go to restaurants.
- These are for fast food.
- One restaurant is McDonald's.
- One restaurant is Burger King.

- There is a second alternative.
- It is to order take-out food.
- One example is pizza.
- Another example is Chinese food.

- There is another option that parents have.
- They can buy TV dinners.
- The dinners are frozen.
- They can be made quickly.
- The making is in microwave ovens.

- There is a final option.
- The option is the worst one of all.

- Family members can eat their own quick meals.
- The eating is at different times.
- The eating is at different places.

- The family should eat dinner together.
- The dinner should be around a table at home.

- Dinner is not just the sharing of a meal.
- It is time spent talking about events of the day.
- It is time spent sharing each other's lives.

- The family dinner is a ritual.
- The ritual is an important one.
- The ritual is a human one.
- The ritual should not be lost.

2 Kids and Mud

- Two toddlers sit on the ground.
- They play in the mud.
- The mud is wet and gooey.

- The children bury their hands in the mud.
- The children bury their toys in the mud.
- The children bury their feet in the mud.

- Mud is the pal of kids.
- Mud makes great pies and cakes.

- Kids don't need expensive toys.
- Kids don't need a television set.
- Kids don't need their parents' help.

- They do need some wet dirt.
- They do need nice parents.
- Nice parents won't yell about their clothes.

- Kids have imaginations.
- Their imaginations are marvelous.
- Their imaginations turn mud into cakes.
- Their imaginations turn dust into icing.
- Their imaginations turn twigs into candles.

- Kids are lucky.
- Mud can't be taken away by adults.
- Mud can't be improved upon.

- No one will package mud in a can.
- No one will sell it on television.

- Mud will always be clean fun.

3 English Class

- The teacher said to John,
  "Name three famous poets."
- She did this in a loud voice.

- John rose slowly.
- He hesitated.
- He didn't want to make a mistake.

- The teacher repeated the question.
- She did this in an encouraging voice.

- John began to answer.
- His voice was cracking.
- His palms were sweating.
- His heart was thumping.

- John named Shakespeare.
- He named Frost.
- He couldn't name a third.

- The teacher felt sorry for John.
- She tried to help.
- She did this by giving him a hint.

- The other students snickered.
- They did this when the teacher asked,
  "What's taking you so long, fellow?"

- Several tense minutes passed.
- John blurted, "Longfellow."
- Then he sat down.

- The teacher acknowledged John's
  correct answer.
- The teacher chuckled.
- The other students laughed out loud.

- One student called out, "What took you so long, fellow?"
- He did this in a teasing tone.

- John realized why everyone was laughing.
- He felt embarrassed.

- But he had a good sense of humor.
- He joined in the laughter.

4 Our First Camping Trip

- My husband and I went camping.
- It was for the first time.
- It was an experience.
- The experience was unforgettable.

- We borrowed a tent.
- We borrowed a propane stove.
- We borrowed them from my brother-in-law.
- He had not used them in years.

- We arrived at the campground.
- We chose a spot.
- The spot was to pitch our tent.

- We had forgotten something.
- It was the sheet of directions.
- The directions were for setting up the tent.
- This was unfortunate.

- We tried to put up the tent.
- We used a trial-and-error process.
- The process took us four hours.

- The tent collapsed.
- The collapsing was sudden.
- It was nearly dark.

- We made a dinner later.
- We did this with difficulty.
- The stove at first refused to light.
- The food refused to cook.

- We finished cleaning up.
- We crawled into our sleeping bags.
- We were exhausted.

- A rain awoke us.
- The awakening was brief.
- The rain was light.
- The rain was at 4 A.M.

- Morning came.
- We were damp.
- We were tired.
- We were miserable.

- We had learned the lesson.
- The lesson was important.
- It was that "roughing it" was too rough.
- It was too rough for us.

5   Do-It-Yourself Special

- Mike and Mandy decided to move out of their apartment.
- The apartment was cramped.
- The apartment was a one-bedroom.

- They went to a real estate agent.
- They told her they didn't have much money to spend.

- They looked at lots of houses.
- All the houses were too expensive.

- Finally, they found a house that they could afford.
- The house was little.
- The house was run-down.

- Mr. Perez had built it himself.
- Mr. Perez is a do-it-yourselfer.

- He had used odds and ends to construct the house.
- The odds and ends were from junkyards.

- The front steps had a railing.
- The railing was made from pipes.
- The pipes were rusty.

- Some window frames were metal.
- Others were wooden.

- Inside, the floors tilted.
- The door frames tilted.
- They tilted like the ones in a fun house.

- A crazy quilt of tiles covered the walls.
- The tiles were different-colored.

- The kitchen cabinets were the oddest things in the house.
- The kitchen cabinets were made of scrap lumber and chicken wire.

- Mike and Mandy bought the do-it-yourself special.
- They did this despite all the work that needed to be done.
- They knew it was a place they could call home.

6 Bargain Flight

- Frank planned to visit his grandparents.
- He planned to do this during the semester break.

- His grandparents live in Florida.
- He looked for a cheap flight to Miami.

- One airline offered a fare.
- It was a no-frills fare.
- It was a one-way fare.
- It was a seventy-five-dollar fare.

- So Frank bought a ticket.
- He bought it from Florida Express.

- Frank couldn't find the terminal for Florida Express.
- This happened when he arrived at the airport.

- He saw a sign.
- He saw it after driving around for twenty minutes.
- The sign read: ''Florida Express—North Cargo Terminal.''

- Frank began to have doubts about his bargain flight.
- He did this as he entered the terminal.
- The terminal was dingy.
- The terminal was little-used.

- He imagined a fleet of planes.
- The planes were old.
- The planes were propeller planes.
- The planes were flown by ninety-five-year-old pilots.

- The clerk charged Frank three dollars apiece for his suitcases.
- This happened at the Florida Express counter.

- Frank ran for the plane.
- He did this when the signal to board was given.

- He wedged himself into a seat.
- The seat was worn.
- The seat was narrow.
- He did this after pushing his way down the crowded aisle.

- The cabin attendant asked Frank if he wanted to buy a snack.
- This happened after the plane took off.

- Frank dug four dollars out of his pocket.
- The attendant handed him a plastic dish.
- The dish was tiny.
- The dish was cellophane-wrapped.

- The dish held a brownie.
- The brownie was limp.
- The dish held two crackers.
- The crackers were small.
- The dish held a stick of dried beef.
- The stick was skinny.

- Frank bought a soda.
- The soda cost two dollars.

- Frank sighed with relief.
- He did this when the plane landed in Miami.

- He had spent more money than he had planned.
- At least he was still alive.

7 Practical Joker

- Mark is the practical joker in our family.
- Mark is my older brother.

- He would send away for all the tricks advertised in comic books.
- He would do this when we were kids.

- He sent away for exploding cigars.
- He sent away for black soap.
- He sent away for plastic insects.
- He sent away for sneezing powder.

- He handed me what looked like a kaleidoscope.
- He did this one day.

- You're supposed to twist the tube.
- You're supposed to watch the patterns.
- The patterns are made by bits of glass inside.

- I twisted and turned.
- I couldn't see anything.

- Mark grabbed the kaleidoscope.
- He told me I must need glasses.

- I could tell something was up.
- Mark was almost bursting with held-in laughter.

- I rushed to the bathroom.
- I looked in the mirror.
- I saw a black ring around my right eye.

- Mark had struck again.
- Mark is the practical joker.

- However, Mark outsmarted himself.
- He did this one Sunday evening.

- My sisters and I always took showers then.
- We did this in order to be ready for school the next day.

- Mark had unscrewed the shower head.
- He had poured in a packet of Rit dye.
- We didn't know it.

- Then he replaced the shower head.
- He waited for one of his victims to take a shower.

- My father put on his striped robe.
- He headed for the bathroom.
- He did this while Mark was in the kitchen.
- This was unfortunate.

- A shout pierced the bathroom walls.
- The shout was deafening.
- This happened five minutes later.

- My father burst through the door.
- His face and hands were splattered with navy blue.

- Mark did the sensible thing.
- He did this when he heard the commotion.

- He took off through the back door.
- He didn't return until my father had cooled off.

- Mark was grounded for a month.
- The "Rit incident" failed to cure him of his passion for pranks.

- Today, Mark is still likely to put a fake ice cube with a plastic fly in your drink.
- Or he is likely to leave a rubber snake in your bathtub.

8   Dishwashing Job

- One of the worst experiences of my life began.
- This happened when I showed up for my first night of work.
- It was work as a restaurant dishwasher.

- I was assigned a spot in the kitchen.
- It was in front of the machine I would run.
- The machine was stainless steel.

- My boss showed me how to scrape the dishes.
- He showed me how to spray them.
- He showed me how to load them into a plastic rack.

- Silverware went into another plastic rack.
- The rack was divided into compartments.
- The compartments were for knives, forks, and spoons.

- I was supposed to open the machine.
- I was supposed to stack the various kinds of dishes into piles.
- This would happen when the machine's wash cycle was over.

- Then a busboy would grab the clean dishes and silver.
- He would bring them back into the dining room.

- Business started to pick up.
- This happened at six o'clock.
- The dishes came in faster and faster.

- I tried to scrape and load the dishes as fast as I could.
- I couldn't keep up.

- The counter was piled high with dishes.
- The busboys began to stack pans of them on the floor.

- I was hot.
- I was sweaty.
- My arms were spotted with bits of parsley.
- They were spotted with blobs of mashed potatoes.
- They were spotted with splashes of gravy.

- My fingertips were burned.
- They were burned from grabbing the dishes and silver out of the machine.
- The dishes and silver were hot.

- My boss burst through the double doors of the kitchen.
- He told me to hurry up.
- He told me the dining room was almost out of clean dishes.

- My back was aching.
- My head was splitting.
- I smelled like the garbage can next to me.
- This happened by the end of the night.

- It took all my courage to return to this job the next night.
- The job was tough.
- The job was dirty.

- But I stuck it out.
- I did this even though the work was hard.
- I needed the money.

9 Fish Story

- I decided to go fishing.
- I did this during my vacation.

- I packed a bucket of bait.
- I packed a fishing rod.
- I packed several hooks.
- I packed a sharp knife.

- I unloaded my gear.
- I did this when I arrived at the municipal fishing pier.

- Dozens of people were lined up along the railings.
- They were casting their lines out into the water.
- Or they were waiting patiently for a telltale tug.

- I was filled with anticipation.
- I staked out a spot.
- I cast my line into the water.

- I waited for a long time.
- I was telling myself that a fish would bite soon.

- I ate a ham sandwich.
- I popped open a can of orange soda.

- I felt some resistance on my line.
- I began to reel in my catch.
- This happened finally.

- I knew I must have snagged a fish.
- It must be gigantic.
- I knew this from the pull on the line.
- The pull was strong.

- A teenaged girl was about twenty feet away from me.
- She was also reeling in her line.
- She was doing this anxiously.

- My line began to reach the surface.
- This happened after a great struggle.

- Then, my stomach sank.
- It sank when I saw what had happened.
- My line was hooked together with the girl's.
- It was hooked firmly.

- We had been pulling against each other.
- We had been doing this for the last ten minutes.

- We unsnagged our lines.
- We were embarrassed.
- We began to wait again for the ''big one.''

10 First Day of School

- The first day of school is tough on kids.
- I think it can be even tougher for adults.

- I came to this conclusion last week.
- Last week, two red-letter days occurred.

- I got my six-year-old daughter ready for school.
- I did this on Monday.

- I remembered what it was like to enter the scary world of school.
- I did this as I wiped her face.
- Her face was teary.

- The following day was *my* first day of school.
- The following day was Tuesday.

- I was starting college.
- I was doing this after eight years as a homemaker.

- I drove to the college.
- I was wondering if I had worn the right thing.
- I was wondering if I would look like a grandmother among the young students.

- I consulted my map of the campus.
- I began to look for Asbury Hall.

- I looked at my watch.
- I did this after taking a couple of wrong turns.
- I realized I was going to be late for my first class.

- I crept in.
- I took a seat in the last row.
- I did this when I finally found the right room.

- The professor was already lecturing.
- The students were taking notes.
- The professor was a young woman.
- She was wearing blue jeans.

- That was only the beginning of a day.
- The day was disastrous.
- The day was confusing.

- For example, I hadn't brought any money to buy books.
- I got a warning for parking in a ''faculty-only'' area.

- I cried in sheer frustration.
- I did this when I got home.

- Then my daughter ran into the room.
- She did this to show me a drawing.
- It was a drawing she had done in school.

- She told me that she liked school a lot.
- She told me that she had made lots of new friends.

- My tears turned to laughter.
- This happened as I compared the six-year-old with her mother.
- The six-year-old was confident.
- The mother was frightened.

- I discovered that people of all ages need courage.
- They need it to begin something new.

Writing Assignments

INTRODUCTION

Part Four provides a number of writing assignments so that you can apply the sentence skills practiced in the earlier parts of the book. Applying these skills *in actual writing* is the surest way to master the rules of grammar, mechanics, punctuation, and usage. Part Four begins with a brief description of four key steps that will help you write effectively. Most of the assignments that follow ask you to write simple paragraphs in which you support an opening point, also known as a *topic sentence*. Later assignments give you some practice at writing essays in which you support an overall point, also known as a *thesis statement*.

Note: Make a special effort to apply the sentence skills you have already learned to each assignment. To help you achieve such a transfer, your instructor may ask you to rewrite a paper as many times as necessary for you to correct a sentence-skills mistake. A writing progress chart on pages 501–502 (in Appendix C) will help track your performance.

Writing
Effectively

Here, in a nutshell, is what you need to do to write effectively.

STEP 1: EXPLORE YOUR TOPIC
THROUGH INFORMAL WRITING

First of all, explore the topic that you want to write about or that you have been assigned to write about. You can explore your topic through *informal writing,* which usually means one of three things.

You can *freewrite* about your topic for at least ten minutes. In other words, write for ten minutes whatever comes into your head about your subject. Write without stopping, and without worrying at all about spelling or grammar or the like. Simply get down on paper all the information about the topic that occurs to you.

A second thing you can do is to *make a list of ideas and details* that could go into your paper. Simply pile these items up, one after another, like a shopping list, without worrying about putting them in any special order. Accumulate as many details as you can think of.

A third way to explore your topic is to *write down a series of questions and answers* about the topic. Your questions can start with words like *What, Why, How, When,* and *Where.*

Getting your thoughts and ideas down on paper will help you think more about your topic. With some raw material to look at, you are now in a better position to decide on just how to proceed with the topic.

STEP 2: PLAN YOUR TOPIC
WITH AN INFORMAL OUTLINE

After using informal writing to explore what you want to write about, plan your paper using an *informal outline*. Do two things:

1 *Decide on and write out the point of your paper.* This opening point is also known as a *topic sentence*.
2 *List the supporting reasons that back up your point.* In many cases, you should have at least three supporting reasons. Number them 1, 2, and 3.

Check your reasons carefully. Make sure that each reason truly supports and explains your point. Your outline should be the logical backbone of your paper.

STEP 3: USE TRANSITIONS

Once your outline is worked out, you should have a clear "road map" for writing your paper. As you write the early drafts of the paper, use *transitions* to introduce each of the separate reasons you present to back up your point. For example, you might introduce your first supporting reason with the transitional words *First of all*. You might begin your second reason with the words *Another reason*. And you might begin your final reason with the words *Last of all* or *A final reason*.

STEP 4: EDIT AND PROOFREAD YOUR PAPER

After you have a solid draft, edit and proofread your paper. To evaluate it, ask yourself four questions:

1 Is the paper *unified*? Is all the material in the paper on target in support of the opening point?
2 Is the paper *well supported*? Do I have plenty of specific evidence to back up my opening point?
3 Is the paper *clearly organized*? Does the material proceed in a way that makes sense? Do I use transitions to connect ideas?
4 Is the paper *well written* in terms of sentence skills? When I read the paper aloud, do the sentences flow smoothly and clearly? Have I checked the paper carefully for sentence-skills mistakes?

A number of writing assignments appear on the pages that follow. Most of them are single-paragraph assignments. A few closing assignments give you some practice with the five-paragraph essay form as well.

Writing a Paragraph

The paragraphs you write for these assignments should consist of about eight to twelve sentences. Typically, the point or topic sentence should be the first sentence of the paragraph. All the sentences that follow should support or develop the point expressed in the topic sentence.

1 Best or Worst Job

Write a paragraph on the best or worst job you ever had. Provide three reasons why your job was the best or worst, and provide plenty of details to develop each of your three reasons.

First read the student paper below, and then do the activity that follows. This will prepare you to proceed with your own paragraph.

BATTERY LOADER

The worst job I ever had was working as a loader in a battery plant near my home. For one thing, the work was physically hard. During a nine-hour shift, I had to lift hundreds of assembled batteries off a steadily moving production belt and place them onto wooden skids. I once figured that I was lifting over twenty tons of batteries during each shift. Another drawback of the job was that my partner was uncooperative. He had a sixth sense for when the boss was near, and only then would he do a fair share of work. Otherwise, he found so many ways to avoid work that I lifted three batteries for every two that he lifted. But the worst part of the job was the acid vapor always in the air. The vapor irritated my sinuses and often left me with a headache at the end of a shift. I was afraid that some of the battery chemicals I was inhaling would start building up in my body. I wasted no time, then, in finding another job where I could work in a safer environment.

Activity

Complete the following outline of the student paragraph. Summarize in a few words the details that develop each reason, rather than writing the details out in full.

Point: _____

Reason 1: _____

   Details that develop reason 1: _____

_____

Reason 2: _____

   Details that develop reason 2: _____

_____

_____

Reason 3: _____

   Details that develop reason 3: _____

_____

_____

How to Proceed

1 Think of a job that might be a promising topic. Then write about that job for ten minutes or so, getting down on paper all the good and bad details about it that occur to you. Ask yourself these questions: ''Was this mostly a good job or mostly a bad one? What was its best or worst single feature? Do I have enough details here to write about this job, or should I choose another one?''

2 If the job seems like a promising one to write about, express in a clear, direct sentence exactly what the job was and whether it was the best or worst job you ever had. Do *not* begin by just stating what the job was:

No: I once worked as a loader in a battery plant near my home.

Yes: The worst job I ever had was working as a loader in a battery plant near my home.

Your point: _____

_____

3 Work up a brief outline of the reasons why you liked or disliked the job. Here, for example, is the list of reasons prepared by the author of the student paper above:

The worst job I ever had was working as a loader in a battery plant near my home.

1 Hard work
2 Uncooperative partner
3 Acid smell in air

4 Use your list as a guide to write the first rough draft of your paper. As you write the draft, try to think of details that will make each of your supporting reasons very clear.

For example, the writer above develops his first reason, ''hard work,'' by stating how many tons of batteries he lifted during every shift. He develops his second reason, ''uncooperative partner,'' by telling us how the partner would lift only two batteries to his own three. He develops his third reason, ''acid smell in air,'' by explaining that the vapor irritated his sinuses and gave him a headache.

5 Do *not* expect to finish your paper in a single draft. Writing is a *process*: it happens one step at a time, not all at once. Each step—from informal writing (*prewriting*) to scratch outline to rough draft to second draft—brings you closer to where you want to be. One step helps you go on to the next step. Step by step, you will move toward your goal: a paper that makes a point, supports the point, organizes the support, and is well written in terms of sentence skills.

6 Use transitions to introduce each of your supporting reasons. Here are words to use:

To introduce reason 1: *First of all* or *For one thing*
To introduce reason 2: *Second* or *A second reason* or *Another reason*
To introduce reason 3: *Finally* or *Last of all* or *A final reason*

7 Check the next-to-final draft of your paper for sentence-skills mistakes by reading it aloud. Make sure you are reading exactly what is on the page. If there are rough spots where your writing is hard to read, make the changes needed to ensure that the paper reads smoothly and clearly.

If there are any words whose spelling you are unsure about, check their spellings in a dictionary. You should definitely own a recent paperback dictionary and keep it handy.

Finally, use the checklist on the inside back cover of this book to proofread your paper for specific sentence-skills mistakes.

8 Add a title to the paper. The title should give the reader a quick sense of what your paper is about. It should usually be several words rather than a complete thought.

Be sure to skip a line between the title and the first sentence of your paper. Also, make sure that the first sentence of your paper stands on its own, independent of the title:

No

	Battery Loader
	I once worked as one in a plant near my home.

(The first sentence in the example above depends on the title to make sense; only by looking at the title do we know what *one* refers to.)

Yes

	Battery Loader
	I once worked as a battery loader in a plant near my home.

(Here, the first sentence stands on its own, independent of the title.)

2   Best or Worst Teacher or Boss

Write a paragraph about one of the best or worst teachers or bosses you have ever had. Give three reasons why that person was a best or worst one, and provide details to develop each reason. First, read the short paper below.

MY WORST TEACHER

My seventh-grade algebra teacher, Mrs. Jamison, was the worst teacher I ever had. First of all, she seemed to know little about algebra. If you asked her a question about something that was not in the textbook, her answer was, ''I'm not going to cover things that are not in the book.'' At least once a week, the class had to correct mistakes she made in doing equations on the board. Another reason I disliked Mrs. Jamison is that she favored the girls in the class. She always excused them for the washroom, but she almost never gave permission to the boys. She spoke to the girls in a friendly tone of voice and would smile or say ''Thank you'' when they gave an answer. On the other hand, she seldom thanked a boy and seemed to regard us in general with suspicion. Finally, Mrs. Jamison was often late or absent. She would usually come into the class about four minutes after the start of the hour. We had more substitute teachers in her class than in any other—about three times a month. And since she seldom left any work for the substitute teacher to give us, we would just sit there and do nothing until the class ended. I was not surprised to hear that Mrs. Jamison was fired at the end of the school year.

Activity

Complete the following outline of the paragraph. Summarize in a few words the details that develop each reason rather than writing the details out in full.

Point: _____

_____

Reason 1: _____

Details that develop reason 1: _____

_____

Reason 2: _____

Details that develop reason 2: _____

_____

Reason 3: _____

Details that develop reason 3: _____

_____

_____

How to Proceed

1 Think of a teacher or boss who might be a promising topic. Then make up a list of all the large and small reasons for liking or disliking that teacher or boss.

2 Now, in a clear, direct sentence identify the teacher or boss and state exactly why he or she is or was "best" or "worst." Do *not* begin by just stating who the teacher or boss is or was:

No: My seventh-grade algebra teacher was Mrs. Jamison.
Yes: My seventh-grade algebra teacher, Mrs. Jamison, was the worst teacher I ever had.

Your point: _____

_____

3 Work up a brief outline of your reasons for liking or disliking this teacher or boss. Here, for example, is the list prepared by the author of the student paper above:

My seventh-grade algebra teacher, Mrs. Jamison, was the worst teacher I ever had.

1   Didn't know her subject
2   Favored the girls
3   Often late or absent

4 Use your list as a guide to write the first rough draft of your paper. As you write the draft, try to think of details that will make each of your supporting reasons very clear.

For example, the writer above develops his first reason, "didn't know her subject," by telling us about his teacher's unwillingness to go outside the book and about her mistakes in class. He develops his second reason, "favored the girls," by telling us just how she treated girls differently from boys. He develops his third reason, "often late or absent," by explaining how late she came to class and how often substitute teachers were used.

5 As noted in assignment 1, you should *not* expect to finish your paper in a single draft. Writing is a *process*: it happens one step at a time, not all at once. Each step—from informal writing (or *prewriting*) to scratch outline to rough draft to second draft— brings you closer to where you want to be. One step helps you go on to the next. Step by step, you move toward your goal: a paper that makes a point, supports the point, organizes the support, and is well written in terms of sentence skills.

6   Use transitions to introduce each of your supporting reasons. Here again, as a reminder, are words to use:

To introduce reason 1: *First of all* or *For one thing*
To introduce reason 2: *Second* or *A second reason* or *Another reason*
To introduce reason 3: *Finally* or *Last of all* or *A final reason*

7   Remember: Check the next-to-final draft of your paper for sentence-skills mistakes by reading it aloud. Make sure you are reading exactly what is on the page. If there are rough spots where your writing is hard to read, make the changes needed to ensure that the paper reads smoothly and clearly.

If there are any words whose spelling you are unsure about, check the dictionary. You should own a recent paperback dictionary and keep it handy.

Also remember to use the checklist on the inside back cover of this book to proofread your paper for specific sentence-skills mistakes.

8   Add a title to the paper. Remember that your title should give the reader a quick sense of what your paper is about. It should be several words (usually, no more than five words) rather than a complete thought. Be sure to skip a line between the title and the first sentence of your paper. Remember to make the first sentence of your paper stand on its own, independent of the title:

No

	My Worst Teacher
	This was my seventh-grade algebra teacher, Mrs. Jamison.

(The first sentence here depends on the title to make sense; only by looking at the title do we know what *This* refers to.)

Yes

	My Worst Teacher
	My seventh-grade algebra teacher, Mrs. Jamison, was the
	worst teacher I ever had.

(Here, the first sentence stands on its own, independent of the title.)

3   Living Where You Do

Do you share an apartment or a dormitory room? Do you live with your parents or another family member? Do you own your own home? Write a paragraph about three advantages or disadvantages of living in the place where you live.

How to Proceed

1   First of all, *outline your paragraph,* using the following form. To begin, you might "think on scratch paper" about how to develop the outline.

  Decide on your *point*. (For example, you may decide to write on the disadvantages of living at home.) At the same time, decide on the three *reasons* you can use to support the point. Then summarize in a few words the *details* that develop each reason (rather than writing the details out in full).

Point: There are three advantages (*or* disadvantages) to (sharing an apartment *or* living in a dorm *or* living at home with my family *or* owning my own home, etc.).

Reason 1: _____

  Details that develop reason 1: _____

  _____

  _____

Reason 2: _____

  Details that develop reason 2: _____

  _____

  _____

Reason 3: _____

  Details that develop reason 3: _____

  _____

  _____

2   Use your outline to write the first rough draft of your paper. As you write the draft, think of details to make each of your supporting reasons very clear.

3   Remember: Do not expect to finish your paper in a single draft. Writing is a *process*: it happens one step at a time. Each step—from informal writing (*prewriting*) to scratch outline to rough draft to second draft—brings you closer to where you want to be. One step helps you go on to the next step. Step by step, you move toward your goal: a paper that makes a point, supports the point, organizes the support, and is well written in terms of sentence skills.

4   Use transitions to introduce each of your supporting reasons:

To introduce reason 1: *First of all* or *For one thing*
To introduce reason 2: *Second* or *A second reason* or *Another reason*
To introduce reason 3: *Finally* or *Last of all* or *A final reason*

5   Check the next-to-final draft of your paper for sentence-skills mistakes by reading it aloud. Make sure you are reading exactly what is on the page. If there are rough spots where your writing is hard to read, make the changes needed to ensure that the paper reads smoothly and clearly.

If there are any words whose spelling you are unsure about, check the dictionary. Own a recent paperback dictionary and keep it handy.

Finally, use the checklist on the inside back cover of this book to proofread your paper for specific sentence-skills mistakes.

6   Add a title to the paper, to give the reader a quick sense of what your paper is about. The title should be several words (usually, no more than five) rather than a complete thought.

Be sure to skip a line between the title and the first sentence of your paper. Also, make sure that the first sentence of your paper stands on its own, independent of the title:

No

	Advantages of Living at Home
	There are several advantages.

(The first sentence above depends on the title to make sense; only by looking at the title do we know what *several advantages* refers to.)

Yes

	Advantages of Living at Home
	There are several advantages of living at home.

(The first sentence here stands on its own, independent of the title.)

4 Owning a Car or Using Public Transportation

Write a paragraph about three separate advantages or disadvantages of your car, or of the public transportation you use to get around town.

How to Proceed

1 First of all, outline your paragraph. Use the form below. (However, you may want to use scratch paper first as you "think on paper" about how to develop the outline.) Decide on your point. At the same time, decide on the three reasons you can use to support it. Then summarize in a few words the details that develop each reason (rather than writing the details out in full).

Point: There are several advantages (*or* disadvantages) of (my car *or* of using public transportation in my town).

Reason 1: _____

   Details that develop reason 1: _____

   _____

   _____

Reason 2: _____

   Details that develop reason 2: _____

   _____

   _____

Reason 3: _____

   Details that develop reason 3: _____

   _____

   _____

2 Use your list as a guide to write the first rough draft of your paper. As you write the draft, try to think of details that will make each of your supporting reasons very clear.

3 Do *not* expect to finish your paper in a single draft. Writing is a *process*: it happens step by step, *not* all at once. Each step—from informal writing (*prewriting*) to informal outline to rough draft to second draft—brings you closer to your goal, and one step helps you go on to the next. Gradually, you move toward a paper that makes a point, supports the point, organizes the support, and is well written in terms of sentence skills.

4   Use transitions to introduce each of your supporting reasons:

To introduce reason 1: *First of all* or *For one thing*
To introduce reason 2: *Second* or *A second reason* or *Another reason*
To introduce reason 3: *Finally* or *Last of all* or *A final reason*

5   Check the next-to-final draft of your paper for sentence-skills mistakes by reading it aloud. Make sure you are reading exactly what is on the page. If there are rough spots where your writing is hard to read, make the changes needed to ensure that the paper reads smoothly and clearly.

If there are any words whose spelling you are unsure about, check your dictionary. You should have a recent paperback dictionary and keep it nearby.

Finally, use the checklist on the inside back cover of this book to proofread your paper for specific sentence-skills mistakes.

6   Add a title to the paper, giving the reader a quick sense of what your paper is about. The title should usually be several words rather than a complete thought. (As a general rule of thumb, it should be no longer than five words.)

Be sure to skip a line between the title and the first sentence of your paper. Also, make sure that the first sentence of your paper stands on its own, independent of the title, as illustrated in assignments 1, 2, and 3.

5   Quality of a Parent or Relative

Write a paragraph about one quality of a parent or stepparent, or some other member of your family (a brother, sister, uncle, aunt, cousin, etc.). Below are some qualities you might consider:

self-centered	trustworthy
other-directed	unreliable
generous	neat
stingy	sloppy
hardworking	honest
lazy	dishonest

The quality you focus on might be one of the above, or it might be any other specific quality.

How to Proceed

1 Decide on the topic sentence of your paper and write it down. It should include the name of the person you want to write about, your relationship to that person, and the specific quality you are focusing on. For example:

My brother Ralph is the laziest student I have ever known.

Dolly is an aggressive cousin I know at work.

My sister Eileen has always been self-centered.

My father, Phil, has always been a quick-tempered person.

Write your topic sentence here: _____

_____

2 Make a list of examples that will support your topic sentence. For instance, ask yourself, "What are specific occasions when Ralph really showed what a lazy person he is?" Then write down all the occasions that you can think of when your brother Ralph showed himself to be a lazy person. You may want to freewrite a bit—for ten minutes or so—just writing down everything you can think of about the person and the quality without worrying about spelling, grammar, or the like.

If you cannot think of enough specific examples that will really *show* readers what you want them to see (how lazy Ralph is, for instance), then you may want to write about another quality. Remember that it is not enough to simply *tell* your reader that a certain person is lazy (or hardworking or impatient or ambitious or whatever). Instead, you must give readers supporting details so that they can *see for themselves* the quality you are writing about. You must provide your readers with the evidence needed to prove your point about the person.

3 If you think you have enough material, see if you can prepare a scratch outline of your paragraph. Perhaps you will have three examples that show what a lazy person Ralph is. Decide which example you will present first, which you will describe second, and which you will close with. Always close with the strongest and most dramatic example.

4   Use your scratch outline as a guide to write the first rough draft of your paper. As you write, try to think of additional details that will support your topic sentence.

5   Be sure to use transitions as you develop your paper:

One example of Ralph's laziness is . . .
Another instance . . .
The final and best example of how lazy my brother is . . .

6   Check the next-to-final draft of your paper for sentence-skills mistakes by reading it aloud. Be sure to read exactly what is on the page. If there are places where your writing is hard to read, make the changes needed to ensure that the paper reads smoothly and clearly.

    If there are any words whose spelling you are unsure about, check your dictionary. Remember that you should own a recent paperback dictionary and keep it handy.

    Finally, use the checklist on the inside back cover of this book to proofread your paper for specific sentence-skills mistakes.

7   Add a title to the paper. Remember that the title should give the reader a quick sense of what your paper is about. It should consist of several words that do at least two things: (1) state what quality you are writing about; (2) give the name of the person you are writing about or your relationship to that person or both.

    Here are possible titles for the four sample topic sentences given above:

My Lazy Brother
An Aggressive Cousin
Self-Centered Eileen
A Quick-Tempered Father

Be sure to skip a line between the title and the first sentence of your paper. Also, make sure that the first sentence of your paper stands on its own, independent of the title, as illustrated in assignments 1, 2, and 3.

6 Writing a Story

Write a paragraph about an occasion when you experienced a certain emotion. The emotion might be one of the following, or some other:

disappointment
relief
nervousness
sympathy
happiness
frustration
fear
anger
jealousy
rejection
sadness
regret
surprise
pride

How to Proceed

1   Think of an experience or event in your life in which you felt a certain emotion strongly. Then spend ten minutes freewriting about the experience. Don't worry about spelling or grammar or putting things in the right order. Instead, just try to get down all the details you can think of that may be related to the experience.

2   This preliminary writing will help you decide whether your topic is promising enough to develop further. If it is not, choose another emotion. If it *is*, do two things:

   a   First, write out your topic sentence, underlining the emotion you want to focus on. For example:

   The time I witnessed a mugging was the most <u>frightening</u> moment of my life.

   Taking my driver's test made me more <u>nervous</u> than almost any other experience I can remember.

   One of the <u>happiest</u> moments of my life was winning an award in high school.

   I had a date several years ago that resulted in an <u>embarrassing</u> moment.

b Second, make up a list of all the details involved in the experience. Then prepare a scratch outline in which you arrange these details in time order. *Time order* simply means that details are listed as they occur in time. *First* this happened; *next* this; *then* this; *after* that, this; and so on. Here is a list of time words that you can use:

first, then, next, after, as, before, while, during, now, finally

3 Write the first rough draft of your paper. Be sure to use time words to connect details as you move from the beginning to the middle to the end of your story.

Do not expect to finish your paper in a single draft. Remember that writing is a *process*: it happens one step at a time, not all at once. Each step—from freewriting to list to scratch outline to rough draft to second draft—brings you closer to where you want to be. One step helps you go on to the next step. Step by step, you move toward your goal: the finished paper.

4 Check the next-to-final draft of your paper for sentence-skills mistakes by reading it aloud. Make sure you are reading exactly what is on the page. If there are rough spots where your writing is hard to read, make the changes needed to ensure that the paper reads smoothly and clearly.

If there are any words whose spelling you are unsure about, check the dictionary. You should own a recent paperback dictionary and keep it handy.

Finally, use the checklist on the inside back cover of this book to proofread your paper for specific sentence-skills mistakes.

5 Add a title to the paper. The title should give the reader a quick sense of what your paper is about. It should be several words that identify the emotion you are writing about.

Here are possible titles for the four sample topic sentences given above:

A Frightening Moment
A Nervous Time
A Happy Moment
An Embarrassing Moment

Be sure to skip a line between the title and the first sentence of your paper. Also, make sure that the first sentence of your paper stands on its own, independent of the title, as illustrated in assignments 1, 2, and 3.

7 Describing a Process

Many everyday activities are processes—series of steps carried out in a definite order. Most of these processes are familiar and automatic: for example, getting dressed, preparing breakfast, or traveling to work or school. We are therefore seldom aware of the steps that make up each activity. The purpose of this assignment is to write a paragraph clearly explaining all the steps in a process.

Write a set of specific instructions for *one* of the following two processes:

Option 1

The steps involved in performing your job effectively. Imagine that your boss asks you to write a job description. Detail, one step at a time, the sequence of tasks that you perform in the course of a typical day on the job.

Option 2

Specific instructions for going from your writing classroom to your house. Imagine that you are giving these instructions to a stranger who has just come into the room and who wants to deliver a million dollars to your home. The stranger does not know the area. You want, naturally, to give *exact* directions, including various landmarks that may guide the way.

How to Proceed

1 Write your topic sentence. For example:

There are a series of tasks that a waiter must carry out during a typical day of work at the Four Seas Restaurant.

Here is the way to get from the Resource Center at Atlantic Community College to my home at 33 Tanner Drive in Linwood, New Jersey.

2 Freewrite on your topic for at least ten minutes. Without stopping and without worrying about spelling or grammar, write down all the details you can think of that might go into your paper.

   Freewriting gives you a good start; it gets some raw material down on paper. Now, using your freewriting as a base, make up a list of all the different steps you can think of that are part of the process. After completing your list, look it over and then number your items in time order.

3 Use your list as a guide to write the first rough draft of your paper. As you write, try to think of additional details that will support your opening sentence. Don't expect to finish your paper in one draft. You should, in fact, be ready to write at least several drafts.

4   As you develop your paper, use time words like *first, then, next, now, during, after,* and *finally* to help the reader follow clearly as you move from one step to the next.

5   Check the next-to-final draft of your paper for sentence-skills mistakes by reading it aloud. Make sure you are reading exactly what is on the page. If there are rough spots where your writing is hard to read, make the changes needed to ensure that the paper reads smoothly and clearly.

If there are any words whose spelling you are unsure about, check your dictionary. Remember that you should own a recent paperback dictionary and keep it handy.

Add a title to your paper: several words that give the reader a quick sense of what the paper is about.

Finally, use the checklist on the inside back cover of this book to proofread your paper for specific sentence-skills mistakes.

8   Examining Causes

Why did Ellen drop the course? What caused Patrick to quit his job? Why are jobs so scarce in our town? How has divorce affected Bonnie? Every day we ask questions like these and look for answers. We realize that actions do not take place without causes. By examining the reasons for an action, we seek to understand and explain things that happen in our lives.

How to Proceed

1   In this paragraph, you will analyze the reasons for a certain attitude or behavior. Read the following topic sentences, and then on separate paper prepare scratch outlines for *two* of them.

There are several reasons why I have stopped smoking.

My relationship with _____ (name a relative or friend) is a good one (*or* not a good one) for several reasons.

Television is a bad influence on my life for several reasons.

There are several causes for my not doing well in high school.

Because of certain things that have happened to me, I am here in college at this time.

People enjoy (*or* do not enjoy) eating at _____ (name a particular dining place) for several reasons.

Probably several factors account for my being (*or* not being) a good reader.

There are several reasons my child is doing well (*or* not doing well) in school.

2   Now choose the scratch outline that you think is most promising to develop. That outline should have *three separate reasons* backing up the point, and *good potential details* to support each of the three reasons. To develop your outline, use the form below. Summarize in a few words the details that you think can develop each reason, rather than writing the details out in full.

Point: _____

_____

Reason 1: _____

   Details that develop reason 1: _____

   _____

   _____

Reason 2: _____

   Details that develop reason 2: _____

   _____

   _____

Reason 3: _____

   Details that develop reason 3: _____

   _____

   _____

3   Use your outline as a guide to write the first rough draft of your paper. As you write the draft, concentrate on providing good details that will make each of your supporting reasons very clear.

4   Use transitions to introduce each of your supporting reasons:

To introduce reason 1: *First of all* or *For one thing*
To introduce reason 2: *Second* or *A second reason* or *Another reason*
To introduce reason 3: *Finally* or *Last of all* or *A final reason*

5   Check the next-to-final draft of your paper for sentence-skills mistakes by reading it aloud. Make sure you are reading exactly what is on the page. If there are rough spots where your writing is hard to read, make the changes needed to ensure that the paper reads smoothly and clearly.

   If there are any words whose spelling you are unsure about, check the dictionary. You should own a recent paperback dictionary and keep it nearby.

   Add a title to your paper: several words that give the reader a quick sense of what the paper is about.

   Finally, use the checklist on the inside back cover of this book to proofread your paper for specific sentence-skills mistakes.

9   Three Paragraph Topics: Personal

Using what you have learned from the previous assignments about how to write effectively, write a paragraph on any *one* of the following topics:

A problem that is worrying you right now

The quality you like most (*or* least) about yourself

A silly or embarrassing moment in your life

Be sure to begin with a topic sentence that states what your paragraph will be about. For example:

Money problems are foremost in my thoughts these days.

The quality that I like least about myself is my impatience.

A Thanksgiving dinner was the scene of one of my most embarrassing moments.

Also, be sure to provide enough details to develop and support your topic sentence. And after reading your paper aloud for smoothness and clarity, use the checklist on the inside back cover to proofread your work for sentence-skills mistakes.

10   Three Paragraph Topics: Persuasive

Using what you have learned from the previous assignments about how to write effectively, write a paragraph on *one* of the following topics:

Why fast-food restaurants are more popular than ever

Why teenage marriages often fail

Why everyone must learn how to use a computer

Begin with a topic sentence that states what your paragraph will be about. Then provide at least three reasons that support your topic sentence. Use word signals such as *first of all, second,* and *finally* to introduce each reason. After reading your paper aloud for smoothness and clarity, use the checklist on the inside back cover to proofread for sentence-skills mistakes.

11   Writing a Paragraph Summary: 1

Making a summary is an excellent way to improve your writing and reading skills. To summarize a selection, you must first read it carefully. Only after you understand fully and clearly what it says can you reduce it to a few sentences. For this assignment, you will be asked to read a selection titled ''Students' Defense Mechanisms'' (on pages 457–459) and condense it to 100 to 125 words.

Here are the reading and writing steps for an effective summary.

Steps to Follow in Summarizing

1   Take a few minutes to preview the work. You can preview an article by taking a quick look at the following:
   a   ***Title.***   The title often summarizes what the article is about. Think about the title and how it may condense the meaning of an article.
   b   ***Subtitle.***   A subtitle or caption, if given, consists of words in special print appearing under or next to the title. Such words often summarize the article or provide a quick insight into its meaning.
   c   ***First and last paragraphs.***   In the first paragraphs, the author may introduce you to the subject and state the purpose of the article. In the last paragraphs, the author may present conclusions or a summary. These previews or summaries can give you a quick overview of the article.

2   Read the article for all you can understand the first time through. Don't slow down or turn back. Look for general statements and for details or examples that support those statements. Mark off what appear to be the main points and key supporting details.

3   Go back and reread more carefully the areas you identified as most important. Also, focus on other key points you may have missed in your first reading.

4   Take notes on the material. After you have formulated what you think is the main idea of the selection, ask yourself, ''Does all or most of the material in the article support the idea in this statement?'' If it does, you have probably identified the main idea. Write it out in a sentence. Then write down the main supporting details for that idea.

5   Remember these points when working on the drafts of your summary:
   a   Express the main idea and supporting ideas in your own words. Do not imitate or stay too close to the style of the original work.
   b   Don't write an overly detailed summary. Your goal is a single paragraph not less than 100 words and not more than 125 words in length.
   c   Preserve the balance and proportion of the original work. If the original devoted 70 percent of its space to one idea and only 30 percent to another, your summary should reflect that emphasis.
   d   Use the checklist on the inside back cover to proofread your summary for sentence-skills mistakes, including spelling.

STUDENTS' DEFENSE MECHANISMS

Michael, a college sophomore, has spent an entire afternoon perfecting his basketball game in the university gym. Karen, a junior, has volunteered to put in overtime at her off-campus job as a store cashier. Gary, a freshman, has been sitting at the desk in his bedroom for hours, but not one page of his textbook has been turned. Looking at these students, a casual observer would be surprised to learn that there are only three weeks left in the semester and that all three students have not even begun to prepare for the numerous papers and exams facing them. But actually, Michael, Karen, and Gary are typical of many college students. Rather than focus on their studies, they have found ways to escape work that—for whatever reason— they don't want to do. To ignore the fact that deadlines are quickly approaching, each student is using *defense mechanisms*—unconscious mental techniques that help people avoid unpleasant truths. Although defense mechanisms are very human, understandable reactions to anxiety, they can get out of hand and be detrimental to success in school.

One of the most common defense mechanisms is *repression,* a tendency to "forget" unpleasant realities. People who repress threatening thoughts deny that those problems exist; they subconsciously tell themselves that nothing is wrong. Indeed, many students use repression around midsemester. Feeling overwhelmed by quickly approaching paper deadlines and final exams, they put their assignments out of mind. Then, having successfully forgotten their responsibilities, they spend their time watching TV, socializing, or just hanging out—doing anything but completing the work that, as far as they are concerned, "doesn't exist." If an instructor or a friend reminds such a student of impending tests, a light of recognition may flicker in his or her eyes for a moment, but then quickly dies out. Students who repress the truth pay an unpleasant price for their procrastination. During the last week of the semester, they find themselves writing, typing, and studying frantically through long, sleepless nights. Moreover, as they can't do their best work under such physical strain and time pressures, their grades suffer.

Students who use the defense mechanism of *rationalization* know that there is work to be done, but they offer plenty of reasons for not doing it. People who rationalize make excuses; they create "logical" explanations for unacceptable behaviors and motivations. For instance, Ms. X, who is neglecting an intimidating sociology report, will not admit—to herself or to other people—that she fears she will fail at it. Instead, she will say, "I'm not going to spend much time on that report because sociology is irrelevant to my career goals in business management." Similarly, Mr. Y, who would rather spend time with his girlfriend than prepare for exams, might say, "Developing relationships is just as important as succeeding in school." And Mr. Z, who is too lazy to do his schoolwork, will say "I can't do it" when he really means "I don't want to try." Another typical rationalization for not doing work is "I'm bored with the subject." If a course is not interesting for students, they should be all the more motivated to do the work so that they can leave it behind once and for all. Finally, some students will rationalize by saying, "I'm too busy." Some students make themselves too busy, working more than they need to or getting overly involved in social activities on or off campus.

People rationalize not only to justify their behavior, but also to minimize their shortcomings and disappointments. They try to convince themselves that a failure doesn't matter (''Things always work out for the best'') or that an unreached goal was not important or worthwhile after all (remember Aesop's fox, who couldn't reach the vine and concluded that the grapes were probably sour anyway?). A student who receives a poor grade might rationalize that ''grades don't matter as much as practical experience in the job market'' or that ''grades signify little more than one's ability to tell instructors what they want to hear.'' Students who rationalize eventually believe their own lies about their goals and responsibilities. This cannot help working against their productivity and performance.

Through another defense mechanism, *compensation,* people make up for their inadequacies in certain areas by doing well in other areas. A student might compensate for a poor academic performance by excelling at a part-time job, or by heading an intramural sports team, or by becoming involved in campus government. Perhaps more than any other defense mechanism, compensation can yield positive results: rather than being defeated by a weakness, a student can be uplifted by achieving something. Nonetheless, compensation can get out of hand; students who make their diversions a priority may leave little time for much-needed studying.

Some people deal with threatening problems simply by *withdrawal.* This defense mechanism is most apparent in students with the ''sleepiness syndrome.'' As soon as it's time to write a paper or study a book or go to class, these students say they are ''too tired.'' Likewise, they imagine that they need naps during the day and ten hours or more of sleep at night. Needless to say, their weariness clears up in time for meals and favorite TV shows. Another form of withdrawal is fantasizing in order to avoid undesirable tasks. The unsuccessful student may waste valuable study time daydreaming, picturing himself or herself as an eminent physician or a powerful corporate executive. Everyone daydreams to some extent, and psychologists agree that occasional fantasies can be a harmless escape from the demands of everyday life. The problem develops when fantasy is used to excess; in such cases, it becomes an unhealthy substitute for activity.

All these defense mechanisms bring only temporary relief. Although they may protect a student from anxieties and feelings of inadequacy, they solve no problems, and they don't help the student get work done. In fact, defense mechanisms usually aggravate problems. They lead students to do sloppy, last-minute work. They also erode self-confidence, making students feel—if only subconsciously—that they have little control over their lives. As a result, students may become even less capable of performing well in the future.

Fortunately, a person can defeat defense mechanisms before they trigger a vicious circle of low self-esteem and failure. The key to overcoming these mental obstacles is being aware of them. If you find yourself avoiding your schoolwork—by making excuses, by finding time for less significant activities, by devoting time to other ''priorities,'' or by daydreaming—you should admit to yourself that you are using defense mechanisms. More important, you must then identify your problem. Why don't you want to do the work? Do you fear failure? Are you feeling lazy? Do you have doubts about being in school? It may be difficult to answer such questions honestly, but self-understanding is the first step to success. You must then come to terms with the fact that the work will not go away—you simply have to get it done, despite any feelings of insecurity or lack of desire. (You may even want to repeat to yourself aloud, "The work will not go away. I have to do the work.") Having truly accepted this, you must develop a strategy for ending your escape tactics and forcing yourself to do the work you should. This means creating an organized study schedule which gives you plenty of time to complete papers and study for tests. At first, it may be quite difficult to turn off the TV or resist the urge to daydream. You will have to develop a new habit—of doing work on a regular basis as it needs to be done. The payoff is that steady work habits will lay the foundation for future success. By proving to yourself that you *can* do it, you'll be less likely to resort to defense mechanisms in the future.

12 Writing a Paragraph Summary: II

Obtain a copy of *Time* or *Newsweek* that is no more than three months old. Write a summary of its cover story. Follow the guidelines given in assignment 11. Attach a copy of the article to the summary before turning the summary in to your instructor.

Writing an Essay

You will probably be asked in college to write papers consisting of several paragraphs that support a single point. The central idea or point developed in a several-paragraph essay is called a *thesis statement,* rather than, as in a paragraph, a *topic sentence.* The thesis statement appears in the introductory paragraph, and specific support for the thesis statement appears in the paragraphs that follow.

Read through the clearly organized student essay on page 461 and consider the following comments.

Comments: This essay begins with an *introductory paragraph* that attracts the reader's interest. The introductory paragraph also presents the thesis statement: "In order to make our dream of being homeowners come true, we decided to take certain steps." The last sentence of this paragraph outlines a plan of development, a preview of the major points that will support the thesis: "By moving in temporarily with my parents, severely limiting our leisure expenses, and taking extra jobs, we hope to have enough money for a down payment on a modest house within two years."

The *second paragraph* presents the first supporting point, or topic sentence ("As the first part of our strategy, we moved in with my parents instead of renting our own apartment"), and specific evidence for that point.

The *third paragraph* presents the second supporting point ("In addition, we are saving money by agreeing to limit our expenses for recreation") and specific evidence for the second point.

The *fourth paragraph* presents the third supporting point ("The most important part of our plan is working at extra jobs") and specific evidence for the third point.

The brief *concluding paragraph* restates the main point of the paper and makes a closing comment or two.

SAVING FOR A HOUSE

Introductory paragraph

It is harder than ever now for a couple to buy that first house. This is a frustrating fact of life that my husband and I learned after we were married. In order to make our dream of being homeowners come true, we decided to take certain steps. By moving in temporarily with my parents, severely limiting our leisure expenses, and taking extra jobs, we hope to have enough money for a down payment on a modest house within two years.

First supporting paragraph

As the first part of our strategy, we moved in with my parents instead of renting our own apartment. Luckily, they have a house with a finished basement, and they were willing to have us live with them. Tom and I set up a bedroom and a living room for ourselves in the basement, and we eat our meals with my parents. We pay $200 a month for room and board, which is a considerable saving over the $400 that we would have to pay in rent alone for an apartment in this area. We do not have total privacy, and we sometimes feel more like kids than married adults because we live at home, but we are willing to make the sacrifice in order to afford a house.

Second supporting paragraph

In addition, we are saving money by agreeing to limit our expenses for recreation. We watch television instead of going to the movies. We have a radio, but we have to put off buying stereo equipment. We don't eat out, except for a rare $7 meal at Pizza Hut. Tom has given up the pro basketball games he used to attend several times a season. I have dropped out of my exercise classes at a health club and now do my workouts on a mat at home. When we feel deprived, as we sometimes do, we add up how much money we are putting away for our house by giving up costly leisure activities. Often, the total is $100 or more a month.

Third supporting paragraph

The most important part of our plan is working at extra jobs. In addition to his job as a TV cable installer, Tom works at night in the appliance department of a Sears store. I type in a title company office five days a week; on weekends I am a hostess in a local restaurant. The hours are long for both of us, and we miss spending time together. Often we are tired and cranky when we get home. But the two extra jobs allow us to save an added $5,500 a year. Once we save the $12,000 we estimate we will need for our down payment, I will probably quit my extra job. Until then, we are willing to work doubly hard for these two years.

Concluding paragraph

Tom and I always assumed that we would live in our own house someday. Once we were married, though, we learned how expensive houses are in today's market. But we decided that, instead of giving up or getting angry, we would make sacrifices now to reach our goal in the future.

1: Providing Reasons or Examples

Write an essay in which you provide reasons or examples to support a thesis statement. Listed below are several thesis statements, any one of which you might develop into an essay. Choose one of the statements and fill in three reasons or examples you can use to support it. Then check your work by answering the questions below.

> There are several reasons why I have decided to come to school.
>
> There are several reasons why the _____ won (*or* lost) their league championship.
>
> There are three ways my town could be made a safer place in which to live.
>
> Students who work at the same time they are going to school face special difficulties.
>
> Several people in my life have helped me appreciate the meaning of courage.

Your thesis: _____

_____

Support 1: _____

Support 2: _____

Support 3: _____

Take your time with the outline. Be prepared to do some plain hard thinking to come up with a strong outline. The outline is probably the most important single step you can take to write an effective paper.

Questions to Consider: Check the logic of your outline by seeing if you can answer *yes* to the following questions:

● Does each of my three reasons or examples truly support the thesis statement?
● Can I back up each of my three reasons or examples with good supporting details?

Now write your paper, taking it through the three or four drafts that may be necessary to complete it satisfactorily. Use the checklist on the inside back cover of the book to proofread the paper for sentence-skills mistakes, including spelling.

2:   Self-Analysis

Many people use New Year's Day as an occasion for identifying changes they would like to make in their lives. At any time of the year, most of us could probably think of three qualities or habits that we would be better off without. Write an essay describing three things you would like to change in yourself. One student who did such a paper used as his thesis the following statement: ''There are three flaws in my character—laziness, jealousy, and impatience—that have created some difficult times in my life in the past few months.''

Use the five-part structure of introduction, three supporting paragraphs, and a conclusion. And refer to the checklist of sentence skills on the inside back cover to proofread your paper for sentence-skills mistakes.

3:   A Letter of Praise or Criticism

Most of us watch at least some television, and we can all name certain shows we find especially enjoyable or especially offensive. Write a letter to one of the major television networks in which you compliment or criticize a particular show. Don't just say that you like or dislike the show. Instead, give two or three detailed reasons that support your feelings either way.

Your letter should take the essay form already discussed—an introduction, a paragraph for each supporting reason, and a conclusion. It should use a standard address format and should begin with the salutation *Dear Sir or Madam*. Use the checklist on the inside back cover to proofread your letter carefully for sentence-skills mistakes.

The networks are sensitive to thoughtful letters from viewers. Your letter, if carefully constructed and neatly written, is almost sure to get a reply.

Here's where to send your letter:

Capital Cities/ABC, 24 East 51st Street, New York, NY 10022
CBS, 51 West 52d Street, New York, NY 10019
NBC, 30 Rockefeller Plaza, New York, NY 10020
PBS, 475 L'Enfant Plaza West, S.W., Washington, D.C. 20024

Appendixes

INTRODUCTION

Three appendixes follow. Appendix A consists of diagnostic and achievement tests that measure many of the skills in this book. The diagnostic test can be taken at the outset of your work; the achievement test can be used to measure your progress at the end of your work. Appendix B supplies answers to the introductory projects and the practice exercises in Part One. The answers, which should be referred to only after you have worked carefully through each exercise, give you responsibility for testing yourself. (To ensure that the answer key is used as a learning tool only, answers are *not* given for the review tests in Part One or for the reinforcement tests in Part Two. These answers appear only in the Instructor's Manual; they can be copied and handed out at the discretion of your instructor.) Finally, Appendix C provides handy progress charts that you can use to track your performance on all the tests in the book and the writing assignments as well.

Appendix A

Diagnostic and Achievement Tests

SENTENCE-SKILLS DIAGNOSTIC TEST

Part I

This diagnostic test will help check your knowledge of a number of sentence skills. In each item below, certain words are underlined. Write *X* in the answer space if you think a mistake appears at the underlined part. Write *C* in the answer space if you think the underlined part is correct.

The headings within the text ("Sentence Fragments," "Run-Ons," and so on) will give you clues to the mistakes to look for. However, you do not have to understand the heading to find a mistake. What you are checking is your own sense of effective written English.

Sentence Fragments

_____ 1. Because I didn't want to get wet. I waited for a break in the downpour. Then I ran for the car like an Olympic sprinter.

_____ 2. The baby birds chirped loudly, especially when their mother brought food to them. Their mouths gaped open hungrily.

_____ 3. Trying to avoid running into anyone. Cal wheeled his baby son around the crowded market. He wished that strollers came equipped with flashing hazard lights.

_____ 4. The old woman combed out her long, gray hair. She twisted it into two thick braids. And wrapped them around her head like a crown.

467

Run-Ons

_____ 5. Irene fixed fruits and healthy sandwiches for her son's <u>lunch, he</u> traded them for cupcakes, cookies, and chips.

_____ 6. Angie's dark eyes were the color of <u>mink they</u> matched her glowing complexion.

_____ 7. My mother keeps sending me bottles of <u>vitamins, but</u> I keep forgetting to take them.

_____ 8. The little boy watched the line of ants march across the <u>ground, he</u> made a wall of Popsicle sticks to halt the ants' advance.

Standard English Verbs

_____ 9. When she's upset, Mary <u>tells</u> her troubles to her houseplants.

_____ 10. The street musician counted the coins in his donations basket and <u>pack</u> his trumpet in its case.

_____ 11. I tried to pull off my rings, but they <u>was</u> stuck on my swollen fingers.

_____ 12. Belle's car <u>have</u> a horn that plays six different tunes.

Irregular Verbs

_____ 13. I've <u>swam</u> in this lake for years, and I've never seen it so shallow.

_____ 14. The phone <u>rung</u> once and then stopped.

_____ 15. Five different people had <u>brought</u> huge bowls of potato salad to the barbecue.

_____ 16. The metal ice cube trays <u>froze</u> to the bottom of the freezer.

Subject-Verb Agreement

_____ 17. The records in my collection <u>is</u> arranged in alphabetical order.

_____ 18. There <u>was</u> only one burner working on the old gas stove.

_____ 19. My aunt and uncle <u>gives</u> a party every Groundhog Day.

_____ 20. One of my sweaters <u>have</u> moth holes in the sleeves.

Consistent Verb Tense

_____ 21. After I turned off the ignition, the engine <u>continued</u> to sputter for several minutes.

_____ 22. Before cleaning the oven, I lined the kitchen floor with newspapers, <u>open</u> the windows, and shook the can of aerosol foam.

Pronoun Reference, Agreement, and Point of View

_____ 23. All visitors should stay in <u>their</u> cars while driving through the wild animal park.

_____ 24. At the library, <u>they</u> showed me how to use the microfilm machines.

_____ 25. As I slowed down at the scene of the accident, <u>you</u> could see long black skid marks on the highway.

Pronoun Types

_____ 26. My husband is more sentimental than <u>me</u>.

_____ 27. Andy and <u>I</u> made ice cream in an old-fashioned wooden machine.

Adjectives and Adverbs

_____ 28. Brian drives so <u>reckless</u> that no one will join his car pool.

_____ 29. Miriam pulled <u>impatiently</u> at the rusty zipper.

_____ 30. I am <u>more happier</u> with myself now that I earn my own money.

_____ 31. The last screw on the license plate was the <u>most rusty</u> one of all.

Misplaced Modifiers

_____ 32. I stretched out on the lounge chair <u>wearing my bikini bathing suit.</u>

_____ 33. I replaced the shingle on the roof <u>that was loose.</u>

Dangling Modifiers

_____ 34. <u>While doing the dishes,</u> a glass shattered in the soapy water.

_____ 35. <u>Pedaling as fast as possible,</u> Todd tried to outrace the snapping dog.

Faulty Parallelism

_____ 36. Before I could take a bath, I had to pick up the damp towels on the floor, gather up the loose toys in the room, and the tub had to be scrubbed out.

_____ 37. I've tried several cures for my headaches, including drugs, meditation, exercise, and massaging my head.

Capital Letters

_____ 38. This fall we plan to visit Cape Cod.

_____ 39. Vern ordered a set of tools from the spiegel catalog.

_____ 40. When my aunt visits us, she insists on doing all the cooking.

_____ 41. Maureen asked, ''will you split a piece of cheesecake with me?''

Numbers and Abbreviations

_____ 42. Before I could stop myself, I had eaten 6 glazed doughnuts.

_____ 43. At 10:45 A.M., a partial eclipse of the sun will begin.

_____ 44. Larry, who is now over six ft. tall, can no longer sleep comfortably in a twin bed.

End Marks

_____ 45. Jane wondered if her husband was telling the truth.

_____ 46. Does that stew need some salt?

Apostrophe

_____ 47. Elizabeths thick, curly hair is her best feature.

_____ 48. I tried to see through the interesting envelope sent to my sister, but couldnt.

_____ 49. Pam's heart almost stopped beating when Roger jumped out of the closet.

_____ 50. The logs' in the fireplace crumbled in a shower of sparks.

Quotation Marks

_____ 51. Someone once said, ''A lie has no legs and cannot stand.''

_____ 52. ''This repair job could be expensive, the mechanic warned.''

_____ 53. ''My greatest childhood fear,'' said Sheila, ''was being sucked down the bathtub drain.''

_____ 54. ''I was always afraid of everybody's father, said Suzanne, except my own.''

Comma

_____ 55. The restaurant's ''sundae bar'' featured bowls of whipped cream chopped nuts and chocolate sprinkles.

_____ 56. My sister, who studies karate, installed large practice mirrors in our basement.

_____ 57. When I remove my thick eyeglasses the world turns into an out-of-focus movie.

_____ 58. Gloria wrapped her son's presents in pages from the comics section, and she glued a small toy car atop each gift.

Spelling

_____ 59. When Terry practises scales on the piano, her whole family wears earplugs.

_____ 60. I wondered if it was alright to wear sneakers with my three-piece suit.

_____ 61. The essay test question asked us to describe two different theorys of evolution.

_____ 62. A theif stole several large hanging plants from Marlo's porch.

Omitted Words and Letters

_____ 63. After dark, I'm afraid to look in the closets or under the bed.

_____ 64. I turned on the television, but baseball game had been rained out.

_____ 65. Polar bear cubs stay with their mother for two year.

Commonly Confused Words

_____ 66. Before your about to start the car, press the gas pedal to the floor once.

_____ 67. The frog flicked it's tongue out and caught the fly.

_____ 68. I was to lonely to enjoy the party.

_____ 69. The bats folded their wings around them like leather overcoats.

Effective Word Choice

_____ 70. If the professor <u>gives me a break</u>, I might pass the final exam.

_____ 71. Harry <u>worked like a dog</u> all summer to save money for his tuition.

_____ 72. Because Monday is a holiday, <u>sanitation engineers</u> will pick up your trash on Tuesday.

_____ 73. Our family's softball game <u>ended in an argument</u>, as usual.

_____ 74. <u>As for my own opinion</u>, I feel that nuclear weapons should be banned.

_____ 75. This law is, <u>for all intents and purposes</u>, a failure.

Part 2 (Optional)

Do the following at your instructor's request. This second part of the test will provide more detailed information about skills you need to know. On separate paper, number and correct all the items you have marked with an *X*. For example, suppose you had marked the word groups below with an *X*. (Note that these examples are not taken from the actual test.)

4. <u>When I picked up the tire.</u> Something in my back snapped. I could not stand up straight as a result.

7. The phone started <u>ringing, then</u> the doorbell sounded as well.

15. <u>Marks</u> goal is to save enough money to get married next year.

29. Without checking the rearview <u>mirror the</u> driver pulled out into the passing lane.

Here is how you should write your corrections on a separate sheet of paper:

4. When I picked up the tire, something in my back snapped.

7. The phone started ringing, and then the doorbell sounded as well.

15. Mark's

29. mirror, the driver

There are over forty corrections to make in all.

SENTENCE-SKILLS ACHIEVEMENT TEST

Part 1

This achievement test will help check your mastery of a number of sentence skills. In each item below, certain words are underlined. Write *X* in the answer space if you think a mistake appears at the underlined part. Write *C* in the answer space if you think the underlined part is correct.

The headings within the test (''Sentence Fragments,'' ''Run-Ons,'' and so on) will give you clues to the mistakes to look for.

Sentence Fragments

_____ 1. <u>When the town bully died</u>. Hundreds of people came to his funeral. They wanted to make sure he was dead.

_____ 2. <u>Suzanne adores junk foods, especially onion-flavored potato chips</u>. She can eat an entire bag at one sitting.

_____ 3. My brother stayed up all night. <u>Studying the rules in his driver's manual</u>. He wanted to get his license on the first try.

_____ 4. Hector decided to take a study break. He picked up *TV Guide*. <u>And flipped through the pages to find that night's listings</u>.

Run-Ons

_____ 5. Ronnie leaned forward in his <u>seat, he</u> could not hear what the instructor was saying.

_____ 6. Our television set obviously needs <u>repairs the</u> color keeps fading from the picture.

_____ 7. Nick and Fran enjoyed their trip to <u>Chicago, but</u> they couldn't wait to get home.

_____ 8. I tuned in the weather forecast on the <u>radio, I</u> had to decide what to wear.

Standard English Verbs

_____ 9. My sister Louise <u>walks</u> a mile to the bus stop every day.

_____ 10. The play was ruined when the quarterback <u>fumble</u> the handoff.

_____ 11. When the last guests left our party, we <u>was</u> exhausted but happy.

_____ 12. I don't think my mother <u>have</u> gone out to a movie in years.

Irregular Verbs

_____ 13. My roommate and I <u>seen</u> a double feature this weekend.

_____ 14. My nephew must have <u>growed</u> six inches since last summer.

_____ 15. I should have <u>brought</u> a gift to the office Christmas party.

_____ 16. After playing touch football all afternoon, Al <u>drank</u> a quart of Gatorade.

Subject-Verb Agreement

_____ 17. The cost of those new tires <u>are</u> more than I can afford.

_____ 18. Nick and Fran <u>give</u> a New Year's Eve party every year.

_____ 19. There <u>was</u> only two slices of cake left on the plate.

_____ 20. Each of the fast-food restaurants <u>have</u> a breakfast special.

Consistent Verb Tense

_____ 21. After I folded the towels in the basket, I <u>remembered</u> that I hadn't washed them yet.

_____ 22. Before she decided to buy the wall calendar, Joanne <u>turns</u> its pages and looked at all the pictures.

Pronoun Reference, Agreement, and Point of View

_____ 23. All drivers should try <u>their</u> best to be courteous during rush hour.

_____ 24. When Bob went to the bank for a home improvement loan, <u>they</u> asked him for three credit references.

_____ 25. I like to shop at factory outlets because <u>you</u> can always get brand names at a discount.

Pronoun Types

_____ 26. My brother writes much more neatly than <u>me</u>.

_____ 27. Vonnie and <u>I</u> are both taking Introduction to Business this semester.

Adjectives and Adverbs

_____ 28. When the elevator doors closed <u>sudden</u>, three people were trapped inside.

_____ 29. The bag lady glared <u>angrily</u> at me when I offered her a dollar bill.

_____ 30. Frank couldn't decide which vacation he liked <u>best</u>, a bicycle trip or a week at the beach.

_____ 31. I find proofreading a paper much <u>more difficult</u> than writing one.

Misplaced Modifiers

_____ 32. The car was parked along the side of the road <u>with a flat tire</u>.

_____ 33. We bought a television set at our neighborhood video store <u>that has stereo sound</u>.

Dangling Modifiers

_____ 34. <u>While looking for bargains at Sears</u>, an exercise bike caught my eye.

_____ 35. <u>Hurrying to catch the bus</u>, Donna fell and twisted her ankle.

Faulty Parallelism

_____ 36. Before she leaves for work, Agnes makes her lunch, does fifteen minutes of calisthenics, and <u>her two cats have to be fed</u>.

_____ 37. Three remedies for insomnia are warm milk, <u>taking a hot bath</u>, and sleeping pills.

Capital Letters

_____ 38. Every <u>Saturday</u> I get up early, even though I have the choice of sleeping late.

_____ 39. We stopped at the drug store for some <u>crest</u> toothpaste.

_____ 40. Rows of crocuses appear in my front yard every <u>spring</u>.

_____ 41. The cashier said, ''<u>sorry</u>, but children under three are not allowed in this theater.''

Numbers and Abbreviations

_____ 42. Our train finally arrived—<u>2</u> hours late.

_____ 43. Answers to the chapter questions start on page <u>293</u>.

_____ 44. Three <u>yrs.</u> from now, my new car will finally be paid off.

End Marks

_____ 45. I had no idea who was inside the gorilla suit at the Halloween party<u>.</u>

_____ 46. Are you taking the make-up exam<u>.</u>

Apostrophe

_____ 47. My <u>fathers</u> favorite old television program is _Star Trek._

_____ 48. I <u>couldnt</u> understand a word of that lecture.

_____ 49. My <u>dentist's</u> recommendation was that I floss after brushing my teeth.

_____ 50. Three <u>house's</u> on our street are up for sale.

Quotation Marks

_____ 51. <u>Garfield the cat is fond of saying, ''I never met a carbohydrate I didn't like.''</u>

_____ 52. <u>''This restaurant does not accept credit cards, the waiter said.''</u>

_____ 53. <u>Two foods that may prevent cancer,'' said the scientist, ''are those old standbys spinach and carrots.''</u>

_____ 54. <u>''I can't get anything done,'' Dad complained, if you two insist on making all that noise.''</u>

Comma

_____ 55. The snack bar offered <u>overdone hamburgers rubbery hot dogs and soggy pizza.</u>

_____ 56. My sister, <u>who regards every living creature as a holy thing, cannot</u> even swat a housefly.

_____ 57. When I smelled something <u>burning I</u> realized I hadn't turned off the oven.

_____ 58. Marge plays the musical saw at <u>parties, and</u> her husband does Dracula imitations.

Spelling

_____ 59. No one will be <u>admited</u> without a valid student identification card.

_____ 60. Pat <u>carrys</u> a full course load in addition to working as the night manager at a supermarket.

_____ 61. Did you feel <u>alright</u> after eating Ralph's special chili?

_____ 62. My parents were disappointed when I didn't enter the family <u>busines</u>.

Omitted Words and Letters

_____ 63. <u>Both high schools in my hometown offer evening classes for adults.</u>

_____ 64. <u>I opened new bottle of ketchup and then couldn't find the cap.</u>

_____ 65. <u>Visiting hour for patients at this hospital are from noon to eight.</u>

Commonly Confused Words

_____ 66. Shelley has always been <u>to</u> self-conscious to speak up in class.

_____ 67. <u>Its</u> not easy to return to college after raising a family.

_____ 68. "Thank you for <u>you're</u> generous contribution," the letter began.

_____ 69. Nobody knew <u>whose</u> body had been found floating in the swimming pool.

Effective Word Choice

_____ 70. My roommate keeps <u>getting on my case</u> about leaving clothing on the floor.

_____ 71. Karla decided to <u>take the bull by the horns</u> and ask her boss for a raise.

_____ 72. Although Lamont <u>accelerated his vehicle</u>, he was unable to pass the truck.

_____ 73. When the movie <u>ended suddenly</u>, I felt I had been cheated.

_____ 74. <u>In light of the fact that</u> I am on a diet, I have stopped eating between meals.

_____ 75. <u>Personally, I do not think</u> that everyone should be allowed to vote.

Part 2 (Optional)

Do the following at your instructor's request. This second part of the test will provide more detailed information about which skills you have mastered and which skills you still need to work on. On separate paper, number and correct all the items you have marked with an *X*. For example, suppose you had marked the word groups below with an *X*. (Note that these examples were not taken from the actual test.)

4. <u>When I picked up the tire.</u> Something in my back snapped. I could not stand up straight as a result.
7. The phone started <u>ringing, then</u> the doorbell sounded as well.
15. <u>Marks</u> goal is to save enough money to get married next year.
29. Without checking the rearview <u>mirror the</u> driver pulled out into the passing lane.

Here is how you should write your corrections on a separate sheet of paper:

4. When I picked up the tire, something in my back snapped.
7. The phone started ringing, and then the doorbell sounded as well.
15. Mark's
29. mirror, the driver

There are over forty corrections to make in all.

Appendix B

Answers to Introductory Projects and Practice Exercises

This answer key can help you teach yourself. Use it to find out why you got some answers wrong—to uncover any weak spot in your understanding of a skill. By using the answer key in an honest and thoughtful way, you will master each skill and prepare yourself for the many tests in this book that have no answer key.

SUBJECTS AND VERBS

Introductory Project (page 9)

Answers will vary.

Practice 1 (11)

1. Fran froze
2. company offered
3. announcer talked
4. Jill peeled
5. sunshine felt
6. backyard is
7. Alicia snagged
8. comb scratched
9. pen leaked
10. store carries

Practice 2 (12)

1. shows . . . were
2. burp . . . is
3. sunglasses . . . look
4. voice sounds
5. Tina became
6. lotion smells
7. Visitors . . . appear
8. vibrations are
9. cold feels
10. change . . . seems

Practice 3 (12)

1. light glowed
2. kite soared
3. Manuel caught
4. skaters shadowed
5. lights emphasized
6. Tracy reads
7. glasses slipped
8. Jane allowed
9. squirrel jumped
10. Carpenters constructed

Practice (13–14)

1. Stripes of sunlight glowed on the kitchen floor.
2. The black panther draped its powerful body along the thick tree branch.
3. A line of impatient people snaked from the box office to the street.
4. At noon, every siren in town wails for fifteen minutes.
5. The tops of my Bic pens always disappear after a day or two.
6. Joanne removed the lint from her black socks with Scotch tape.
7. The mirrored walls of the skyscraper reflected the passing clouds.
8. Debris from the accident littered the intersection.
9. Above the heads of the crowd, a woman swayed on a narrow ledge.
10. The squashed grapes in the bottom of the vegetable bin oozed sticky purple juice.

Practice (15)

1. Einstein could have passed
2. She could have been killed
3. children did not recognize
4. strikers have been fasting
5. I could not see
6. People may be wearing
7. He should have studied
8. Rosa has been soaking
9. lines were flying
10. brother can ask

Practice (16)

1. trees creaked and shuddered
2. girl fell and landed
3. I will vacuum and change
4. sun shone and turned
5. Sam and Billy greased
6. man and friend rode
7. sister and I race
8. Amy breathed and began
9. Phil draped and pretended
10. wrestler and opponent strutted and pounded

SENTENCE FRAGMENTS

Introductory Project (18)

1. verb
2. subject
3. subject . . . verb
4. express a complete thought

Practice 2 (23)

Note: The underlined part shows the fragment (or that part of the original fragment not changed during correction).

1. Since she was afraid of muggers, Barbara carried a small can of Mace on her key ring.
2. When I began watching the TV mystery movie, I remembered that I had seen it before.
3. Tulips had begun to bloom until a freakish spring snowstorm blanketed the garden.
4. Whenever I'm in the basement and the phone rings, I don't run up to answer it. If the message is important, the person will call back.

5. Since she is a new student, Carla feels shy and insecure. She thinks she is the only person who doesn't know anyone else.

Practice 1 (25–26)

1. Julie spent an hour at her desk, staring at a blank piece of paper.
2. Rummaging around in the kitchen drawer, Bob found the key he had misplaced a year ago.
3. As a result, I lost my place in the checkout line.

Practice 2 (26)

1. I tossed and turned for hours.
   Or: Tossing and turning for hours, I felt like a blanket being tumbled dry.
2. It fluffed its feathers to keep itself warm.
   Or: A sparrow landed on the icy windowsill, fluffing its feathers to keep itself warm.
3. The reason was that she had to work the next day.
   Or: Alma left the party early, the reason being that she had to work the next day.
4. Grasping the balance beam with her powdered hands, the gymnast executed a handstand.
5. To cover his bald spot, Walt combed long strands of hair over the top of his head.

Practice 1 (28)

1. For instance, he folds a strip of paper into the shape of an accordion.
2. Marco stuffed the large green peppers with hamburger meat, cooked rice, and chopped parsley.
3. For example, he craves Bugles and Doritos.

Practice 2 (28–29)

1. For instance, he has his faded sweatshirt from high school.
2. For example, she borrows my sweaters.
3. To improve her singing, Donna practiced some odd exercises, such as flapping her tongue and fluttering her lips.
   Or: She flapped her tongue and fluttered her lips.
4. For example, she had put on forty pounds.
5. Stanley wanted a big birthday cake with candles spelling out STAN.

Practice (30)

1. Then she quickly folded her raggedy towels and faded sheets.
2. Wally took his wool sweaters out of storage and found them full of moth holes.
   Or: He found them full of moth holes.
3. Also, she is learning two computer languages.
4. Then he hides under the bed.
5. A tiny bug crawled across my paper and sat down in the middle of a sentence.
   Or: And it sat down in the middle of a sentence.

RUN-ONS

Introductory Project (36)

1. period
2. but
3. semicolon
4. although

Practice 1 (39)

1. coffee. His
2. way. She
3. coughing. A
4. me. It
5. time. The
6. machine. We
7. closely. They
8. Lauren. She
9. victims. They
10. late. The

Practice 2 (40)

1. cockroaches. Both
2. blood. The
3. counselor. She's
4. death. He
5. seen. One
6. beautiful. Now
7. penalty. The
8. down. It
9. Germany. In
10. request. He

Practice 1 (42–43)

1. , but
2. , for
3. , so
4. , for
5. , and
6. , so
7. , so
8. , but
9. , for
10. , so

Practice 2 (43)

Answers will vary.

Practice (44)

1. backwards; his
2. indestructible; it
3. cards; she
4. moth; it
5. book; it

Practice 1 (45)

1. month; on the other hand, they
2. sick; therefore, she (*or* consequently *or* as a result *or* thus)
3. hydrant; however, she
4. guests; furthermore, he (*or* also *or* moreover *or* in addition)
5. money; consequently, she (*or* therefore *or* as a result *or* thus)

Practice 2 (46)

1. wait; however, she
2. computers; as a result, she
3. abused; moreover, many
4. smoking; otherwise, I
5. carefully; nevertheless, the

Practice 1 (47)

1. After
2. before
3. When
4. If
5. until

Practice 2 (47–48)

1. Even though I had a campus map, I still could not find my classroom building.
2. When a cat food commercial came on, Marie started to sing along with the jingle.
3. Since the phone in the next apartment rings all the time, I'm beginning to get used to the sound.
4. After Michael gulped two cups of coffee, his heart began to flutter.
5. As a car sped around the corner, it sprayed slush all over the pedestrians.

STANDARD ENGLISH VERBS

Introductory Project (52)

played . . . plays
hoped . . . hopes
juggled . . . juggles

1. past time . . . -d or -ed
2. present time . . . -s

Practice 1 (54)

1. wears
2. says
3. subscribes
4. rides
5. sees
6. distributes
7. C
8. feeds
9. overcooks
10. polishes

Practice 2 (55)

Lou works for a company that delivers singing telegrams. Sometimes he puts on a sequined tuxedo or wears a Cupid costume. He composes his own songs for birthdays, anniversaries, bachelor parties, and other occasions. Then he shows up at a certain place and surprises the victim. He sings a song that includes personal details, which he gets in advance, about the recipient of the telegram. Lou loves the astonished looks on other people's faces; he also enjoys earning money by making people happy on special days.

Practice 1 (56)

1. turned
2. bounced
3. paged
4. crushed
5. C
6. washed
7. cracked
8. collected
9. pulled
10. lacked

Practice 2 (56)

Mrs. Bayne strolled across the street to her neighbor's yard sale. She examined the rack of used clothes, checked the prices, and accidentally knocked a blouse off its hanger. She poked through a box of children's toys, spilling a carton full of wooden blocks. She leafed through some old issues of *National Geographic* and *Life,* ripping a few of the brittle pages. At a table of kitchen equipment, she pushed down the buttons on a toaster and forced them up again. Mrs. Bayne then wandered off without buying anything.

Practice 1 (58)

1. is
2. has
3. is
4. does
5. did
6. was
7. had
8. was
9. did
10. was

Practice 2 (59)

1. is
2. has
3. has
4. are
5. are
6. do
7. do
8. has
9. does
10. are

Practice 3 (59)

My friend Brad is a real bargain-hunter. If any store has a sale, he runs right over and buys two or three things, whether or not they are things he needs. Brad does his best, also, to get something for nothing. Last week, he was reading the paper and saw that the First National Bank's new downtown offices were offering gifts for new accounts. "Those freebies sure do look good," Brad said. So he went downtown, opened an account, and had the manager give him a Big Ben alarm clock. When he got back with the clock, he was smiling. "I am a very busy man," he told me, "and I really need the free time."

IRREGULAR VERBS

Introductory Project (62)

1. screamed . . . screamed
2. wrote . . . written
3. stole . . . stolen
4. asked . . . asked
5. kissed . . . kissed
6. chose . . . chosen
7. rode . . . ridden
8. chewed . . . chewed
9. thought . . . thought
10. danced . . . danced

Practice 1 (66)

1. took
2. chosen
3. caught
4. stolen
5. saw
6. gone
7. fallen
8. sworn
9. shrunk
10. spoken

Practice 2 (66–68)

1. (a) loses
   (b) lost
   (c) lost
2. (a) brings
   (b) brought
   (c) brought
3. (a) swim
   (b) swam
   (c) swum
4. (a) goes
   (b) went
   (c) gone
5. (a) begins
   (b) began
   (c) begun
6. (a) hides
   (b) hid
   (c) hidden
7. (a) choose
   (b) chose
   (c) chosen
8. (a) speak
   (b) spoke
   (c) spoken
9. (a) takes
   (b) took
   (c) taken
10. (a) wake
    (b) woke
    (c) woken

Practice (69)

1. laid
2. lay
3. laid
4. lying
5. lay

Practice (70)

1. set
2. set
3. sit
4. set
5. setting

Practice (71)

1. rise
2. raised
3. raised
4. rose
5. raised

SUBJECT-VERB AGREEMENT

Introductory Project (73)

Correct: There were many applicants for the position.
Correct: The pictures in that magazine are very controversial.
Correct: Everybody usually watches the lighted numbers in an elevator.

1. applicants . . . pictures
2. singular . . . singular

Practice (75)

1. leaders of the union have
2. One of Robin's pencil sketches hangs
3. days of anxious waiting finally end
4. members of the car pool chip
5. woman with the teased, sprayed hairdo looks
6. addition of heavy shades to my sunny windows allows
7. houses in the old whaling village have
8. stack of baseball cards in my little brother's bedroom is
9. puddles of egg white spread
10. box of Raisinets sells

Practice (76)

1. were . . . trucks
2. are . . . coyotes
3. are rows
4. are . . . boots
5. was . . . boy
6. was . . . animal
7. is . . . shampooer
8. was . . . stream
9. is . . . box
10. is . . . sign

Practice (77)

1. is
2. remembers
3. fit
4. has
5. wanders
6. needs
7. keeps
8. sneaks
9. is
10. eats

Practice (78)

1. look
2. are
3. confuse
4. are
5. star

Practice (79)

1. roam
2. begins
3. thunder
4. fear
5. tastes

CONSISTENT VERB TENSE

Introductory Project (81)

Mistakes in verb tense: Alex discovers ... calls a ... present ... past

Practice (82–83)

1. smeared
2. started
3. breathed
4. saw
5. rolled
6. points
7. swallows
8. pushed
9. coat
10. notices

ADDITIONAL INFORMATION ABOUT VERBS

Practice (Tense; 88)

1. had watched
2. has written
3. am taking
4. had lifted
5. has improved
6. are protesting
7. have dreaded
8. has vowed *or* is vowing
9. were peeking
10. are getting *or* have gotten

Practice (Verbals; 89)

1. *P*
2. *G*
3. *I*
4. *G*
5. *I*
6. *P*
7. *P*
8. *P*
9. *G*
10. *I*

Practice (Active and Passive Verbs; 90–91)

1. The beautician snipped off Kate's long hair.
2. The parents protested the teachers' strike.
3. The alert bank teller tripped the silent alarm.
4. Relentless bloodhounds tracked the escaped convicts.
5. A famous entertainer donated the new CAT scanner to the hospital.
6. A stock clerk dropped a gallon glass jar of pickles in the supermarket aisle.
7. A car struck the deer as it crossed the highway.
8. My doctor referred me to a specialist in hearing problems.
9. Family photographs cover one wall of my living room.
10. Fear gripped the town during the accident at the nuclear power plant.

PRONOUN REFERENCE, AGREEMENT, AND POINT OF VIEW

Introductory Project (92)

1. b
2. b
3. b

Practice (94–95)

Note: The practice sentences could be rewritten in various ways; the following are examples.

1. When we pulled into the gas station, the attendant told us one of our tires looked soft.
2. Nora broke the heavy ashtray when she dropped it on her foot.
3. Ann asked for a grade transcript at the registrar's office, and the clerk told her it would cost three dollars.

4. Don't touch the freshly painted walls with your hands unless the walls are dry.

5. Maurice's habit of staying up half the night watching *Chiller Theater* really annoys his wife.

6. Robin went to the store's personnel office to be interviewed for a sales position.

7. Matt told his brother, ''You need to lose some weight.''

8. I wrote to the insurance company but haven't received an answer.

9. I went to the doctor to see what he could do about my itchy, bloodshot eyes.

10. I took the loose pillows off the chairs and sat on the pillows.
   Or: I sat on the loose pillows, which I had taken off the chairs.

Practice (96)

1.	it	4.	their
2.	them	5.	it
3.	they		

Practice (98)

1.	her	6.	its
2.	he	7.	her
3.	his	8.	his
4.	his	9.	their
5.	she	10.	his

Practice (99–100)

1.	we saw	6.	I get depressed
2.	I can buy	7.	I save
3.	we were given	8.	he or she could make
4.	we relax	9.	she can buy
5.	they serve	10.	I can stop

PRONOUN TYPES

Introductory Project (103)

Correct sentences:

Andy and I enrolled in a computer course.

The police officer pointed to my sister and me.

Lola prefers men who take pride in their bodies.

The players are confident that the league championship is theirs.

Those concert tickets are too expensive.

Our parents should spend some money on themselves for a change.

Practice 1 (106)

2.	I (*S*)	7.	We (*S*)
3.	her (*O*)	8.	she (*S*)
4.	me (*O*)	9.	me (*O*)
5.	her and him (*O*)	10.	he (*S*)
6.	I (*can* is understood) (*S*)		

Practice 2 (107)

Answers will vary; the following are possibilities.

2. me *or* her *or* him *or* them
3. I *or* she *or* he
4. I *or* she *or* he *or* they
5. me *or* him *or* her *or* them
6. I *or* he *or* she *or* they
7. them
8. him *or* her *or* them
9. I *or* he *or* she
10. I *or* she *or* he

Practice 1 (109)

1. who
2. which
3. whom
4. who
5. who

Practice (111)

1. hers
2. mine
3. ours
4. its
5. their

Practice 1 (112)

1. This
2. Those
3. Those
4. Those
5. that

Practice (113)

1. ourselves
2. himself
3. themselves
4. yourself
5. ourselves

ADJECTIVES AND ADVERBS

Introductory Project (116)

Answers will vary for 1–4.
adjective . . . adverb . . . <u>ly</u> . . . <u>er</u> . . . <u>est</u>

Practice 1 (118)

kinder . . . kindest
more ambitious . . . most ambitious
more generous . . . most generous
finer . . . finest
more likable . . . most likable

Practice 2 (119)

1. thickest
2. lazier
3. harshest
4. more flexible
5. worse
6. best
7. less
8. less vulnerable
9. most wasteful
10. shinier

Practice (120)

1. hesitantly
2. easily
3. sharply
4. abruptly
5. aggressively
6. regretfully
7. quickly
8. messily
9. enviously
10. terribly

Practice (121)

1. well
2. good
3. well
4. good
5. well

MISPLACED MODIFIERS

Introductory Project (123)

1. Intended: The farmers were wearing masks.
   Unintended: The apple trees were wearing masks.
2. Intended: The woman had a terminal disease.
   Unintended: The faith healer had a terminal disease.

Practice 1 (124–125)

Note: In the corrections below, the underlined part shows what had been a misplaced modifier. In some cases, other corrections are possible.

1. <u>Driving along the wooded road</u>, we noticed several dead animals.
2. <u>In her mind</u>, Bobbi envisioned the flowers that would bloom.
3. <u>In my tuxedo</u>, I watched my closest friends being married.
4. Sue Ellen carried her new coat, <u>which was trimmed with fur</u>, on her arm.
5. We just heard <u>on the radio</u> that all major highways were flooded.
6. Fresh-picked blueberries covered <u>almost</u> the entire kitchen counter.
7. <u>Making sounds of contentment</u>, Betty licked the home-made peach ice cream.
   Or: Betty, <u>making sounds of contentment</u>, licked the homemade peach ice cream.

8. <u>With a grin</u>, the salesman confidently demonstrated the vacuum cleaner.
9. <u>Dressed in a top hat and tails</u>, Gena is delivering singing telegrams.
10. The local drama group <u>badly</u> needs people to build scenery.

Practice 2 (126)

1. With a pounding heart, I opened my mouth for the dentist.
2. Newspapers all over the world announced that the space shuttle pilots had landed.
3. Newborn kangaroos, which resemble blind, naked worms, crawl into their mothers' pouches.
4. Bruce Springsteen's latest album has sold almost five million copies.
5. Joanne proudly deposited in her savings account the fifty dollars she had earned typing term papers.

DANGLING MODIFIERS

Introductory Project (129)

1. Intended: The giraffe was munching leaves.
   Unintended: The children were munching leaves.
2. Intended: Michael was arriving home.
   Unintended: The neighbors were arriving home.

Practice 1 (131–132)

1. The dog warden had the stray, which was foaming at the mouth, put to sleep.
2. Marian finally found her slippers, which had been kicked carelessly under the bed.
3. I tried out the old swing set, which was rusty with disuse.
4. The manager decided to replace his starting pitcher, who had given up four straight hits.
5. The farmers lost their entire tomato crop, which had frozen on the vines.
6. *C*
7. The audience cheered wildly as the elephants, which were dancing on their hind legs, paraded by.
8. Marta took the overdone meat loaf, which was burned beyond all recognition, from the oven.
9. We decided to replace the dining room wallpaper, which was tattered, faded, and hanging in shreds.
10. A person can keep membership cards clean by sealing them in plastic.
    Or: When sealed in plastic, membership cards can be kept clean.

FAULTY PARALLELISM

Introductory Project (135)

Correct sentences:

I use my TV remote control to change channels, to adjust the volume, and to turn the set on and off.

One option the employees had was to take a cut in pay; the other was to work longer hours.

The refrigerator has a cracked vegetable drawer, a missing shelf, and a strange freezer smell.

Practice 1 (137)

1. waved pennants
2. to stay indoors
3. make a cream sauce
4. turn down the heat
5. overdone hamburgers
6. coughed
7. demanding
8. drinking two milk shakes
9. puts a frozen waffle into the toaster
10. to leave the company

PAPER FORMAT

Introductory Project (141)

In "A," the title is capitalized and centered and has no quotation marks around it; there is a blank line between the title and the body of the paper; there are left and right margins around the body of the paper; no words are incorrectly hyphenated.

Practice 1 (143)

2. Do not use quotation marks around the title.
3. Capitalize the major words in the title ("Too Small to Fight Back").
4. Skip a line between the title and the first line of the paper.
5. Indent the first line of the paper.
6. Keep margins on both sides of the paper.

Practice 2 (143–144)

Here are some possible titles:

1. My First-Grade Teacher
2. My Hardest Year
3. My Father's Sense of Humor
4. Ways to Conserve Energy
5. Violence in the Movies

Practice 3 (144–145)

1. Lack of communication is often the reason why a relationship comes to an end.
2. Educational TV programs are in trouble today for several reasons.
3. Correct
4. The worst vacation I ever had began when my brother suggested that we rent a large van and drive to Colorado.
5. Most professional athletes have been pampered since grade school days.

CAPITAL LETTERS

Introductory Project (146)

1–13: Answers will vary, but all should be capitalized.
14–16: On . . . "Let's . . . I

Practice (149)

1. Fourth . . . July . . . Veterans' Day
2. When . . . I
3. Toyota . . . Long Island Expressway
4. *Guide* . . . *Sixty Minutes*
5. National Bank . . . General Electric
6. Melrose Diner . . . Business Institute
7. A Sound . . . Thunder
8. Pacific School . . . Cosmetology
9. Sears . . . Ninth Street
10. Tang . . . Swift's

Practice (152)

1. Uncle Harry
2. Bic . . . Snoopy
3. Congressman Hughes
4. Indian . . . West Coast
5. Introduction . . . Astronomy . . . General Biology

Practice (152–153)

1. high school . . . principal . . . discipline
2. father . . . creature . . . wing
3. skull . . . hair . . . bones
4. monument . . . settlers' . . . plague . . . locusts
5. motorcycle . . . tractor-trailer . . . motel

NUMBERS AND ABBREVIATIONS

Introductory Project (155)

Correct choices:

First sentence: 8:55 . . . 65 percent
Second sentence: Nine . . . forty-five
Second sentence: brothers . . . mountain
Second sentence: hours . . . English

Practice (157)

1. five
2. eight . . . fifty-six
3. 10:30
4. five o'clock
5. 65
6. seventy-two
7. 12
8. 600 . . . 80
9. November 3, 1982,
10. *The Three Musketeers* . . . two

Practice (158)

1. department . . . purchase
2. Route . . . Florida
3. America . . . pounds
4. pair . . . inch
5. appointment . . . doctor . . . month
6. library . . . minutes . . . magazine
7. teaspoon . . . French
8. license . . . driving . . . road
9. finish . . . assignment . . . point
10. limit . . . senator . . . representative

END MARKS

Introductory Project (160)

1. depressed.
2. paper?
3. parked.
4. control!

Practice (162)

1. house?
2. it.
3. tiger!
4. mower?
5. chip.
6. working?''
7. Shark!''
8. bottle.
9. drain.
10. leaflets.

APOSTROPHE

Introductory Project (164)

1. The apostrophes indicate omitted letters: *You are, he is, does not.*
2. In each case, the apostrophe indicates possession or ownership.
3. In the first sentence in each pair, the *s* in *books* and *cars* indicates plural number; in the second sentence in each pair, the *'s* indicates possession.

Apostrophe in Contractions

Practice 1 (165)

shouldn't	won't	who's
doesn't	they're	wouldn't
isn't	can't	aren't

Practice 2 (166)

1. you'll . . . it's
2. hadn't . . . couldn't
3. isn't . . . doesn't
4. I'm . . . I'm
5. Where's . . . who's

Practice (167)

1. It's . . . it's
2. they're . . . their
3. You're . . . your
4. whose . . . who's
5. it's . . . your . . . who's

Apostrophe to Show Ownership or Possession

Practice 1 (168–169)

1. The assassin's rifle
2. his mother's legacy
3. Mark's throat
4. Sam's parking space
5. The chef's hat
6. the president's wife
7. The mugger's hand
8. Harry's briefcase
9. Sandy's shoulder bag
10. The dog's leash

Practice 2 (169)

2. instructor's
3. astrologer's
4. Ellen's
5. lemonade's
6. sister's
7. Brian's
8. Sue's
9. Charles's
10. hypnotist's

Practice 3 (170)

Sentences will vary.

2. friend's
3. cashier's
4. teammate's
5. brother's

Practice (171–172)

1. diners: diner's, meaning ''the hamburgers of the diner''
   hamburgers: simple plural meaning more than one hamburger
   steaks: simple plural meaning more than one steak
2. San Franciscos: San Francisco's, meaning ''the cable cars of San Francisco''
   cars: simple plural meaning more than one car
   hills: simple plural meaning more than one hill
3. brothers: brother's, meaning ''the collection of my brother''
   cards: simple plural meaning more than one card
   boxes: simple plural meaning more than one box
4. toothpicks: simple plural meaning more than one toothpick
   years: year's, meaning ''the fashions of this year''
   fashions: simple plural meaning more than one fashion
5. Pedros: Pedro's, meaning ''the blood pressure of Pedro''
   minutes: simple plural meaning more than one minute
   spaces: simple plural meaning more than one space

6. write-ups: simple plural meaning more than one write-up
Ellens: Ellen's, meaning "the promotion of Ellen"
coworkers: simple plural meaning more than one co-worker

7. sons: son's, meaning "the fort of my son"
pieces: simple plural meaning more than one piece
nails: simple plural meaning more than one nail
shingles: simple plural meaning more than one shingle

8. mayors: mayor's, meaning "the double-talk of the mayor"
reporters: simple plural meaning more than one reporter
heads: simple plural meaning more than one head
notebooks: simple plural meaning more than one notebook

9. cuts: simple plural meaning more than one cut
boxers: boxer's, meaning "the left eye of the boxer"
rounds: simple plural meaning more than one round

10. cafeterias: cafeteria's, meaning "the loudspeakers of the cafeteria"
loudspeakers: simple plural meaning more than one loud-speaker
exams: simple plural meaning more than one exam

Practice (173)

1. stores' windows
2. friends' problems
3. Cowboys' new quarterback
4. students' insect collections
5. voters' wish

QUOTATION MARKS

Introductory Project (176)

1. Quotation marks set off the exact words of a speaker.
2. Commas and periods following quotations go inside quotation marks.

Practice 1 (178)

1. "This is the tenth commercial in a row," complained Maureen.
2. The police officer said sleepily, "I could really use a cup of coffee."
3. My boss asked me to step into his office and said, "Joanne, how would you like a raise?"

4. "I'm out of work again," Miriam sighed.
5. "I didn't know this movie was R-rated!" Lorraine gasped.
6. "Why does my dog always wait until it rains before he wants to go out?" Clyde asked.
7. A sign over the box office read, "Please form a single line and be patient."
8. "Unless I run three miles a day," Marty said, "my legs feel like lumpy oatmeal."
9. "I had an uncle who knew when he was going to die," claimed Dan. "The warden told him."
10. The unusual notice in the newspaper read, "Young farmer would be pleased to hear from young lady with tractor. Send photograph of tractor."

Practice 2 (179)

1. The officer said, "I'm giving you a ticket."
2. "Please wait your turn," the frantic clerk begged.
3. Phil yelled, "Where's the Drano?"
4. "These directions don't make any sense," Laura muttered.
5. "Inside every fat person," someone once said, "is a thin person struggling to get out."

Practice 1 (180–181)

2. Marian exclaimed, "It was the worst day of my life."
3. Lew said, "Tell me all about it."
4. Marian insisted, "You wouldn't understand my job problems."
5. Lew said, "I will certainly try."

Practice 2 (181)

1. He said that he needed a vacation.
2. Martha said that purple was her favorite color.
3. She asked the handsome stranger if she could buy him a drink.
4. My brother asked if anyone had seen his frog.
5. Fran complained that she married a man who falls asleep during horror movies.

Practice (182–183)

1. My recently divorced sister refused to be in the talent show when she was told she'd have to sing "Love Is a Many-Splendored Thing."

2. Disgusted by the constant dripping noise, Brian opened his copy of Handy Home Repairs to the chapter entitled "Everything about the Kitchen Sink."

3. My little brother has seen the movie Star Wars at least eight times.

4. Before they bought new car tires, Nick and Fran studied the article "Testing Tires" in the February, 1993, issue of Consumer Reports.

5. Many people mistakenly think that Huckleberry Finn and The Adventures of Tom Sawyer are children's books only.

6. I just found out that the musical My Fair Lady is taken from a play by George Bernard Shaw called Pygmalion.

7. The ending of Shirley Jackson's story "The Lottery" really surprised me.

8. I sang the song "Mack the Knife" in our high school production of The Threepenny Opera.

9. Unless he's studied the TV Guide listings thoroughly, my father won't turn on his television.

10. Stanley dreamed that both Time and Newsweek had decided to use him in their feature article "Man of the Year."

COMMA

Introductory Project (186)

1. a. news, a movie, a *Honeymooners* rerun,
    b. check, write your account number on the back,
    (commas between items in a series)

2. a. indoors,
    b. car,
    (commas after introductory words)

3. a. opossum, an animal much like the kangaroo,
    b. Derek, who was recently arrested,
    (commas around interrupters)

4. a. pre-registration, but
    b. intersection, and
    (commas between complete thoughts)

5. a. said, "Why
    b. interview," said David, "I
    (commas with direct quotations)

6. a. 1,500,000
    b. Highway, Jersey City, New Jersey
    January 26, 1994,
    (commas with everyday material)

Practice 1 (188)

1. rackets, a volleyball, and a first-aid kit
2. comics, the sports page, and the personals
3. birdbath, two stone deer, a flagpole, and a plastic daisy

Practice 2 (188)

1. A metal tape measure, a pencil, a ruler, and a hammer dangled from the carpenter's pockets.
2. The fortune-teller uncovered the crystal ball, peered into it, and began to predict my fortune.
3. That hairdresser is well-known for her frizzy perms, butchered haircuts, and brassy hair colorings.

Practice 1 (189)

1. hands,
2. storm,
3. help,

Practice 2 (189)

1. In order to work at that fast-food restaurant, you have to wear a cowboy hat and six-guns. In addition, you have to shout "Yippee!" every time someone orders the special Western-style double burger.
2. Barely awake, the woman slowly rocked her crying infant. While the baby softly cooed, the woman fell asleep.
3. When I painted the kitchen, I remembered to cover the floor with newspapers. Therefore, I was able to save the floor from looking as if someone had thrown confetti on it.

Practice 1 (191)

1. gadget, ladies and gentlemen,
2. Tigers, because they eat people,
3. dummy, its straw-filled "hands" tied with rope,

Practice 2 (191)

1. My brother, who only likes natural foods, would rather eat a soybean patty than a cheeseburger.
2. That room, with its filthy rug and broken dishwasher, is the nicest one in the building.
3. My aunt, who claims she is an artist, painted her living room ceiling to look like the sky at midnight.

Practice (192–193)

1. hour, or
2. fine, but
3. releases, and
4. manual, but
5. *C*
6. *C*
7. housecleaning, and
8. melted, and
9. telephone, but
10. *C*

Practice 1 (193)

1. asked, ''Do
2. wrote, ''2
3. of,'' said Richie, ''is

Practice 2 (193)

1. ''Could you spare a quarter,'' the boy asked passersby in the mall, ''for a video game?''
2. ''Man does not live by words alone,'' wrote Adlai Stevenson, ''despite the fact that sometimes he has to eat them.''
3. ''That actress,'' said Vicki, ''has promoted everything from denture cleaner to shoelaces.''

Practice (195)

1. A new bulletproof material has been developed that is very lightweight.
2. The vet's bill included charges for a distemper shot.
3. Since the firehouse is directly behind Ken's home, the sound of its siren pierces his walls.
4. Hard sausages and net-covered hams hung above the delicatessen counter.
5. The students in the dance class were dressed in a variety of bright tights, baggy sweatshirts, and wooly leg warmers.
6. A woman in the ladies' room asked me if she could borrow a safety pin.
7. Telephone books, broken pencils, and scraps of paper littered the reporter's desk.
8. The frenzied crowd at the game cheered and whistled.
9. Splitting along the seams, the old mattress spilled its stuffing on the ground.
10. To satisfy his hunger, Enrique chewed on a piece of dry rye bread.

OTHER PUNCTUATION MARKS

Introductory Project (199)

1. Artist:
2. life-size
3. (1856–1939)
4. track;
5. breathing—but alive.

Practice (200)

1. follows:
2. things:
3. life:

Practice (201)

1. outlets; otherwise,
2. spider; he
3. 9 A.M.; . . . 10:00;

Practice (202)

1. well—
2. see—
3. hoped—no, I prayed—

Practice (203)

1. first-rate . . . brand-new
2. worn-out . . . wall-to-wall
3. great-looking . . . two-bit

Practice (203)

1. prices (ten to twenty-five dollars) made
2. election (the April primary), only
3. you (1) two sharpened pencils and (2) an eraser.

DICTIONARY USE

Introductory Project (205)

1. fortutious (fortuitous)
2. hi/er/o/glyph/ics
3. be

4. oc/to/ge/nar ′ /i/an
5. (1) an identifying mark on the ear of a domestic animal
    (2) an identifying feature or characteristic

Answers to the activities are in your dictionary. Check with your instructor if you have any problems.

SPELLING IMPROVEMENT

Introductory Project (214)

Misspellings:

> akward . . . exercize . . . buisness . . . worryed . . . shamful . . . begining . . . partys . . . sandwichs . . . heros

Practice (217)

1.	carried	6.	permitted
2.	revising	7.	gliding
3.	studies	8.	angrily
4.	wrapping	9.	rebelling
5.	horrified	10.	grudges

Practice (219)

1.	crashes	6.	potatoes
2.	matches	7.	twenties
3.	doilies	8.	wives
4.	crosses	9.	passersby
5.	dozens	10.	media

OMITTED WORDS AND LETTERS

Introductory Project (222)

> bottles . . . in the supermarket . . . like a wind-up toy . . . his arms . . . an alert shopper . . . with the cry...g

Practice (223–224)

1. In the rest room, Jeff impatiently rubbed his hands under the mechanical dryer, which blew out feeble puffs of cool air.

2. On February 10, 1935, *The New York Times* reported that an eight-foot alligator had been dragged out of a city sewer by three teenage boys.

3. Gene dressed up as a stuffed olive for Halloween by wearing a green plastic garbage bag and a red knitted cap.

4. Mrs. Hanson nearly fainted when she opened the health insurance bill and saw an enormous rate increase.

5. At 4 A.M., the all-night supermarket where I work hosts an assortment of strange shoppers.

6. With a loud hiss, the inflated beach ball suddenly shrank to the size of an orange.

7. The boiling milk bubbled over the sides of the pot, leaving a gluey white film on the stove top.

8. Susan turned to the answer page of the crossword book, pretended to herself that she hadn't, and turned back to her puzzle.

9. In order to avoid stepping on the hot blacktop of the parking lot, the barefoot boy tiptoed along the cooler white lines.

10. The messy roommates used hubcaps for ashtrays and scribbled graffiti on their own bathroom walls.

Practice I (224–225)

1. shaves . . . blades
2. legs . . . hurdles
3. fads . . . ants
4. owners . . . monkeys
5. photographers . . . sharks
6. spores . . . leaves
7. cages . . . plants
8. pounds . . . grapes . . . cents
9. soles . . . shoes
10. cheeseburgers . . . shakes

COMMONLY CONFUSED WORDS

Introductory Project (227)

1.	Incorrect: your	Correct: you're
2.	Incorrect: who's	Correct: whose
3.	Incorrect: there	Correct: their
4.	Incorrect: to	Correct: too
5.	Incorrect: Its	Correct: It's

Homonyms (228–236)

already . . . all ready	plane . . . plain
brake . . . break	principal . . . principle
course . . . coarse	right . . . write
hear . . . here	then . . . than
whole . . . hole	There . . . their . . . they're
It's . . . its	through . . . threw
knew . . . new	two . . . to . . . too
know . . . no	where . . . wear
pair . . . pear	weather . . . whether
passed . . . past	whose . . . Who's
peace . . . piece	your . . . you're

Other Words Frequently Confused (237–242)

an . . . a	desert . . . dessert
accept . . . except	dose . . . does
advise . . . advice	fewer . . . less
effect . . . affects	former . . . latter
Among . . . between	learn . . . teach
Besides . . . beside	loose . . . lose
can . . . may	quiet . . . quite
cloths . . . clothes	Though . . . thought

Incorrect Word Forms

being that (243)

1. Because the boss heard my remark,
2. because my diet
3. because his dad

can't hardly/couldn't hardly (243)

1. They could hardly
2. I can hardly
3. We could hardly

could of/must of/should of/would of (244)

1. Thelma must have
2. You should have
3. I would have
4. No one could have

irregardless (244)

1. Regardless of what anybody else does,
2. Regardless of the weather,
3. Regardless of what my parents say,

EFFECTIVE WORD CHOICE

Introductory Project (247)

Correct sentences:

1. After the softball game, we ate hamburgers and drank beer.
2. Someone told me you're getting married next month.
3. Psychological tests will be given on Wednesday.
4. I think the referee made the right decision.

1 . . . 2 . . . 3 . . . 4

Practice (248–249)

1. The scene in the movie where Rocky ate six raw eggs made me sick.
2. Ex-offenders have a hard time adjusting after leaving prison.
3. Manny went through the multiple-choice questions quickly but had trouble with the essay section.
4. The professional assassin killed over twenty victims before someone informed on him.
5. That book on suicide is depressing; it really bothered me.

Practice 1 (250)

1. Substitute make me very angry for make my blood boil.
2. Substitute depressed for down in the dumps.
3. Substitute wonderful for one in a million.
4. Substitute have a celebration for roll out the red carpet.
5. Substitute free for free as a bird.

Note: The above answers are examples of how the clichés could be corrected. Other answers are possible.

Practice (252)

1. I do not understand that person's behavior.
2. He erased all the mistakes in his notes.
3. She thought about what he said.
4. The police officer stopped the car.
5. Inez told the counselor about her career hopes.

Practice (253–254)

1. I am a vegetarian.
2. Last Tuesday, I started going to college full time.
3. Since I'm broke, I can't go to the movies.
4. I repeated that I wouldn't go.
5. Everything I say and do annoys my father.

Appendix C

Progress Charts

PROGRESS CHART FOR MASTERY TESTS

Enter Your Score for Each Test in the Space Provided

Individual Tests	1 Mastery	2 Mastery	3 Mastery	4 Mastery	5 Ditto	6 Ditto	7 IM	8 IM
Subjects and Verbs								
Sentence Fragments								
Run-Ons								
Standard English Verbs								
Irregular Verbs								
Subject-Verb Agreement								
Consistent Verb Tense								
Pronoun Reference, Agreement, and Point of View								
Pronoun Types								
Adjectives and Adverbs								
Misplaced Modifiers								
Dangling Modifiers								
Parallelism								

Individual Tests (continued)	1 Mastery	2 Mastery	3 Mastery	4 Mastery	5 Ditto	6 Ditto	7 IM	8 IM
Capital Letters								
Numbers and Abbreviations								
End Marks								
Apostrophe								
Quotation Marks								
Comma								
Other Punctuation Marks								
Dictionary Use								
Spelling Improvement								
Omitted Words and Letters								
Commonly Confused Words								
Effective Word Choice								

Combined Tests	1 Mastery	2 Mastery	3 Mastery	4 Mastery	5 Ditto	6 Ditto	7 IM	8 IM
Sentence Fragments and Run-Ons								
Verbs								
Pronouns								
Faulty Modifiers and Parallelism								
Capital Letters and Punctuation								
Word Use								

PROGRESS CHART FOR
EDITING AND PROOFREADING TESTS

Date	Step	Comments	To Do Next	Instructor's Initials
9/27	1a	Missed -ing frag; 3 copying mistakes	1b	JL
9/27	1b	No mistakes—Good job!	2a	JL

Date	Step	Comments	To Do Next	Instructor's Initials

PROGRESS CHART FOR COMBINED EDITING TESTS

Enter Your Score for Each Test in the Space Provided

Editing Test 1		Editing Test 7	
Editing Test 2		Editing Test 8	
Editing Test 3		Editing Test 9	
Editing Test 4		Editing Test 10	
Editing Test 5		Editing Test 11	
Editing Test 6		Editing Test 12	

PROGRESS CHART FOR
WRITING ASSIGNMENTS

Date	Paper	Comments	To Do Next
10/15	Worst job	Promising but needs more support.	Rewrite
		Also, 2 frags and 2 run-ons.	

(Continues on next page)

Date	Paper	Comments	To Do Next

Index